To Go Free

A TREASURY OF
Iowa's LEGAL HERITAGE

To Go Free

A TREASURY OF
Iowa's LEGAL HERITAGE

Richard, Lord Acton *and* Patricia Nassif Acton

IOWA STATE UNIVERSITY PRESS / AMES

Richard, Lord Acton, born in Shropshire, England, received his B.A. and M.A. degrees in Modern History from Trinity College, Oxford University. He received his legal training at the Inns of Court School of Law, London, and practiced as a barrister in London and Zimbabwe, Africa. He is the fourth Lord Acton and sits as a Cross-Bench (Independent) peer in the British House of Lords. Lord Acton has published numerous articles on Iowa history in the *Palimpsest, Annals of Iowa, The Iowan,* and the *Des Moines Register.* In 1995, he won the State Historical Society of Iowa's Throne/Aldrich Award for the best historical article in the *Palimpsest.*

Patricia Nassif Acton, a life-long resident of Cedar Rapids, Iowa, received her B.A. degree in History from the University of Iowa and her J.D. degree from the University of Iowa College of Law. She practiced law in Cedar Rapids for several years before joining the faculty of the University of Iowa College of Law in 1981, where she currently is a Clinical Professor of Law and the Director of the London Law Consortium. She has published books and articles on a variety of legal subjects.

© 1995 Iowa State University Press, Ames, Iowa 50014
All rights reserved

Authorization to photocopy items for internal or personal use, or the internal or personal use of specific clients, is granted by Iowa State University Press, provided that the base fee of $.10 per copy is paid directly to the Copyright Clearance Center, 27 Congress Street, Salem, MA 01970. For those organizations that have been granted a photocopy license by CCC, a separate system of payments has been arranged. The fee code for users of the Transactional Reporting Service is 0-8138-2178-9/95 $.10.

♾ Printed on acid-free paper in the United States of America

First edition, 1995
Second printing, 1996
Third printing, 1996

Library of Congress Cataloging-in-Publication Data

Acton, Richard, Lord
    To go free: A treasury of Iowa's legal heritage/Richard, Lord Acton and Patricia Nassif Acton.—1st ed.
       p.   cm.
    Includes bibliographical references and index.
    ISBN 0-8138-2178-9
    1. Law—Iowa—History. 2. Law—Iowa—Anecdotes. 3. Lawyers—Iowa—History. 4. Iowa—Constitutional history. 5. Iowa—History. I. Acton, Patricia Nassif. II. Title.
KFI4278.A26   1995
348.777—dc20
[347.7708]   95-19307

Title page photo: A panel from the ceiling of the Iowa Supreme Court chamber, state capitol building, Des Moines (State Historical Society of Iowa; photographer, Chuck Greiner).

CONTENTS

PREFACE

THE YEAR 1996 MARKS THE SESQUICEN-
tennial of the statehood of Iowa. It seems appropriate to commemorate the
occasion with reflections on those aspects of statehood that distinguish the
last 150 years. Our subject is the law.

This undertaking presupposes that law somehow can be classified and
described. However, we tend to agree with former U.S. Supreme Court Justice Oliver Wendell Holmes, Jr., who said: "The life of the law has not been
logic: it has been experience."

We suspect that law, like other nebulous bodies, assumes different
forms depending on the viewpoint of the observer. It seems only fair, then,
to tell the reader something about our own points of view.

We are both lawyers, one an English barrister, the other a University of
Iowa law professor. Trained in the law, we recognize the importance of constitutions, codes, and court decisions in defining legal history.

However, we also recognize that constitutions, codes, and court decisions do not exist in a vacuum. They apply to human problems; their meaning is defined within the ever-changing contours of family, society, and government. Law is as much about defendants and jurors as it is about judges
and legislators.

Given the many aspects of law, how can we write a legal history of
Iowa? By manifestly *not* attempting to write a "history" at all, but rather, to
give an *impression* of history. And to form this impression chiefly through
reliance on primary sources—the opinions of judges, the texts of statutes,
eyewitness reports, governors' speeches, the anecdotes of lawyers, and the
confessions of their clients. We include original essays throughout the book
to elaborate some important or colorful features of law, but these essays are
the servants, not the masters, of the primary sources themselves.

Although written by lawyers to commemorate a historical period, this
book is not just for lawyers or historians. Rather, it is for *all* Iowans with a
lively interest in their state, its people, and its past.

ACKNOWLEDGMENTS

WE WISH TO THANK THE FOLLOWING individuals for their invaluable assistance and support:

Mark Schlenker, chairman, and the members of the Legal Heritage Committee of the Iowa State Bar Association.

The family of the late Wilber W. Sackett, Esq.

Karen Laughlin and Susan Rogers, formerly librarians with the State Historical Society of Iowa, Iowa City.

Mary Bennett of Special Collections, State Historical Society of Iowa, Iowa City; Becki Peterson and Ellen Sulser with the State Archives, State Historical Society of Iowa, Des Moines; and other staff members of the State Historical Society of Iowa in Iowa City and in Des Moines.

Tom Eicher, Legal Bibliographer and Reference Librarian at the University of Iowa College of Law Library.

Beverly Heitt, secretary with the University of Iowa College of Law.

Legal research assistants Blair Bennett, Richard Swartzbaugh, Mary Kennedy, Emily Colby, Lisa Bandy, and Melissa Biederman.

The editors and staff of the Iowa State University Press.

Special thanks to Merle Davis of the University of Iowa College of Law Library, and Susan Kuecker, formerly with the Masonic Library in Cedar Rapids.

And we wish to thank all those individuals in so many libraries, courthouses, and historical societies across the state whose kindness and appreciation of Iowa history made this book possible.

RICHARD, LORD ACTON / PATRICIA NASSIF ACTON

To Go Free

A TREASURY OF
Iowa's LEGAL HERITAGE

PROLOGUE

In the Beginning

"You will plant corn where my dead sleep ...."

— Chief Poweshiek

The Pre-Territorial Years

WHEN THE FIRST KNOWN EUROPEAN explorer set eyes on the future Iowa in 1673, he found a land he believed to be largely uninhabited. The Frenchman Louis Jolliet, whose party included the Jesuit priest Jacques Marquette, traveled for days down the Mississippi River before finding a small village of Indians, apparently an offshoot of a larger tribe east of the great river.

Had Jolliet moved inland from the Mississippi, he might have found other Indians who lived on, hunted, and crossed the Iowa lands. And he surely would have discovered the mounded earth that bespoke a human presence in the region many hundreds of years before.

White settlers did not soon follow this first European "discovery." Indeed, the earliest known settler was French-Canadian trapper and trader Julien Dubuque, who in 1788 obtained from the Indians an exclusive right to mine lead in the area that would soon bear his name.

The Louisiana Purchase of 1803—by which France sold to envoys of President Thomas Jefferson land stretching from the Mississippi to the Rockies—marked a turning point for the vast, largely unexplored territory. Within two years, Meriwether Lewis and William Clark had explored the Missouri River, and Zebulon Pike had explored the upper Mississippi River, great waters that later would define the west and east boundaries of the state of Iowa. This area was included in what was first known as the District of Louisiana, and then, in 1805, the Territory of Louisiana.

One of the military outposts built to protect the upper Mississippi River was Fort Madison. The site proved susceptible to attacks by Indians led by the Sauk Chief Black Hawk and allied to the British during the War of 1812. A besieged United States military command finally abandoned Fort Madison in September 1813, setting fire to its buildings.

In 1812, the Territory of Louisiana was renamed the Territory of Missouri. Under the Missouri Compromise of 1820, a part of that territory became the slave state of Missouri. Slavery was prohibited in an area that included the future Iowa, which for the moment was left without formal government status.

The unregulated area included Indian peoples pushed ever westward by the white migration, and sometimes hostilities ensued. The United States negotiated treaties in 1825 and 1830 that sought to divide the Iowa lands among Indian tribes and establish a "neutral ground" between the Sioux in the north and the Sauk and Meskwaki in the south.

In 1831, Chief Black Hawk signed what has been called the "Corn Treaty," agreeing to remove his followers from Illinois to their assigned lands along the Iowa River and accept the authority of the younger Chief Keokuk. In exchange, the United States guaranteed the sanctity of the Sauk and Meskwaki lands west of the Mississippi River.

In the spring of 1832, Chief Black Hawk re-crossed the Mississippi River into Illinois and began a fruitless drive to reclaim his former lands. Black Hawk engaged in brief skirmishes with the United States military before the massacre of his band of followers and the collapse of his hopes.

Following this "Black Hawk War," General Winfield Scott dictated the terms of peace. The guaranteed lands along the Iowa River were forfeited; the Sauk and Meskwaki were to leave the area by June 1, 1833. Even before the June 1 removal date, white settlers began locating on the rich west bank of the Mississippi—the formal beginnings of Dubuque, Bellevue, Muscatine, Burlington, Fort Madison, and Keokuk. However, the future Iowa still was in a state of governmental limbo, a situation remedied in 1834 when Congress made it part of the Territory of Michigan.

A census taken in 1836 showed that over 10,000 people had settled in the Iowa lands. In that year, the District of Iowa was made a part of the new Territory of Wisconsin. President Andrew Jackson appointed Colonel Henry Dodge of Mineral Point, Wisconsin as the first governor of the Territory of Wisconsin.

Soon a convention of Iowa counties pressed for independent territorial status. The prospect was opposed by certain southern members of Congress concerned about the creation of another "free" territory. Still, the momentum for territorial status was irresistible. The population had more than doubled since 1836, and stood at over 22,000 in 1838. Congress gave its approval, and on June 12, 1838, President Martin Van Buren signed the Organic Act creating the Territory of Iowa, effective "from and after the third day of July."

For many, the new territorial status was an unmitigated blessing. For others, it represented the end of a way of life. When Poweshiek, the great Meskwaki chief, was told why his white neighbors were engaged in special celebration on this Fourth of July, 1838, he declared:

> I want to live where men are free! Soon I will go to a new home. You will plant corn where my dead sleep, our towns, the paths we have made, the flowers we have loved will soon be yours. I have moved many times, I have seen the white man put his foot in the track of the Indian and make the earth into fields and gardens. I know I must go far away, and you will be so glad when I am gone. You will soon forget the lodge fire, and the meat of the Indian has ever been free to the stranger and he has asked for, what he has fought for, the right to be free.

On July 13, 1787, Congress passed the Ordinance for the Government of the Territory of the United States North West of the River Ohio (the "North West Ordinance"). This ordinance applied to the area that included the future Territory of Iowa, and guaranteed its inhabitants certain fundamental rights and privileges.

Article the First. No person demeaning himself in a peaceable and orderly manner shall ever be molested on account of his mode of worship or religious sentiments in the said territory.

Article the Second. The Inhabitants of the said territory shall always be entitled to the benefits of the writ of habeas corpus, and of the trial by Jury; of a proportionate representation of the people in the legislature, and of judicial proceedings according to the course of the common law ....

Article the Third. Religion, Morality and knowledge being necessary to good government and the happiness of mankind, Schools and the means of education shall forever be encouraged. The utmost good faith shall always be observed towards the Indians, their lands and property shall never be taken from them without their consent; and in their property, rights and liberty, they never shall be invaded or disturbed, unless in just and lawful wars authorised by Congress ....

Article the Fourth. ... The navigable Waters leading into the Mississippi and St. Lawrence, and the carrying places between the same shall be common highways, and forever free ....

Article the Sixth. There shall be neither Slavery nor involuntary Servitude in the said territory otherwise than in the punishment of crimes, whereof the party shall have been duly convicted; provided always that any person escaping into the same, from whom labor or service is lawfully claimed in any one of the original States, such fugitive may be lawfully reclaimed and conveyed to the person claiming his or her labor or service as aforesaid.

. . . .

The North West Ordinance, Art. 1-4, 6, reprinted in *Journals of the Continental Congress 1774-1789* (Washington: U.S. Gov't Printing Office, 1936), vol. XXXII, pp. 334, 340, 342-43.

In 1820, amidst controversy over the expansion of slavery in the territories carved out of Louisiana Purchase land, Congress enacted what is known as the "Missouri Compromise." Missouri was admitted as a slave state, but slavery was to be "forever" excluded from an area that encompassed the future Iowa. Hence Iowa would become "the first free child of the Missouri Compromise."

Be it enacted by the Senate and House of Representatives of the United States of America, in Congress assembled,

Sec. 8. ... That in all that territory ceded by France to the United States, under the name of Louisiana, which lies north of thirty-six degrees and thirty minutes north latitude, not included within the limits of the state, contemplated by this act, slavery and involuntary servitude, otherwise than in the punishment of crimes, whereof the parties shall have been duly convicted, shall be, and is hereby, forever prohibited: *Provided always*, That any person escaping into the same, from whom labor or service is lawfully claimed, in any state or territory of the United States, such fugitive may be lawfully reclaimed and conveyed to the person claiming his or her labor or service as aforesaid.

Approved, March 6, 1820

U.S. Statutes at Large, vol. 3, p. 548.

The settlers in pre-territorial Iowa were left to their own devices to keep the peace and handle their business and personal affairs. Private contracts and compacts were drawn up and enforced. On September 22, 1788, the French-Canadian settler Julien Dubuque contracted with the Meskwaki [Fox] Indians for the right to mine the lead-rich lands that would someday bear Dubuque's name.

Lead mining in pre-territorial Iowa was governed by the miners' private contracts. (From David Dale Owens, Senate Document 407, Congressional Series #437)

Copy of the council held by the Foxes, that is to say, of the branch of five villages, with the approbation of the rest of their people, explained by Mr. Quinantotaye, deputed by them in their presence, and in the presence of us, the undersigned, that is to say, the Foxes, permit Mr. Julien Dubuque, called by them the Little Cloud, to work at the mine as long as he shall please, and to withdraw from it, without specifying any term to him; moreover, that they sell and abandon to him all the coast and the contents of the mine discovered by the wife [le femme] of Peosta, so that no white man or Indian shall make any pretension to it without the consent of Mr. Julien Dubuque; and in case he shall find nothing within, he shall be free to search wherever he may think proper to do so, and to work peaceably without any one hurting him, or doing him any prejudice in his labors. Thus we, chief and braves, by the voice of all our villages, have agreed with Julien Dubuque, selling and delivering to him this day, as above mentioned, in presence of the Frenchmen who attend us, who are witnesses to this writing.

At the Prairie due Chien, in full council, the 22d of September, 1788.

Blondeau,
Ala Austin, his x mark,
Autaque.

Bazil Teren, his x mark,   )
               marque   )
Blondeau de X Quirneau,   ) Witnesses.
            tobague.   )
Joseph Fontigny.   )

Chouteau v. Molony, 57 U.S. (16 Howard) 203, 223-24 (1853).

Years after Julien Dubuque's death, the Langworthy brothers and others supplanted the Indians who were working the Dubuque lead mines. A committee of five individuals drew up a private agreement for self-government. The document, signed on June 17, 1830, has since been known as the "Miners' Compact" or the "Miners' Code."

Dubuque Mines, June 17, 1830. We, a committee, having been chosen to draft certain rules and regulations, by which we, as miners, will be governed; and, having duly considered the subject, do unanimously agree that we will be governed by the regulations on the east side of the Mississippi River, with the following exceptions, to wit:

Article I.—That each and every man shall hold two hundred yards square of ground by working said ground one day in six.

Article II.—We further agree, that there shall be chosen by the majority of the miners present, a person who shall hold this article, and who shall grant letters of arbitration, on application being made, and that said letter [of] arbitration shall be obligatory on the parties concerned so applying.

To the above, we the undersigned subscribe.

J. L. Langworthy,
H. F. Lander,
James McPheeters,
Samuel H. Scoles,
E. M. Urn.

John C. Parish, "The Langworthys of Early Dubuque and Their Contributions to Local History," *Iowa Journal of History and Politics* VIII (July 1910): 315, 317.

(*Harper's New Monthly Magazine*, March 1858)

Sauk Chief Black Hawk. (Plate from *Dr. Pritchard's Natural History of Man,* original painting by George Catlin)

The United States government acquired the lands constituting the future state of Iowa through a series of treaties from 1824 through 1851 with the Sauk and Meskwaki [the Sac and Fox], the Winnebago, the Potawatomi, the Ioway, and the Sioux. The Indians living in Iowa were pushed ever westward through these concessions. In the Treaty of 1832, the defeated Sauk and Meskwaki ceded a strip of land approximately fifty miles wide along most of the future state's Mississippi River boundary. The area became known as the Black Hawk Purchase.

The first Sauk signatory of the Treaty of 1832 was Chief Keokuk. His conciliatory nature was rewarded with the land concession in Article II. The older Chief Black Hawk, whose attempts to return to his homelands east of the Mississippi had resulted in the small skirmishes known as the Black Hawk War, was not present when the treaty was signed. He had been taken prisoner and sent down the Great River to Jefferson Barracks in St. Louis, Missouri.

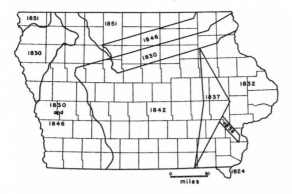

Map showing Indian cessions in Treaties of 1824, 1830, 1832, 1836, 1837, 1842, 1846, and 1851. (From Leland L. Sage, *A History of Iowa,* Ames: Iowa State University Press, 1974)

WHEREAS, under certain lawless and desperate leaders, a formidable band, constituting a large portion of the Sac and Fox nation, left their country in April last, and, in violation of treaties, commenced an unprovoked war upon unsuspecting and defenceless citizens of the United States, sparing neither age nor sex; and whereas, the United States, at a great expense of treasure, have subdued the said hostile band, killing or capturing all its principal Chiefs and Warriors—the said States, partly as indemnity for the expense incurred, and partly to secure the future safety and tranquility of the invaded frontier, demand of the said tribes, to the use of the United States, a cession of a tract of the Sac and Fox country ....

ARTICLE I. Accordingly, the confederated tribes of Sacs and Foxes hereby cede to the United States forever, all the lands to which the said tribes have title, or claim, (with the exception of the reservation hereinafter made) .... And the said confederated tribes of Sacs and Foxes hereby stipulate and agree to remove from the lands herein ceded to the United States, on or before the first day of June next ....

ARTICLE II. Out of the cession made in the preceding article, the United States agree to a reservation for the use of the said conferated tribes, of a tract of land containing four hundred square miles ... so as to include Ke-o-kuck's principal village on its right bank, which village is about twelve miles from the Mississippi river.

ARTICLE III. In consideration of the great extent of the foregoing cession, the United States stipulate and agree to pay to the said confederated tribes, annually, for thirty successive years, the first payment to be made in September of the next year, the sum of twenty thousand dollars in specie.

ARTICLE IV. It is further agreed that the United States shall establish and maintain within the limits, and for the use and benefit of the Sacs and Foxes, for the period of thirty years, one additional black and gun smith shop, with the necessary tools, iron and steel; and finally make a yearly allowance for the same period, to the said tribes, of forty kegs of tobacco, and forty barrels of salt, to be delivered at the mouth of the Ioway river.

ARTICLE V. The United States, at the earnest request of the said confederated tribes, further agree to pay to Farnham and Davenport, Indian traders at Rock Island, the sum of forty thousand dollars without interest, which sum will be in full satisfaction of the claims of the said traders against the said tribes ....

ARTICLE VII. [T]he following named prisoners of war, now in confinement, who were Chiefs and Headmen, shall be held as hostages for the future good conduct of the late hostile bands, during the pleasure of the President of the United States, viz: — Muk-ka-ta-mish-a-ka-kaik (or Black Hawk) and his two sons; Wau-ba-kee-shik (the Prophet) his brother and two sons; Na-pope; We-sheet Ioway; Pamaho; and Cha-kee-pa-shi-pa-ho (the little stabbing Chief).

Done at Fort Armstrong, Rock Island, Illinois, this twenty-first day of September, in the year of our Lord one thousand eight hundred and thirty-two, and of the independence of the United States the fifty-seventh.

Winfield Scott,
John Reynolds.
 Sacs.
Kee-o-kuck, or he who has been every where, his x mark,
(and other signers)

Treaty with the Sac and Fox, September 21, 1832, reprinted in Charles J. Kappler (ed.), *Indian Affairs. Laws and Treaties* (Washington: U.S. Gov't Printing Office, 1904), vol. II, pp. 349-51.

After the formal removal of the Sauk and Meskwaki Indians from the land ceded in the Black Hawk Purchase, white settlers began streaming across the Mississippi River. They did so without official government sanction, and at a time when the political status of the ceded lands was unclear. In 1834, this legal limbo was resolved by including the Iowa lands as part of the Territory of Michigan.

One of the early settlers was Eliphalet Price, who lived in Dubuque during the years 1832-1835. During his forty years in Iowa, Price was a farmer, lawyer, judge, politican, and writer. His first-hand account of the "trial" and execution of Patrick O'Connor at Dubuque vividly illustrates how the early settlers, without the benefit of organized courts, dealt with the problems of crime and punishment.

Black Hawk Purchase Treaty Council, 1832. (Courtesy, State Historical Society of Iowa, Iowa City)

Soon after the treaty between the United States and the Sac and Fox Indians at Rock Island in 1832, which resulted in the extinguishment of the Indian Title to the lands embraced in the present State of Iowa, permanent mining locations and settlements began to be made in the vicinity of the present city of Dubuque; and at the close of the winter of 1834, Congress attached the country acquired under the treaty, to the Territory of Michigan, for election and judicial purposes.

Up to that period no judicial tribunals existed in the country, except those created by the people for special purposes. Difficulties of a civil character were investigated and settled by arbitrators; while those of a criminal character were decided by a jury of twelve men, and, when condemnation was agreed upon the verdict of guilty was accompanied by the sentence. Such was the judicial character of the courts which were held at that time, in what was known as the "Blackhawk Purchase."

Patrick O'Conner [sic], the subject of this memoir, was born in the year 1797 in the county of Cork, Ireland,—came to the United States in the year 1826, and soon after arrived at Galena .... [H]e left Galena and came to the Dubuque mines in the fall of 1833, where he entered into a mining partnership with George O'Keaf, also a native of Ireland. ...

On the 19th of May, 1834, O'Keaf came up to Dubuque and purchased some provisions, when he returned to his cabin about 2 o'clock in the afternoon, accompanied by an acquaintance. Upon arriving at his cabin and finding the door fastened upon the inside, he called to O'Conner to open it. O'Conner replied:

"Don't be in a hurry, I'll open it when I get ready."

O'Keaf waited a few minutes when he again called to O'Conner, saying: "It is beginning to rain, open the door quick."

To this, O'Conner made no reply; when O'Keaf, who had a bundle in one hand and a ham of bacon in the other, placed his shoulder against the door and forced it open. As he was in the act of stepping into the house, O'Conner, who was sitting upon a bench on the opposite side of the room in front of the door, immediately leveled a musket and fired at O'Keaf. Five slugs entered his breast and he fell dead. ... In a short time a large concourse of miners were assembled around the cabin, when O'Conner being asked why he shot O'Keaf, replied, "That is my business," and then proceeded to give directions concerning the disposition of the body. Some person present having suggested that he be hung immediately upon the tree in front of his cabin, a rope was procured for that purpose. But the more discreet and reflecting portion of the bystanders insisted that he should be taken to Dubuque, and the matter there fully and fairly investigated. Accordingly O'Conner was taken up to Dubuque. And on the 20th of May, 1834, the first trial for murder, in what is now known as the State of Iowa, was held in the open air beneath the wide-spreading branches of a large elm tree, directly in front of the dwelling then occupied by Samuel Clifton. A large concourse of people had assembled and stood quiety gazing upon the prisoner, when upon the motion of some person, Captain White was appointed prosecuting attorney, or counsel in behalf of the people. O'Conner being directed to choose from among the bystanders some person to act as his counsel, observed: "Faith, and I'll tind to my own business," and appeared perfectly indifferent about the matter. At length he selected Capt. Bates of Galena, who happened to be present, and in whose employ O'Conner had formerly been engaged. The two counsel then summoned from among the bystanders twenty-four persons, who were requested to stand up in a line; when Capt. White directed O'Conner to choose from among those persons twelve jurors. ...

... The jury being seated upon some house logs, Capt. White observed to O'Conner, "Are you satisfied with that jury?" O'Conner replied, "I have no objection to any of them; ye have no laws in the country, and ye cannot try me."

Capt. White continued, "you, Patrick O'Conner, are charged with the murder of George O'Keaf, do you plead guilty or not guilty?"

O'Conner replied, "I'll not deny that I shot him, but ye have no laws in the country, and cannot try me."

Three or four witnesses were then examined; when Capt. White addressed the jury for a few minutes and was followed by Capt. Bates, who endeavored to urge upon the jury to send the criminal to the State of Illinois, and there have him tried by a legal tribunal. Capt. White replied that offenders had been sent to Illinois for that purpose, and had been released upon "Habeas Corpus," that state having no jurisdiction over offences committed upon the west side of the Mississippi River. After this, the jury retired, and having deliberated for an hour, returned to their seats, upon the logs, with Woodbury M[a]ssey as their foreman, who read from a paper the following verdict and sentence:

> "We the undersigned, residents of the Dubuque Lead Mines, being chosen by Patrick O'Conner, and empanneled as a Jury to try the matter wherein Patrick O'Conner is charged with the murder of George O'Keaf, do find that the said Patrick O'Conner is guilty of murder in the first degree, and ought to be, and is by us sentenced to be hung by the neck until he is dead; which sentence shall take effect on Tuesday the 20th day of June, 1834, at one o'clock P.M."

Signed by all the jurors, each in his own hand writing.

There was a unanimous expression of all the bystanders in favor of the decision of the jury. No dissenting voice was heard, until a short time before the execution, when the Rev. Mr. Fitzmaurice, a Catholic priest from Galena, visited O'Conner and inveighed against the act of the people, denouncing it as being illegal and *unjust*. ...

... Application was made to the Governor of Missouri to pardon him; but he replied that he had no jurisdiction over the country, and referred the applicants to the President of the United States. President Jackson replied to an application made to him, that the laws of the United States had not been extended over the newly acquired purchase, and that he had no authority to act in the matter. ... [O]n the morning of the 20th of June, 1834, one hundred and sixty-three men, with loaded rifles formed into line on Main street. ... Two steamers had arrived that morning from Galena and Prairie Du Chien, with passengers to witness the execution. The concourse of spectators could not have been less than one thousand persons.

The company having marched to the house occupied by O'Conner, now owned by Herman Chadwick, halted and opened in the center, so as to admit into the column the horse and cart containing the coffin. The horse was driven by William Adams, who was seated upon the coffin, and was employed as executioner. He had on black silk gloves, and a black silk handkerchief secured over and fitted to his face by some adhesive substance. ... The Marshals soon came out of the house, followed by O'Conner and the Rev. Mr. Fitzmaurice. ...

... O'Conner being now seated upon the coffin, the column commenced moving forward, to quarter minute taps of the drum, and arrived about twelve o'-clock at the gallows, which was erected on the top of a mound in the vicinity of the present Court House. The company here formed into a hollow square, the cart being driven under the arm of the gallows, at the foot of which the grave was already dug. ... Even many of the spectators removed their hats, while the priest offered up, in a clear and distinct tone of voice, a fervent and lengthy prayer, parts of which were repeated by O'Conner, who, at the close of the prayer, addressed a few remarks to the people, saying that he had killed O'Keaf, that he was sorry for it, and he hoped that all would forgive him. ... The hangman now spoke to O'Conner and assisted him to re-ascend the cart, when he adjusted around his person a white shroud; then securing his arms behind him at the elbows, he drew the cap over his face, fixed the noose around his neck, and lastly, he removed his leg of wood; then decended from the cart, and laid hold of the bridle of his horse and waited for the signal, which was given by one of the Marshals, who advanced into the open area, where he stood with a watch in one hand and a handkerchief at arm's length in the other. As the hand of the watch came around to the moment, the handkerchief fell, and the cart started. There was a convulsive struggling of the limbs for a moment, followed by a tremulous shuddering of the body, and life was extinct. The body hung about thirty minutes, when Dr. Andros stepped forward, felt of his pulse, and said, "He is dead." ...

Eliphalet Price, "The Trial and Execution of Patrick O'Conner at the Dubuqe Mines in the Summer of 1834," *Annals of Iowa* 1st Series, no. XII (October 1865): 566-73.

*I*n 1836, the Iowa District—a part of the Territory of Michigan since 1834—was made part of the new Territory of Wisconsin. While a permanent capital was being readied in Madison, the Wisconsin territorial legislature temporarily met first at Belmont, Wisconsin, and then at Burlington in Des Moines County—much to the dismay of the Iowa District's other county, Du Buque.

A sampling of the enactments of the Wisconsin territorial legislature illustrates the conditions and needs of the rapidly settling Iowa District.

*A*n Act Prescribing The Duties Of Coroners.

Be it enacted by the council and house of representatives of the territory of Wisconsin ....

[E]very coroner, as soon as, and whenever he shall be informed, or know of the body of any person being found dead, supposed to have come to his or her death by violence, calamity or any undue means, shall forthwith proceed to summon a jury of twelve good and lawful men, of the neighborhood where said dead body shall be found lying or being, to repair at such time as he shall direct, to the place where said dead body may be, to inquire (upon a view of said body,) how and in what manner, and by whom or what he or she came to his or her death ....
Approved November 29, 1836.

An Act To Provide For The Election Of County Treasurers And To Define Their Duties.

[T]here shall be elected at the time and place of electing county commissioners, a county treasurer ....

[T]he county treasurer shall have for his services, one and a half per centum for all moneys received, and one and a half per centum for all moneys paid out for the county ....
Approved December 20, 1837.

An Act For The Relief Of The Poor.

The board of county commissioners of any county in this territory, may if they think proper, cause to be built or procured in their respective counties, work-houses for the accommodation and em-

ployment of such paupers, as may from time to time become a county charge; and said work-house, and pauper, shall be under such rules and regulations as said board of commissioners may deem proper and just ....
Approved January 3, 1838.

An Act To Authorize The ... Erecting [Of] Court Houses And Jails.

[T]he boards of county commissioners, of the several counties in this territory, be, and they are hereby authorized to borrow, on the credit of their respective counties, at any interest not exceeding seven per centum per annum, such sum or sums of money as may be necessary for the erection, at the county seats of the several counties, a court house, jail, and fire proof offices ....
Approved January 15, 1838.

An Act To Regulate Ferries.

The board of county commissioners in each of the counties in this territory shall grant licenses for keeping ferries in their respective counties, to as many suitable persons as they may think proper; which license shall continue in force for a time to be fixed by the board of commissioners, not exceeding three years.
Approved January 18, 1838.

Laws of the Territory of Wisconsin, 1836-38, reprinted in Benjamin F. Shambaugh, (ed.), *Documentary Material Relating To The History of Iowa* (Iowa City: State Historical Society, 1901), vol. III, pp. 3-4, 9-10, 23-24, 26-27, 34.

When Iowa became part of the Wisconsin Territory in 1836, there were a few lawyers who plied their profession on both sides of the Mississippi River. The following reminiscences of two of these men give a flavor of the first courts and judges of the Iowa District.

There were but two counties in what is now Iowa [in 1836]—DuBuque and Des Moines. ... There was no title to our lands west of the Mississippi river. The Indians had ceded on the west side only a strip of land about sixty miles wide. The towns of Davenport, Burlington, and DuBuque had about three dry-goods stores each, filled only with some of the necessaries of life. ... There was not a railroad in the United States, and if any one had then told us that there would be in our day, a railroad from the Atlantic to the Pacific, passing through Iowa, he would have been regarded as a lunatic. When navigation closed our only communication, with the east, was by mail through Chicago, carried either on horse-back, or in dilapidated wagons in which no man could safely ride. The frozen river was our turn-pike from the head of the upper rapids to Prairie du Chien. When travelling on the river was not safe we went from DuBuque to Burlington, the then temporary seat of government, on horse-back, following the bank of the river. ...

The first court was held by Judge David Irving [sic] in the spring of 1837, at DuBuque. His district was established by the [Wisconsin territorial] legislature at Belmont during the session of 1836-7, and embraced the whole of the territory situated on the west side of the Mississippi river; the next term by Judge Dunn, of Elk Grove, Wisconsin, to whose district the counties of DuBuque and Jackson were subsequently attached by the Wisconsin Territorial Legislature at Burlington.

"Address of Judge T. S. Wilson at the Opening of the Supreme Court-Room," *Iowa Historical Record* X (April 1887): 457-59.

David Irvin was one of the first Territorial Judges after the organization of Wisconsin Territory. He was a Virginian. He was assigned to the first district west of the Mississippi River. He was about forty-five years of

Territory of Wisconsin }
Des Moines County } ss.

The United States of America
to the Sheriff of said County. You are hereby
~~Commanded~~ to take the body of Martin Wheeler
if he shall be found in your county and
him safely keep so that you have his body before
the next District Court of said County to be
holden at the Court House in the town of Burlington on Monday the Fourth day of September
next to answer James Bell and Nicholas Bois
Merchants trading and doing business in the name
style and firm of Bell and Bois in a Plea
of Debt. — Debt Sixty nine dollars and sixty three
cents. — Damag Fifty dollars. And of this Writ
make legal Service and due return as the
Law directs. —

Witness the Hon. David Irwin Judge
of the second Judicial District
of the territory aforesaid at Burlington
with the temporary seal of the said
Court hereto affixed there being no
regular official seal provided
this twenty fourth day of June
Anno Domini 1837.
William R Ross Clerk of
Des Moines County, Wisconsin Terr.

Original court paper in the case of *Bell v. Wheeler,* June 24, 1837, commanding the presence of the defendant at the next term of court before the Hon. David Irvin, Judge of the Second Judicial District of the Territory of Wisconsin in Burlington, Des Moines County, Iowa District.

age; a genuine 'high-toned' gentleman; well informed upon all the current events of the day, even to horses, dogs and guns; at all times ready to attend to any fun. He could show a tailor how to cut and fashion a garment, a bootmaker how to make and fit a boot, a barber how to strop a razor; in fact, he could teach a housekeeper how to cook meals and make beds, and upon all occasions he imparted this knowledge. ... When upon the bench he was a fair and able jurist enough, but one of the most technical Judges it has been my fortune to meet in a constant attendance on the courts of more than fifty years. This anecdote was told about him: A man had an important case before him and having obtained a decree in his favor, was about leaving the court room when he met the Judge's dog and gave him a violent kick. This was too much for the Judge, and he directed the Clerk to make an entry setting aside the decree. Whether he ever reinstated it I don't know, but I presume he did after he cooled down. He was so strict and technical that upon one occasion when Washington County was organized and the county seat had been located a half mile from Gobles—the nearest house—at a place called Astoria, he would not hold court at the house, but rode out to where the town site was located, and improvised my buggy for the Judge's seat, and the Clerk used the top of the buggy for his desk.

James W. Woods, quoted in Edward H. Stiles, *Recollections and Sketches of Notable Lawyers and Public Men of Early Iowa* (Des Moines: Homestead Publishing Co., 1916), pp. 265-66.

One of the men who practiced law in Iowa before it became a separate territory was none other than Charles Mason—the first Chief Justice of the Iowa Territorial Supreme Court and the principal author of the State of Iowa's first code of laws. He later recalled the humorous and harrowing aspects of the life of a pioneer lawyer.

In April, 1838, the first court in the Third Wisconsin District was held at Farmington in the County of Van Buren, Judge Irvin presiding. Mr. Rorer [a fellow lawyer] and myself started in a buggy the day previous to the opening of the court and after a toilsome journey reached West Point about nightfall, where we became guests for the night of Col. William Patterson, now a resident of Keokuk, who was then the keeper of a public house. The next day about noon we reached the seat of justice and preparations were soon made to commence the business of the court. ...

As soon as supper was finished each day most of the guests of the hotel stole off to bed, it being well understood that the first three who took possession of a couch had a pre-emption thereto, no one expecting a less number of occupants. Some of us preferred later hours and taking our chances—the consequence was that almost, if not quite every night there were five men left with only one bed for them all. This was spread lengthwise before the fire, and we lay across it with our feet to the fire. I was generally fireman and kept a rousing fire in the broad, old-fashioned chimney, replenished from time to time during the night. ... The next court was to be held at Mount Pleasant commencing the following Monday. Sunday morning after gaining the best information as to our route within our reach, we started off without guide or compass, over the trackless prairie. Fortunately we had sunshine to aid us. Our main purpose was to strike the Skunk River at a point some six or seven miles from Mount Pleasant, where there was the only known ferry across that river for twenty miles up and down its course. About noon we reached a farmer's cabin, where we found no means of satisfying our own appetites, though we found an indifferent feed for our horses. ... Arriving at Big Creek, we found it very much swollen. I endeavored to find someone

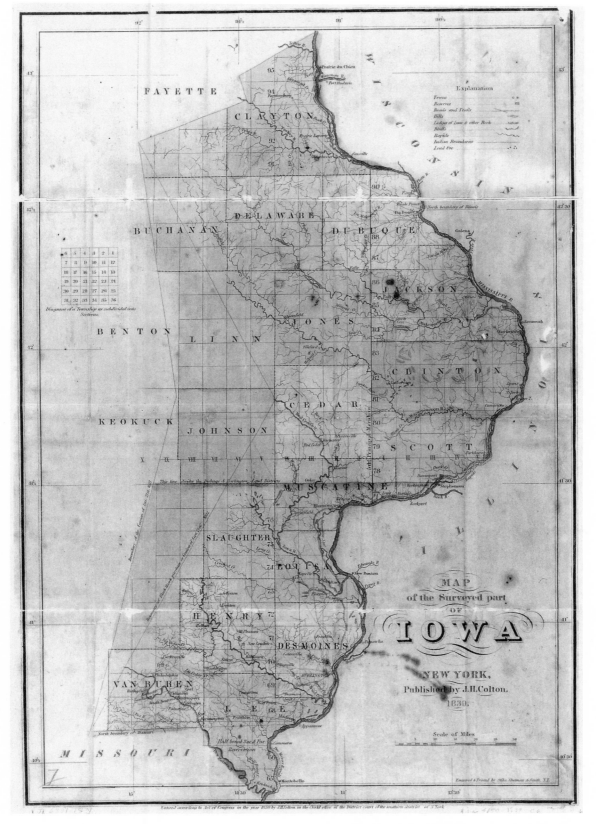

Map of Iowa, 1839. (Courtesy, State Historical Society, Iowa City)

who would carry us over on horseback, and while I was parleying with a settler with that intent, Mr. Rorer became impatient and plunged into the stream, though the water came up to his middle, while I by waiting a few minutes was enabled to go across dry shod.

After the business of the court at Mount Pleasant was finished, we started for home at about the middle of the day. No such thing as a bridge was known on that route, and the spring rains had rendered the prairie sloughs next to impassable. ... By this time it was sunset, and we had not proceeded a mile when we were met by a thunderstorm which came directly in our faces. ... Dense darkness rendered eyesight useless except when the occasional flashes of lightning enabled us to see our way imperfectly. When these ceased to aid us I went ahead of the buggy, and where I found the deepest mud supposed myself in the right way. ... These and like experiences, though lightly regarded at the time, were probably laying the foundation for the bilious fever which in August following came very nearly terminating my earthly existence.

Charles Mason, quoted in Edward H. Stiles, *Recollections and Sketches of Notable Lawyers and Public Men of Early Iowa* (Des Moines: Homestead Publishing Co., 1916), pp. 29-30.

The United States established land offices in Dubuque and Burlington in June 1838. Surveyed land was offered for sale at public auction for $1.25 an acre. However, by 1838 there were nearly 23,000 settlers already living in the future Iowa. Thousands had taken possession of land, built homes, and planted crops. Technically, they were trespassers, or "squatters," but they sought to protect their interests through extra-legal groups known as "claim clubs" or "squatters associations." Many of these clubs were tightly organized and adopted formal rules regarding membership, officers, and land qualifications.

The first government surveys of Iowa were undertaken in 1836-1837. One of the surveyors, Willard Barrows, gave a first-hand account of the influence of claim clubs in pre-territorial Iowa.

All lands, from the time of the departure of the Indians, until they were offered for sale by the government, were under the rule of "squatter sovereignty." Any man had a right to select for himself any portion of the public domain, not otherwise appropriated, for his home, and by blazing the lines bounding his "claim" in timber, or staking it out on the prairie, he was legally possessed of title. Societies were formed, or "claim clubs," who organized themselves to protect one another in their rights. The Secretary kept a book in which all claims had to be recorded. ... These claims were respected and held in peace (when properly taken) until the sale of the lands by government, when the owners were permitted to purchase them at the minimum price of $1.25 per acre. ...

Some trouble occurred this year [1836] among claim-holders. ... Individuals, not in actual possession, were liable to have their claims jumped. Several cases of this kind occurred, when the Society, which had been organized in March of this year, interfered. Having tried one man by the name of Stephens, who had jumped a claim of Maj. Wilson's ... and he refusing to vacate the premises, on application of the Major, the Sheriff of Du Buque county was sent for, there being then no nearer seat of Justice than Du Buque. On the arrival of Sheriff Cummings, he found Mr. Stephens snugly ensconced in the Major's cabin, armed with the instruments that would terminate life if properly handled, and threatening entire annihilation to any and all who might dare to touch him. The Sheriff soon summoned his posse, and with them came a yoke of oxen, which were soon hitched to one corner of the log cabin, and as the timbers began to show signs of parting, Mr. Stephens very willingly vacated the premises, and was shown the most feasible, as well as the quickest route to Stephenson, and never afterward made any attempt to recover his claim on this side of the river.

Willard Barrows, "History of Scott County, Iowa," *Annals of Iowa* 1st Series, no. II (April 1863): 49, 58-59, 61.

Burlington, the second temporary capital of the Wisconsin Territory and first capital of the Territory of Iowa. (Painted by Henry Lewis in 1848, reproduced from *Das Illustrirte Mississippithal,* 2d ed., 1923)

No sooner had the Iowa District become part of the Wisconsin Territory than pressure began to mount for a separate Territory of Iowa. A convention of the newly created seven southern counties was held at Burlington in November 1837, and passed a resolution requesting territorial status.

The following year, Congress took action. Despite the opposition of a few southern members, the Organic Act for the Territory of Iowa was passed in June 1838, and was signed into law by President Martin Van Buren. The law created the new Territory of Iowa, effective July 4, 1838.

An Act to divide the Territory of Wisconsin and to establish the Territorial Government of Iowa.

Be it enacted by the Senate and House of Representatives of the United States of America in Congress assembled, That from and after the third day of July next, all that part of the present Territory of Wisconsin which lies west of the Mississippi river, and west of a line drawn due north from the head waters or sources of the Mississippi to the Territorial line, shall, for the purposes of temporary government, be and constitute a separate Territorial Government by the name of Iowa ....

Sec. 2. And be it further enacted, That the executive power and authority in and over the said Territory of Iowa shall be vested in a Governor, who shall hold his office for three years ....

Sec. 4. And be it further enacted, That the legislative power shall be vested in the Governor and a Legislative Assembly. The Legislative Assembly shall consist of a Council and House of Representatives. ...

Sec. 5. And be it further enacted, That every free white male citizen of the United States, above the age of twenty-one years, who shall have been an inhabitant of said Territory at the time of its organization, shall be entitled to vote at the first election, and shall be eligible to any office within the said Territory ....

Sec. 9. And be it further enacted, That the judicial power of the said Territory shall be vested in a supreme court, district courts, probate courts, and in justices of the peace. The supreme court shall consist of a chief justice, and two associate judges ... and

they shall hold their offices during term of four years. ...

Sec. 11. And be it further enacted, That the Governor, secretary, chief justice, and associate judges, attorney and marshal, shall be nominated, and by and with the advice and consent of the senate, appointed by the President of the United States. ...

Sec. 12. And be it further enacted, That the inhabitants of the said Territory shall be entitled to all the rights, privileges and immunities heretofore granted and secured to the Territory of Wisconsin and to its inhabitants ... subject, nevertheless, to be altered, modified, or repealed, by the Governor and Legislative Assembly of the said Territory of Iowa ....

Approved June 12, 1838

U.S. Statutes at Large, vol. 5, pp. 235-39, 241.

CHAPTER ONE

The Iowa Territory

1838-1846

"Oh, God of Heaven and Earth, bless Iowa."

— TERRITORIAL GOVERNOR Robert Lucas

1838-1846

T HE NEW IOWA TERRITORY NEEDED ITS
own governor. Democrat President Martin Van Buren nominated the former governor of Ohio, Robert Lucas, for this position, and the Senate confirmed the nomination. Lucas arrived at Burlington in August 1838.

In accordance with the Organic Act establishing the Territory of Iowa, President Van Buren also appointed three judges of the territorial Supreme Court. They were Chief Justice Charles Mason, a West Point graduate and Burlington resident; the youthful Thomas S. Wilson of Dubuque; and Joseph Williams, a Pennsylvanian who settled in Bloomington (now Muscatine).

The territorial Legislative Assembly consisted of a Council, whose thirteen members held two-year terms, and a House of Representatives, whose twenty-six members held one-year terms. The election of the first Legislative Assembly was held in September 1838; the legislature convened at Burlington in November.

Governor Lucas had chosen the river town of Burlington as the first capital of the Territory of Iowa. Thereafter, the Legislative Assembly authorized a new, more western site to serve the expanding territory. Iowa City became the territorial capital in December 1841, and the stone capitol building was occupied one year later.

Soon after his arrival in the Iowa Territory, Governor Lucas faced an issue more weighty than choosing a territorial capital. The state of Missouri claimed as its northern border the "Brown Line," which was farther north than the "Sullivan Line" that apparently had been accepted by Congress when Missouri was admitted to statehood. The Territory of Iowa claimed a border farther south than the Sullivan Line. Residents of the disputed area (over 2,500 square miles) were confronted by Missourian attempts to collect taxes and the prospect of living in a slave state rather than in the free Territory of Iowa.

While a United States commission tried to sort matters out, local residents became embroiled in skirmishes. In November 1839, a Clark County, Missouri sheriff accompanied by other Mis-

23

sourians tried to collect taxes in Van Buren County. The sheriff was met with a force of Iowa farmers, and was arrested and taken to Governor Lucas. Missouri called up the militia; Governor Lucas responded in kind. The only real casualties appear to have been some bee trees cut down by raiding Missourians—hence the name sometimes applied to the conflict, "The Honey War."

The militias disbanded without incident, but the controversy remained unsettled even when Iowa attained statehood in 1846. The border dispute was handed back to Congress, and finally to the United States Supreme Court. In 1849 and 1851 decisions, the Court adopted the Sullivan line and approved the results of a new survey.

In 1841, after the election of Whig William Henry Harrison as President of the United States, Governor Lucas was replaced by John Chambers of Kentucky, Iowa's second territorial governor. The Democrats under James K. Polk regained control of the White House in the 1844 election, and in 1845 a Democrat again was appointed governor. This third and last territorial governor of Iowa was James Clarke, who had been territorial secretary under Governor Lucas.

Governor Lucas had himself hoped to guide the Iowa Territory to full statehood. To this end, in 1839 he proposed that the Legislative Assembly ask Congress to call a constitutional convention. The Assembly did not do so, but in July 1840, it decided to submit the question to a popular vote. The following month, by a margin of 2,907 to 937, voters rejected the proposition.

Lucas's successor, Governor Chambers, proposed that the Legislative Assembly again submit the question to the people. And again, in August 1842, voters defeated a proposition for a constitutional convention. Among other reasons, the negative vote reflected concern that statehood would mean increased costs and a greater tax burden.

In 1844, a third vote to assemble a constitutional convention at last succeeded. The population had grown from approximately 43,000 in 1840 to over 75,000 in mid-1844, and statehood appeared both inevitable and desirable. Delegates convened in Iowa City in October and drafted the Constitution of 1844. The constitution and a petition for statehood were sent to Congress.

On March 3, 1845, President John Tyler—who had succeeded President Harrison after his untimely death—signed an act admitting Iowa (a free state) and Florida (a slave state) to statehood. However, Congress had narrowed the proposed western and northern boundaries of Iowa, apparently to enable more "free" states to be carved out of the upper Mississippi valley. When submitted to a vote in April, Iowans narrowly rejected the amended constitution. Another referendum in August brought the same result.

A second constitutional convention was called for May 1846, and the delegates drafted the Constitution of 1846. Congress in the meantime reconsidered and expanded the proposed boundary to the Missouri and Big Sioux Rivers. On August 3, 1846, Iowans approved the constitution by a slim margin of 9,492 to 9,036 votes. Outgoing territorial Governor Clarke called an election for October, and Democrat Ansel Briggs was selected the first governor of the State of Iowa.

On December 28, 1846—while the nation was engaged in a war with Mexico—President Polk signed the bill formally admitting Iowa as the twenty-ninth state. With a population nearing 100,000, Iowa began a new political life.

The Organic Act establishing the Territory of Iowa divided the territory into three judicial districts. Each of the three Territorial Supreme Court judges was assigned to hold district court and reside in one of these judicial districts.

Ohio-born Thomas S. Wilson served on the Iowa Supreme Court from 1838 until his resignation in 1847. He was not yet twenty-five years old at the time of his appointment. Judge Wilson lived in Dubuque and is credited as presiding over the first district court in the new Territory of Iowa, held at Prairie La Porte (now Guttenburg) in September 1838. His reminiscences give a flavor of the vicissitudes of life in the pioneer courts of Iowa.

The first court held in Iowa after its organization as a Territory, was held by me at Prairie La Porte, (now Guttenburg) Clayton county. There were then but three houses in the place and they were log cabins. There was no wagon road to Prairie La Porte .... There was then no dwelling house there, the nearest being that of C. W. Hobbs, clerk of the court, which was a mile from the court house. The attendants at court dined out of their wagons. ... The court house was a one story log house on the bank of the lake, with one room below for the court, and one for the petit jury in the half story above. The floors were made of loose plank, and when the jurors walked over the loose boards above our heads, we were in constant apprehension that they would return into court without due deliberation. There being no place provided for the grand jury, they held their sessions in the adjacent grove with the foreman, Moreland, seated on a stump. ...

The first term of the court in Jackson county, after the organization of our territory, was held in Bellevue in a building of Mr. Heffly, a grocer, erected for a dwelling house, but not yet occupied as such, but contained supplies for the store. To make room for the court a hogshead of molasses, which was there, was rolled against the side wall with the end upwards, back of a projection made for folding doors. Judge Grant was then trying his first case in that county, as an attorney. Many of you know his power-

Many court proceedings in territorial Iowa were held in log cabins. (Courtesy, State Historical Society of Iowa, Iowa City)

ful, shrill voice. The day was warm. The attendants at court with the exception of those engaged in the trial of the case, were sitting near the court house, on the bank of the river, under the shade of the trees. Among them was Peterson the court bailiff, who was about five feet high, and four feet broad with legs about two feet long. When Grant commenced to speak to the jury it was in his usual tone of voice, which could be heard for a mile. The outsiders when they heard his voice, thinking there was a row in court, rushed there. The bailiff, whose short legs left him in the rear, cried "Silence," repeatedly, and vociferously on his way. Being in the rear of the crowd his low stature prevented his seeing what was taking place before the court, and he climbed upon the molasses hogshead to obtain a view of the situation. ... When the bailiff stood upon his toes and shouted, "Silence," the head of the hogshead gave away, and the bailiff sank to the chin in the molasses cask. ... I suspended proceedings until he could be resurrected, and when that was done he rushed to the river and went in for total immersion. ...

In 1840, when the first court was held in Jones county, there was but one dewling [sic] house at the county seat, and that was a log cabin about fifteen feet square, with but one room, and but one bed. ... There being but one bed in the house and that being occupied by the landlord and his wife, Mr. Malony, the deputy United States Marshal and I slept on a pile of straw at the side of the stove. The only other building in town was the log court house, consisting of one room. At the next term the members of the bar who went from Dubuque, the Marshal and I lodged at Farmer Hosterrer's on our way to court. Mr. H. offered to load his wagon with beds, bedding and provisions, and proposed that we should encamp in the court house. We accepted his offer, and he fulfilled his promise. After court adjourned, and after we had taken our lunch, our beds were spread upon the court house floor, and at bed time we retired to rest. Many of the jurors and other persons attending court sought repose with us and laid upon the floor, which had been swept. But little did we know what was before us. We were not aware that the court house had been used as a stable and hog dormitory during the summer previous. ... This, I think, was the last court ever held there. Whether the flea insurrection had anything to do with it or not, I do not know, but the county seat was removed to Anamosa, where there were comfortable accommodations.

Thomas S. Wilson, *Pioneer Law-Makers Association of Iowa: Reunions of 1886 and 1890* (Des Moines: State Printer, 1890), Reunion of February 27-29, 1890, pp. 85, 81, 86-87.

The recollections of lawyers who practiced in the territorial courts corroborate the rugged—and often humorous—conditions that attended the practice of law.

My professional life in Iowa dates from early in 1840. ... At this time we must bear in mind that courts were not held west of Jefferson and Van Buren counties. The immense and rich country beyond these counties and to the south line of the Territory were in the undisputed possession of the Indian, and but few of the counties north of Henry and Jefferson were organized, or if so, they had but few inhabitants. ...

Think of these things, judges and lawyers, in the early days of Iowa. Think of the forded Iowa, the overflowing Cedar, the muddy Turkey, the deceitful English, the quagmiry Fox Run, the Skunk and Coon, the Wapsy, and even for the most part the beautiful, placid and gentle Des Moines; and think of them as I have known them, without bridges, without boats, out of their banks and without bottom. Think too of the muddy roads and bottomless sloughs, of the mere blind paths from one village or settlement to another. ...

Our first term in B— for the first half was held in the room about twenty feet square, where we all ate and slept. The other half was held in a log house without floor, the judge occupying a block as a judicial bench, the clerk a like substitute with a small rough board table as his desk and the lawyers a plank placed upon logs. The grand jury was kept to one side of what was called "a run" between two hills on the prairie, with officers to keep off as best they could the curious crowd; while the petit jury in the case tried, was kept in the like manner on the opposite side. So in B. court was held in a log cabin five miles from the present county seat in the midst of thick timber. The good old lady of the house removed her pots and kettles to the shelter of a neighboring tree, to give room for the learned judge and the officers of the law. ...

In Story County the court was held ... in a small log house. The petit jury occupied a stable; one of the jurors being kicked by a horse while in the jury room. The grand jury had a retired spot on the prairie where rumor says they discussed many matters, including a jug of whiskey—assisted in the last by the judge "at the earnest solicitation of the jury."

George G. Wright, "Judge Wright's Last Lecture Before The Law Class. The Pioneer Bar of Iowa," *Iowa Historical Record* XII (January 1896): 401, 402, 405-08.

I had in my district eight counties, and was often out from home eight weeks at a time .... I was district Attorney, and in that position frequently represented the United States Attorney. It was with Judge Williams holding court that I first came to Johnson county. ... The Indians had just been removed to near Marengo. All about here was open country, and the only building, the old trading house, south of the city, was taken for a court room. It had no windows, and the only way to light the room was to leave the door open. We organized the county and held the first term of court, and occasionally some lookers-on would stand in the door-way obstructing the light, and the court would order it cleared. A man had committed an offense, and I had him indicted; of course there was no room in the old trading house for the grand jury to deliberate, and in preparing the indictment we went out on the prairie, a distance from the trading house, where as I remember I stood on a log and addressed the grand jury. ...

When Judge Williams was holding court in Muscatine some unruly people in the audience kept up a disturbance, greatly annoying the court and lawyers. As the Judge and I were going to our hotel after adjournment, we met a man who looked like the typical bully of the State, over six feet high and of great frame. He stopped us, and said to my friend ... "Appoint me bailiff, and I'll see that you have order, if I have to kill a man." The Judge did not care to have any controversy on the street—so said "I'll see

about it." I said to the Judge, "appoint him, perhaps he can really keep order, and at any rate we will not be any worse off than we are now." So the next morning, when court opened, the Judge said, "I appoint J. L. ... bailiff of this court, and he will preserve order." Just as soon as he was sworn in, he stepped out in front of the Judge and called, "gentlemen, you will keep order; I have been appointed to see that you do, and if you don't I will throw the first man that makes a disturbance out of the window." ... [N]o Judge ever presided over a court in which he had better order.

At another term of court, when I went out to meet the grand jury, I found them by no means as "sober as a judge," in fact they were unmistakably drunk. I saw there was no use of trying to do anything and told the Judge the jury was drunk. He called the jury in, reprimanded them and told them to come back sober, or he would put them in prison. The jury came back next morning, perfectly sober and retired for deliberation. ...

Theodore S. Parvin, *The Early Bar of Iowa: An Address Delivered Before the State Historical Society of Iowa* (Iowa City: State Historical Society, 1894), pp. 15-17.

Our early courts in [Louisa County] were held in log cabins. The sessions of the grand jury were held at first in an adjacent ravine. Mr. Thomas and I were the first resident lawyers in the county. At our first term of court, held in 1839, we were engaged in some forty cases. ...

Louisa County was then in the Second Judicial District, presided over by Judge Joseph Williams, of Muscatine. He and my friend, Edward H. Thomas, were the life and center of attraction of the social circles of evenings when on court circuits, both being adept in vocal and instrumental music. The Judge was at home on almost any instrument, banjo, drum, fife, as well as on instruments of a higher grade. ... The Judge's gift as a comedian would keep a crowd in a roar ....

Francis Springer, quoted in Edward H. Stiles, *Recollections and Sketches of Notable Lawyers and Public Men of Early Iowa* (Des Moines: Homestead Publishing Co., 1916), p. 534.

A high drama in the frontier territory involved David Rorer, one of early Iowa's most prominent and brilliant attorneys. Rorer came to Iowa in 1836 and settled in Burlington, where he practiced law until his death in 1884. He wrote several books on law and argued numerous important cases before the Iowa Supreme Court, including the first reported decision, In the matter of Ralph.

David Rorer was one of twenty lawyers admitted in the first term of the Iowa Territorial Supreme Court in November 1838. But one month earlier, Rorer in self-defense had shot and killed Cyrus Jacobs, the first district attorney of the Iowa Territory and a newly elected member of the Legislative Assembly. Animosity between the two men appears to have grown during Rorer's unsuccessful bid for election as Iowa's territorial delegate to Congress.

The events of October 29, 1838, were recounted by Rorer during a "preliminary trial" in Burlington, following which he was exonerated of all charges.

As I passed Mr. [James] Clarke I gave him a friendly salutation and he returned it. As I approached Mr. [Cyrus] Jacobs I [did] the same, spoke friendly to him. … He replied to my salutation by commanding me to stop placing his hand in his bosom on a pistol as I supposed. His appearance and attitude was offensive …. I asked him what he meant mildly, and in a low tone of voice. He said … "I mean to have an apology from you you Damn Rascal" … [t]hat I should make it or he would cane me or kill me and I can not absolutely say which. I replied to him in a mild tone that I was surprised at him to attempt to extract an apology from a gentleman in the streets by force, and observed that we had better converse friendly upon that subject and that we would understand each other without any "fuss."

He repeated his demand and threat a second time. I told [him] I had nothing against him and advised him to be peaceable. He observed then I will "kill you God damn you." When he said that I put my hand in my pocket. He then said if you draw your pistol I will shoot you …. At that I attempted to turn and

Lawyers' advertisements in territorial Iowa. James Grimes (*top*) later became governor of Iowa. (*Burlington Hawk-Eye & Patriot,* October 31, 1839)

walk off. At the time he spoke of drawing a pistol and killing of me, he drew his pistol from his bosom either partly or entirely—I think entirely. As I was in the act of turning with a view to retire, I received the blow from the cane upon my head. The severity of it caused me to reel and stagger back several steps. While reeling and staggering back I drew my pistol. He was advancing on me, and making an effort to draw his pistol again which was partly out.

The blow had produced a concussion of the brain so as to cause my recollection to leave me. See[ing] that he was drawing his pistol and feeling like falling from the blow I shot.

… I placed my hands on my head and discovered that it was wet with blood …. I have a very in-

Attorney David Rorer of Burlington. (Courtesy, State Historical Society of Iowa, Iowa City)

distinct recollection of the report of the second pistol.

[W]hen I did shoot ... I had an indubitable belief that if I did not shoot, I should be shot myself.

Statement of David Rorer, November 2, 1838, *United States contra David Rorer,* Papers of David Rorer, State Historical Society of Iowa, Manuscript Division, Iowa City.

The Jacobs shooting led to the first official call for "gun control" in Iowa. During his first annual message to the Legislative Assembly of the Territory of Iowa, Governor Robert Lucas alluded to the recent tragic event in Burlington.

The recent transaction in this city, that deprived the Legislative Assembly of one of its members elect, as well as all other transactions of a similar character, should meet with the indignant frown of every friend of morality and good order in community; and the practice of wearing concealed about the person, dirks, pistols, and other deadly weapons, should not only be considered disreputable, but criminal, and punished accordingly. There certainly cannot be a justifiable excuse offered for such a practice; for in a civil community, a brave man never anticipates danger, and an honest man will always look to the laws for protection.

Governor Robert Lucas, First Annual Message, November 12, 1838, reprinted in Benjamin F. Shambaugh (ed.), *The Messages and Proclamations of the Governors of Iowa* (Iowa City: State Historical Soc'y, 1903), vol. I, p. 84.

The first session of the Legislative Assembly of the Territory of Iowa convened in Burlington on November 12, 1838. The Legislative Assembly included future governors Stephen P. Hempstead and James W. Grimes—the latter, at twenty-two, being the youngest member. One of the legislators, Hawkins Taylor, later described the conditions facing this first territorial assembly.

It was a long time ago when I was in the Legislature. ... We then had nothing, no House, no library; we passed about six hundred pages of law at that session .... We did not believe then that this part of the State [Des Moines] would be occupied while we lived except by wolves and gophers. That was a brainy Legislature, and I think was equal to the average, yet we had a quarrel with the Governor because we elected officers and employees of the Legislature and paid them $3.00 per day, the same as we received, and he thought it was entirely too much. We learned to eat with knives and forks, and were honest, because there was no object to be dishonest. I have never seen a House presided over with greater dignity, either here or in Washington, than was that Legislature, and I think we are entitled to credit for laying a good foundation.

Hawkins Taylor, *Pioneer Law-Makers Association of Iowa: Reunions of 1886 and 1890* (Des Moines: State Printer, 1890), Reunion of February 24-25, 1886, pp. 11-12.

"Old Zion" Methodist Church, Burlington, where the first sessions of the Legislative Assembly of the Territory of Iowa were held. (Courtesy, State Historical Society of Iowa, Iowa City)

be inflicted with a view to reform, rather than exterminate the criminal. In these conclusions I heartily concur, and would wish to see confinement at hard labor, for life, substituted in all cases, in lieu of capital punishment, when suitable prisons for the purpose can be had .... I would recommend to your consideration the propriety of providing by law, for executing capital punishment (should such punishment be necessary) privately, in the county prison, in the presence of the sheriff, and such other persons as the court passing sentence might direct.

In preparing a system of criminal jurisprudence, the whole catalogue of vices ... pass in review ... and we frequently see the most disastrous consequences proceed from practices, that in some places are considered as only fashionable vices—namely: *gambling and intemperance.*

These two vices may be considered the fountains from which almost every other crime proceeds, as the statistical reports of many of the penitentiaries conclusively show. ... Could you in your wisdom devise ways and means to check the progress of gambling and intemperance in this Territory, you will perform an act that would immortalize your names and entitle you to the gratitude of posterity.

Governor Robert Lucas, First Annual Message, November 12, 1838, reprinted in Benjamin F. Shambaugh (ed.), *The Messages and Proclamations of the Governors of Iowa* (Iowa City: State Historical Society, 1903), vol. I, pp. 82-84.

Territorial Governor Robert Lucas quickly established a reputation for vigorous leadership. In his first annual message to the Legislative Assembly, he questioned the wisdom of capital punishment and warned against the twin evils of gambling and alcohol.

The compilation of a criminal code ... is a subject of deep interest to the community. It is one which of late has occupied the attention of some of the greatest statesmen and philanthropists of the age; and the general conclusion has been ... that the general policy of all criminal laws should be to prevent crimes, rather than to inflict punishment, and that all punishments should

Governor Lucas charged the first Legislative Assembly to appoint a committee of three persons "of known legal experience and weight of character, to digest and prepare a complete code of laws .... " However, not until 1848 was a commission—headed by former Chief Justice Charles Mason—appointed to draft such a code, finally issued as the Code of 1851.

In the meantime, the territory was governed by statutes passed in the 1838-1839 legislative session, known as "The Old Blue Book" because of its blue cardboard backing. This was succeeded four years later by the Revised Statutes of the Territory of Iowa, 1842-1843, known as "The Blue Book."

Robert Lucas, Iowa's first territorial governor. (Courtesy, State Historical Society of Iowa, Iowa City)

The enactments of the Legislative Assembly cover hundreds of pages. Even a small selection of these statutes gives a vivid glimpse of life and attitudes in territorial Iowa.

An Act Defining Crimes And Punishments. EXCUSABLE HOMICIDE: Excusable homicide, by misadventure, is when a person is doing a lawful act without any intention of killing, yet unfortunately kills another; as where a man is at work with an axe, and the head flies off and kills a bystander; or where a parent is moderately correcting a child, or master his servant or scholar, or an officer punishing a criminal, and happens to occasion death, it shall be only misadventure, for the act of correction was lawful ....

DUELLING: If any person shall challenge another to fight a duel, or shall accept of a challenge to fight a duel, or shall knowingly be the bearer of a challenge for the purpose aforesaid, or shall be a second to any person who fights a duel, or shall aid, assist or promote any duel, every such person so offending, upon conviction thereof, shall forfeit and pay a sum not exceeding two thousand dollars, nor less than five hundred dollars, and shall moreover be rendered incapable of holding or being elected to any office of profit, trust, or emolument, either civil or military, in this Territory, or of voting at an election within the same.

ATTEMPT TO POISON: Every person who shall wilfully and maliciously administer, or cause to be administered to or taken by any person, any poison or other noxious or destructive substance ... with the intention to procure the miscarriage of any woman being with child, and shall thereof be duly convicted, shall be imprisoned for a term not exceeding three years, and fined in a sum not exceeding one thousand dollars.

. . . .

HOG STEALING: Any person who shall steal any hog, shoat, or pig, or mark or alter the mark of any hog, shoat, or pig, with an intention of stealing the same, for every such offence, upon being thereof duly convicted, shall be fined in any sum not exceeding one hundred dollars, and moreover shall be imprisoned for a term not exceeding five years ....

PERSONS SETTING FIRE TO PRAIRIES: If any person shall at any time hereafter willfully, intentionally, or negligently and carelessly, set on fire, or cause to be set on fire, any woods, prairies, or other grounds whatsoever in the inhabited parts of this Territory, persons so offending shall, on conviction, be fined in any sum not less than fifty, nor more than one hundred dollars ....

THE PUNISHMENT OF DEATH: The manner of inflicting the punishment of death shall be by hanging the person convicted by the neck until dead, at such time as the court shall direct, which time shall not be less than fifteen, nor more than twenty-five days from the time sentence is pronounced ... and the court, at their discretion, may order such execution to take place in public ....

Approved January 25, 1839.

An Act To Prevent The Selling Of Spirituous Liquors To Indians.

[I]f any tavern keeper, grocery keeper, or other person, or persons, shall sell, or barter, or in any manner dispose of, any spirituous liquor, or any other liquor of intoxicating quality, to any Indian or Indians, within this Territory, such person, or persons, shall forfeit and pay, for the use of the county, a fine not exceeding one hundred dollars, nor less than twenty-five dollars ....
Approved January 3, 1839.

An Act To Prevent Disasters On Steam Boats. ...

... It shall not be lawful for steam boats to run races, for the trial of speed, or for any other purpose, and the owner and officers, severally and jointly, shall be liable and responsible for all damages which any one may sustain, from any accident, or casualty, which may happen during said race.
Approved January 4, 1839.

An Act To Preserve Good Order In All Worshiping Congregations In This Territory.

[A]ny person who shall, by menace, profane swearing, vulgar language, or any disorderly, or immoral conduct, interrupt and disturb any congregation, or collection of citizens assembled together for the purpose of worshiping Almighty God ... shall be deemed guilty of a high misdemeanor, and upon conviction, shall be fined in any sum not exceeding fifty dollars.
Approved January 24, 1839.

The Statute Laws of the Territory of Iowa, 1838-1839 (Du Buque: Russell & Reeves, 1839), pp. 144-45, 150, 169-70, 274, 447-48, 513-14 ("The Old Blue Book").

An Act Regulating Marriages.
... All marriages of white persons with negroes or mulattoes are declared to be illegal and void.
. . . .
Approved January 6, 1840.

An Act to encourage the destruction of wolves.

[T]he board of commissioners of the several counties in this Territory, be and they are hereby authorized and empowered, at their discretion, to offer a reward of not less than twenty-five cents nor over one dollar, to any person who shall kill any wolf within their respective counties, not exceeding six months old; and the sum of not less than fifty cents nor more than three dollars for every wolf over that age. ...
Approved January 7, 1840.

An Act Regulating The Keeping Of Stallions And Jacks And To Improve The Breed Of Horses.

[I]t shall not be lawful for any person to keep or let to mares any stallion or jack, within the limits of any town or village in this Territory, or within two hundred yards thereof, unless such person shall provide an enclosure, so arranged as to obstruct the view from all the inhabitants in the town and vicinity as aforesaid ....
Approved January 28, 1843.

An Act For The Prevention Of Certain Immoral Practices.

[I]f any person of the age of fourteen years or upwards, shall be found on the first day of the week commonly called Sunday, rioting, quarreling, fishing, shooting, or at common labor, (works of necessity and charity only excepted) he or they shall be fined in any sum not exceeding five dollars ....

[I]f any grocery keeper or other person shall sell or barter any spirituous liquors on the first day of the week, commonly called Sunday, (except prescribed by a physician, or if such grocery keeper or other person shall know that such spirituous liquors are wanted to be used as medicine) such grocery keeper or other person so offending, shall be fined in any sum not exceeding five dollars.
    . . . .

Approved 10th February, 1843.

Revised Statutes of the Territory of Iowa, 1842-43 (Iowa City: Hughes & Williams, 1843), pp. 295, 436, 602-03, 653 ("The Blue Book").

Building where the Iowa territorial legislature met in Iowa City before completion of the limestone capitol building. (Courtesy, State Historical Society of Iowa, Iowa City)

The Legislative Assembly moved quickly to establish a permanent territorial capital. In January 1839, it authorized a three-man commission to locate the capital—to be called "Iowa City"—within Johnson County. In May, the commission selected the site for the future Iowa City on the east bank of the Iowa River. On July 4, 1840, the cornerstone of the limestone capitol building was laid. The seat of government moved from Burlington to Iowa City in December 1841, with the fourth Legislative Assembly meeting in temporary quarters. One year later, the fifth Legislative Assembly occupied the still unfinished capitol building. Iowa City remained the capital of the territory (and subsequently the state) of Iowa for fifteen years, until Des Moines became the seat of government in 1857.

When territorial Governor Robert Lucas first visited the site selected for the new capital, he was filled with dreams for Iowa's future.

One of the most interesting bits of Iowa history was related to me by the late Hon. Abraham Owen, who had a cabin located near the bank of the river where the English river enters the Iowa. One bright day in Spring when all nature seemed in tune, two men appeared on the opposite bank of the river, calling to Mr. Owen, asked "if he could direct them to the site selected for the Capitol of the state of Iowa." Owen said he could and would, if they would cross over and eat dinner with him. Owen rowed over and brought them to his cabin by boat. During the meal Owen asked his distinguished looking guest who he might be. "Well, sir, my name is Lucas, Governor of the state of Iowa".

… Returning by boat to the opposite side of the river, they mounted the horses, Owen walking by the side of the Governor's Kentucky mare, to begin their journey to the site where now stands the once pioneer capitol building of Iowa.

On reaching historic Indian Lookout, Lucas called a halt, removing his hat, standing erect in the stirrups. running his fingers through his curling, slightly greying hair, looking thoughtfully upon the broad expanse of flower decked prairies, the vivid green of the vast forest, the river sparkling in the distance said, "Oh what a country this of ours, so vast in production, so varied in beauty," turning his glowing face to the Heavens, continuing, "Oh, God of Heaven and Earth, bless Iowa."

"Reminiscences," Memoirs of M. Etta Cartwright Coxe, State Historical Society of Iowa, Manuscript Division, Iowa City.

The selection of Johnson County as the site for the permanent territorial capital roused concern among the settlers that a tide of immigrants and speculators would jeopardize their land claims. On March 9, 1839, nearly every settler in the county met to adopt the "Constitution and Laws for the Government of the Citizens of Johnson County in Making and Holding Claims." This remarkable document was signed by 282 individuals, including territorial Governor Robert Lucas. It contained descriptions and salaries of officers, membership requirements, and rules for the staking off, recording, and adjudication of claims.

The practical value of the Johnson County Claim Association is shown in the following account of the members' pilgrimage to Dubuque for a public sale of Johnson County lands.

"Old Capitol" in Iowa City, occupied by the territorial legislature and later the state legislature from 1842 through 1857. (Courtesy, State Historical Society of Iowa, Iowa City)

On the 30th day of July [1840] a number of settlers started to the land sales that were to take place at Dubuque on the 3rd of August. A majority of them were provided with money to buy their claims, though some were expectant of meeting capitalists at the sale, of whom they could borrow the money. Some forty or fifty settlers composed our company and we started for Dubuque in two-horse wagons, supplied with provisions and camp equipage. We traveled by easy stages, and reached Dubuque on Saturday, August 1st. On Monday morning early we had made all arrangements for the sale. The bidder and assistant bidder had furnished themselves with large plats of the two townships to be sold, with each claimant's name plainly written on the subdivision which he wished to

purchase. When the time came for the sale to begin, the crier stepped out on the platform, and inviting the bidder and assistant to take places on the platform beside him, took hold of one side of the plat, and began at section No. I, and called out each eighty acre subdivision as rapidly as he could speak. When he came to a tract with a name written on it, he would strike his hammer down, and give the name to the clerk. He thus proceeded, taking the sections in numerical order. The two townships were offered in less than thirty minutes. During this time the claimants stood in a compact semicircle in front of the platform in breathless silence, not a sound being heard except the crier's voice. The purchasers were then admitted, two or three at a time, to pay for the land and receive their certificates. This was a tedious process, as the land office accepted no money for land except United States coin, or notes on the State Bank of Missouri. Nearly all the money paid was in silver, and it consumed a great deal of time to count it and sort out the spurious coin. On the 5th of August we started for home, many of us enjoying the comfortable feeling of being owners of real estate for the first time in our lives.

Account of Cyrus Sanders, Member of the Johnson County Claim Association, reprinted in Benjamin F. Shambaugh, *Constitution and Records of the Claim Association of Johnson County, Iowa* (Iowa City: State Historical Society, 1894), pp. xvii-xviii.

Governor Lucas was not the only early lawmaker in sympathy with the individuals who had laid claim to and made improvements on Iowa lands before obtaining formal title. In an 1840 Iowa Territorial Supreme Court opinion, Chief Justice Charles Mason expressed admiration for the contribution of these first, extra-legal settlers.

It is notorious that when this territory was organized, not one foot of its soil had ever been sold by the United States, and but a small portion of it (the half breed tract) was individual property. Were we a community of trespassers, or were we to be regarded rather as occupying and improving the lands of the government by the invitation and for the benefit of the owner? ...

Let us suppose that the next week after our territorial organization, the President had directed the Marshall to remove with the least possible delay the whole of our twenty-five thousand people, (excepting the few settlers on the half breed lands and the still fewer who would have been entitled to remain by virtue of pre-emption privileges,) ought such a command to have been obeyed? ... We have no hesitation in saying that such a command would have been altogether illegal, and ought not to have been obeyed.

... Whole communities of unoffending citizens find themselves liable to heavy amercements, and long incarceration for doing acts which they had every reason to believe would be deemed patriotic and praiseworthy, for leading the way in the introduction of wealth and civilization and happiness into the almost illimitable west; for sacrificing the comforts and endearments of home and enduring the hardships and privations, and encountering the diseases of a new and untried country; for building up great communities in the wilderness, enlarging our bounds of empire and vastly augmenting the current of our national revenue. For doing these acts which have redounded so much to the national advantage— done too in accordance with the almost express invitation of the national legislature, and when encouragement to western emigration had become a part of our settled national policy, these individuals where they had every reason to expect rewards—nay, while on the one hand they are actually receiving such rewards, they feel themselves on the other, condemned to severe and even ignominious punishment. Does the spirit of our institutions justify such stupendous deception and wholesale tyranny? We answer emphatically, NO.

Hill v. Smith, 1 Morris 70, 77-78 (Iowa 1840) (Mason, C.J.).

The border dispute between Missouri and the Iowa Territory, given the inflated name in history of the "Honey War," occupied the attention of the governor and Legislative Assembly in the last half of 1839. When the state of Missouri called up its militia, Governor Lucas responded by calling for Iowa militia. John P. Cook, a respected lawyer and legislator who practiced in both Tipton and Davenport, gave a first-hand account of Iowa's enthusiastic—but primitive—volunteer force.

On the day appointed for the first drill, the whole country marched to the standard of the gallant Colonel in command, and Davenport witnessed one of the most spirited military reviews that ever took place within her limits. The line was formed on the banks of the river, fronting towards the enemy's country, the right wing resting against a cotton wood tree, the left in close proximity to the ferry house. There they stood, veterans of iron nerve and dauntless courage, presenting a sight that would have daunted the most desperate foe, and assuring the women and children that they would defend their homes to the death, against the "border ruffians" from the Des Moines river.

The weapons carried by some of these volunteer patriots, were not satisfactory to the commanding officers, and about one fourth of the army were ordered out of the ranks, and their services dispensed with, unless they would procure others of a different character, and more in accordance with the army regulations. The objectionable weapons consisted of a plough colter, carried in a link of a large log chain, which the valiant soldier had over his shoulder. Another was a sheet iron sword about six feet in length, fastened to a rope shoulder strap. Another was an old fashioned sausage stuffor. Another with an old musket without a lock, and the balance of like character.

John P. Cook, quoted in Willard Barrows, "History of Scott County, Iowa," *Annals of Iowa* 1st Series, no. II (April 1863): 49, 70.

*G*overnor Lucas tried to restore calm and order by characterizing the border conflict essentially as one of law. When the House of Representatives passed resolutions decrying the dispute between Missouri and Iowa, Lucas returned them with his objections. He reminded the House that Iowa's government was "entirely under the control of the United States," and that the dispute therefore was between Missouri and the federal government. Governor Lucas's diplomacy bore fruit, and the border incidents ceased while Congress considered the controversy. (Ultimately the United States Supreme Court resolved the dispute.)

In his Third Annual Message to the Legislative Assembly, Lucas reported that the border was calm. Iowa's bloodless "war" with its neighbor to the south was effectively over.

*T*he excitement produced by the intrusions upon the rights of the citizens of Iowa, by the authorities of Missouri, near the boundary line, has subsided. The prosecution commenced under the laws of the Territory against a Sheriff of Missouri, has been dismissed, and no far-

ther attempts have been made by the authorities of that State to exercise jurisdiction north of Sullivan's line. The committee of Congress, in the House of Representatives, at the last session, after an elaborate examination of the subject ... recommended the adoption of the line commonly known as the old Indian boundary, or Sullivan's line .... [W]e therefore trust that the bill, as reported, will be passed by Congress at the ensuing session, and that the line thus designated may be finally established as the boundary between the State of Missouri and this Territory.

Governor Robert Lucas, Third Annual Message, November 3, 1840, reprinted in Benjamin F. Shambaugh (ed.), *The Messages and Proclamations of the Governors of Iowa* (Iowa City: State Historical Soc'y, 1903), vol. 1, pp. 147-48.

*O*ne of the first laws passed by the Legislative Assembly provided: "[T]he first session of the supreme court of the Territory shall be held at the city of Burlington, on the twenty-eighth day of November one thousand eight hundred and thirty-eight." In fact, the Supreme Court Order Book indicates that the first session was held two days earlier, on November 26, 1838. The Court admitted twenty lawyers to practice, appointed a clerk and court reporter, granted a procedural writ of error, and adjourned.

Chief Justice Charles Mason and Judges Joseph Williams and Thomas Wilson comprised the Iowa Territorial Supreme Court. (Associate "judges" of the Supreme Court were not popularly known as "justices" until much later in Iowa's history.) From contemporary accounts, it appears that the three men were temperamentally and judicially well matched.

*C*hief Justice Mason] was a man over six feet in height, thin and somewhat angular. His movements were energetic, and he carried himself erect, a habit formed during his military education at West Point. His mind was by nature a judicial one. He was an attentive listener; arranged his thoughts carefully before clothing them

Charles Mason, Chief Justice of the Iowa Territorial Supreme Court. (Courtesy, State Historical Society of Iowa, Iowa City)

Associate Judge Joseph Williams. (Courtesy, State Historical Society of Iowa, Iowa City)

in words; not much given to talking; rather reticent than otherwise, yet capable of being very interesting when he did talk, and having a quick sense of humor that brought with it a cheery smile and a twinkle of the eye.

George H. Yewell, quoted in Edward H. Stiles, *Recollections and Sketches of Notable Lawyers and Public Men of Early Iowa* (Des Moines: Homestead Publishing Co., 1916), p. 21.

My association with Judges Williams and Wilson was always of the most harmonious and agreeable character. The former was one of the most affable and amusing men I have ever known and although not a very close legal student was a man of very quick parts and seemed to arrive at just conclusions as if by intuition. The latter was a closer legal student and formed his opinions after more thought and reflection. We rarely disagreed ultimately in our views with respect to any questions that were argued before us as

Associate Judge Thomas S. Wilson. (Courtesy, State Historical Society of Iowa, Iowa City)

Judges of the Supreme Court. I do not now remember more than one case in which there was a dissenting opinion written by either of us, for although many of the decisions made by each of us [as district court judges] were reversed by the Supreme Court the judge making such decisions respectively cheerfully concurred in such reversals.

Charles Mason, quoted in Edward H. Stiles, *Recollections and Sketches of Notable Lawyers and Public Men of Early Iowa* (Des Moines: Homestead Publishing Co., 1916), p. 25.

Associate Judge Joseph Williams showed his true mettle and spirit when it came time for President Tyler to re-appoint the judges of the Iowa Territorial Supreme Court. An account of his efforts to secure re-appointment was given by a contemporary lawyer.

These three Judges appointed for four years [Mason, Wilson, and Williams], were all Democrats, but when their terms expired there was a Whig President, Tyler, and it was expected by many that he would appoint Whigs to the positions. Mason was rich, had his farm, and did not care for the place. Wilson had his law practice and felt he could do as well at that as on the bench; but Williams, having nothing to fall back on, was very anxious for reappointment and started to Wash-

ington to secure a renewal of his commission. In those days all the travel from east to west was by land and mostly by stage. When the Judge reached Wheeling, he fell in with a handsome lady going east, and being a very gallant man and quite at ease among the ladies, he had no trouble in making himself agreeable and made known to the lady the nature of his business at Washington. They were traveling companions all the way to Baltimore, and strangely enough the Judge never found out the lady's name. When he got to Washington he fixed himself up in his best manner and called upon the President. He was very cordially received. "What can I do for you Judge Williams?" said the President. The Judge suggested, as delicately as he could, that he would like to have his commission renewed. "Oh," was the reply, "that is already fixed, but I would like to have you stay awhile." He was taken into the parlor and there met the lady who had been his traveling companion—the President's wife, who greeted him most affably and said, "I spoke to my husband about you and he said you should have the appointment." The Judge was as gallant to men as to ladies, and having been so fortunate in his own case, determined to put in a plea for Mason and Wilson. So he asked the President to re-appoint his associates. Madam seconded the request, and they were accordingly all three re-appointed and served eight years, until Iowa was admitted as a State.

Theodore S. Parvin, *The Early Bar of Iowa: An Address Delivered Before the State Historical Society of Iowa* (Iowa City: State Historical Society, 1894), pp. 7-8.

[*Opposite*] Handwritten record of the first session of the Iowa Territorial Supreme Court on November 26, 1838, from the Supreme Court Order Book, vol. A, 1838-1853. Twenty lawyers were admitted to practice before the court, including David Rorer and future state governors James Grimes, Stephen Hempstead, and Ralph P. Lowe. (Courtesy, State Historical Society of Iowa, Des Moines)

At a Supreme Court of the Territory of Iowa,
begun and holden at the Court House in Burlington
in and for the Territory aforesaid, on Monday, the
the 26th, day of November A.D. 1838
Present

    The Honorable Charles Mason, Chief Justice
Honorable Joseph Williams, and Thomas S. Wilson,
Associate Judges

    And now, this, day, came, into Court
how, the following persons, to wit —
    William S. Conway, William
A. Starr, W. Henry Starr, M. L. Browning, James W. Grimes,
David Rorer, Stephen Whicher, G. W. Teas, Stephen Hempstead,
Isaac Van Allen, J. P. Leak, S. C. Hastings, Philip Vich,
J. G. Parvin, R. P. Lowe, Alpha Rich, James W. Woods, B. Rush
Petrikin, Ira C. Clay, and Charles Weston Esqrs. who were
duly admitted as attorneys and Counsellors at Law in this Court
and thereupon the persons aforesaid were duly sworn as attorneys
and Counsellors at Law aforesaid, according to Law

    It is ordered, that Thornton Bayless be hereby appointed Clerk of
this Court, upon on entering into bond and Security according
to Law and thereupon the Said Thornton Bayless with
George H. Palen and Enos Lowe, as his Securities, came
into Court and entered into a bond, in the penalty of
Conditioned according to Law, and thereupon
the Said Thornton Bayless was duly Sworn as Clerk aforesaid

    On motion ordered that Charles Weston Esqr. be hereby appointed
Reporter of this Court

    And now this, day, Came William Gordon
with Counsel by Rorer & Starr his attorneys and moved the Court
for a writ of Error to the District Court of the County of
Musquitine requiring Said Court to certify to this Court
at, the next term thereof, the record and proceedings, in the
judgement of a certain proceeding had in Said District Court
on an appeal from the decision of a justice of the peace at the
last October term of Said District Court wherein Jonas
M. Higby was Plaintiff, and the Said William Gordon, and
Arthur Washburn were defendants, and the Said writ of
Error was awarded accordingly

    Ordered that Said Court

Court adjourned Sine die

Charles Mason
Chief

*D*uring its first terms in Burlington, the Iowa Territorial Supreme Court—like the Legislative Assembly—had no permanent home. Judge Thomas Wilson later recalled that "[a]s no court-house had been erected we consecrated churches, school-houses and empty store-rooms to the purpose."

The humble surroundings of the early Court belied the important issues that awaited decision. The Court reconvened on July 1, 1839, for its first full term since adjourning the previous November. On July 4, it heard arguments in a case Judge Wilson described as "[t]he most important case in the early judicial history of Iowa ...." The Court's first reported decision, In the matter of Ralph (a colored man), on Habeas Corpus, 1 Bradford 3, 1 Morris 1 (Iowa 1839), *addressed issues that twenty years hence would plunge the nation into war—slavery, state sovereignty ... and the right "To Go Free."*

"To Go Free": The Case of Ralph, a Former Slave

THERE WERE SLAVES IN EARLY IOWA. THE first star-spangled banner ever hoisted at Dubuque, on the 4th of July, 1834, was made by a black slave woman. Dred Scott is believed to have built a wooden shack on his master's plot near Davenport in the mid-1830s. Sixteen slaves, all at Dubuque, were counted in the Iowa census of 1840, compared to 172 "free colored persons." The previous year one former slave had been dramatically judged to belong in the ranks of the free. His name was Ralph.

Ralph was born a slave in Virginia, about 1795, under the name of "Rafe Nelson." In infancy he was given the name of his owner, Ralph Montgomery. Later master and slave moved to Kentucky, where—having grown tall and strong—Ralph was sold as a field hand to Montgomery's brother, William. On November 5, 1830, William Montgomery sold five of his slaves for $820 to his son, Jordan. The bill of sale read: "sold to the said Jordan J. Montgomery one negro man by the name of Ralph aged about thirty five years .... "[1] The bill of sale was registered in Lincoln County, Kentucky.

In 1832, Jordan Montgomery moved Ralph and his other slaves to Marion County in northeast Missouri. He registered the Kentucky bill of sale at the county seat, Palmyra, on May 21st of that year. The twenty-seven-year-old Montgomery and his wife Susan had a young family—by 1840 it had grown to seven children under the age of fifteen. Montgomery owned a block of land near Palmyra, and Ralph's life in Missouri was presumably spent as a field hand. Montgomery's cash position seems to have deteriorated in the next years, and he took a paid job as County Assessor of State Taxes for the year 1835. But the previous year he had already taken a step to raise money. He had made a written contract with Ralph to sell him his freedom.

The contract was undoubtedly made for reasons of commerce rather than sentiment. Jordan Montgomery was no abolitionist. He already owned two slaves when he bought Ralph, and he still held a young woman slave in 1840. The price of Ralph's freedom was $500, with an additional $50 payment for his hire. The sale price was about average in Missouri then for a male slave of Ralph's age. Slaves were often hired out by the year, and the going rate for a year's hire was slightly above ten percent of a slave's market value. So the $50 hire fee indicates that the parties envisaged Ralph would pay the full amount in a year. Fortunes had been made mining lead in Dubuque, and Ralph hoped to make the necessary money in the mines to buy his freedom. As a precautionary measure, the contract stipulated interest from January 1, 1835. Jordan Montgomery gave Ralph permission to go to Dubuque.

Ralph set out from Palmyra with the contract in his pocket and traveled the 300 miles to Dubuque. He arrived there in the first half of 1834 and commenced mining for lead. Little is known of his home life. There is reference in a Dubuque miner's 1845 diary to Ralph's wife, but when the marriage took place is unknown. One historian records that a woman named Tilda—who contributed $.25 to the building of the Dubuque Methodist Church in 1834—was a sister of Ralph, and Ralph himself was of a religious bent.

Ralph's lead mining was not a great success. Despite being industrious, he hardly made enough money for food and clothes, let alone to pay Montgomery for his freedom. References to Ralph's lead mining show his diggings a little to the west of Dubuque. Slightly to the east were the crevices worked by Alexander Butterworth, an Irishman who was to play a vital part in Ralph's life.

A portion of the 1830 Kentucky bill of sale, filed in Marion County, Missouri,
recording the sale to Jordan Montgomery of "one negro man by the name of Ralph .... "

Alexander Butterworth left Missouri to mine lead in Dubuque the same year as Ralph. Unlike Ralph, he prospered—in addition to his mine he had a wheat and cattle farm near the town and was a partner in one of early Dubuque's few grocery stores. In 1838, Butterworth was elected a trustee of the town council of Dubuque and served on the town committee to arrange the dinner to celebrate the birthday of the Territory of Iowa on July 4th.

Thomas S. Wilson, then district court judge resident at Dubuque, described Butterworth as "noble-hearted,"[2] a quality he undoubtedly inherited from his spirited old mother. The ancient Mrs. Butterworth was able to date her birth by the fact that she was sixteen when the Catholic Stuart cause had been finally defeated in 1746 at the Battle of Culloden in Scotland. When Butterworth was married in 1837, his mother—then an incredible 107—danced "quite briskly" at the wedding.[3]

The early population of Dubuque was so small that everybody must have known everybody else. Alexander Butterworth and Ralph had adjacent mines, and doubtless Ralph and everyone else frequented the Quigley and Butterworth grocery store. Ralph and Butterworth were obviously acquainted. But in May 1839, Butterworth would prove they were more than just fellow miners who had both come from Missouri. They were friends.

While Ralph was still toiling in the lead mines, the Iowa Territorial Assembly passed "An Act to Regulate Blacks and Mulattoes" in January 1839. Under section 6 of the act, if any person (or their agent) applied to a justice of the peace and proved

An advertisement for "Quigley & Butterworth" grocery store, frequented by Ralph and other early Dubuque miners. (*Du Buque Visitor,* May 11, 1836)

Quigley & Butterworth,

RESPECTFULLY inform their friends and the public in general, that they have just received an assortment

GROCERIES,

Suitable for family use, which they offer cheap for cash, lead, or mineral—Among which will be found

Sugar, Coffee, Young H. Tea,
Imperial, Gunpowder Souchoung do.,
Molasses, Mackerel, Cheese.
Crackers, Almonds, Raisins, Figs;
Loaf Sugar, Dried Peaches,
Dried Apples, Chewing Tobacco,
Smoking Tobacco, Pepper, Allspice.
Cloves, Ginger, Nutmegs, Starch, Indigo,
Soap, Candles, Flour, Corn Meal, Corn,
Mustard, Paste Blacking, Playing Cards.
Writing and Letter Paper;
Kegs Oysters, 10 barrels Porter,
French Brandy, American do.,
Holland Gin, American do.,
Madeira, Tenerieffe, Malaga & Port Wines
Rum, Claret in bottles, (sup.)
Lemon Syrup, Spanish Cigars, Melee do:
Nails, Brooms, Flasks, Powder and Ink;
Stoughton Bitters by the gallon or bottle;
3,500 lbs. well cured Bacon.
Du Buque, May 11, 1836.   1tt

that a black person was their property, the justice of the peace was required to direct the sheriff to arrest the individual and deliver him to the claimant or his agent. This law would affect Ralph's future.

Meanwhile in Missouri Jordan Montgomery had become county clerk of Marion County. In November 1838, he entered deep financial waters. With three partners he borrowed $4,000 from the Bank of the State of Missouri. The terms of the loan required the money to be repaid on May 15, 1839, and Montgomery was liable for the full amount. Montgomery's financial position was extremely weak at the time—in February he was taking advantage of his position as county clerk to borrow $60.95 from the county. With May approaching there was nothing like the necessary money to repay the huge loan to the bank. Montgomery was owed $550 and five years' interest by Ralph. Slave prices had risen since their contract. One source of funds could be tapped; an asset could be realized. Jordan Montgomery sent an agent or agents to Dubuque.

In the last week of May 1839, the Virginians (as the agents have always been known to historians) swore an affidavit in front of a justice of the peace that Ralph was the property of Jordan Montgomery and that they were his representatives. The justice issued his precept under the Blacks and Mulattoes Act directing the sheriff to deliver Ralph to Montgomery's agents. Ralph was working on his mineral lot a little to the west of Dubuque when he was seized by the sheriff and handed over to the Virginians. They handcuffed him, put him in a wagon, and—deliberately avoiding Dubuque—drove to Bellevue. There Ralph was taken on board a boat bound for Missouri, and the boat's master confined him in the vessel.

Word of Ralph's fate reached the ears of Alexander Butterworth, who was plowing on his farm on the outskirts of Dubuque. Butterworth reacted without regard to any possible public disapproval. As soon as he heard what had happened to Ralph, he rushed to the house of Judge Wilson and demanded a writ of habeas corpus on Ralph's behalf. The application was drawn up by an attorney, and Judge Wilson issued the writ of habeas corpus. The sheriff in obedience to the writ galloped off to Bellevue, and Ralph was rescued from the boat. The sheriff returned to Dubuque with Ralph, who appeared before Judge Wilson.

There is no court record of Ralph's appearance in the District Court. The *Iowa News* in Dubuque reported on June 1, 1839: "A case of importance to the owners of slaves in this Territory was last week brought before Judge Wilson, which has not yet been determined, time having been granted for bringing up witnesses at a distance." Judge Wilson later explained how he proceeded: "The case was heard, but at my suggestion was transferred to the Supreme Court of the Territory, because of its importance."[4] The Supreme Court opinion stated that this transfer occurred by agreement of the parties.

The Supreme Court of the Territory of Iowa consisted of Chief Justice Charles Mason, a brilliant New York lawyer, Associate Judge Joseph Williams, a clever and witty Pennsylvanian, and Associate Judge Thomas S. Wilson, a popular Ohioan appointed at the amazing age of twenty-four. Each Supreme Court judge was in addition responsible for the district court in one of the three districts into which Iowa was divided.

At 8:00 a.m. on July 4, 1839—the first birthday of the Territory of Iowa—the Supreme Court sat to hear what would become the first case reported in the Iowa

Law Reports. The case was *In the matter of Ralph (a colored man) on Habeas Corpus.*[5] The Supreme Court Order Book signed by the chief justice records that only Chief Justice Mason and Judge Williams heard the case. Presumably it was thought unsuitable for Judge Wilson to sit, as he had declined to adjudicate the matter when it came before him as judge in the district court.

The lawyer for Ralph (the Petitioner) was the brilliant David Rorer of Burlington, who represented Ralph without charge. Rorer was a native Virginian who had manumitted his own slaves while living in Arkansas. Rorer gave the oral presentation before the Supreme Court and was assisted by his partner W. Henry Starr. J.D. Learned of St. Louis assisted by John V. Berry of Dubuque represented Jordan Montgomery (the Claimant). The facts had been agreed by the parties, and the argument was purely on the law.

David Rorer began a lengthy argument to the Court on Ralph's behalf. He first urged that the Articles of Compact contained in the 1787 Ordinance for the Government of the Territory of the United States North West of the River Ohio (known in history as the North West Ordinance) applied to Ralph. Ralph had resided at Dubuque when it was part of the Territory of Wisconsin and later when it became part of the Territory of Iowa. By means of section 12 of the Organic Laws (the constitutions) of both territories, the North West Ordinance governed. The ordinance provided: "There shall be neither Slavery nor involuntary Servitude in the said territory .... "[6] Therefore, Rorer reasoned, Ralph was free.

Rorer then argued that apart from the North West Ordinance, Ralph became free as soon as he came to reside in what was now the Territory of Iowa with his master's consent, as a consequence of the 1820 Act of Congress known as the Missouri Compromise. Section 8 of the Missouri Compromise began: "In all that territory ceded by France to the United States, under the name of Louisiana, which lies north of thirty-six degrees, and thirty minutes north latitude, not included within the limits of the State contemplated by this act [Missouri], slavery and involuntary servitude ... shall be, and is hereby, forever prohibited."[7] As the Territory of Iowa lay in the area where slavery was prohibited, and as there was no law by which Ralph could be removed, he was free to exercise his right to remain in Iowa. In support of this argument Rorer relied on various authorities, and concluded with an appeal to "much earlier and higher authority"[8]—the law of the prophet Moses.

The Blacks and Mullatoes Act of 1839 had prohibited blacks from settling in Iowa without evidence of freedom and the posting of a $500 bond.[9] But Rorer argued that as Ralph had come to Dubuque before the Territory of Iowa was founded (in fact, before there was even a civil government in the area at all), Ralph could not be said to have violated that law. Furthermore, Ralph was not a fugitive slave within the Blacks and Mulattoes Act or under the laws of the United States. He had come to Iowa by the voluntary consent and agreement of his former owner. By permitting Ralph to come to that part of the United States in which slavery had been prohibited for an indefinite period, Jordan Montgomery had virtually manumitted Ralph. Indeed, the very fact that Montgomery had contracted with a slave presupposed a state of freedom.

Rorer concluded by urging that if Montgomery had a remedy at all, it was on the contract for the money agreed upon. The contract, however, was not before the Court, and was irrelevant to the question of Ralph's freedom.

Jordan Montgomery's lawyer, J.D. Learned, then addressed the Court. He argued that, as Ralph had failed to perform his part of the contract by not paying the price of his freedom, he should be regarded as a fugitive slave. Accordingly, he could be claimed under that section of the Missouri Compromise that provided: "[A]ny person escaping into [the territory thus set apart], from whom labor or service is lawfully claimed, in any State or Territory of the United States, such fugitive may be lawfully reclaimed and conveyed to the person claiming his or her labor or service as aforesaid."[10]

He further urged that slavery was not prohibited in the Territory of Iowa. The Missouri Compromise was not intended to affect the rights of individuals without additional legislative action. It was merely meant to direct local legislatures to pass laws prohibiting slavery. And the Missouri Compromise contained no sanction and consequently had no binding force.

Alternatively, even if the Missouri Compromise was intended to operate without further legislation, it did not work as a forfeiture of slave property. So it would go no further in this case than to merely require Montgomery to remove his property (Ralph) out of the territory. The case was comparable to that of property invested in private banking contrary to the provisions of a statute where, although the owner might be made liable, the property would not be confiscated.

The Supreme Court issued its decision the same day. In the handwritten record of its proceedings of July 4, 1839, were the following words: "It is therefore ordered and adjudged that he (Ralph) be discharged from further duress and restraint, and that he go hence."[11]

The Supreme Court Order Book, vol. A, 1838-1853, states the court's decision in *Jordan J. Montgomery vs. Ralph, a man of color*. (Courtesy, State Historical Society of Iowa, Des Moines)

The unanimous opinion of the Supreme Court (made available to the press within two days) was written by Chief Justice Mason. The opinion first dealt with procedural irregularities—the case had come before the Supreme Court by none of the ordinary methods of application in an appellate court. Nevertheless, "[t]he proceedings having been transferred to this court, it will be proper for us to make such a disposition of the matter as might have been made by the District Judge while the subject was before him."

The Court roundly dismissed the argument of Montgomery's lawyer that since Ralph had failed to pay the price of his freedom he should be regarded as a fugitive slave: "Such a construction would introduce almost unqualified slavery into all the free States .... We cannot countenance such a doctrine .... [T]he claimant permitted his slave to come to this Territory. The permission seems to have been absolute, but there was also an understanding that the latter was to pay the former a certain amount as the price of his freedom. How the failure to comply with this understanding could render a removal, undertaken with the master's consent, an escape, we cannot comprehend." Although Ralph should, indeed, pay the debt, "no man in this territory can be reduced to slavery" for failure to do so.

The Court also rejected the argument that the Missouri Compromise was a mere naked declaration requiring further action and sanction by the given territory: "Congress possesses the supreme power of legislation in relation to the Territories and its right to prohibit slavery, at least in relation to slaves subsequently introduced, is doubtless legitimate. Has that right been exercised in relation to this Territory? The language of the Act of 1820 in relation to the district of country in which this Territory is embraced, is, that slavery therein 'shall be, and is hereby, forever prohibited.' This seems to us an entire and final prohibition, not looking to future legislative action to render it effectual."

The Court dealt with the additional argument that the Missouri Compromise, if applicable, did not work a forfeiture of slave property: "It is true that the Act ... does not, in express terms, declare a forfeiture of slave property, but it does, in effect, declare that such property shall not exist."

The opinion continued: "The master who, subsequently to that Act, permits his slave to become a resident here, cannot, afterwards, exercise any acts of ownership over him within this Territory. The law does not take away his property in express terms, but declares it no longer to be property at all."

The Court went on to reject the argument that private banking was indistinguishable from slave holding: "Property, in the slave, cannot exist without the existence of slavery: the prohibition of the latter annihilates the former, and this, being destroyed, he becomes free."

In the light of its ruling under the Missouri Compromise, the Court apparently felt it was unnecessary to consider Rorer's argument that Ralph was also free by virtue of the North West Ordinance. The opinion ended with a powerful statement of principle: "When, in seeking to accomplish his object, [the Claimant] illegally restrains a human being of his liberty, it is proper that the laws, which should extend equal protection to men of all colors and conditions, should exert their remedial interposition. We think, therefore, that the petitioner should be discharged from all custody and constraint, and be permitted to go free .... "[12]

The Iowa Supreme Court decision was a major item of news. It was prominently reported by both Burlington newspapers in their next editions, and the following week both newspapers printed Chief Justice Mason's opinion in full. One of the papers, the *Iowa Patriot,* commented: "This decision will doubtless receive the approbation of all who profess to be the friends of humanity and law throughout the Country, and obtain for the Judiciary of the infant Territory of Iowa a name abroad, which could not, under other circumstances, have been granted."[13]

The immediate reaction of the slave owners in the Territory of Iowa is not recorded. The following year, however, the heads of eleven Dubuque families announced their defiance of the law to the assistant marshall who took the federal census. He enumerated sixteen slaves among these eleven households. Instances of slavery continued to be reported, and as late as 1852 a man called L.P. "Tune" Allen brought two young slaves into Iowa from North Carolina. He held them there a year and then sold them to someone in Missouri.

Following the Supreme Court's decision, Ralph continued his mining in Dubuque. Judge Wilson reported that "he afterwards struck a big lode but gambled it away."[14] Certainly the scattered references to Ralph in the contemporary diary of Richard Bonson, an Englishman who ran a blast furnace and mined lead, showed that Ralph had erratic fortunes. In August 1841, the diarist was "weighing Rafe's mineral." A year later he went to Mackenzie's diggings "to take [over] Rafe's part of the diggins." In October 1844, however, Bonson was "in town and weighing for Black Rafe" again.

Ralph's fortunes seem to have taken a new plunge in 1845. In May Bonson's wife was sick, and needing domestic help, Bonson went to town "to get Black Rafe's wife to stop with us." On July 14th, Bonson "had … Raf[e] spading in garden."[15] Later that month Ralph was back in front of Judge Wilson in the Dubuque County District Court. A blacksmith called William Newman had judgment awarded against "Rafe Montgomery" for $17.37 with court costs of $1.64.

Ralph continued mining all his life, and in his last years lived at times in lodgings and at times in the county poorhouse. Ralph was very popular in Dubuque. His friendly disposition and religious bent showed themselves in his final action. On July 22, 1870, "Old Rafe" died in the pesthouse of small pox, "having contracted the disease while nursing a sick patient."[16] Ralph was buried in Linwood Cemetery, Dubuque.

Jordan Montgomery emerged in December 1839 as Colonel J.J. Montgomery of the state militia commanding a regiment of 200 men during the boundary dispute, or "Honey War," between Missouri and Iowa. In 1840, Montgomery resigned as county clerk and was elected sheriff of Marion County that year and again two years later. In 1840, judgment had been entered against Montgomery and his partners for the $4,000 debt and interest owed to the Missouri bank. In 1843, the coroner of Marion County (acting for Sheriff Montgomery) sold some real property of Montgomery and his partners under court order towards satisfying the debt.

A Freemason of Palmyra Lodge, Montgomery was appointed steward of the Masonic College near Palmyra in 1844. It proved not to be a suitable vocation. His successor wrote: "The late Steward, Col. Montgomery erected [an ice house] last winter, the roof of which fell in with the first heavy rain last spring … if it were repaired, its location is so distant from the refectory that it would be comparatively of little value." Montgomery's farming efforts were similarly unfortunate: "The farm has been occupied by ... the Steward for the purposes of husbandry, and so far as the Steward is concerned, has yielded no profit this year. ... The yield of the crop would have been considerably larger, but for the wretched condition of the fencing, allowing much to be destroyed by horses and hogs."[17] In June 1845, the Board of Curators of the Masonic College reported that they had ended Montgomery's career as steward. Jordan Montgomery moved to St. Louis, where he became an insurance agent and lived in the house of one of his sons. His net assets in 1860 were listed as $1,400.

The decision in Ralph's case stood for seventeen years and was followed in such lower Iowa court cases as Rachel Bundy (1841) and Jim White (1848).[18] The principle of law in *In the matter of Ralph* was annulled by the majority of the U.S. Supreme Court in the 1857 decision *Dred Scott v Sandford*[19], which Abraham Lincoln called "an astonisher in legal history."[20] Ralph's case was not cited by any of the justices in their opinions in *Dred Scott*.

A very eminent jurist considered the place of *In the matter of Ralph* in history. In 1906, the Hon. John F. Dillon said: "True it is that the Dred-Scott decision afterwards rendered was in direct conflict with Judge Mason's decision on Ralph's case. But in the civil war, a higher body than either of those courts, namely the American people, in their primary and sovereign capacity, overruled the Dred-Scott decision and re-established the doctrines of the Iowa court in Ralph's case."[21]

Although Ralph had benefited from the law of habeas corpus, many laws of the first years of Iowa discriminated against black residents. From the very beginning, the congressional act establishing the Territory of Iowa in 1838 had given the vote to white male citizens only. During the next four years a battery of racist laws were passed: schools were opened only to whites; the militia was confined to free white males; blacks coming to Iowa were required to produce a certificate of freedom and a $500 bond; blacks were prohibited from being witnesses against whites in any court case; marriages of blacks and whites were declared illegal and void; and in 1842 statutory relief of the poor was denied to blacks.[22] Just six months after the decision in his case, Ralph was even denied the vote in his own town—the "Act to incorporate the City of Du Buque" limited the municipal franchise to white male citizens.[23]

But to Ralph the freedom of Iowa was infinitely preferable to the slavery of Missouri. One morning several years after the court case Judge Wilson, who had issued the writ of habeas corpus, found Ralph working in his Dubuque garden. The judge asked him why he was there. Ralph replied: "I want to work for you one day every spring to show you that I never forget you."[24]—A gesture of gratitude for the right to go free.

There were over 200 reported opinions of the Iowa Territorial Supreme Court in the period 1838-1846, dealing with such diverse subjects as claim jumping, horse racing, treaties, debt collection, and murder. The Court's rulings extended from its lofty pronouncements in the case, In the matter of Ralph, to the more mundane question of whether an accusation that one is "a dirty, trifling, thieving puppy" constitutes slander (it does).

The Court also heard cases on the vital subject of navigation. In an important 1844 decision, while acknowledging the principle that the Mississippi River was a common highway and "forever free," the Court upheld a legislative grant of the exclusive right to operate a ferry crossing.

The legislature has not exceeded its lawful powers in granting such a charter to the appellee [Timothy Fanning of Dubuque]. True, the Mississippi river and all the navigable waters leading into it are common highways and must be forever free. The legislature can make no law for obstructing the navigation of these streams.

But the establishment of public roads traversing the country in various directions is a rightful subject of legislation … [and a] ferry (properly so called) is merely the continuance of a road across a river. It is only a substitute for a bridge.

… Nor will it we think be doubted that the legislature may for the purpose of encouraging individuals to construct such bridge, grant them an exclusive privilege to a reasonable extent and prohibit all other persons from interfering therewith. The rule would be the same in relation to a ferry which is a floating bridge. The granting of an exclusive privilege to establish such a public convenience within certain reasonable limits, would be no violation of that provision of the ordinance of 1787 [the North West Ordinance], which declares the Mississippi and its tributaries common highways and forever free, provided the navigation proper of the river be not thereby interfered with or obstructed.

· · · ·

The conclusion to which we are brought on this subject therefore is, that the Mississippi river so far as it affords facilities for transportation, cannot be obstructed or monopolized. … But so far as it presents an obstruction to land carriage it is left to the sound discretion of the legislature to provide means for surmounting such obstructions by means of ferries, and that they may even for this purpose give individuals exclusive privileges within reasonable limits when done in good faith for the purpose of furnishing an indispensable link in the chain of transportation on dry land.

United States, *ex rel.* Jones v. Fanning, 1 Morris 348, 351, 353 (Iowa 1844).

In May 1845, three men broke into a cabin near West Point and murdered two occupants. The motive was believed to be robbery. Two young Mormon brothers, William and Stephen Hodges, were convicted of murder and sentenced to die.

The Hodges brothers protested their innocence at trial, and witnesses placed them in Nauvoo, Illinois, at the time of the murder. Both men again asserted their innocence as they stood on the gallows awaiting execution. The Hodges—and others who felt certain they were guiltless—believed that popular feeling against the growing Mormon population in Nauvoo and southern Iowa contributed to their conviction.

In his first message to the Legislative Assembly in 1838, Governor Lucas (who opposed capital punishment) had urged that the death penalty be carried out in private. But—as shown in the newspaper report of the Hodges' execution in Burlington—a public execution was an event that aroused curiosity and excitement.

The brothers, William and Stephen Hodges were hung in this town on Tuesday last. From dawn until the time appointed for the execution the principal avenues to town were crowded with people. The Steamer Mermaid brought down a large number from Bloomington [Muscatine] …. In the meantime one of the Steam ferry boats from Fort Madison—the Caroline—came loaded to the guards with passengers—the "New Purchase,"—with a large multitude from Nauvoo, and places adjacent, arrived too late for the passengers to witness the execution. Long before the time appointed our streets were literally filled with men, women, and children.

At 12 o'clock, the guard, composed of three or four companies of riflemen under the command of Col. Geo. Temple, arrived at the Jail, and soon after the prisoners were placed in a wagon, which contained their coffins .... The Band and Martial music played appropriately solemn tunes during the progress of the march. The procession crossed the square from the jail and down Court to Third street, through Third to Jefferson street, through Jefferson to the place of execution.

The place selected was on the Mt. Pleasant road, immediately west of town. It was a perfect natural amphitheatre. The gallows was in the centre of the dell and in full view of and immediately contiguous to the thousands of spectators who covered the hills. ...

The gallows was occupied by the Sheriff and his Deputy, the Prisoners and a friend that had just arrived in town, the Rev. Mr. White of the Cumberland Presbyterian, the Rev. Mr. Coleman of the Methodist, the Rev. Bishop Loras of the Catholic and the Rev. Mr. Hutchinson, of the Congregational churches, together with the Counsel for the prisoners, Messrs Mills and Hall.

The exercises commenced with the reading of the 51st Psalm by Mr. Coleman. This Psalm was read at the request of the prisoners, and we cannot but believe from all their conduct and their refusal to confess their crimes to their fellow-men, that they clung to this psalm and adopted its language as an excuse for their refusal. They may have thought their confessions to their Maker were sufficient, and thus they may have palliated their consciences.

After the reading of the Psalm, Mr. White gave out the appropriate hymn, "Now in the heat of youthful blood." After the singing Mr. White offered a most fervent and pertinent prayer, calling upon God to shield the youth then present as spectators, from temptation and sin, and ending their lives as those before them were about to do. Immediately after the prayer, Stephen Hodges came forward to address the crowd. He was very much agitated. ... He said

Gentlemen and Fellow citizens I stand before you a dying man about to be launched into eternity. I have not much to say and shall not detain you long. There never was a trial where men were convicted under such slight evidence as was brought against us. ... He then alluded to the evidence and in a sort of special pleading lawyer like style attempted to show that it was inadequate to convict them. He asked why the jury did not believe the witnesses who swore that they were at Nauvoo at the time of the murder and answered that it was because they were Mormons. ...

Here he became almost frantic and came near, we thought, of bursting assunder the ropes that bound his arms. The froth issued from his mouth and he gave other signs of extreme rage and madness. ... He asked how could any citizen go home and tell his wife what he had seen—two men hung without evidence—and sleep quietly. ...

William Hodges came forward and said, Friends and fellow citizens, I am on the step that is soon to place me in eternity. I am innocent of shedding man's blood. He then in a much more subdued spirit than Stephen reviewed the evidence educed at his trial, complained of its insufficiency—and decided that it was not strong enough to convict a man in a common case of assault and battery. He became quite animated and addressed the crowd at one time as "gentlemen of the Jury." ... He then said I am prepared to go—and when I drop I expect to go right straight into Heaven. I bid you all farewell. I am going home in glory. I die in peace and hope to meet you all in that better world of glory. He claimed the forgiveness of all and said he forgave all and again bid the audience farewell.

Mr. White then said there was still time for religious exercises and as the prisoners requested the time might be so filled up, they proceeded to sing a few hymns in which all could join. ...

Their chains were then knocked off, and the Sheriff conducted William to the drop and put the rope around his neck. While the rope was being put round the neck of Stephen we could see that William was apparently engaged in prayer. The caps were pulled over their faces, and in a few moments the Sheriff with one blow severed the cord, the drop fell, and both were launched into eternity. Stephen's neck broke and he died without a struggle. William struggled nearly ten minutes before he was apparently dead. ...

After the bodies were taken down they were placed in the coffins and handed over to their friends

The spectacle of a public execution. (From Edward Bonney, *The Banditti of the Prairies,* 1855)

Although lynchings occurred periodically in Iowa from 1834 onward, the Hodges' execution in July 1845 was the first legal execution in the Iowa Territory. In April 1846, a legal hanging took place in Van Buren County of one William McCauley, convicted of murdering a man and his daughter. The costs associated with the execution give a gruesome reality to the details of public execution.

John Pease had in 1845 been allowed by the County Commissioners Court the sum of nine dollars for work on and erection of a gallows and by the same body the sheriff was allowed the following:

April 4, 1846 removing irons from McCauley $1.25, for rope $2.50.

Repairing gallows, making coffin and digging grave $12.00.

For hauling McCauley to the blacksmith shop $2.50.

For grave clothes $3.19.

There was allowed also Phillip Hartzell bailiff in McCauley case $3.00.

J.C. Knapp, prosecuting attorney, McCauley case $45.00.

E. R. Harlan (ed.), *The Execution of William McCauley* (privately printed, 1905), p. 11 (reprinted from the *Keosaqua Republican,* April 13, 1905).

on board the steam ferry boat "New Purchase." His sister accompanied their remains to Nauvoo.

The number of people at the execution has been variously estimated. We think there were from eight to ten thousand. Never have we seen more decorum or better behavior exhibited at a public execution. … We understand that several fainted and we heard a few screams from the females as the drop fell. All seemed to realize that it was an awful and melancholy sight to see two young men, who might have been ornaments in society thus cut off in health and in the vigor of manhood and we hope some good impression may have been made.

The Burlington Hawk-Eye, July 17, 1845.

In 1845, the accused, twenty-four-year-old William McCauley, had entered a plea of guilty (which was later withdrawn), and had made a full written confession of murder. In his confession, McCauley warned others to avoid the temptations that had led to his crime of passion.

Confession
....
In conclusion, and as I am about to appear before the Judge of all the earth, I here solemnly say, so far from any person advising me to do the deed, or knowing it was to be done, that

I did not even know it myself until the fatal deed was done; it was not either advised by any person, or premeditated by myself, but was done from the impulse of the moment .... But the fatal deed is done and I am now about to suffer the penalty of the law. I deeply regret my criminal connection and intimacy with the wife of [the deceased man] who by her imprudence has drawn a young man from the path of virtue and caused him to commit a crime against his God, his friend, and society by violating the matrimonial state and creating discord between man and wife, by giving ground for the seeds of jealousy to spring up, and the hatred of the husband to ripen into revenge, from which to escape, through fear, was influenced to take the life of a fellow man; for which I am now condemned to die. Let me advise all young men to take warning from me, never contract an intimacy with a married woman, the crime is one that will lead you to ruin—and I see now when too late, my fatal error and think it to be my duty to warn the young to beware of the rock upon which I have been wrecked; hoping by an exposition of all the circumstances connected with the fatal deed for which I am condemned to die, I may be instrumental in warning some young man of his approaching danger, has induced me to make this, my last confession. And now having made my peace with my God, and received the pardon of all my sins, as I believe, I am now ready to pay the debt, and hope that my sad case may be a warning to all, both male and female, never to depart from the path of virtue, but live a virtuous life, that they may die an honorable death. May the Lord of his infinite compassion have mercy on me, and bless you all—farewell.

His
William   X   McCauley.
mark.
Attest,
Jonathan Riggs.

E. R. Harlan (ed.), *The Execution of William McCauley* (privately printed, 1905), pp. 5, 9 (reprinted from the *Keosaqua Republican,* April 13, 1905).

Although Iowa did not achieve statehood until 1846, the possibility of this legal status was a constant theme during the territorial years. Indeed, scarcely a year into his governorship of the Iowa Territory, Governor Lucas asked the Legislative Assembly to consider taking steps toward eventual statehood.

When we consider the rapidly increasing population, and advancing prosperity of the Territory, we may, in my opinion, with propriety proceed to measures preparatory to the formation of a Constitution and State Government, and for our admission into the Union as an independent State. I know it is the opinion of some, that such measures would be premature at this time, inasmuch as our expenses are defrayed by the United States. This consideration is entitled to weight; but when we consider the imperfect organization of the Territorial Government, and the consequent embarrassment in the administration of its internal affairs ... the preponderance is much in favor of a State Government .... With these facts before us, I would earnestly recommend to the Legislative Assembly the early passage of a memorial to Congress, respectfully asking of that body the passage of an Act, at their ensuing session, granting to the inhabitants of Iowa Territory, the right to form a Constitution and State Government, and to provide for their admission into the Union upon an equal footing with the original States.

Governor Robert Lucas, Second Annual Message, November 5, 1839, reprinted in Benjamin F. Shambaugh (ed.), *The Messages and Proclamations of the Governors of Iowa* (Iowa City: State Historical Society, 1903), vol. I, p. 95.

The territorial legislature and Iowans generally did not share Governor Lucas's enthusiasm for immediate statehood. In 1840 and again in 1842, voters rejected proposals to call a constitutional convention.

Within two years, however, public opinion had turned around. In April 1844, a majority of voters decided to call a constitutional convention.

In August, seventy-three delegates were chosen (of whom seventy-two attended). Democrats predominated over Whigs by a two to one majority. The delegates convened in Iowa City on October 7, 1844, and adjourned on November 1.

The convention was charged with the solemn duty of drafting a document to establish the framework of a new state government. During their twenty-five days of deliberations, the delegates confronted issues ranging from the prohibition of banking to the banning of black residents in Iowa. Before they could begin their substantive work, however, the delegates were faced with a particularly knotty problem—should they begin each day's session with a prayer?

Thursday, Oct. 10, 1844.

The Convention took up Mr. Sells' motion to have daily prayer.

Mr. Chapman spoke in favor of the resolution, stating that no outlay would be occasioned, as the ministers would gladly attend and render the service without compensation.

Mr. Gehon said it would not be economical, for the Convention sat at an expense of $200 to $300 per day, and time was money. ...

Mr. Lucas [the former governor] regretted that there should be contention on this subject, and could not believe that any disbelieved in a superintending Providence. If ever an assemblage needed the aid of Almighty Power, it was one to organize a system of Government. ...

Mr. Kirkpatrick said if the Convention had a right to pass the resolution, they had a right to establish a religion. It had no right to bring the members on their knees every morning. If it had, it might do it noon and night; and had a right to require the people of the Territory to do the same. ...

Mr. Bailey said whenever politics and religion were mingled, excitement was created. ... If individuals wish prayer, there were meetings in town almost every night; let them go there and not take up the time of the Convention. ...

Mr. Fletcher said, that having made the motion by which the Convention was opened with prayer on the first day, and voted to take up this resolution, he felt bound to say something. He regretted the opposi-

tion that he saw, and he was unwilling that it should go forth to the world that Iowa refused to acknowledge a God. ...

Friday, Oct. 11, 1844.

The Convention resumed the consideration of the resolution of Mr. Sells, providing for daily prayer ....

Mr. Galbraith moved the indefinite postponement of the resolution. Carried; yeas 44, nays 26 ....

Excerpts from *The Iowa Standard,* reprinted in Benjamin F. Shambaugh (ed.), *Fragments of the Debates of the Iowa Constitutional Conventions of 1844 and 1846* (Iowa City: State Historical Society, 1900), pp. 11-12, 14-16, 20-21.

The Constitution of 1844 did not lead immediately to statehood. The delegates had included a provision that the Constitution of 1844—with any conditions attached by Congress—would be submitted to a vote. In April 1845, dissatisfied with Congress's imposition of smaller boundaries, Iowans rejected the constitution by a vote of 7,019 to 6,023. A second referendum in August was similarly defeated.

The Legislative Assembly called for the election of another constitutional convention. Thirty-two delegates met in Iowa City on May 4, 1846, and voted to accept the compromise boundary lines proposed by Congress. The convention made few changes to the 1844 constitution. It adjourned its work on May 18, having drafted the Constitution of 1846.

The Constitution of 1846.

Article 1.

Preamble and Boundaries.

We, the People of the Territory of Iowa, grateful to the Supreme Being for the blessings hitherto enjoyed, and feeling our dependence on Him for a continuation of those blessings, do ordain and establish a free and independent government, by the name of the State of Iowa ....

Article 2.

Bill of Rights.

1. All men are by nature free and independent, and have certain unalienable rights, among which are those of enjoying and defending life and liberty, acquiring, possessing, and protecting property, and pursuing and obtaining safety and happiness.

. . . .

3. The General Assembly shall make no law respecting an establishment of religion, or prohibiting the free exercise thereof ....

5. Any citizen of this State who may hereafter be engaged, either directly or indirectly, in a duel, either as principal or accessory before the fact, shall forever be disqualified from holding any office under the constitution and laws of this State.

. . . .

7. ... No law shall be passed to restrain or abridge the liberty of speech or of the press. ...

8. The right of the people to be secure in their persons, houses, papers and effects, against unreasonable seizures and searches, shall not be violated ....

9. The right of trial by jury shall remain inviolate ....

10. In all criminal prosecutions, the accused shall have a right to a speedy trial by an impartial jury ....

19. No person shall be imprisoned for debt in any civil action on mesne or final process, unless in cases of fraud ....

23. Neither slavery nor involuntary servitude, unless for the punishment of crimes, shall ever be tolerated in this State.

. . . .

Article 3.
Right of Suffrage.

1. Every white male citizen of the United States, of the age of twenty-one years, who shall have been a resident of the State six months next preceding the election, and the county in which he claims his vote twenty days, shall be entitled to vote at all elections which are now or hereafter may be authorized by law.

. . . .

Article 4.
Legislative Department.

1. The Legislative authority of this State shall be vested in a Senate and House of Representatives, which shall be designated the General Assembly of the State of Iowa ....

3. The members of the House of Representatives shall be chosen every second year, by the qualified electors ....

4. No person shall be a member of the House of Representatives who shall not have attained the age of twenty-one years [and] be a free white male citizen of the United States ....

5. Senators shall be chosen for the term of four years, at the same time and place as representatives, they shall be twenty-five years of age, and possess the qualifications of representatives as to residence and citizenship.

. . . .

25. Each member of the General Assembly shall receive a compensation ... [which] shall not exceed two dollars per day for the period of fifty days from the commencement of the session, and shall not exceed the sum of one dollar per day for the remainder of the session ....

29. No lottery shall be authorized by this State; nor shall the sale of lottery tickets be allowed.

. . . .

Article 5.
Executive Department.

1. The supreme executive power of this State shall be vested in a chief magistrate, who shall be styled the Governor of the State of Iowa.

2. The Governor ... shall hold his office four years from the time of his installation, and until his successor shall be qualified.

. . . .

Article 6.
Judicial Department.

1. The Judicial power shall be vested in a Supreme Court, District Courts, and such inferior courts, as the General Assembly may from time to time establish.

2. The Supreme Court shall consist of a Chief Justice and two Associates, two of whom shall be a quorum to hold court.

3. The Judges of the Supreme Court shall be elected by joint vote of both branches of the General Assembly ... and hold their offices for six years ....

4. The District Court shall consist of a Judge who shall be elected by the qualified voters of the district in which he resides, at the township election, and hold his office for the term of five years .... The first session of the General Assembly shall divide the State into four districts, which may be increased as the exigencies require.

. . . .

Article 7.

Militia.

1. The Militia of this State shall be composed of all able bodied white male citizens between the ages of eighteen and forty-five years ....

Article 9.

Incorporations.

1. No corporate body shall hereafter be created, renewed, or extended, with the privilege of making, issuing, or putting in circulation, any bill, check, ticket, certificate, promissory note, or other paper, or the paper of any bank, to circulate as money. ...

Done in Convention, at Iowa City, this 18th day of May, in the year of our Lord, one thousand eight hundred and forty-six, and of the Independence of the United States of America, the seventieth.

The Constitution of 1846, reprinted in Benjamin F. Shambaugh (ed.), *Documentary Material Relating to the History of Iowa* (Iowa City: State Historical Society, 1897), vol. I, pp. 190-95, 198-200, 202-05, 210.

O n August 3, 1846, Iowa voters approved *the Constitution of 1846 by the fragile margin of 9,492 to 9,036 votes. Congress passed a bill admitting Iowa to statehood, which was signed by President James K. Polk on December 28, 1846.*

Thus Iowa became the twenty-ninth state of the United States of America.

A n Act for the Admission of the State of Iowa into the Union.

Whereas the people of the Territory of Iowa, did on the eighteenth day of May, anno Domini eighteen hundred and forty-six, by a convention of delegates called and assembled for that purpose, form for themselves a constitution and State government—which constitution is republican in its character and features—and said convention has asked admission of the said Territory into the Union as a State, on an equal footing with the original States, in obedience to "An Act for the Admission of the States of Iowa and Florida into the Union," approved March third, eighteen hundred and forty-five, and "An Act to define the Boundaries of the State of Iowa, and to repeal so much of the Act of the third of March, one thousand eight hundred and forty-five as relates to the Boundaries of Iowa," which said last act was approved August fourth, anno Domini, eighteen hundred and forty-six: Therefore—

Be it enacted by the Senate and House of Representatives of the United States of America in Congress assembled, That the State of Iowa shall be one, and is hereby declared to be one, of the United States of America, and admitted into the Union on an equal footing with the original States in all respects whatsoever. ...

Approved December 28, 1846.

U.S. Statutes at Large, vol. 9, p. 117.

CHAPTER TWO

Statehood

1846-1860

"Come then, I say to all, to Western Iowa ...."

— Amelia Bloomer

1846-1860

THE STORY OF IOWA DURING THE DEC-
ade and a half after statehood is one of growth—in population, in formation of counties, and in expansion to its westward boundary.

In 1846, Iowa's population was recorded as 97,588; in 1860, it was 674,913. The number of counties had grown from forty-four to ninety-nine. With an influx of immigrants from other states and other lands—and the final Sioux cession of northwestern land in 1851—the tide of settlement spread steadily westward to the Missouri River border.

Iowa was a beacon of hope for many in search of a new and better life. Iowa also was a beacon of faith for some individuals seeking to establish religious or utopian societies. These social experiments largely were short-lived, like the Swedenborgians' communistic colony in Iowa County in the early 1850s. A notable exception were the German Pietists who moved to Iowa from New York and southern Canada, and in 1855 founded the Amana communal society in Iowa County that would endure well into the twentieth century.

Iowa was not the promised land for thousands of Mormons, who—after the murder in 1844 of their imprisoned prophet, Joseph Smith, near Nauvoo, Illinois—followed Brigham Young's footsteps to the Great Salt Lake of Utah. But the new state did offer temporary respite along the routes of the Mormons' westward trek in the late 1840s and the 1850s.

Iowa's growth spurred efforts to traverse Iowa with the symbol of progress and prosperity— the railroad. In 1856, large congressional land grants set the stage for four major railroads to cross Iowa within the next decade and a half; a fifth major railroad soon followed. In coming years, a growing network of rail lines joined wagons and steamboats as important modes of transport and commerce.

The new State of Iowa found its formative years shaped by national events that led ultimately to civil war. The 1846 war with Mexico raised anew questions about the status of territory acquired by the United States. In Henry Clay's Compromise of 1850—supported by Iowa's Democrat Senators Augustus Caesar Dodge and George W. Jones—Congress passed five measures designed to maintain the tenuous balance between slavery and non-slavery interests. California was admitted as a free state; the territories of New Mexico and Utah would determine the status of slavery by popular vote; Texas would cede disputed territory to New Mexico in exchange for federal assumption of Texan debts; slave trading in Washington, D.C., was prohibited; and a stronger fugitive slave law was enacted.

In 1854, Congress passed the Kansas-Nebraska Act, which created the two new territories of Kansas and Nebraska, repealed the Missouri Compromise, and allowed the people of Kansas and Nebraska to determine by popular vote whether their territories would be slave or free. Opposition to this act solidified anti-slavery sentiment in Iowa, and changed the state's political landscape.

The anti-slavery Whig candidate, James W. Grimes, endorsed by the Free Soil Party, was narrowly elected Governor of Iowa in 1854. The Whigs won sufficient seats in the General Assembly to replace Democrat Senator Dodge with Whig Senator James Harlan (United States Senators were not then popularly elected, but were chosen by the state legislature). Whigs, Free Soilers, and others re-formed themselves into the nascent Republican Party.

Iowa found itself at the heart of developing events. Many individuals crossed the state to cast their ballots—or to fight—in "Bleeding Kansas" and the Nebraska territory. Aided fervently by Iowa Quakers and other abolitionists, the underground railroad defied the fugitive slave law to transport slaves northward to freedom. Radical reformer John Brown used Iowa as a base to train recruits for his ill-fated raid on Harpers Ferry, Virginia.

While the United States was moving inexorably toward civil conflict, Iowa was moving to solidify its legal base. Five years after statehood, the legislature had approved the first comprehensive state code, the Code of 1851. After his election, Governor Grimes strongly urged the calling of a constitutional convention, which was approved by a large margin in the 1856 general election.

The predominantly Republican convention took under seven weeks to draft the Constitution of 1857. A major change from the 1846 constitution was a provision removing restrictions on banking corporations. Other provisions confirmed a change in the state capital from Iowa City to Des Moines, and made the Iowa Supreme Court judges subject to election by the people, rather than the legislature. Iowa voters ratified the Constitution of 1857 by the narrowest of margins— only 1,630 votes out of nearly 79,000 cast.

Black male suffrage had been a hotly debated subject during the constitutional convention, and the delegates determined to let the voters decide. At the same election in which Iowans approved their new constitution, they overwhelmingly defeated black suffrage—by a margin of nearly six to one.

In 1858, the solidly Republican Iowa General Assembly elected Governor James Grimes (now the leading member of that newly formed party) to the United States Senate, for a term commencing in 1859. That year, Republican Samuel Kirkwood was elected governor. In the 1860 general election, Iowans cast a sizable majority of their votes to help elect Republican Abraham Lincoln as President of the United States.

In its fourteen years of statehood, Iowa had built a firm legal and political foundation. But as it prepared to enter the tumultuous 1860s, the young state's commitment to the principles of federalism and anti-slavery would soon be measured by more than the ballot box.

*A*part from the more settled eastern portion of Iowa, much of the new state was still frontier. The lawyers who set out to practice law in the middle and western regions during the decade after statehood often found their profession as challenging as did the early lawyers in territorial Iowa.

In the fall of 1853 I made a trip west through the southern tier of counties, attending the courts at Davis, Appanoose, Wayne, and Decatur counties. I made the trip on horseback with a pair of saddle-bags that contained my necessary baggage.

From Bloomfield I was accompanied by several attorneys of that bar, and at Centerville two or three additional lawyers joined our party. The counties west of Centerville were very sparsely settled and the road consisted merely of two paths worn by the horses and wagon wheels on the prairie grass. In Wayne county we applied at one settler's house for accommodations for the night, but the housewife informed us that her husband was away from home, had gone to mill, and that she had nothing in the house to eat save a little bacon. She said if we would remain she would entertain us with such accommodations as the place afforded. ...

... The next morning we rode into Corydon, the county seat of Wayne county. The only hotel in the place was a small one and one-half story frame house, with a shed addition for kitchen and dining hall.

Our bed room was the upstairs, and our beds were in two rows, with our heads under the eaves and our feet touching each other in the center of the room. We had no separate apartment or separate beds, our wearing apparel furnishing the pillows.

The court was held in a frame school house on the public square. ... An enterprising peddler with two large peddling wagons came through with us from Centerville and erected a large tent in the center of the square for the display and sale of his goods, and whenever the court was not in actual session his store was opened for business. ...

From Wayne county we went to Decatur, the peddler also keeping us company with his itinerant dry goods establishment.

Charles Clinton Nourse, *Autobiography of Charles Clinton Nourse* (privately printed, 1911), pp. 25-26.

In 1857 this portion of Iowa [Woodbury County] was very sparsely settled. Most of the unorganized counties in northwestern Iowa were attached to Woodbury for revenue and judicial purposes, and whatever law business there was in this vast region of country was done at Sioux City. ...

The early bar of Woodbury county was composed largely of young men who had received their education and legal training in eastern colleges, and came to their work well prepared by the training of the schools. The supposition that the extensive land grant made in 1856 to the state of Iowa, to aid in the construction of a railroad from Dubuque to Sioux City, would secure its early completion, induced a large number of young men of more than ordinary ability and energy, to locate at Sioux City, and commence here the practice of their profession. To-day one can hardly realize under what difficulties they labored. ...

During the winter time, and in seasons of high water, these journeys, across the wide prairies and swollen streams, were fraught with many dangers. ... Many of the early members of the bar recall nights spent wandering upon the bleak prairie, searching amid blinding snow and piercing winds for the dim trail; days and nights spent in wet clothing, journeying through drenching rains and swollen streams, crossing the almost trackless prairies; trips on foot made through mud and water .... Then, too, for many years the possibility was ever before them in their journeys that the red man might be lurking for them in every ravine and clump of trees. This constant exposure to danger made them fearless almost to recklessness.

History of the Counties of Woodbury and Plymouth, Iowa (Chicago: A. Warner & Co., 1890-91), pp. 134, 150.

Iowa had achieved the exalted goal of state-hood, but some of its courthouses were still in less than exalted states. Lawyers, judges, jurors, and litigants endured conditions that tested their commitment to the law—and their physical vigor.

The old court-house [in Monroe County] was built in 1846 by Job Rogers, who had the contract for its construction. Oliver Rowles furnished him some of the logs that went into the construction .... [I]t was 20x20 feet, with half story above. This was reached by a common ladder from the court room below. The jurors ascended this ladder to the half story above, and returned by way of the ladder to the court below, and reported their verdict. This was done in the celebrated trial of Ross for the killing of N. Wright. Jacob Webb, who still survives, was one of the jury in that case, and with the jury returned a verdict of not guilty. ... The jury climbed the ladder leading to the loft, and in the same way descended the ladder leading to the court room below and delivered its verdict in that case.

Chester C. Cole & E. C. Ebersole (ed.), *The Courts and Legal Profession of Iowa* (Chicago: H. C. Cooper, Jr., & Co., 1907), vol. II, p. 856.

The first district court held in Afton [Union County] ... was at the house of Elbert H. Smith. The building was of logs—an old-fashioned chimney built of clay and sticks being laid up on the outside thereof. A heavy rain coming on, the clay moistened, and, while the honorable Court was in session, the whole chimney suddenly collapsed and came to the ground of its own weight. This unforeseen occurrence compelled the immediate adjournment of court, *nem con.*—smoked out.

Biographical and Historical Record of Ringgold and Union Counties, Iowa (Chicago: Lewis Publishing Co., 1887), p. 710.

The district court judges in the new state were often as singular and resourceful as the structures they occupied as courts. By all accounts, one of the most colorful was Judge C.J. McFarland of Boone, who in 1854 became judge of the fifth judicial district.

Judge McFarland was certainly a unique, and I might say, the most grotesque character that ever presided over an Iowa Court. I know nothing of his origin or bringing up, but one would judge that his early life had been amid the rough conditions of the frontier. It must be confessed that the drink habit was much in vogue among the early lawyers, and it would seem that Judge McFarland, at least at times, indulged pretty freely, and there was nothing half way about him. He was a very tall, stalwart, well-shaped man, with a beard as long and flowing as that of Aaron. He was a delegate to the National Democratic Convention of 1856, and it is said that his striking appearance and manner attracted general attention. He was a man of decided ability and had it not been for the weakness referred to, would probably have distinguished himself. On the bench he usually presided with force and propriety, but sometimes showed the effects of the previous night's indulgence in ways that in these modern days would have invoked the public censure if not impeachment or removal. ...

... Judge J. C. Knapp, of Keosauqua, one of Iowa's ablest lawyers ... said he was trying a case before Judge McFarland, in which an aged father was endeavoring to have cancelled a deed made by him to his son, in consideration of the support promised him by the latter. The gravamen of the complaint was, that the son had failed in his promise and had mistreated his father. Judge Knapp was for the defense. In the course of the trial a witness testified that on a certain occasion the defendant shamefully abused his father and struck him a blow. Upon this, Judge McFarland, who had been seemingly drowsy, almost dozing, suddenly raised himself in his seat, and bending forward towards the defendant, exclaimed: "You strike your old father! You strike your old father! I'll show you not to strike your poor old father!" The effect on Judge Knapp can be imagined by anyone who knew him. He seized his hat and started for the door with

Examples of some of the finer courthouses in the new state of Iowa. *Clockwise from upper left:* Henry County (built 1839-1840), Van Buren County (built 1841-1843), Scott County (built 1840-1842), and Clayton County (built 1843-1844). (Courtesy, State Historical Society of Iowa, Iowa City)

the exclamation that he could be of no further use in the case. "Hold on, Baldy!" (Knapp was somewhat bald) "Hold on, Baldy," said the Judge. But Baldy did not hold on, he stalked in disgust from the court room. This is the greatest breach of judicial decorum that Judge McFarland is reported to have committed. But while it was flagrant and unpardonable, it nevertheless showed that he had an irresistible sense of natural justice and filial duty.

Edward H. Stiles, *Recollections and Sketches of Notable Lawyers and Public Men of Early Iowa* (Des Moines: Homestead Publishing Co., 1916), pp. 262-63.

Many anecdotes are related of Judge McFarland, some of which are too good to be lost. He had nick-names for many of the attorneys who practiced before his court, James W. Wood[s] he called "Old Timber," and Gov. Eastman "Old Spot," from the fact of his being marked with small-pox. On one occasion, while Old Timber was addressing the court, an ass walked up near one of the windows and set up a terrible bray. The Judge quickly turned to Mr. Wood and cried out: "Sit down, Old Timber, sit down; one at a time, if you please."

History of Hardin County, Iowa (Springfield, Illinois: Union Publishing Co., 1883), p. 263.

A sober contrast to Judge McFarland was the sedate and temperate Judge John H. Gray of Des Moines, who became judge of the fifth judicial district in 1858.

Judge Gray and his wife arrived in Des Moines in a stage coach, late one night in 1856. As the coach drove into town and through the street, the occupants were singing songs, young Gray and his wife leading the singing. They were both active members of the Methodist Episcopal church; Mrs. Gray especially so. He was a small, delicate, spare man. He had received a good education, and had been a school teacher. Not long after his arrival he formed a partnership with W. W. Williamson in the law practice. He was industrious, conscientious, patient and studious, though neither brilliant nor profound; and made a very satisfactory judge. He had been raised a Puritan, had exemplary habits, and was a strong temperance advocate. ... He was universally respected, and he held this responsible position as sole judge of the district for the longest period accorded to any judge up to that time, being re-elected October 14, 1862, and remaining upon the bench until his death, October 14, 1865.

Chester C. Cole & E. C. Ebersole (ed.), *The Courts and Legal Profession of Iowa* (Chicago: H.C. Cooper, Jr., & Co., 1907), vol. II, pp. 903-04.

In its March 3, 1845, law supplemental to the act admitting Iowa and Florida to statehood, Congress established a United States judicial district called the District of Iowa, to be served by a single federal judge. In 1846, John J. Dyer of Dubuque was appointed Iowa's first United States district court judge. He remained on the federal bench until his death in 1856. In 1849, the District of Iowa was divided into northern, middle, and southern divisions, with court sessions held in Dubuque, Iowa City, and Burlington.

During his tenure, Judge Dyer presided over many important federal court cases, but two stand out as involving issues of special significance to the new state—the aiding of fugitive slaves, and title to land in the city of Dubuque. The first of these was the 1850 case of Daggs v. Frazier, in which a Missouri slave owner sought damages against a number of Henry County residents for interfering with the recovery of fugitive slaves, contrary to the Fugitive Slave Law of 1793. A federal jury in Burlington awarded the plaintiff $2,900 against several of the defendants.

The attorney for the slave owner was none other than David Rorer who, a decade earlier, had successfully vindicated the rights of Ralph, a former slave. Although personally opposed to slavery (he had freed his own slaves in Arkansas), Rorer forcefully argued for adherence to established law in the Daggs case.

Concluding Argument by Mr. Rorer. (attorney for the plaintiff)
Gentlemen of the Jury—I come now to perform my last duty to my client in this cause. This is, as the opposite counsel have said, an important trial. It is important to the plaintiff; for it is an inquiry as to whether he shall be compensated for the injury he has sustained by the acts of the defendants, done in violation of all law, and in contempt of the Constitution. It is important to the people of Iowa; for it will determine whether we are willing to abide by the compact we made when we entered into and became one of this great family of States. ...

Iowa is almost the youngest State in the Union. Missouri is the oldest of those west of the Mississippi. She was one of the Union when we knocked at the door for admission. It was the suggestion of our own minds. We knew what the Constitution was—the terms upon which we could be made a party to that compact—that not only Missouri, but many other States tolerated and sanctioned the institution of Slavery, and that every State was bound by the Constitution to deliver up fugitives when claimed. Shall we now repudiate the contract we have made—shall we be the first to violate it? ...

[The defendants'] sympathy for the negroes was their excuse! Their high sense of the turpitude of slavery—of its injury to the rights of man, and the great laws of God and Nature are pleaded as their apology! But who has made them the judges of that law? When were they made the oracles of wisdom and of God? Can their private opinions be set up in extenuation of their guilt, when they invade the province of the law and violate its most positive sanctions, under the pretence that the law is wrong! ...

I have said that this is an important case, and I repeat it. ... The very subject upon which you are called to decide, is now agitating our country from Washington to the most distant borders. It has been a source of contention and distrust among the people of both North and South—of slave-holding and non-slave-holding States. Your verdict will show whether there is just ground for this suspicion, as to us. Whether fanaticism is to be encouraged among us of the North, or the wild and maniac cry of disunion in the South. ... Above all, the law should be vindicated—its supremacy confirmed. The idea that any man or society of men, may be permitted to trample upon the plain letter of the law and Constitution, should be severely rebuked, and the offenders convinced that the impunity they have enjoyed in other places, will never be found in Iowa. ...

Gentlemen, I have done. I commend the case to your hands with the firmest conviction that you will meet out to us nothing more or less than impartial justice.

George Frazee (reporter), "An Iowa Fugitive Slave Case—1850," Daggs v. Frazier (D. Iowa, Southern Div., 1850), reprinted in *Annals of Iowa* 3rd Series, vol. VI (April 1903): 9, 29, 32, 35, 37-38.

Another important case presided over by Judge Dyer in the early years of statehood was Chouteau v. Molony. *Henry Chouteau, who claimed title as a successor in interest to Julien Dubuque, brought a lawsuit for the recovery of lands, including the city of Dubuque. The defendant Patrick Molony was a settler who claimed title under a patent from the United States government. Chouteau argued that Julien Dubuque's interest derived from a purchase agreement with the Indians and was confirmed by a grant from the Spanish authorities in Louisiana, thus antedating the United State's in-*

terest in the lands under the Louisiana Purchase.

Judge Dyer ruled for the settler Molony. The United States Supreme Court affirmed, finding that the Indians had intended to sell only mining privileges, and that the Spanish authorities had merely confirmed this limited grant. Hence, Chouteau, as the assignee of Julien Dubuque, could not claim a complete title in the lands exempt from the United States patent. Chouteau v. Molony, *57 U.S. (16 Howard) 203 (1853).*

The attorney who argued the settler's case before the United States Supreme Court was Thomas S. Wilson, the former associate judge of the Iowa Territorial Supreme Court. Judge Wilson later spoke about the unique manner in which he learned about the Court's favorable decision.

The case in our early judicial history which involved the greatest amount of property was the [Chouteau] case ... finally taken from the court of Iowa to the Supreme Court of the United States, and decided at the December term, 1853 ....

... After the case had been argued and submitted, and we had waited in great suspense for the decision, one morning when Mrs. Wilson and myself had taken our seats at the breakfast table at the hotel in Washington, Judge McLean, of the United States Supreme Court, with his wife and daughter, sat down at the same table; and after bidding us good-morning and alluding to what I said to the court in my argument, and when trying to represent what the condition of the settlers in our town and county would be if the decision should be adverse to them, that when turned out of home on the cold prairies they would be in a worse condition than the Israelites were when in the desert, having no manna placed upon our pathway, no pillar of cloud by day or fire by night, the judge said to my wife: "Mrs. Wilson, are you ready to turn out upon the desert this snowy morning?" She replied: "No, Judge, and I hope you will make no decision of our case that will render that necessary." I immediately arose from the table without breakfast, for I had not been served, and went rapidly to [associate counsel Platt] Smith's room. It was then nine o'clock, but I found him asleep, and, as usual, with his door unlocked. Clapping him on the shoulder to

The penitentiary at Fort Madison, as it appeared in 1846. (Courtesy, State Historical Society of Iowa, Iowa City)

arouse him, I said, "Smith, awake, we have gained our case." "How do you know?" said he. I then told him what Judge McLean had said at the table, remarking that the Judge would not have jested with us upon the subject, if the conclusion had been adverse to us. We immediately went to the clerk's office to learn the facts. The court sustained our objection to Julian DuBuque's title, viz.: that it was only an inchoate grant.

"Address of Judge T. S. Wilson at the Opening of the Supreme Court-Room," *Iowa Historical Record* X (April 1887): 457, 463, 465.

The first Great Seal of Iowa was adopted by the General Assembly in 1847. The state motto appears thereon: "Our liberties we prize and our rights we will maintain." (Courtesy, State Historical Society of Iowa, Iowa City)

The most pressing legislative task for the new state was the drafting of a revised code of laws. As early as December 2, 1846—twenty-six days before President Polk signed the act formally admitting Iowa as the twenty-ninth state—the first General Assembly of the State of Iowa had met in joint session to hear outgoing territorial Governor James Clarke address this need.

The period has arrived when a complete revision of the laws of Iowa is on all hands expected. The want of such a code has been felt and acknowledged for years, but it was deemed inexpedient to commence its compilation until after the organization of a State Government. ... The confusion which pervades our statute enactments is injurious in its tendencies, as, if permitted to continue, it will be disreputable to the character of the State. Nor will it be an easy task to collect, harmonize, and put into proper shape, the incongruous legislation of eight years; but a work of time and labor, which should be committed to none but able hands. I cannot but express the hope that, in authorizing such a revision, the State will avail itself of its best legal talent, whether it be deemed advisable to institute a special commission for the purpose, or, as has been done elsewhere, some gentleman learned in the law be authorized to perform the work, with a guarantee that the State will subscribe and pay a stipulated price for a certain number of copies upon their delivery. In either case, the State should prescribe the arrangement and execution of the work in the fullest manner possible.

Governor James Clarke, Second Annual Message, December 2, 1846, reprinted in Benjamin F. Shambaugh (ed.), *The Messages and Proclamations of the Governors of Iowa* (Iowa City: State Historical Society, 1903), vol. 1, p. 345.

The call for a new code was echoed by Iowa's first state governor, Ansel Briggs, in a message to a special session of the General Assembly in January 1848. Within the month, the legislature passed an act appointing a code commission. The commissioners were former territorial Chief Justice Charles Mason, lawyer (and future Supreme Court judge) William G. Woodward, and lawyer Stephen Hempstead, who in 1850 would be elected the second governor of the State of Iowa. At the end of 1848, the commissioners reported to Governor Briggs that they would need more time to complete their important work.

To His Excellency the Governor of Iowa: The undersigned who were appointed by an act of January 25th, 1848, to draft, revise and prepare a code of laws for the State of Iowa, beg leave to report:

That they have not been able to complete the task assigned them, and that it will require from three to five months in order to mature their work.

The great mass of the work is in writing, but we have not been able to give it that consideration which it demands before it is presented. The work of revis-

ing and writing *alone* has required the greater portion of the time since it was commenced. To *digest* it is the more important part of our task, and which remains to be done.

The importance of the work, and the consequences which will flow from a good or bad performance of it, are so great, that the undersigned are not willing to pass it without the most mature care. The revised code is intended to be a *permanent* work. All future legislation will have relation to it. If it is made complete and harmonious, but little legislation will be hereafter required on subjects of a general nature. If it is left incomplete and incongruous, it will require repeated amendments and alterations, until we shall no longer have a *code.* ...

Your excellency will permit us to suggest that in no case, we believe, has a *whole* code of Statute law been prepared in one year. ...

In presenting these views, sir, we have (in the words of our oath) "an eye single to the good of the people of Iowa;" and in presenting them, we trust we shall receive the indulgence of the General Assembly.

. . . .

W. G. Woodward,
Charles Mason,
S. Hempstead.
Iowa City, Dec. 4th, 1848.

Report of 1851 Code Commissioners to Governor Ansel Briggs, December 4, 1848, reprinted in Benjamin F. Shambaugh (ed.), *The Messages and Proclamations of the Governors of Iowa* (Iowa City: State Historical Society, 1903), vol. 1, pp. 393-94.

The Third General Assembly convened in biennial session in December 1850. The chief business before it was consideration of the voluminous report of the code commission. The General Assembly ordered a large portion of the commissioners' manuscript to be printed for the use of the legislators—an act that caused some newspapers to opine that the Assembly unfortunately anticipated a number of amendments. The Muscatine Journal *gave a tongue-in-cheek description of how the House of Representatives digested the 495-page printed report.*

The process is some thing like this: A chapter is read by the Clerk of the House, to thirty-nine persons, whose qualifications to judge of its merits or demerits, are equal to those of any equal number of persons selected indifferently from the counties of the State. The law required them to approve each chapter before it becomes a law; they feel the importance of their position—and in order to show to their constituents that they know and understand what is going on, each one feels called upon to leave, if possible, his mark upon each chapter. After the Clerk has read the chapter, each solon begins to scratch his head, and wonder if some portion can't be altered without doing much damage. The reading of the chapter by sections is then called for; by the time the first section is read, about three of them are on their feet, having caught an idea—Mr. Speaker! Mr. Speaker!! Mr. Speaker!!! is heard from east, south and west: The Speaker recognizes the gentleman from "Buncombe" county, and the other two, in a discontented mood, take their seats more determined than ever, the world shall have the benefit of the idea which is struggling within them for utterance.

Muscatine Journal, January 11, 1851.

In the end, the General Assembly made few amendments to the proposed code—a tribute to the excellent and thorough work of the code commissioners. The code was approved as a single act, and signed by the governor on February 5, 1851, effective July 1.

The Code of 1851 served the early period of statehood, until the Revision of 1860. The 1851 code was both a fusion of existing statutory law into a unified and comprehensive format, and a vehicle for new and revised laws. One of the most important (and controversial) changes was the centralization of county government and the creation of a county judge, whose broad administrative and judicial powers included those formerly exercised by the probate court.

County Judge

Sec. 105. Powers. The county judge is hereby invested with the usual powers and jurisdiction of county commissioners and of a judge of probate, and with such other powers and jurisdiction as are conferred by this statute ....

Sec. 106. Duties. ... He is the accounting officer and general agent of the county, and as such is authorized and required:

1. To take the management of all county business, and the care and custody of all the county property, except such as is by law placed in the custody of another officer ....

2. To audit all claims for money against the county ....

3. To audit and settle the accounts of the treasurer ....

8. To institute and prosecute civil actions brought for the benefit of the county;

9. To superintend the fiscal concerns of the county and secure their management in the best manner;

10. To keep an account of the receipts and expenditures of the county ....

Sec. 129. The county court has authority to provide for the erection and reparation of court houses, jails, and other necessary buildings within and for the use of the county, and such authority in relation to roads, ferries, the poor, and cases of bastardy, as is given in the chapters relating to those subjects, and has such other powers as are or may be given it by law. It shall determine the amount of tax to be levied for county purposes, according to the provisions of law in force at the time, and cause the same to be collected.

. . . .

Sec. 138. ... As the judge of probate, the county judge has jurisdiction of the probate of wills, the administration of the estates of deceased persons, and of the guardianship of minors and insane persons.

. . . .

Code of 1851, ch. 15, §§ 105, 106, 129, 138.

*The Code of 1851 contained provisions reg-
ulating liquor sales that were satisfactory
to neither side in the temperance debate.
Section 924 provided: "The people of this state
will hereafter take no share in the profits of re-
tailing intoxicating liquors, but the traffic in
those commodities as articles of merchandise is
not prohibited." Section 925, on the other hand,
prohibited "[t]he retail of intoxicating liquors in
the manner which is commonly denominated 'by
the glass' or 'by the dram' ...."*

*These laws spurred efforts by pro- and anti-
temperance groups to influence future legislation.
In his inaugural address, new Whig Governor
James Grimes added his voice to the call for temperance reform.*

SONS OF TEMPERANCE.

Iowa Division, No. 12

SIR—

You are invited to attend a Select Meeting, at TEETOTALERS' HALL,
No. 71 Division Street, on THURSDAY EVENING, Sept. 29, 1842, at half-
past 7 o'clock.

The object of the meeting is, to organize a Beneficial Society based on
Total Abstinence, bearing the above title. It is proposed to make the initia-
tion fee, at first, $1, and dues 6¼ cents a week;—in case of sickness, a
member to be entitled to $4 a week—and in case of death $30 to be appropriated for funeral expenses.

A Constitution will be submitted on the above evening, and if the
principles adopted meet your approbation, you are invited to become a
member of the Division.

Advertisement for an organizational meeting of a temperance society. (*Keokuk Register,* September 29,
1842)

There is a strong public sentiment in favor of
a radical change of the present laws regulating the manufacture and sale of intoxicating liquors. Every friend of humanity
earnestly desires that something may be done to dry
up the streams of bitterness that this traffic now pours
over the land. I have no doubt that a prohibitory law
may be enacted, that will avoid all constitutional objections, and meet the approval of a vast majority of
the people of the State.

Governor James Grimes, Inaugural Address, December 9,
1854, reprinted in Benjamin F. Shambaugh (ed.), *The Messages
and Proclamations of the Governors of Iowa* (Iowa City: State
Historical Society, 1903), vol II, p. 10.

*The temperance issue figured in many polit-
ical contests, including judicial elections.
A lively example was the 1854 election for
the judgeship of the fifth judicial district—in
which the* anti-*temperance candidate prevailed.*

Judge McKay occupied the bench for about five
years, and held his last term of court in the
early spring of 1854. He was renominated by
the whigs. P. M. Casady repeatedly refused to
be a candidate for the democrat nomination, but was
nominated by the democratic convention in spite of
his protests, and the convention adjourned in confusion, while he was standing upon the floor in a vain
effort to decline the nomination. The campaign was a
memorable one, but good natured, as Casady and
McKay were warm, personal friends. One of the features of the contest was a great meeting held by Judge
McKay at Newton, Iowa, at which he made a strong
temperance speech, induced a number of voters to
sign the pledge, and had an immense bon-fire, in
which he burned up a barrel of whiskey. The election
was held April 3, 1854. Mr. Casady was elected ....

Chester C. Cole & E. C. Ebersole (ed.), *The Courts and Legal
Profession of Iowa* (Chicago: H. C. Cooper, Jr., & Co., 1907),
vol. II, p. 901.

*The efforts of temperance reformers were
rewarded with the passage of "An Act for
the suppression of intemperance," signed
by Governor Grimes on January 22, 1855. The
act was subject, however, to a provision requiring
approval by popular vote. In April 1855, Iowans*

approved the prohibitory measure by a vote of 25,555 to 22,645. The act was immediately challenged on constitutional grounds, and was upheld by the Iowa Supreme Court.

An Act For The Suppression Of Intemperance

Be it enacted by the General Assembly of the State of Iowa:

Section 1. No person shall manufacture or sell by himself, his clerk, steward or agent, directly or indirectly, any intoxicating liquors, except as hereinafter provided. And the keeping of intoxicating liquor, with the intent, on the part of the owner thereof, or any person acting under his authority or by his permission, to sell the same within this state, contrary to the provisions of this act, is hereby prohibited, and the intoxicating liquors so kept, together with the vessels in which it is contained, is declared a nuisance, and shall be forfeited and dealt with as hereinafter provided; ale, porter, lager beer, cider, and all wines are included among intoxicating liquors within the meaning of this act: provided, however, that nothing in this section or in this act shall be construed to forbid the making of cider from apples, or wines from grapes, currants or other fruits grown or gathered by the manufacturer, or the selling of such cider or wine, (if made in the state) by the maker thereof, provided, only, that the quantity sold at any one time be not less than five gallons, and be sold and be all taken away at one time.
. . . .

Sec. 3. The county judge of any county ... shall appoint some suitable person or persons, not more than two in number, residents of said county ... to act as agent or agents of such county, for the purchase of intoxicating liquor, and for the sale thereof within such county, for medicinal, mechanical and sacramental purposes only. ...

Sec. 5. Every person who shall manufacture any intoxicating liquor, as in this act prohibited, shall be deemed guilty of a misdemeanor ....

Sec. 18. At the April election, to be holden on the first Monday in April, A. D., 1855, the question of prohibiting the sale and manufacture of intoxicating liquor, shall be submitted to the legal voters of this State .... [I]f it shall appear from such official statement that a majority of the votes cast as aforesaid upon said question or prohibition shall be for the prohibitory liquor law, then this act shall take effect on the first day of July, A. D. 1855 ....
Approved January 22d, 1855.

Acts of the Fifth General Assembly, 1854-55, § 1, 3, 5, 18.

The prohibitory law did not have an immediate salutary effect on public morals. Temperance and women's rights reformer Amelia Bloomer, writing for The Lily *from her newly adopted city of Council Bluffs, complained that the law had failed to stem the flow of intoxicating beverages.*

Council Bluffs, Iowa, Aug. 30, 1855.
I hoped, by this time, to have a good report to make in regard to the workings of the prohibitory liquor law of this State—which was passed last winter and went into operation the first of July. But whatever may have been done in other sections, I am sorry to say that so far as our city is concerned, it amounts to nothing. Notwithstanding the passage of such a law, our merchants and saloon keepers brought on a full supply of liquors, and have been as actively and openly engaged in their sale as though the law had not pronounced it a criminal business, and imposed fines and imprisonment on both the seller and the drinker. Only one case has been tried under the law, and that proved a failure. Though positive proof of sale was produced, the jury returned a verdict of "not guilty," and the criminal was discharged. And there the matter rests. Men say it is useless to enter complaints—for though the justices are temperance men, the constables are not; and as these latter have the summoning of juries there is no hope that any will be chosen to sit on a trial for violation of the liquor law, except the hangers-on of grogshops—and from whom there is no hope of conviction, even if the proof of guilt be positive and undeniable. And so they have abandoned the field, leaving the rumseller in full possession, to pursue his work unmolested. ...

I have hoped that some of the Lily readers in the eastern part of this State would report thro' its columns something in relation to the success of the law in their different localities—but as yet I have seen nothing. I am assured, however, by travelers who come through, that it is quite generally observed, and that in many places no liquor can be obtained. I hope this is true, and that the same influence that operates farther east to make them an order-loving and law-abiding people, may speedily extend to our city—and even go beyond into Nebraska, where the law is equally disregarded.

Amelia Bloomer, "Editorial Correspondence," *The Lily*, October 1, 1855, p. 143.

Amelia Bloomer. (Courtesy, State Historical Society of Iowa, Iowa City)

Despite Amelia Bloomer's fond hope that the eastern portion of the state would exhibit greater diligence than western Iowa in enforcing the temperance law, the situation there also was less than ideal. A Burlington newspaper reported that the general populace was reluctant to involve itself in law enforcement efforts.

Seizure of Liquors.—Complaint was made, a day or two since, against the "American House," corner of Front and Valley streets, as an institution at which liquors were vended in all quantities contrary to the statute in such case made and provided. Warrants were issued accordingly, and Constables Wedge and Kirkpatrick proceeded to lay legal hands on the contraband liquids aforesaid.—The size and weight of the vessels containing the inhibited luxuries proved rather too much for the worthy officials, so they were compelled to call for assistance. Although there was a crowd of persons present, they respectfully declined to take any part or lot in the matter. In this emergency, the Constables, not knowing what else to do, fell back upon the informers, whose muscles were put in requisition to aid and assist in accomplishing the seizure. Having rolled the barrels upon the pavement the next thing to be done was to store the same in some secure place. A drayman happening to pass, he

was bailed, and his services demanded. Upon a sober second thought, Pat told them to be after attinding to their own business—it was'nt convanient just thin for him to be bothering himself about other paple's matthers. Failing to elicit aid or comfort from any quarter, the Constables and the informers again put their shoulders under the law, and after considerable heaving, tugging, and grunting, they succeeded in making a deposit of their trophies in some neighboring store house. A story is told of a shower bath descending in golden sheets from a second story window upon one of the informers, but the particulars could hardly add to the interest of the event.

It will thus be seen that although there is no resistance made to the law, it is pretty much left to execute itself. We are far from wishing any thing but success to those who are honestly striving to extend the area of temperance among us, but when a law is so odious in its features that not one in a hundred of our citizens will aid in its execution, it is certainly time to enquire whether both public and private morality would not be more certainly promoted by the adoption of a different policy?

[Burlington] Daily Iowa State Gazette, February 7, 1856.

There were widespread violations of the new prohibition law, due at least in part to vacillating efforts at enforcement. Many individuals began to press for modifications, and in 1857 additional measures were approved that diluted, without repealing, the general prohibitory law. One of these measures authorized a county license scheme subject to popular vote. Within a year, the Iowa Supreme Court had declared the 1857 license law unconstitutional.

This act authorizes the county judge of any county, to issue a license to any person, making application according to its provisions, for the sale of malt, spirituous and vinous liquors .... By the seventeenth and eighteenth sections, it is provided, that the act entitled "an act for the suppression of intemperance," approved January 22, 1855, is not repealed in any county of the state, unless the people of such county shall, by vote taken upon the question of licensing the sale of spirituous or vinous liquors, adopt the said act of January 29, 1857; and if a majority of the legal voters in any county, shall vote in favor of the act, then the county judge shall proceed to issue license, as by the said act is provided.

In *Santo v. The State,* 2 Iowa, 203 [1856], it was held, that the eighteenth section of the act for the suppression of intemperance, approved January 22, 1855, which provided for submitting to the people of the state, the question of prohibiting the sale of intoxicating liquors, was not a submission in its largest and broadest sense of the question, whether the act aforesaid should become a law; that such a submission would have been unconstitutional and void ....

The position seems to us too clear to admit of any doubt, that if the act of January 29, 1857, receives its vitality and force from a vote of the people, such vote is an exercise of legislative power, and the law is unconstitutional and void. The legislative power is vested in the General Assembly, and can be exercised by that body alone.

The act of January 29, 1857 ... attempts to abrogate the uniform operation, and consequently, the force and validity, of a law general in its nature, and intended to secure the entire prohibition of the sale of intoxicating liquors in the state, and to provide for li-

censing the sale thereof, in any county of the state desiring the change, not by virtue of an act of the legislature passed into a law, according to the form of the constitution, but by the vote of a majority of the people of such county expressed at the polls.
. . . .

It results from the foregoing considerations, that the act entitled "an act to license and regulate the sale of malt, spirituous and vinous liquors, in the state of Iowa," approved January 29, 1857, is unconstitutional and void.

Geebrick v State of Iowa, 5 Clarke 491, 493-95, 499 (Iowa 1858).

Although Amelia Bloomer was disappointed with efforts to enforce Iowa's prohibition law, she was more generous in her assessment of the legal status of women. Writing in The Lily in 1855, she urged women to come to western Iowa and take advantage of the state's relatively liberal property laws.

Come then, I say to all, to Western Iowa— and to Council Bluffs. Send here your money and your Land Warrants, and secure a part in these rich prairie lands which border the Missouri, and you will secure for yourselves and families a patrimony at once ample and abundant for all your, or their wants. ...

And especially would I urge those women who can command one or two hundred dollars of their own, or "coax it out of their husbands," to invest that amount at least, in western lands, in their own name. By the laws of this State women can hold and control property, both real and personal, and I am desirous that they should take advantage of this liberality by securing to themselves a share of these fine prairie farms. ... I know that those women who are dependent upon their own exertions, can scarcely expect to save enough of their meagre wages to make even a small investment of this kind; yet with prudence and economy there are some who may secure a forty or an eighty acre interest in land at one dollar and a quarter per acre,—and it can be obtained at even less than that by the purchase of Land Warrants. I am happy to know that there are some who are making such disposition of their earnings, and I hope the number may increase.

Amelia Bloomer, "Editorial Correspondence," *The Lily*, June 15, 1855, p. 93.

The territorial Legislative Assembly in 1846 had passed a law that ameliorated to some extent the restrictive common law rules regarding married women and property ownership. Thereafter, the Code of 1851 embodied provisions regarding married women that were among the most progressive in the nation.

Married Women.
An Act Concerning The Rights Of Married Women.
Be it enacted by the Council and House of Representatives of the Territory of Iowa.

Section 1. That any married woman may become seized or possessed of any real estate by descent, bequest, demise, gift, purchase or distribution, in her own name and as of her own property. Provided, the same does not come from her husband, nor is, nor has been purchased with the funds or property of the husband during coverture.

Sec. 2. That hereafter when any married woman shall become possessed of any real estate as aforesaid, or shall have possessed any real estate before coverture, she shall possess the same in her own right and the same shall in no case be liable to the debts of her husband.

Sec. 3. The control and management of such real estate, and the annual productions and rents and profits of the same, shall remain in the husband agreeably to the laws heretofore in force. ...

Approved January 2d, 1846.

Territorial Laws of Iowa, 1845-46, ch. 5, §§ 1-3.

Husband and Wife: Of The Domestic Relations.

Section 1447. The personal property of the wife does not vest at once in the husband ....

Sec. 1448. If the wife has such property which she leaves under [the husband's] control she must, in order to avoid the entire surrender of her interest therein, file for record with the recorder of deeds a notice, stating the amount in value of such property and that she has a claim therefor out of the estate of her husband. ...

Sec. 1450. Specific articles of personal property may be owned by the wife exempt from the husband's debts, although left under his control, if during his lifetime and prior to its being disposed of by him or levied upon for his debts notice of her ownership is filed for record with the recorder of deeds of the county.

. . . .

Sec. 1454. Contracts made by a wife in relation to her separate property or those purporting to bind herself only, do not bind the husband.

. . . .

Sec. 1456. Married women abandoned by their husbands may obtain authority from the district court of the county in which they reside to act and to transact business as though unmarried.

. . . .

Sec. 1462. The husband cannot remove the wife nor their children from their homestead without the consent of the wife, and if he abandons her she is entitled to the custody of their minor children, unless the district court upon application for that purpose shall for good cause otherwise direct.

Code of 1851, ch. 84, §§ 1447, 1448, 1450, 1454, 1456, 1462.

Subsequent decisions of the Iowa Supreme Court embodied the state's more liberal position on the subject of women's property rights.

By the whole spirit of our law ... the wife is recognized as having a right to hold and control property, and to have an existence in the marital relation, not merged into that of the husband. ... While our law in no manner weakens the obligations of this most sacred relation; yet in its letter and spirit, it does recognize that she may have a separate property, which she can hold exempt from the debts of the husband; that she may be authorized to transact business in her own name, when abandoned by her husband; that she cannot be removed from their homestead without her consent; and that courts will protect her rights, and give her, either in property or otherwise, what is right and proper. ... [The property] has been accumulated in most instances by the joint labor of the parties, each in their appropriate sphere. While technically, perhaps, it is recognized as the husband's, yet rightly and properly, it is also the wife's. He cannot convey or dispose of it without her consent, nor do any act that would directly incumber her interest therein. It is not his nor hers, but theirs. ... [W]e are clear that under our law, the court has full power to give to the wife in these cases, a specific portion of the husband's property, and that this may be real or personal. And is it not clearly equitable and just, that the wife shall be given a home—a place to reside—if the circumstances justify it, rather than be turned from that which she has assisted to obtain, improve, and make pleasant and comfortable, with an annual or other allowance, to seek a new home?

Jolly v. Jolly, 1 Clarke 9, 12-13 (Iowa 1855).

Despite the advances in women's property rights, the legal status of Iowa women during the mid-19th century was still considerably inferior to men, as shown in an Iowa Supreme Court decision concerning child custody rights.

The law of England, the principle of which, so far as it has not been changed by our statutes is in force here, is "that the very being or legal existence of the woman is suspended during marriage, or at least is incorporated and consolidated into that of the husband." 1 Black. Com., 468.

The control of the child, follows as a consequence. ... The father has legal power over the child until it arrive at the age of twenty-one years. There can be no doubt of the paramount right of the father to the possession, care and control of his minor child, when the child—as this one is—is of such age that it can, without injury or violence to nature, be withdrawn from maternal nursing. ...

What are the facts of this case, as certified by the district judge of record here? It is expressly stated that the father and mother are both capable and able to take charge of the child, and to support it. The child is now about five years old, and therefore may be separated from the mother without doing violence to it, on the score of natural support and comfort. ... The right of the father to the possession and control of the person of his minor child, when his disability is not established, is paramount.

... We are aware that in this, our day, the spirit of progress is abroad in the land, but, whilst we would not obstruct its onward career to triumph over error and oppression, we think that it is well to observe and maintain those great and cardinal principles upon which the integrity of the social compact must ever depend. The just appreciation of the rights and duties of the marriage contract, and its incidents, is essential to the existence of civil and christian society. ...

The order of the court below is reversed, and ordered that the child be delivered to John B. Hunt, the father.

Hunt v. Hunt, 4 Greene 216, 219, 221, 222-23 (Iowa 1854).

Although there was a strong anti-slavery sentiment in Iowa—as shown by the efforts of Quakers and others to aid fugitive slaves through the "underground railroad"—attitudes about blacks, Indians, and people of mixed race were largely discriminatory. This was reflected in a number of Iowa laws. One such law in the Code of 1851 (subsequently repealed in December 1856) concerned the ability to give testimony in a court of law.

The exclusion of blacks from giving testimony "in any cause wherein a white person is a party" was held by the Iowa Supreme Court to apply even when a white defendant sought to introduce the testimony and the objecting party was a black plaintiff.

The competency of the witness, Hinton, must depend upon the construction to be given to the concluding part of section 2388, of the Code [of 1851]. This provides, that an Indian, a negro, a mulatto, or a black person, shall not be allowed to give testimony in any case wherein a white person is a party. This language is explicit, and most clearly renders the witness incompetent. ...

It is urged, however, that this provision was designed for the benefit of, and to protect the white person; and that the defendants having waived this objection, by offering to introduce the witness, the plaintiff, being a negro, cannot object. ... This position would be tenable, if the provision contained in section 2388, was alone for the benefit of the white person. But as already shown, this is not the language of the Code, and so far as relates to the reason and policy of the law, we can conceive of quite as weighty considerations for excluding the testimony, when offered by, as when offered against, a white man. If the plaintiff was a white man, it would be clear that the witness would, if objected to, be incompetent, when offered by the defendants. So also, if offered by the plaintiff, a negro, against the defendants. Why, then, should the law make him competent for a white person against a negro? It is said that the reason he is incompetent for the black against the white person, is, that the blacks are clannish, and might confederate to the great injury and prejudice of

white suitors. But, on the other hand, it is not to be disguised, that from the dependent position of this unfortunate portion of our population upon white persons, they might be used as instruments by them, to injure and prejudice black suitors. ... When both parties are black, such witnesses are competent; otherwise not, if objection is made.

Motts v. Usher, 2 Clarke 82, 83-84 (Iowa 1855).

An extreme example of the bias against non-whites in the period of early statehood was an act passed in the Third General Assembly "to prohibit the immigration of free negroes." Bearing the same approval date as the Code of 1851—February 5, 1851—this restrictive legislation did not appear in the code itself. The law was virtually unenforced until the Civil War years, was declared unconstitutional by an Iowa district court in 1863, and the following year was repealed by the General Assembly.

An Act To Prohibit The Immigration Of Free Negroes Into This State.
Be it enacted by the General Assembly of the State of Iowa:

Section 1. That from and after the passage of this act, no free negro or mulatto, shall be permitted to settle in this state.

Sec. 2. It shall be the duty of all township and county officers, to notify all free negroes who may immigrate to this state, to leave the same within three days from the time of notice, and upon their failure to do so, it shall be the duty of the constable of the proper township, sheriff of the county, marshal or other police officer of the town, to arrest such free negro, and take him or her before a justice of the peace or county judge, and it shall be the duty of such justice or judge to fine such free negro, the sum of two dollars, for each day he may remain in the state after such notice, and costs of such prosecution; and to commit such free negro to the jail of the county or the nearest one thereto, until such fine and costs are paid, or until he will consent to leave the state ....

Sec. 3. That all free negroes now living in this state, who have complied with the laws now in force, shall be permitted to remain here, and enjoy such property as they may now possess, or may hereafter acquire.

. . . .

Approved February 5th, 1851.

Acts of the Third General Assembly, 1850-51, ch. 72, §§ 1-3.

Iowa Governor (later U.S. Senator) James W. Grimes. (Courtesy, State Historical Society of Iowa, Iowa City)

While abhorring the institution of slavery and strongly opposing its extension, most Iowans did not endorse total abolition. In his inaugural address on December 9, 1854, Whig Governor James Grimes expressed the delicate balance existing in the Iowan consciousness on the question of slavery.

I trust that there is no citizen of Iowa, who desires the general government to interfere with slavery in the States of this Union. It is a local institution, and to the States that maintain it, belong its responsibilities and its perils. But whilst the people of the North should scrupulously regard the rights of others, they should manfully maintain their own. They are recreant to their own interests; they betray the rights of their posterity; they give a fatal blow to the principles of free and equal government, when they consent to the creation of new slave States and a consequent further representation of slave property.

The removal of that great landmark of freedom, the Missouri Compromise line—when it had been sacredly observed until slavery had acquired every inch of soil south of it, has presented the aggressive character of that system broadly before the country. It has shown that all compromises with slavery, that are designed to favor freedom, are mere ropes of sand, to be broken by the first wave of passion or interest that may roll from the South. ...

It is both the interest and duty of the free States to prevent the increase and extension of the slave element of power, by every constitutional means. ... Freedom being the natural condition of all men; and no authority being delegated to the general government to establish or protect slavery, Congress can pass no law establishing or protecting it in the territories. If Congress can pass no such law, much less can it delegate such authority to the territorial legislatures, over whose acts it has ever exercised a supervisory and restraining power. By a wide departure from constitutional principles, slavery has been tolerated in some of the territories. Let such toleration forever cease. Let the government be brought back to its original purity. Let the principle be authoritatively announced and persistently adhered to, that there can be no slavery outside of State sovereignties. ... It is only by an entire disconnection of the general government from the institution of slavery, that the people of the free States can find safety and honor. ...

It becomes the State of Iowa—the only free child of the Missouri Compromise—to let the world know, that she values the blessings that compromise has secured to her, and that she will never consent to become a party to the nationalization of slavery.

Governor James Grimes, Inaugural Address, December 9, 1854, reprinted in Benjamin F. Shambaugh (ed.), *The Messages and Proclamations of the Governors of Iowa* (Iowa City: State Historical Society, 1903), vol. II, pp. 12-14.

Governor Grimes followed with keen interest a fugitive slave case in his hometown of Burlington. In June 1855, Dr. Edwin James, an eminent scientist and ardent abolitionist, had attempted to aid the escape of a fugitive slave called Dick. A Missourian claiming to be Dick's owner sought his return under the provisions of the Fugitive Slave Law, whose penalties had been strengthened by the Compromise of 1850.

Governor Grimes wrote to his wife (who was visiting relatives in Maine) about the case—and about the conflict between his private feelings and his duties as governor.

June 24th [1855]—Exciting times here. Yesterday morning Dr. James was captured on the Illinois side of the river, with a fugitive slave in his carriage. Bowie knives and revolvers were drawn on him by the Missourians in pursuit, and he and the negro were forced back to town. A process was afterward obtained, the negro thrown into jail, where he is to remain to await his trial on Tuesday. ... I shall certainly furnish no aid to the man-stealers [slave catchers], and it has been determined that the negro shall have able counsel, and a resort to all legal means for release, before any other is resorted to. I am sorry I am Governor of the State, for, although I can and shall prevent the State authorities and officers from interfering in aid of the marshal, yet, if not in office, I am inclined to think I should be a lawbreaker. It is a very nice question with me, whether I should act, being Governor, just as I would if I were a private individual. I intend to stand at my post, at all events, and act just as I shall think duty may require under the circumstances.

Governor James Grimes, letter to Elizabeth Grimes, June 24, 1855, reprinted in William Salter, *The Life of James W. Grimes* (New York: D. Appleton & Co., 1876), p. 72.

The Fugitive Slave Law of 1850 had required the appointment of federal commissioners to dispose of claims under the law. Attorney George Frazee of Burlington, in his capacity as commissioner for the United States District of Iowa, issued the warrant for Dick's arrest upon the application of the claimant's agent. Dick was represented by the brilliant David Rorer—whose previous clients had included a former slave in the 1839 case, In the matter of Ralph, and a slave owner in the 1850 case, Daggs v. Frazier.

George Frazee later recalled the dramatic events of June 26, 1855.

When the doors were opened and the alleged fugitive, in custody of the marshal, was brought in, the large court room was immediately filled to suffocation by excited people. It was never so crowded before or since. The doors had to be closed and guarded to keep out a great mass of others, all anxious to witness the proceedings. The mayor of the city, Mr. S. A. Hudson ... voluntarily installed himself as doorkeeper. Mr. M. D. Browning again appeared on behalf of the claimant, and Judge David Rorer ... and Mr. T. D. Crocker, were counsel for Dick. Along with Mr. Browning came young Rutherford, son of the claimant, who was of course supposed to be well acquainted with his father's negroes, and very certainly with the man, Dick, who was said to have escaped into Iowa. Everybody was agog to see the witness upon whose testimony the fate of Dick depended. ... Mr. Browning offered the son as his witness, who was duly sworn. Next, Mr. Browning asked that the negro, who occupied a seat some distance from the witness, might be required to stand up, so that the witness might obtain a clear view of him. Without any hesitation Dick assumed a standing position and boldly confronted the witness. Mr. Browning then interrogated the witness as to the identity of "Dick." The answer was a surprise to all present, quite as much to me as to anyone. ... Instead of affirming that Dick was his father's, the witness promptly responded that the negro before him was not; that he did not know him and that he had never seen him before. No other evidence was offered, and Judge Rorer then moved that the fugitive should be released from custody and whatever property had been taken from him should be restored, and so it was ordered.

George Frazee, "The Iowa Fugitive Slave Case," *Annals of Iowa* 3rd Series, vol. IV (July 1899): 118, 132-33.

Illustration of a slave catcher.

Lowe was brought from Keokuk Monday in the night, and a writ of habeas corpus was ready to be served, if the decision had been adverse to us. Writs were sued out against the negro-stealers for kidnapping, assault, etc., but, unfortunately, they escaped, before service could be made upon them. I am satisfied that the negro would never have been taken into slavery from Burlington. …

Thus has ended the first case under the [1850] fugitive-slave law in Iowa. The State, the town, and the people, thank God, are saved from disgrace. How opinions change! Four years ago, Mr. _____ and myself, and not to exceed three others in town, were the only men who dared express an opinion in opposition to the fugitive-slave law, and, because we did express such opinions, we were denounced like pickpockets. Now I am Governor of the State; three-fourths of the reading and reflecting people of the county agree with me in my sentiments on the law, and a slave could not be returned from Des Moines County into slavery.

Governor James Grimes, letter to Elizabeth Grimes, June 27, 1855, reprinted in William Salter, *The Life of James W. Grimes* (New York: D. Appleton & Co., 1876), pp. 72-73.

Governor Grimes rejoiced in the outcome of Dick's hearing. His letter to his wife suggests that the Iowa authorities were prepared to resort to other legal measures, if necessary, to prevent Dick's return to slavery.

June 27th.—The negro is free, and is on his way to Canada. A great crowd yesterday in town. … Marion Hall was filled, and guards were stationed at the door, to prevent any more people entering, and around the house. Rorer and Crocker appeared for the negro. When the decision was made, such a shout went up as was never heard in that hall before, and then it was caught up by the people outside the building, and the whole town reverberated. A thousand men followed Dr. James and the negro to the river, and rent the air with their cheers, as the boat was unlashed from her moorings, and started with the poor fellow on his road to freedom. Judge [Ralph P.]

The Sioux Treaty of 1851 was the final agreement between the federal government and the Indian tribes in Iowa, and effectively removed from the state the last formal Indian presence. Nine years earlier, the Treaty of 1842 had ceded the remaining Sauk (Sac) and Meskwaki (Fox) lands in Iowa, with removal from all portions of the state to be completed in three years. After 1845, some individual Sauk and Meskwaki undoubtedly remained in the state, but most were removed to Kansas, where they found the land inhospitable compared to their lush hunting grounds in Iowa.

In 1856, some members of the Meskwaki tribe sought to realize by legal barter what they had failed to achieve by treaty—a permanent homeland in Iowa. They found willing sellers of land in Tama County, and their efforts were supported by petitions from friendly settlers. In 1856, the Iowa legislature passed a law permitting a limited Indian residence in the state; the follow-

ing year, the Meskwaki purchased eighty acres of land west of Tama, whose title was held by Iowa's governor as trustee. Additional land acquisitions would bring the Meskwaki holdings to over 4,500 acres by the mid-1990s.

An Act Permitting Certain Indians To Reside Within The State.
Be it enacted by the General Assembly of the State of Iowa,

Section 1. That the consent of the state is hereby given that the Indians now residing in Tama county known as a portion of the Sacs and Foxes, be permitted to remain and reside in said state, and that the governor be requested to inform the secretary of war thereof, and urge on said department, the propriety of paying said Indians their proportion of the annuities due or to become due to said tribe of Sacs and Fox Indians.

Sec. 2. That the sheriff of said county, shall as soon as a copy of this law is filed in the office of the county court proceed to take the census of said Indians now residing there giving their names, and sex, which said list shall be filed and recorded in said office, the persons whose names are included in said list shall have the privileges granted under this act, but none others shall be considered as embraced within the provisions of said act.

. . . .

Approved July 15th, 1856.

Acts of the Fifth General Assembly Extra Session, 1856, ch. 30, §§ 1-2.

Education was one of the vital subjects to occupy the Iowa General Assembly during the formative years of statehood. Many pieces of legislation concerned the organization and government of schools—both common schools and a university.

In 1845, the territorial Legislative Assembly had passed "An Act to incorporate the University of Iowa." Two years later, the General Assembly committed Iowa's resources to a major institution of learning in Iowa City.

An Act To Locate And Establish A State University.
Be it enacted by the General Assembly of the State of Iowa:

Section 1. [T]here shall be established at Iowa City, the present seat of government of the state of Iowa, an institution to be called the "State University of Iowa," with such branches as, in the opinion of the general assembly, the public convenience may hereafter require.

Sec. 2. The public buildings at Iowa City, together with the ten acres of land on which the same are situated, be, and the same are, hereby granted for the use of said university: provided that the sessions of the general assembly, and the offices of the officers of state, shall be held in the present capitol until otherwise provided for by law.

. . . .

Sec. 10. [S]aid university shall never be under the exclusive control of any religious denomination whatever.

Sec. 11. [T]he grants and donations herein made are upon the express condition that the said university shall, so soon as it shall be in the enjoyment of revenue from the said grant and donations at the rate of two thousand dollars per annum, commence and continue the instruction—free of charge—of fifty students annually, in the theory and practice of teaching, as well as in such branches of learning as shall be deemed best calculated for the preparation of said students for the business of common school teaching.

...

Approved February 25th, 1847.

Acts of the First General Assembly, 1846-47, ch. 125, §§ 1-2, 10-11.

The Constitution of 1857 specified in Article IX that the General Assembly also should encourage "the promotion of intellectual, scientific, moral, and agricultural improvement." Armed with this directive, the legislature in 1858 laid the legal groundwork for a second great institution of learning, which was to become Iowa State University at Ames.

An Act To Provide For The Establishment Of A State Agricultural College And Farm ....

Be it enacted by the General Assembly of the State of Iowa,

Section 1. [T]here is hereby established a state agricultural college and model farm, to be connected with the entire agricultural interests of the state. ....

Sec. 15. The course of instruction in said college shall include the following branches, to-wit: Natural philosophy, chemistry, botany, horticulture, fruit growing, forestry, animal and vegetable anatomy, geology, mineralogy, meteorology, entymology, zoology, the veterinary art, plain mensuration, levelling, surveying, book keeping and such mechanic arts as are directly connected with agriculture. ...

Sec. 17. Tuition in the college herein established shall be forever free to pupils from this state over fourteen years of age and who have been resident of the state six months previous to their admission. Applicants for admission must be of good moral character, able to read and write the English language with ease and correctness, and also to pass a satisfactory examination in the fundamental rules of arithmetic.

Sec. 18. The trustees upon consultation with the professors and teachers shall, from time to time, establish rules regulating the number of hours, to be not less than two in winter and three in summer, which shall be devoted to manual labor and the compensation therefor; and no student shall be exempt from such labor except in case of sickness or other infirmity. ....

Approved March 22, 1858.

Acts of the Seventh General Assembly, 1858, ch. 91, §§ 1, 15, 17-18.

The Constitution of 1857 placed educational interests under the management of an elected Board of Education. Until abolished in 1864, the Board of Education promulgated regulations that had the force and effect of law. During its first session, the Board considered an issue that has since plagued many local school boards—what books should be permitted in the classroom?

Act No. 7.

An Act Prohibiting The Exclusion Of The Bible From The Schools Of The State.

Section 1. Be it enacted by the Board of Education of the State of Iowa, That the Bible shall not be excluded from any school or institution in this State, under the control of the Board, nor shall any pupil be required to read it contrary to the wishes of his parent or guardian.

Oran Faville,
President of the Board of Education.
December 22d, 1858.

Act No. 12.
An Act Relative To The Introduction Of Webster's Dictionary Into The Common Schools Of This State.

Section 1. Be it enacted by the Board of Education of the State of Iowa, That the Board of Directors of each school district in this State may, at any regular or special meeting of said board, determine whether they will purchase for the use of the schools in their district copies of Webster's Unabridged Dictionary. ...

Sec. 4. [S]uch books ... shall be purchased at a cost not exceeding four dollars per copy[,] shall be the latest edition of Webster's Quarto Unabridged, printed on superior paper, well bound in leather, perfect in all respects, and shall be delivered free of charges at any points in this State not exceeding four, one of which shall be Council Bluffs, and the other three not farther west than Des Moines City ....

Sec. 7. Such Dictionaries shall be kept in the schools during the term time, and under the control of the teacher thereof, and when not in school, shall be placed in the district library, subject to the rules established for the government of district libraries. ...

Oran Faville,
President of the Board of Education.
December 24th, 1858.

Acts of the Board of Education, First Session, 1858, Nos. 7, 12 (Des Moines: State Printer, 1859).

The General Assembly passed many statutes governing the state's common schools. It was clear, however, that these schools were not intended to benefit all Iowans. The concept of a "white only" and "separate but equal" educational system was firmly established in the state, until successfully challenged in the post-Civil War years.

The school district directors shall annually take a list of all the persons in their district between the ages of five and twenty-one years ... [and] they shall see ... that said school shall be open and free alike to all white persons in the district between the ages of five and twenty-one years ....
Approved January 24, 1847

Acts of the First General Assembly, 1846-47, ch. 99, § 6.

All real and personal property of blacks and mulattoes in this state shall be exempt from taxation for school purposes.
Approved February 5, 1851.

Code of 1851, ch. 71, § 1160.

The duties of the district board of directors shall be as follows:

... Education of colored children. They may admit pupils not belonging to the district ... to the privileges of their schools on such terms of tuition as may be agreed upon. And they shall provide for the education of the colored youth, in separate schools, except in cases where by the unanimous consent of the persons sending to the school in the sub-district, they may be permitted to attend with the white youth.

. . . .

Approved March 12, 1858.

Acts of the Seventh General Assembly, 1858, ch. 52, § 30(4).

The population of Iowa moved steadily westward. In the early days of the Iowa Territory, the Mississippi River towns were the heart of legislative and judicial activities, and the selection of Iowa City as the second territorial and first state capital seemed a sufficient concession to the westward movement. Now the population had shifted yet further toward the Missouri River, and pressure mounted for a more central capital. Amidst great political controversy, the General Assembly in 1855 voted to relocate the seat of government to Des Moines.

The state government moved to Des Moines in late 1857, although not until 1884 was the gold-domed capitol building completed. The new state had found its permanent political center.

An Act To Re-locate The Seat Of Government.
Be it enacted by the General Assembly of the State of Iowa:

Section 1. [F]ive commissioners ... shall be appointed by the governor to re-locate the seat of government of this state; provided, that the site selected by them shall be within two miles of the junction of the Des Moines and Racoon rivers in Polk county; and provided further, that the governor, before issuing his proclamation, as hereinafter provided, shall approve of the site selected ....

Sec. 10. When buildings are prepared for the accommodation of the general assembly and the officers of state, which in the opinion of the governor, are suitable therefor, he shall issue his proclamation to that effect, and from that time the general assembly shall meet, and the officers of state keep their offices at such new seat of government ....
Approved 25th January, 1855.

Acts of the Fifth General Assembly, 1854-55, ch. 72, § 1, 10.

In compliance with the act of 25th of January, 1855, entitled "an act to re-locate the seat of government," I appointed commissioners for that purpose and they have discharged their duty. The site selected for the future capitol is on a gentle swell of land about three quarters of a mile east of Fort des Moines, and on the east side of the

The first building occupied as a state capitol in Des Moines. (Courtesy, State Historical Society of Iowa, Iowa City)

river. It commands a good prospect and seems to be well adapted to the purpose for which it has been selected.

Governor James Grimes, First Biennial Address, December 2, 1856, reprinted in Benjamin F. Shambaugh (ed.), *The Messages and Proclamations of the Governors of Iowa* (Iowa City: State Historical Society, 1903), vol. II, p. 36.

The Seventh General Assembly assembled at the new capital of Des Moines in January 1858. One of its members, Cyrus C. Carpenter (who later became governor of Iowa), recalled the happy festivities that greeted the legislators.

On the 11th day of January, 1858, this General Assembly came together at Des Moines. It was the first General Assembly that had met in this city. The people of the city were much elated at what they regarded as their good fortune in securing the re-location of the Capitol, and were correspondingly rejoiced at the first assembling of a legislative body in their midst. We were therefore welcomed with a hospitality and friendly warmth that could not well be repeated. I came here two or three days before the time of assembling, traveling by stage down the old State road leading from Fort Dodge to Des Moines, staying over night at Boonsboro, and arriving in the city the evening of the second day.

Des Moines was then a town of about 3,000 inhabitants, as two years thereafter at the Federal census, it only had a population of about 3,900. It was literally a city of "magnificent distances." The site of the Capitol was then a wooded hill, occupied by the old (then new) Capitol building, and perhaps some twenty-five or thirty family residences scattered here and there in the openings of the timber. The bottom intervening between the foot of the hill and the river was a low muddy flat, comparatively unoccupied and unimproved. ...

I have said that a Legislative Assembly was a new thing to the population of that day, and that on every hand was manifested courteous and generous hospitality. The houses of her citizens were not large, but the doors were wide, the hinges swung towards the interior, and the Legislators who had time, and were given to the social amenities, were everywhere generously entertained. During the winter almost the entire population united in giving a reception to the General Assembly. The festivities occurred in the Sherman Hall, situated, I think, at the corner of Third Street and Court Avenue. It was a whole-souled western "blow-out." The lamps (literally) shone over fair women and entranced Legislators until after the midnight hour, and the dance and promenade still went on.

The General Assembly was not to be outdone by the good citizens in the social amenities. So on March 12th the two Houses adopted the following resolution:

> *Resolved* (If the Senate concur), That the use of the Hall of the House of Representatives, Senate Chamber, Supreme Court Room, and Library, be given to Messrs. Coolbaugh, Kirkwood, Patterson, Edwards, Lundy, Jackson, and Clune, on Thursday evening, March 16th, for the purpose of giving a festival to the citizens of Des Moines.

A little discussion sprang up upon the passage of this resolution. One moved to strike out "Library," and another "Supreme Court Room," expressing a doubt as to the constitutionality of using rooms which had been set apart for these purposes for such an affair as a festival. But the imagination of the entire Assembly snuffed the aroma of the forthcoming spread, and before their eyes flitted the beauty and intelligence of the city, so all constitutional scruples were silenced and the resolution passed unanimously. At that day a donation of ten dollars by each Legislator was sufficient to furnish a generous entertainment for the entire city. In fact, at that time, the one hundred and fifty Legislators, with the officers of the two Houses, and the usual quota of lobbyists and visitors which such an assembly calls together, made a very appreciable addition to the population of the city, and the whole thing was thoroughly enjoyed by all the people.

C. C. Carpenter, *Pioneer Law-Makers Association of Iowa: Reunion of 1892* (Des Moines: State Printer, 1893), Reunion of February 10-11, 1892, pp. 54-55.

*T*he importance of the state capital question was underscored when, two years after the General Assembly's Act to Re-locate the Seat of Govern-ment, the move was embodied in a new constitution for the State of Iowa. This was one of many subjects debated during the 1857 constitutional convention.

The Constitution of 1846 had served the purpose of achieving statehood for Iowa. But soon after Iowa became the twenty-ninth state, there were calls for amendment, particularly concerning the subject of banks. The General Assembly in January 1855 passed an act authorizing a popular referendum on a constitu-tional convention.

In August 1856, Iowa voters approved a convention by a majority of over 18,000 votes. On January 19, 1857, thirty-six delegates convened at the stone capitol building in Iowa City. When they adjourned on March 5th, they had drafted a document that—with amendments—would remain the constitutional foundation for the state of Iowa even as it prepared to celebrate its Sesquicenten-nial.

A Lawyers' Convention:
The Making of the
Iowa Constitution of 1857

IN AUGUST 1857, FOLLOWING IOWANS' approval of a new constitution, Abraham Lincoln wrote to James Grimes, the Re-publican governor of Iowa: "Write me again, pointing out the more striking points of difference between your old and new constitutions .... "[1] The fullest answer to Lincoln's inquiry can be found in the 1,066-page record of the debates of the 1857 constitutional convention. These debates also reveal the delegates' prejudices and partisan wrangling as they sought to draft a document that would win the support of their constituents.

Partisan politics had played a similar role in shaping Iowa's earlier constitu-tion, effective from statehood in 1846. After voters had rejected a proposed consti-tution in 1844, a largely Democrat convention drafted another constitution, which the Whigs firmly opposed.

William Penn Clarke—an Iowa City Whig who later would be a leading Re-publican delegate at the 1857 convention—wrote a lengthy address damning the document. Clarke's words became the refrain of the Whigs and their successor party, the Republicans, for the next decade: "I am opposed to the adoption of the proposed [1846] Constitution, in the first place, because it entirely prohibits the es-tablishing of banking incorporations .... "[2]

Those, like Clarke, who favored banks believed them essential to issue suffi-cient paper currency for proper economic expansion of capital-starved Iowa farms and businesses. On the other side, the anti-bank Democrats—or Jacksonians—believed there was sufficient gold and silver in the country to meet its monetary needs. They were wholly opposed to banks, which they regarded as monopolies and swindles, sucking the blood of the industrious.

The referendum on the constitution, held on August 3, 1846, had a happy outcome for the opponents of banking—the constitution was approved by 9,492 votes to 9,036. On December 28, 1846, Iowa entered the Union as the twenty-ninth state, but opposition to its constitution continued. In the first three sessions of the new General Assembly, the Whigs unsuccessfully introduced bills for a constitutional convention, which they hoped would advance their pro-banking views.

Democrat Governor Stephen Hempstead vigorously opposed allowing Iowa institutions to issue bank notes. In his biennial message of 1852, he stressed: "What is to be gained … by the creation of banks among us and the substitution of a paper currency the inevitable tendency of which will be to drive the specie from circulation?"[3] Hempstead even urged the legislature to prohibit the circulation of out-of-state bank notes under $10 to encourage reliance on gold and silver.

However, the fourth General Assembly rejected this hard-money attitude. With Whig lawyer James Grimes of Burlington in the forefront, the Assembly passed legislation enabling voters to call a constitutional convention. Governor Hempstead, largely to avoid "the establishment of banks" by a constitutional convention,[4] twice vetoed the legislation in January 1853.

The following year, James Grimes revolutionized state politics by becoming the first Whig Governor of Iowa. His 1854 election manifesto mostly concerned the great question of slavery, but he also emphasized his hostility to the constitution. Grimes believed "numerous substantial reasons" supported amendment, particularly the need for Iowa banks and for the direct election of Supreme Court judges.[5]

Grimes complained that the constitutional prohibition on banking meant out-of-state banks profited mightily by circulating their notes in Iowa. Indeed, "[i]n place of having a domestic currency, the value of which *might* be known to every one, the country [Iowa] has been furnished with the worst conceivable currency from every State in the Union, and of the value of which nothing *could* be known."[6]

Governor Grimes again called for a new constitution in his December 1854 inaugural address. The Whig majority in the Iowa House of Representatives concurred. Although the Democrats had a majority of one in the Senate, sufficient pro-bank Democrats joined the Whigs to authorize a popular vote on the question of a constitutional convention.

The vote took place in August 1856—32,790 Iowans favored and 14,162 opposed a convention. Although the majority was huge, the turn-out of 47,000 was low (one delegate later said that the voters "were indifferent").[7] On the same day, more than 73,000 voters cast their ballots for each of four statewide offices. All of these offices were easily won by the newly formed Republican Party—the phoenix that had grown out of the ashes of the Whigs. In November 1856, the voters chose delegates to the constitutional convention. In another triumph for Governor Grimes, the preeminent member of the new party, the Republicans won twenty-one seats to the Democrats' fifteen.

The constitutional convention that met in Iowa City on January 19, 1857, was a lawyers' convention if ever there was one. Of the thirty-six delegates elected, fourteen were lawyers. The man elected president of the convention—Francis Springer of Wapello—counted as a fifteenth, as he was both lawyer and farmer.

The leading lights, Republican and Democrat alike, were all lawyers. On the Republican side, William Penn Clarke of Iowa City—ardent foe of slavery and court reporter to the Supreme Court—was the most active. Second to him was Rufus L.B. Clarke (no relation), a Mount Pleasant lawyer. For the Democrats, Jonathan C. Hall, a Burlington lawyer, dominated. Hall had taken part in the abortive 1844 constitutional convention and subsequently had been a state Supreme Court judge.

The convention selected its officers and then settled down to a lawyers' argument about the delegates' oath. Jonathan Hall objected: "[W]e come here for the very purpose of altering and violating the Constitution of the State of Iowa, and I do not therefore, feel that I can take the oath to support that Constitution."[8] Rufus Clarke disagreed: "[W]e meet here under that Constitution, and we will be under it until the one we may get up ... shall have been sanctioned by the people .... "[9] The convention in the end swore to support the *United States* Constitution.

The next problem concerned Iowa City. The legislature was still in session, and the delegates were crammed into the Supreme Court room of the limestone capitol building. Some delegates—miserable in Iowa City—wanted to move to Davenport or Dubuque. The Davenport delegate complained: "Half of the members of the Convention have to sleep three in a bed, and two on a bunk, in consequence of the want of good accommodation .... "[10] Jonathan Hall agreed: "[G]o where we will we cannot get in a worse place .... [T]he people have got into the habit of treating all who come here like sheep who are to be shorn."[11]

However, bad weather had made the roads to Davenport and Dubuque impass-

The delegates to the 1857 constitutional convention met for ten days in the Iowa Supreme Court chamber (shown here as it appeared in 1842-1857) before moving into the roomier Senate chamber. (Courtesy, University Photo Service, University of Iowa, photographer Don Roberts)

able, so the convention stayed in Iowa City. When the legislature adjourned on January 29th, the delegates moved into the roomier Senate chamber.

The convention appointed twelve committees on the constitution, drew up rules, and invited the press to attend. It ordered that 1,500 copies of its debates and proceedings be printed. David P. Palmer, a Bloomfield lawyer, offered a resolution that each delegate be furnished a copy of the Iowa Supreme Court reports. William Penn Clarke—the Supreme Court reporter—modestly abstained, but most of his fellow lawyers enthusiastically agreed.

Lewis Todhunter, an Indianola lawyer and keen moral reformer, moved a resolution that many modern Iowa legislators would applaud: "That there shall be no smoking allowed in this Chamber during the sittings of this Convention."[12] The resolution passed.

The delegates referred temperance and Sabbath observance petitions to committees. One supporter of temperance urged: "However impracticable it may be to carry out that principle at the present ... I hope the time is not far distant when it will be deemed not only practicable but expedient."[13]

After two weeks the convention got down to its real work. The banking issue dominated the debates. Only four delegates supported the hard-money, anti-bank conviction of former Governor Hempstead. Daniel Solomon, a Democrat lawyer from Mills County, spoke for them: "I look upon banking as nothing more or less than a series of tricks of adroit swindlers, invented by ingenious financiers, to rob the laboring man of the fruits of his labor."[14]

But Solomon despaired of victory. "I expect that I am, upon this question, an old fogy; and I expect that my views will be disapproved of by a large majority of the members of this Convention."[15] He was quite right. Pro-bank delegates overwhelmed Solomon and his anti-banking cohorts.

The convention addressed two specific banking questions: first, whether Iowa should have a state bank with branches, or general free banking; and second, whether banking regulation should be a matter for the constitution or for the legislature.

A general system of banking was less anathema to the anti-bank delegates than a state bank, which Daniel Solomon deemed "a more exclusive system of monopoly."[16] Harvey J. Skiff, a strongly pro-bank Jasper County Republican, also thought that a general banking system "is more democratic, because it allows any person, who will furnish the requisite securities to go into banking .... "[17]

Solomon and Skiff represented the two extremes of the convention. The solid middle favored a state bank. Republican James F. Wilson, a brilliant Fairfield lawyer and future U.S. Senator, spoke for those who feared a multiplicity of banks: "Nebraska has flooded our State all over with a currency in which I have never had any faith. Every bank in the western States seems to have sent their paper here, and particularly those which have no credit at home."[18] Wilson stressed that the branches of a state bank would be responsible for each other's issues.

Debate also raged over banking regulation, and a number of constitutional restrictions were agreed. These restrictions appalled William Penn Clarke. He became the only Republican to vote against the article on banking, claiming many Republicans deserved the title of hard-money men.

The convention's provisions on banking (contained in Article VIII of the 1857 constitution) are best summarized by the eminent Iowa historian, Benjamin F. Shambaugh, in his book *The Constitutions of Iowa:* "(1) The power to make laws relative to corporations was conceded to the General Assembly. (2) But acts of the General Assembly authorizing or creating corporations with banking powers must be referred to the people for their approval at a general or special election. (3) The General Assembly was empowered to establish 'a State Bank with branches.' But such a bank if established 'shall be founded on actual specie basis and the branches shall be mutually responsible for each other's liabilities upon all notes, bills and other issues intended for circulation as money.' (4) The General Assembly might provide by a general law for a free banking system under [a number of constitutional restrictions ensuring sound banking practice] .... "[19]

Another matter that consumed the delegates was the rights of black Iowans. The most advanced proposition considered was whether the voters should decide if the word "white" be struck *wherever* it occurred in the constitution (in provisions on suffrage, the census, electoral apportionment, the militia, and qualification for the General Assembly). Only two progressive Republicans voted consistently for this position—Rufus Clarke, and David Bunker, a farmer from Washington County.

Rufus Clarke tried passionately to obtain equal rights. "I came here," he said, "not to insert anything in our constitution recognizing any differences in the classes of men. I came here to establish principles that are eternal."[20]

Jonathan Hall and the Democrats took a racist point of view. Hall and lawyer Daniel Price of Council Bluffs issued a minority report on the right to suffrage. "[Y]our committee ... can never consent to open the doors of our beautiful State, and invite [the negro] to settle our lands. ... [T]he two races could not exist in the same government upon an equality without discord and violence, that might eventuate in insurrection, bloodshed and final extermination of one of the two races."[21]

William Penn Clarke's views lay somewhere between Rufus Clarke and Jonathan Hall. He favored certain civil rights for blacks, but opposed their voting and holding office.

Numerous votes took place. The most significant change made was a section (Article XII, § 14) submitting to a separate vote of the people a proposition to delete the word "white" from the article on suffrage. Even Rufus Clarke did not expect that a majority would vote for it—and indeed, in the end a huge majority rejected the proposition for black male suffrage.

The convention also approved language in the Bill of Rights that "any party to any judicial proceeding shall have the right to use as a witness ... any person not disqualified on account of interest .... " (Article I, §4). The convention had earlier turned down Rufus Clarke's amending language that no one could be disqualified "in consequence of his belonging to any particular sect, class or party of men,"[22] but largely through the influence of William Penn Clarke, the delegates settled on words that nonetheless were intended constitutionally to permit black testimony.

Rufus Clarke also failed in his amendment to guarantee blacks the same property rights as foreigners. His colleagues, thinking such a provision would encourage black immigration to Iowa, strongly opposed his reform.

The question of education for black youths exercised the convention. Ottumwa farmer George Gillaspy was a hard-core segregationist Democrat. He called for "separate and distinct schools," and continued: "I will not have [negroes] made equal with my children, and the children of my constituents, who are white and I thank God they are white." At the opposite pole was A.H. Marvin, a Monticello farmer, who moved that the schools be "free of charge and equally open to all."[23]

The convention finally agreed to a formula that common schools shall be provided "for the education of all the youths of the State. ... " (Article IX, §12). This left open the question of integrated or segregated schools—a question that the Iowa Supreme Court would take up after the Civil War.

The convention can be credited for tabling without debate (by a large majority of 25 votes to 8) a clause introduced by Democrat Amos Harris, a Centerville lawyer, that constitutionally would have excluded black immigration into Iowa. Further, the convention rejected an amendment to remove the guarantee of jury trials "in cases involving the life, or liberty of an individual" (Article I, §10). The delegates agreed that this decision ensured a jury trial to fugitive slaves.

Perhaps the last word about the debates on racial matters should be left with the progressive Republican Rufus Clarke. When a delegate unsuccessfully moved that the word "white" be struck from the article on the militia, Rufus Clarke objected. "[W]hen, by your laws, you ostracize [the negro] and throw him without the pale of society, when you deprive him of all its protection, I ask is it right, is it just, that you should call upon him to serve in the militia?"[24]

Among his constitutional proposals in 1854, James Grimes had urged that the election of Supreme Court judges "should be left with the people, instead of being made the subject for corrupt legislative bargainings."[25] The convention agreed. William Penn Clarke said: "It is conceded on all hands, that these judges ought to be elected by the people." Jonathan Hall, himself a former Supreme Court judge, declared: "I think the sooner [the people] have it given to them now the better."[26]

The main debate was whether the Supreme Court judges should be elected by district or by the state as a whole. William Penn Clarke strongly favored the district system. He pointed to the example of Jonathan Hall. "[A]sk [the general voter] what he knows about Mr. Hall as a lawyer and it is more than likely that he knows nothing about that." However, locally "ask a man what his notions of Mr. Hall as a lawyer are [and] he will say that he stands at the head of the bar in his district."[27]

But the argument of James Wilson for statewide elections triumphed: "Under that system every voter in the State has a voice in selecting all of the judges, while under the district system, he will have a voice in the selection of but one judge."[28] The convention agreed that the three Supreme Court judges "shall be elected by the qualified electors of the State .... " (Article V, §3).

Governor Grimes had raised another constitutional matter. In his message to the Assembly in December 1856, he had pointed out that although the 1846 constitution prohibited the state from creating a debt over $100,000, there was no similar prohibition on local authorities. Subsequently, "many counties and cities in this State have adopted the very doubtful policy of creating large municipal debts, for the purposes of becoming stockholders in railroads and other private corporations."[29] Grimes called for control.

James Wilson, chairman of the committee on state debts, wanted to keep the limit on state borrowing at $100,000. William Penn Clarke sought to allow for inflation: "[F]ive hundred thousand dollars now is not larger, in comparison, than the one hundred thousand dollars which we had ten years ago .... "[30] In the end, the convention increased the limit to $250,000 (Article VII, §2).

The delegates debated county and municipal indebtedness at length. They estimated that vast debts of between six and eleven million dollars had been incurred. Some delegates wanted a constitutional limitation; others believed it should be legislative. After three days of debate, they could not agree.

Two weeks later the delegates tried again. Rufus Clarke proposed that no county or municipal corporation could become indebted "to an amount, in the aggregate, exceeding *six* per centum on the value of [its] taxable property .... "[31] One delegate teased Clarke about his persistence. "I took it for granted that the motion was not made seriously. This is the fourth time the question has been brought before us .... I am tired of it."[32]

After another debate, the convention rejected Clarke's plan. But when Republican lawyer John Edwards of Chariton proposed a substituted limit of *five* percent, the convention at last approved. For the first time the constitution restricted municipal and county debt (Article XI, §3).

The delegates also took novel decisions about Iowa City and Des Moines. The state university had been allocated to Iowa City under 1847 legislation, and in 1855 the General Assembly ordered the state capital moved from Iowa City to Des Moines. William Penn Clarke, as delegate for Johnson County, sought to have the location of the university constitutionally enshrined at Iowa City. The convention decided to leave the matter to the legislature.

But a week later, when delegates wanted the constitution to fix the state capital at Des Moines, they changed their minds. William Penn Clarke was withering: "I rise merely to express my surprise at the sudden change of sentiment on this subject." Robert Gower, a farmer of Cedar County, complained that corrupt methods had influenced the legislature to make Des Moines the state capital. "And what were the means used to induce that General Assembly to pass that act? I believe gentlemen, I have it in my power to satisfy you and posterity, that it was money, town lots, and oyster suppers."[33]

Jonathan Hall countered that the reasons Iowa City had earlier become the capital were equally suspect. "I might show that the seat of government was originally located in this city by a species of management that might not be very creditable to some gentlemen. We know who gave the casting vote, and how he was induced to give it .... "[34]

Rufus Clarke believed that the constitution should endorse both choices to avoid the issue becoming "a football from year to year." He noted that "expression of opinion is almost universal throughout the state" that Iowa City should have the university, and "ninety-nine out of every one hundred who know the condition of Iowa" favored Des Moines as the capital.[35] Clarke's voice proved representative, and the constitution enshrined Des Moines as state capital, with the university at Iowa City (Article XI, §8).

Another matter before the convention was the method of amending Iowa's constitution. Ten years earlier, William Penn Clarke had railed against the current system: "Not a single letter can be stricken from it, without calling a convention."[36] Most of the delegates wanted the system reformed.

The method adopted was that the General Assembly would propose a constitutional amendment. If the succeeding General Assembly agreed to the identical amendment, the measure would be put to a vote of the electorate. Furthermore, to ensure direct voter control (memories were still fresh of Governor Hempstead's 1853 vetoes that shut out the voters from calling a constitutional convention), there was a new safeguard. In 1870 and every ten years thereafter—and at such times as the legislature might decide—the electorate would vote on the question: "Shall there be a Convention to revise the Constitution, and amend the same?" (Article X, §3).

Changes of some sort were made to every article in the constitution, except the article on the militia. Among these changes, the governor's term of office was reduced from four years to two (Article IV, § 2). Important innovations included provisions for a lieutenant governor (Article IV, §3) and a Board of Education (Article IX, §1).

The delegates adopted the new constitution by a vote of twenty-five to seven—the latter all Democrats. At the final session, the delegates passed by acclamation a resolution "that all personal difference which have occurred between members during the sittings of the convention be sunk in oblivion and forgotten from and after this date."[37] On March 5, 1857, after thirty-nine working days, the convention adjourned.

The vote on the new constitution was to take place at the August election. Shortly after the convention adjourned, Governor Grimes predicted: "I am convinced that the new constitution is destined to be popular and that it will be adopted by an overwhelming majority."[38]

However, Grimes was too sanguine. The Democrats—upsetting the trend of recent years—won two of three minor state offices in April 1857. Ex-delegate John Edwards wrote to William Penn Clarke that his local Democrats "have calculated their recent success to be in consequence of the unpopularity of the new constitution. All their cry is the making of negroes better than white men."[39]

In the campaign on the constitution and the separate question of suffrage for black men—known as "the codicil"—the Democrats hammered away on a racist theme. For example, the *[McGregor] North Iowa Times* wrote: "If the Republican Party of Iowa desire to invite a colored immigration and fill our towns and villages with a class of persons who must ever remain socially degraded, they can effectually secure that object by offering the premiums for black citizens which this New Constitution and its *anti-white* codicil embodies."[40]

The horror of permitting banking was another Democrat theme. The *[Davenport] Daily Iowa State Democrat* opined that the new article on banking "opens the door for every species of wildcat banking and rag money institution .... It will drive all the gold and silver out of the State and place you at the mercy of a set of sharpers."[41]

The Republicans took the line that the constitution was a bipartisan effort, and that black suffrage was a completely separate issue. But as the referendum drew nearer, Grimes and the Republicans saw that their bipartisan approach was not working.

Two weeks before the vote, the secretary of the Republican Central Committee wrote to the Republican county committee members. He emphasized the importance to their party of the constitution. "It is unquestionably a Republican measure ... put forth by a Republican Convention. Now it rests with the Republicans of Iowa to ... sustain a measure that will aid to sustain them as a party."[42]

The electorate did sustain the measure—but only just. On August 3, 1857, Iowans voted on the constitution and the "codicil" of black male suffrage. To no one's surprise, they massively rejected the codicil by 49,267 to 8,479 votes.

On the new constitution itself, the Republicans scraped home; 40,811 votes were cast in favor and 38,686 against approval—a majority of just over 2,000. A year earlier, 32,790 voters had favored and 14,162 had opposed holding a constitutional convention. Thus, the apathy of the opposition to holding a convention had become vigorous opposition to the constitution itself. The Republicans had successfully maximized their turn-out and narrowly triumphed.

On September 3, 1857, Governor Grimes formally proclaimed: "I ... hereby declare the said New Constitution to be adopted, and declare it to be the supreme law of the State of Iowa."[43] The lawyers' convention had fashioned the constitution—but Grimes had played a huge part in its making. He had long campaigned for a convention; he defined several key issues that came before the convention; he and his party won the battle for ratification.

Thus, Governor Grimes could have replied with personal pride to Abraham Lincoln's request for "the more striking points of difference between your old and new constitutions." The Constitution of 1857 allowed for a banking system; had sensible limits on state, county, and municipal debts; decreed popular election of Supreme Court judges; fixed the state capital in Des Moines and the university in Iowa City; and established a more practical method of constitutional amendment.

And if Governor Grimes had had the gift of second sight, he also could have pointed to the durability of the constitution. For the Constitution of 1857—albeit with many amendments, including black and woman suffrage—would still remain Iowa's organic law even as the state prepared to celebrate its 1996 Sesquicentennial.

Photograph of the surviving members of the Constitutional Convention of 1857, taken at a reunion in Des Moines on January 19, 1882. (Courtesy, State Historical Society of Iowa, Iowa City)

The introduction of railroads into Iowa produced great excitement in the years immediately preceding the Civil War. In July 1856, Governor James Grimes convened a special session of the General Assembly to consider recent federal land grant legislation for the construction of four major rail lines across the state. Governor Grimes—himself a fine lawyer—anticipated the legal problems that could arise with the introduction of the Iron Horse.

The introduction of Rail Roads within the State has rendered necessary an act more clearly defining the rights, duties and liabilities of railway companies. The law should declare that where death is caused through negligence or misconduct of the agents or servants of such companies, the same remedies shall be open in a suit at law, as for like injuries to the person resulting in disability and not in death. Among other things, the speed of trains passing through cities, and villages and across highways, should be regulated by law, and the disasters that have occurred in a neighboring State, have admonished us of the necessity for a law, prohibiting a company from carrying passengers over a new road, until it has first been examined and pronounced safe by a competent and disinterested Board of Engineers. It is evidently as much the duty of the State to protect the lives and safety of the citizens from accidents, resulting from carelessness, misconduct or cupidity, as from open and premeditated violence.

Governor James Grimes, Special Session Message, July 3, 1856, reprinted in Benjamin F. Shambaugh (ed.), *The Messages and Proclamations of the Governors of Iowa* (Iowa City: State Historical Society, 1903), vol. II, pp. 17-18.

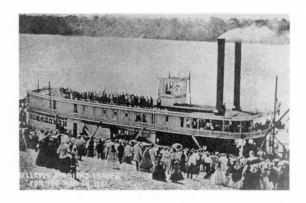

The Iowa Supreme Court deplored the increasing hazards of steamboat and stage coach travel. Here a steamboat prepares to depart Bellevue. (Courtesy, State Historical Society of Iowa, Iowa City)

Governor Grimes's concern over the hazards of railroad travel were well founded. Iowa already had a taste of the risks of public transportation in the form of stage coaches, steamboats, and river ferries. In a case brought to recover for injuries sustained when a stage coach overturned, the Iowa Supreme Court laid down a standard of care for proprietors of stage coaches—and vented its frustration over the increasing number of accidents.

It is objected that the court erred in giving the following instruction, as requested by the plaintiff below: "That the proprietors of stage coaches which ply between different places, and carry passengers for hire and compensation, are responsible for all accidents and injuries happening to the persons of the passengers, which could have been prevented by human care and foresight."

This instruction contemplates a great degree of diligence, care and foresight on the part of stage proprietors, but not more, we think, than sound public policy dictates, nor more than the authorities justify. … [I]n *McKinney v. Neil*, 1 McLean, 540, it is decided that a stage proprietor is bound to furnish good coaches, gentle and well broke horses, good harness, and a prudent, skillful driver, and is liable to any passenger who may receive any injury from any defect in these particulars, and is also liable for the smallest degree of negligence, carelessness or want of skill in the driver. With horses gentle and well broke, with coaches and harness good and strong, with drivers sober, prudent and skillful, a stage coach line might be regarded as managed with human care and foresight. With such an outfit, stage proprietors, in a level prairie country like Illinois and Iowa, would rarely if ever be called upon to pay damages for personal injuries to passengers. In *McKinney v. Neil*, 1 McLean, 540, the upsetting of a stage coach was held to be prima facie evidence of negligence. That doctrine is especially appropriate to a level prairie country, where nearly every accident may be traced to drunken or grossly careless drivers.

The instruction under consideration is quite as moderate towards stage proprietors as the authorities would justify. ...

In a case of gross negligence on the part of a stage proprietor, such as the employment of a known drunken driver, and where a passenger has been injured in consequence of such negligence, we think exemplary damages should be entertained.

... The reason and necessity for this rule is becoming yearly more apparent. The consequences of such negligence on the part of carriers, is becoming more and more appalling. The alarming increase of railroad, steamboat and stage disasters, the frightful destruction of life, and limbs, and property, call loudly for a strict enforcement of the most exemplary rules, in reference to common carriers. If a stage proprietor employs a driver known to be drunken and careless, a more severe measure of damage should be awarded to the injured party, than in a case where some degree of care and diligence had been exercised by the proprietor.

Frink & Co. v. Coe, 4 Greene 555, 557-58, 559-60, (Iowa 1854).

The caseload of the Iowa Supreme Court grew steadily during the period of early statehood. The Court was asked to mediate between such diverse parties as joint adventurers in the California gold rush, warring spouses, and rival claimants to riparian rights. In one of its most important decisions, the Court struck an early blow in favor of freedom of the press.

The case, Dunham v. State of Iowa, *involved a criminal contempt proceeding against the editor and proprietor of Burlington's* Daily Hawk-Eye, *which had published articles critical of a district court judge's rulings.*

From its novelty in this State, and the character of the questions involved, this case has occupied no little space in the public mind. ...

In the examination, we have endeavored to keep constantly in view, what is due from the citizen to the authority and power of the courts of the State. And on the other hand, as was our duty, we have had regard to the liberty of the individual, and the proper freedom of the public press. As the power to punish for contempt, is a necessary one—necessary to the very existence of judicial tribunals, and their efficiency and own preservation—and while it is a power that is not only inherent in every court, but one that is abundantly recognized by the constitution and laws of the several States; so, on the other hand, the personal liberty of the individual—and the liberty of speech and the press—are made no less secure, and are upheld by considerations equally important, and essential to the prosperity and advancement of every free government. In consonance with these rights, our own constitution declares, that no law shall be framed to restrain or abridge the liberty of speech or the press, and that every person may publish his sentiments on all subjects, being responsible for the abuse of that right. ...

The power given to the courts to punish for contempts, is not alone for their own preservation, but also for the safety and benefit of the public. ...

... But to make a party guilty under this clause, the contempt, or insolent behavior must be towards the court—the court must be engaged in the discharge of a judicial duty—and this behavior must tend to impair the respect due to its authority. It would be a perversion of the entire language used, and a palpable violation of the spirit and policy of the provision, to say that a judge could bring before him every editor, publisher, or citizen, who might, in his office—in his house—in the streets—away from the court, by printing, writing, or speaking, comment upon his decisions, or question his integrity or capacity. ...

If ... the respondent did nothing more than comment, though never so severely, upon the action of the court; and though he may have published ever so fully, and, whether truly or falsely, the proceedings upon the first hearing, we cannot think it would amount to a contempt ....

Dunham v. State of Iowa, 6 Clarke 245, 253-56 (Iowa 1858).

T*he decade of the 1850s drew to a close amidst mounting tension between the North and South, between abolitionists and supporters of slavery, between unionists and secessionists. The events leading to the Civil War marked the end of the period of early statehood for Iowa. The new state would come of age during the greatest test of the Union's staying power.*

Iowa's first reported territorial Supreme Court case had upheld the principle that a former slave enjoyed the benefits of a free man on free soil. Now the Iowa legislature in a joint resolution reacted with outrage to the U.S. Supreme Court's decision in the case of Dred Scott v. Sanford.

W*hereas,* The supreme court of the United States in the recent case of Scott vs. Sanford, after expressly deciding that it had not jurisdiction of the case, by deciding that the plaintiff Scott could not by reason of his descent, sue in the courts of the United States, has undertaken to pronounce an extra judicial opinion prohibiting the people of the United States, through congress and the people of the territories through their local government instituted under the authority of congress from any control of the question of slavery within the territories of the United States, and legalizing slavery in all those territories; and

Whereas, Such extra judicial opinion subordinates the political power and interests of our whole people to the cupidity and ambition of a few thousand slave holders who are thereby enabled to carry the odious institution of slavery wherever the national power extends, thereby degrading free labor in all the territories which the United States now have or hereafter may acquire by bringing slave labor in direct competition therewith, and predooming all such territory to all the blighting influences of the system of human slavery; and

Whereas, Such extra judicial opinion of the supreme court is conclusive proof of the settled determination of the slavery propagandists to subvert all those high and holy principles of freedom upon which the American Union was formed, and to degrade it from its intended lofty position of the exemplar and bulwark of freedom, into a mere engine for the extension and perpetration of the barbarous and detestable system of chattel slavery.

Therefore it is, as the sense of the people of Iowa, Resolved, that the extra-judicial opinion of the supreme court in the case of Dred Scott, is not binding in law or conscience upon the government or people of the United States, and that it is of an import so alarming and dangerous as to demand the instant and emphatic reprobation of every good citizen. ...

Resolved, That the state of Iowa will not allow slavery within her boundaries, in any form or under any pretext, for any time however short, be the consequences what they may.
Approved March 23d, 1858.

Acts of the Seventh General Assembly, 1858, Joint Resolution No. 12.

W*hen Governor Samuel Kirkwood gave his inaugural address to the General Assembly on January 11, 1860, civil war was little over a year away. Governor Kirkwood spoke passionately and at some length on the subjects of the Kansas-Nebraska Act and John Brown's raid on Harpers Ferry—so much so that a group of conservative legislators protested he had exceeded the proprieties of a gubernatorial address.*

But even Governor Kirkwood's apt appraisal of the nation's crisis did not predict the grave danger that lay ahead. He ended his inaugural

address on a hopeful note of conciliation with southern interests. His hope soon would prove unfounded.

In conclusion, permit me to say that, although our political horizon is not unclouded, although anger and jealousy have to some extent taken the place of brotherly kindness and good will among our people, although some men occupying high position under our Federal and in some of our State Governments, influenced by pride and passion, utter sentiments disloyal to our Union; and others in like high position, but governed by baser motives, either openly or silently approve these sentiments; still, in my opinion, those who love our Constitution and our Union, have not very great cause for alarm. Passion will subside, reason will resume its sway, and then our southern brethren will discover that they have been deceived and misled, as to our feelings and purposes; that the people of the north, while hoping and praying for the day when no slave shall press our soil, yet do neither claim nor desire any power to interfere with slavery in any of the States where it exists; and that the good old ways wherein we walked, when to talk of disunion openly, or to approve it silently, was to incur the scorn due a traitor, are ways of pleasantness, and that the good old paths our fathers taught us to tread, are paths of peace. And they will join with us in believing that the men who achieved our independence and framed our Constitution, were as true patriots, and understood the Constitution as well as the statesmen of the present day— will unite with us in following their teachings and walking in their footsteps, and in discarding these new measures, and this new policy, which have produced no fruits but those of discord and bitterness; and will again pledge themselves as we today pledge ourselves in the full depth and force of its meaning to the sentiment of the true and stern old patriot of the Hermitage—"The Union—it must and shall be preserved."

Governor Samuel Kirkwood, Inaugural Address, January 11, 1860, reprinted in Benjamin F. Shambaugh (ed.), *The Messages and Proclamations of the Governors of Iowa* (Iowa City: State Historical Society, 1903), vol. II, pp. 17-18.

CHAPTER THREE

The
Civil War
Years
1860-1865

"Iowa. Her affections like the rivers of her borders flow to an inseparable union."

— INSCRIPTION, Washington Monument

1860-1865

IN 1860, IOWA'S POPULATION WAS 674,913, just over two percent of the nation's total population of 31,218,000 in thirty-three states. But Iowa would play a role in the Civil War years disproportionate to its size. Under the leadership of Governor Samuel Kirkwood, the "first free child of the Missouri Compromise" threw itself solidly behind the forces for Union and, ultimately, the abolition of slavery.

The year 1859 was a watershed for events that culminated in southern secession. The radical abolitionist, John Brown, led an ill-fated raid on the federal arsenal at Harpers Ferry, Virginia, as part of a plan to free the slaves. He had recruited and trained men to his cause in Iowa, and four Iowans were with him at Harpers Ferry. The emotions aroused by this act—and Brown's subsequent execution—resonated in the North and South, and increased the tensions that eventually led to the Civil War.

Iowa joined the majority of states to elect Republican Abraham Lincoln as President in November 1860. In December, South Carolina seceded from the Union; six other southern states seceded before Lincoln's inauguration in March 1861. (Four more southern states later left the Union, making a total of eleven states in the Confederacy.)

On April 12, 1861, shots were fired at Fort Sumter in Charleston, South Carolina. President Lincoln requested 75,000 volunteer troops to quell the rebellion and called a special session of Congress. Iowa responded by oversubscribing its quota of 800 men. During the next four years, over 76,000 Iowans served in the Union military cause, including 440 "colored troops." Approximately 13,000 Iowans died—nearly two-thirds from disease. Another 8,800 were wounded.

In 1862, President Lincoln appointed the first Iowan to serve on the United States Supreme Court—Samuel Freeman Miller. Miller, who had practiced medicine before studying law, had moved from his native Kentucky to Keokuk, Iowa, in 1850, where he opened a law firm and became active in the Republican Party. Miller was forty-six years old when appointed to the Supreme Court, and would serve with distinction for the next twenty-eight years.

The 1862 elections resulted in a Republican sweep of Iowa's congressional seats, which had grown from two in 1860 to six. The state was now solidly Republican—in addition to Iowa's congressional seats, both United States Senators, the governor, and both houses of the Iowa General Assembly were Republican. From this solid political foundation, Iowa would remain largely Republican for the next century.

Following the Union victory in the battle at Antietam in September 1862, President Lincoln issued his preliminary Emancipation Proclamation, declaring that on January 1, 1863, slaves held in actively rebellious states would be free. On April 9, 1865, following a bitter and bloody conflict, General Robert E. Lee surrendered the Army of Northern Virginia to General Ulysses S. Grant at the Appomattox Court House, Virginia. Although some Confederate armies remained in the field, the war effectively was over.

In February 1865, Congress proposed the Thirteenth Amendment to the U.S. Constitution, which formally abolished slavery. By December the amendment had been ratified by the required three-quarters of the states. Iowa did not have the opportunity to be among the original ratifying states, because Governor William Stone had not called the legislature back into special session. (Iowa ratified the amendment in the next succeeding legislative session.) Nonetheless, Iowa's Congressman James F. Wilson—who served as chairman of the Judiciary Committee—had been strongly influential in propounding the Thirteenth Amendment.

On April 15, 1865, President Lincoln died from a wound inflicted by an assassin's bullet. He was succeeded by Vice-President Andrew Johnson. Before his death, Lincoln had nominated Iowa's Senator James Harlan to serve as Secretary of the Interior. Harlan took office one month after Lincoln's assassination—the first Iowan to achieve a position in the cabinet of the United States. Amidst the pressures of Reconstruction, Harlan commenced his short-lived service in the troubled administration of President Johnson.

*I*owa's role in supporting the Union cause is well known. The young state is believed to have sustained the greatest proportionate number of deaths among the Union states. Iowa's 76,000 troops represented approximately one-tenth of its population and nearly one-half the men of military age; its war dead and wounded numbered nearly 22,000.

Less well known is the role played by Iowa in provoking South Carolina's secession from the Union in December 1860, a move that led inexorably to civil war. A young Iowan follower of John Brown, his flight from Virginian authorities, and Governor Samuel Kirkwood's legal maneuvers to avoid the young man's extradition were key ingredients cited by the South Carolina convention among its justifications for secession.

Thus a point of Iowa law became a spark of contention that, ultimately, fed the flames of war.

Iowa and Southern Secession: The Story of Barclay Coppoc

WHEN SOUTH CAROLINA DECLARED ITS independence from the Union in December 1860, civil war became inevitable. The convention gathered at Charleston gave as the principal reason for secession the election of Abraham Lincoln as President of the United States. In addition, the delegates cited two constitutional justifications. The first was that various northern states, including Iowa, had broken the constitutional guarantee to deliver up fugitive slaves. The second justification arose out of John Brown's raid on Harpers Ferry, Virginia: *"And the states of Ohio and Iowa have refused to surrender to justice fugitives charged with murder and with inciting servile insurrection in the state of Virginia."*[1] Thus South Carolina immortalized three fugitives from the epic raid on Harpers Ferry—one of them a consumptive Iowa youth named Barclay Coppoc.

Barclay Coppoc was born in Columbiana County, Ohio, on January 4, 1839, the fifth child of a Quaker couple, Samuel and Ann Coppoc. When Barclay was two years old, his father suddenly died of consumption. The family was left destitute, and Ann Coppoc was obliged to farm her children out to various relatives and friends. After she inherited a precious $100 from her father in 1849, Ann moved with most of her children to Springdale, Cedar County, Iowa.

Barclay joined the rest of the family on their farm in 1853. That year his mother had remarried a neighboring Quaker, Joseph Raley. But what should have been a joyous reunion was shattered by the death of Barclay's sister Lydia from consumption, just after he arrived in Iowa. Two years later his sister Maria died from the same disease.

In 1856, Barclay visited Kansas, apparently because he himself seemed consumptive. His movements in that state are unclear, but according to some sources he made the acquaintance of the legendary John Brown.

Iowan Barclay Coppoc served as a rear guard during John Brown's raid on Harpers Ferry. (Courtesy, State Historical Society of Iowa, Iowa City)

Barclay returned to Iowa to help nurse his eldest brother, Levi, who also had developed consumption. Barclay appears to have exhibited some un-Quakerlike tendencies during this period. The local Quaker monthly meeting recorded: "Barclay Coppoc complained of for striking a man in anger."[2]

Levi died of the family scourge in the summer of 1857. Proximity to his sick brother affected Barclay's health, and he journeyed to the lakes of Michigan to recuperate. Barclay returned to Springdale some time before the arrival of John Brown in December 1857.

John Brown was already well known as a veteran and ruthless fighter against slavery in "Bleeding Kansas." Now he had made the astounding decision to invade Virginia and the South to liberate all of the slaves. He came to Springdale from Kansas with ten men, the nucleus of the invading army he envisaged. Brown left his men in Springdale for the winter of 1857/1858, while he went east to raise funds.

The men—most of whom thought they were training for further warfare in Kansas—drilled hard with guns and wooden swords. They spent much of their time studying military manuals and history. John Brown's followers and local youths held a mock legislature in Springdale, where they debated slavery, suffrage, and other reform issues. Deep friendships sprang up between some of the men and the local Quakers. Barclay and his elder brother Edwin were fascinated by the newcomers.

John Brown returned from the east in April 1858, and took his men and two local recruits off to Canada. In February 1859, he reappeared in Springdale with a party of eleven slaves freed in Missouri, and went on with them to Canada.

Unknown to their family and friends, Edwin and Barclay Coppoc had volunteered to join Brown's army. Brown planned to raid the federal arsenal at Harpers Ferry in Virginia as the beginning of his grand design to free the slaves. How much of the plan was known to the young Coppocs is unclear.

In the summer of 1858, Edwin and Barclay sold their oxen, which they used to break prairie, and Edwin hired a black man to run the farm. In July, the brothers departed for Ohio, and from there made their way to the Kennedy farm in Maryland, five miles from Harpers Ferry. Here Brown and his twenty-one men—sixteen white and five black—assembled.

For the first time, Brown told his company the full details of his plan for the raid on Harpers Ferry. They would capture the federal government armory, arsenal, and rifle-works, and thus acquire the arms necessary for the next phase. Slaves and dissident whites would join them. With guns from the arsenal, their army would move south, and more slaves would flock to them from the plantations. Continuing south, the army would raid more arsenals, and yet more slaves would join them—until slavery was destroyed.

After near mutiny by some of his men who thought the raid suicidal, John Brown's plan was accepted. Brown as the commander-in-chief assigned three rearguards, chosen for their physical frailty. His son Owen, who had a withered arm, was in charge of the group. With him were Francis Meriam, who had only one eye and was feeble-minded, and the consumptive Barclay Coppoc.

On the night of Sunday, October 16, 1859, John Brown led his eighteen other men into Harpers Ferry. They captured the arsenal, armory building, and rifle works.

They temporarily freed ten slaves, and took hostage some local slave owners and Harpers Ferry townspeople.

But the insurgents' success was short-lived. Farmers and militia streamed into the town, and a general battle ensued. John Brown's group killed four local men, and subsequently a United States marine. Altogether ten of Brown's men were killed. Ultimately, U.S. marines under Colonel Robert E. Lee captured Brown, Edwin Coppoc, and three others. Four of Brown's men escaped from Harpers Ferry—two of whom were later apprehended. Meanwhile, the three rearguards in Maryland were performing their duties.

Owen Brown has left a full description of the rearguards' adventures during and after the raid. Of Barclay Coppoc he said: "[He] was a medium sized young man, not over twenty-two or twenty-three years old. He did not look very healthy, but could stand a great deal, as you shall see. Still he was not so well educated or so energetic as his brother .... "[3]

On the Monday afternoon, as planned, the rearguards at the Kennedy Farm loaded a wagon with arms and ammunition. One of John Brown's men, back from Harpers Ferry, and a freed slave, took the arms to their chosen base—a school house in Maryland, about a mile from Harpers Ferry. Late in the afternoon, another freed slave arrived on horseback and asked Owen Brown, Meriam, and Barclay to come and help in the fighting at Harpers Ferry.

The three rearguards armed themselves and started on foot. On the way, they met Charles Tidd, one of John Brown's men who had been on guard duty at the school house. He told them all was lost at Harpers Ferry, and they must flee.

The group continued on toward the schoolhouse and came across John Cook, a member of Brown's band who had fled from Harpers Ferry. Cook reported that most of their men were dead. Owen Brown insisted on continuing to the schoolhouse, where they collected some provisions and fled on foot into the Pennsylvania mountains. Thus, Owen Brown, Francis Meriam, and Barclay Coppoc never set foot in the state of Virginia.

All too soon, the five men's provisions gave out. They were reduced to eating raw corn standing in the field and raw potatoes. Cook went to buy food and was captured. But the three rearguards and Tidd continued deeper into the Pennsylvania mountains, having decided to make for the home of an abolitionist widow in Chambersburg. For days they walked—miserable, freezing, and hungry—before reaching her house. Terrified at the arrival of men who were being sought everywhere, the widow urged them to leave.

The men didn't know what to do next, but Meriam's exhausted condition persuaded the others to risk putting him on a train. Barclay wanted to leave with Meriam, but Owen Brown refused to let him go, believing that two men would excite suspicion. Brown recalled Barclay's reaction: "[I] looked at Coppoc, I could see that great tears had fallen and hung quivering on his waistcoat."[4]

The feeble Meriam was placed on a train to Ohio, and the remaining trio continued their journey by foot, bound for Crawford County, Pennsylvania, where Owen Brown had friends. Hunger dominated their wanderings. They supplemented their diet of raw corn by stealing some chickens. Tidd was so hungry that when they roasted the chickens, he ate the bones as well.

The fugitives discovered they were near Bellefonte, Pennsylvania. As they approached the town, they saw a farmhouse with a cheery light. Finding it irresistible, they knocked on the door. The farm family welcomed them and fed them. The farmer produced a newspaper, and the three men learned they had been wandering for three weeks. Their host told them that John Brown had been tried and was to be hanged.

Owen Brown recalled: "Coppoc sat gazing thoughtfully into the blaze of the great fire place, and I happened to be looking at him when our host went on to say that the very latest news was that the man Coppoc had been tried, too, and found guilty. That was his brother Edwin, and the ruddy glare of the fire did not paint out the deathly white in our poor Coppoc's face. He did not speak, but a little while after, he stealthily brushed away a tear from one of his cheeks, and sighed in a half choked way."[5]

The fugitives eventually found some Quakers in Townville, Crawford County, who sheltered them, gave them provisions, and directed them on to another Quaker family forty miles away. When the trio reached that family, they stayed a night and then Owen Brown decided that Barclay could safely leave.

Thus, on November 24, 1859—after six weeks of terror, hunger, cold, and wandering—Barclay went by stagecoach and train to Columbiana County, Ohio, where he had spent his childhood. From there he made his way to Canada, and at last was able to let his mother at Springdale know that he was safe.

While Barclay was escaping, his brother Edwin was being sentenced to hang for treason to Virginia, murder, and inciting slaves to revolt. Ann Raley, the Coppocs' mother, sent Thomas Winn, the Springdale postmaster, to Virginia to plead for Edwin's life. However, Winn's best efforts failed. John Brown had already been executed, and on December 16, 1859, Edwin Coppoc and three others of the band were hanged in Virginia. The following day, Barclay returned to Springdale for Edwin's funeral.

However, Thomas Winn and the Coppocs' Uncle Joshua had decided that Edwin should be buried in Ohio, rather than Iowa. Thousands of mourners and supporters attended Edwin's funeral. When Winn returned to Iowa, Barclay was reported in the *Muscatine Daily Journal* of December 22, 1859, to be among those welcoming him home. An Iowan sympathizer of the South, on reading this news, wrote to Virginia's Governor Wise: "Barclay Coppoc is with his mother in Springdale."[6]

The state of Virginia had earlier offered a $500 reward apiece for the capture of Barclay, Owen Brown, Meriam, and Tidd. Now Virginia's new Governor, John Letcher, sent a special agent to Muscatine to arrest Barclay. The Virginia agent—Courtland Camp—arrived at Muscatine on January 9, 1860, and stayed under an assumed name at the Mason House Hotel. But he apparently made no effort to go to Springdale.

Barclay's mother, Ann Raley, wrote to a friend in Ohio on January 22, describing her son's state of mind: "Barclay is at home and seems determined to stay although there are reports almost continuously of somebody being in search of him. He says he has hurt nobody and will not *run* nor will he be *taken* .... I think B's friends will take care of him."[7]

"B's friends" were apparently a group of Springdale young men, armed and ready to defend Barclay. The Democrat press gleefully reported that they were hypocritical Quakers in arms. The Republican press had it that none of them were Quakers. But Barclay was one Quaker who did go everywhere armed—with no less than four revolvers. The Quaker elders called on him in his mother's house to complain, but he ignored their admonition. Inevitably, the Quaker monthly meeting recorded: "Barclay Coppoc, disowned [expelled] for bearing arms."[8]

The Governor of Iowa in that fateful year of 1860 was Republican Samuel J. Kirkwood. In his inaugural address on January 11, Kirkwood spoke of John Brown

The state of Virginia offered a reward of \$2,000 for the capture of four of John Brown's men, including \$500 for "Barclay Coppie" [Coppoc]. (*The Daily Richmond Enquirer,* November 5, 1859)

> **TWO THOUSAND DOLLARS REWARD.**
> **BY THE GOVERNOR OF VIRGINIA:**
> A PROCLAMATION.
>
> INFORMATION having been received by the Executive, that OWEN BROWN, BARCLAY COPPIE, FRANCIS J. MERIAM and CHARLES P. TIDD, (who are severally charged with the crimes of treason, murder, and conspiring and advising with slaves to rebel in the county of Jefferson, in this Commonwealth,) have escaped from justice, and are now going at large; therefore I do hereby offer a reward of FIVE HUNDRED DOLLARS to any person who shall arrest either of said fugitives and deliver him into the jail of said county of Jefferson, and I do moreover require all Officers of this Commonwealth, civil and military, and request the people generally to use their best exertions to procure their arrest, that they may be brought to justice
>
> { L. S. }   Given under my hand as Governor, and under the Less Seal of the Commonwealth, at Richmond, this 3rd day of November, 1859.
>
>   HENRY A. WISE.

Barclay's brother Edwin Coppoc (*center*) is handcuffed to John Brown at the arraignment. (*Harper's Weekly,* November 12, 1859)

and Harpers Ferry. Although characterizing the invasion as wrong and an act of war, he said: "While the great mass of our northern people utterly condemn the act of John Brown, they feel and they express admiration and sympathy for the disinterestedness of purpose by which they believe he was governed, and for the unfailing courage and calm cheerfulness with which he met the consequences of his failure."[9]

The Virginia agent, Courtland Camp, came to Des Moines on January 23 to meet with Governor Kirkwood. Camp presented a requisition from Governor Letcher to extradite Barclay Coppoc as a fugitive from Virginia justice. Governor Kirkwood was undoubtedly sympathetic to Coppoc, and so refused to extradite him. He produced four technical legal reasons, which he wrote to the Governor of Virginia and later summarized for the Iowa legislature.

First, the affidavit presented was not made before a magistrate, but before a Notary Public.

Second, the affidavit was not authenticated by the Notary seal.

Third, the affidavit did not show, unless inferentially, that Coppoc was in the state of Virginia at the time he "aided and abetted John Brown and others" as stated therein.

Fourth. The affidavit did not legally charge Barclay with commission of "treason, felony or other crime."[10]

Courtland Camp was angered at Kirkwood's refusal of the requisition. Although Camp supposedly was on a secret mission, he ignored the governor's advice to restrain himself, and fumed: "I don't care a damn who knows it now since you have refused to honor the requisition."[11] Anti-slavery legislators who overheard the argument in the governor's office hired a messenger to ride to Springdale and warn Barclay to flee. Obstinately, he refused to budge. Meanwhile, Courtland Camp returned to Muscatine to await a corrected requisition from Virginia.

Jonathan W. Cattell, state senator from Cedar County, recognized the great folly of Barclay remaining at Springdale. Having written the original warning to Barclay, he now wrote to the Coppoc family friend, Dr. Henry C. Gill, at Springdale. Catell warned that a second corrected affidavit would inevitably be acted on, and he feared bloodshed if Barclay didn't leave.

Barclay's mother, Ann Raley, added her voice to the fray over the requisition. She wrote a powerful letter to Virginia Governor Letcher, and sent a copy to the *Chicago Press and Tribune*. She first castigated Virginia for the killing of John Brown's men during the raid, the "farcical representations of the forms of law," and the hanging of her son Edwin and the others. But the "most disgraceful part" was the hunting of Barclay. His mother argued that Barclay had signed no constitution or pledge of allegiance to John Brown. Nor had he been in Virginia during the raid or injured anyone, "yet you are chasing him with biped bloodhounds and big bloated marshalls, secret patrols and spies, and most inhuman of all, the … reward for him dead or alive."

Barclay's mother wrote of his asthma and consumption, and she assailed Governor Letcher: "You are hanging men for treason, when thou thyself hath uttered treasonable sentiments in thy inaugural message." She ended her letter: "As thou seems very anxious to have Barclay visit you, if he chooses to go, I shall expect him to receive that kind hospitality at thy house that one of thy sons would receive from me. Perhaps a few months in the genial climate of Virginia might prove beneficial to his health. I think you would soon become attached to him, as he is a pleasant boy, and loves dry jokes."[12]

A few days later, Barclay gave in to pressure and left Iowa for Chicago. He arrived there on February 8 and subsequently went on to Canada. Two days later, Virginia Governor Letcher's second requisition reached Des Moines. This time the document was based on grand jury indictments charging Barclay Coppoc with conspiracy, advising slaves to revolt, and murder.

Governor Kirkwood could find no legal errors, and accepted the requisition. He issued a warrant for Barclay's arrest. The Cedar County sheriff went through the motions of searching Springdale, but by then, of course, Barclay had vanished.

THE COMMONWEALTH OF VIRGINIA,

To the Executive Authority of the State of *Iowa*

Whereas it appears by the annexed documents, which are here as authentic, that Barclay Coppoc *fugitive from justice, from this state, charged with* advising slaves to revolt, with conspiring with slaves to rebel & make insurrection, & with conspiring with slaves to rebel & make insurrection; and, with the crime of murder;

Now, therefore, I, John Letcher *Governor of Virginia, have thought proper, by virtue of the provisions of the C of the United States in such case made and provided, and of the act of passed in pursuance thereof, to demand of the Executive authority of* Iowa *the surrender of* the said Barclay Coppoc *as a fugitive from justice, to be delivered to* C. Camp *who* agent to receive him on the part of this Com*

Given under my hand as Governor, and Great Seal of the State, at Rich. fourth day of February *hundred and* sixty *and year of the Commonwealth.*

John Letc

George Mumford

Secretary of the Commonwealth.

Virginia's Governor Letcher made a second written demand that Iowa surrender Barclay Coppoc to Virginia, dated February 4, 1860. (Samuel J. Kirkwood papers, 1841-1894, State Historical Society of Iowa, Des Moines)

Governor Letcher had not responded directly to Governor Kirkwood's refusal of the first requisition, but on February 13, he sent a lengthy message to the Virginia legislature about Kirkwood's failure to honor that requisition. He dismissed Kirkwood's legal reasons as "exceedingly frivolous."

Letcher accused Kirkwood of "giving notice to the criminal [Barclay] to make his escape" by publishing Kirkwood's letters to Letcher in the Iowa newspapers. He castigated Kirkwood's inaugural address as showing "his feelings and sympathies are warmly enlisted on the side of John Brown and his associates." Letcher angrily concluded: "The denial of this requisition ... ought to impress upon us the necessity of adopting prompt, energetic and decided measures *to ... achieve southern independence.*"[13]

When the press published Governor Letcher's message, the Barclay Coppoc affair became a national issue. The *New York Times* criticized Virginia in a lengthy editorial entitled "Preaching and Practice." On the same day, the *Chicago Press and Tribune* printed in full Ann Raley's voluminous letter to Governor Letcher.

The Virginia agent, Courtland Camp, was still lurking in Muscatine. The Iowa newspapers made him into a figure of fun. Articles appeared mocking his talkativeness when supposedly on a secret mission, his drinking, and his billiards. One historian records: "Even the boys hooted at him in the streets, and Mrs. Ann Raley, the mother of Coppoc, sent an invitation for him to come to her house and she would give him his dinner."[14]

Courtland Camp departed from Muscatine, having failed in his mission, on February 25. The newspapers dubbed him "(S)camp," and gleefully reported that he had left the town with "a disreputable woman" and an unpaid board bill of $38.[15]

Barclay Coppoc did not stay long in Canada. On March 16, 1860, he was at Jefferson, Ashtabula County, Ohio. There he attended a public meeting to show sympathy for two of John Brown's men who were hanged that day in Virginia. Brown's eldest son, John Brown, Jr., spoke on behalf of Barclay. He said Barclay could not talk himself because of his asthma, which had been worsened by his flight from Harpers Ferry.

John Brown, Jr., pointed out that his brother, Owen Brown, Meriam, and Barclay were in Maryland throughout the Harpers Ferry raid, and had never gone into Virginia. He told how Barclay believed that Canada would have to comply with any request for extradition to Virginia. Therefore, "he had come to Ashtabula county—where he had resolved to sell his life as dearly as possible in case of an attempt to arrest him."[16]

A week earlier, on March 8, 1860, Virginia Governor Letcher had demanded that Governor Dennison of Ohio surrender Owen Brown and Francis Meriam. The governor of Ohio referred the requisition to his attorney general. The latter stated that no "legal" demand had been made or proper papers submitted. He went on, "[i]n all these documents from beginning to end there is no word, no letter, from which human ingenuity can draw the vaguest hint that Owen Brown or Meriam had fled from Virginia, nor was there any proper proof of either of the men being within the bounds of Ohio."[17]

The Ohio governor forwarded this opinion to Governor Letcher with a brief note stating that, for the reasons set forth by his attorney general, he refused to issue the warrants requested. On March 14, Governor Letcher laid a furious message before the Virginia legislature concerning this fresh northern refusal to surrender fugitives from justice.

Governor Letcher ominously concluded his message: "If the course which has been pursued by the authorities of the states of Ohio and Iowa is to become the settled policy of the non-slaveholding States towards us, we must adopt such measures for protection against these grave outrages upon our rights as will be suited to the case. *We must adopt retaliatory measures ....* "[18]

With the election of Abraham Lincoln as President in November of 1860, the hunt for the Harpers Ferry fugitives died away. But the tremendous depth of feeling about Barclay Coppoc and the others was shown by those words in South Carolina's declaration of independence from the Union: "[A]nd the States of Ohio and Iowa have refused to surrender to justice fugitives charged with murder, and with inciting servile insurrection .... "[19]

When the Civil War came, twenty-two-year-old Barclay joined a Kansas regiment as a lieutenant, and came home to Springdale to enlist recruits. He left Iowa and took a train at Hannibal, Missouri, bound for St. Joseph. Confederate guerillas had set fire to a bridge across the Platte River, and the train carrying Coppoc plunged into the river.

Barclay died of his injuries the following day and was buried at Leavenworth, Kansas. His rifle was recovered from the train wreck and was brought home to his mother—but as a Quaker, she refused to accept it. Thus ended the short, extraordinary story of Barclay Coppoc, Iowa's main link with Southern secession.

General Francis M. Drake, lawyer, governor of Iowa, and founder of Drake University. Drake rose to the rank of brigadier general in the Civil War. (Courtesy, State Historical Society of Iowa, Iowa City)

Many Iowa lawyers were among those who left home, family, and professions to serve in the Civil War. A prominent example was Francis M. Drake, principal founder of Drake University in Des Moines, who raised a military company at Centerville, Iowa, when Fort Sumter was fired upon in the spring of 1861. Over the course of the war Drake rose to the rank of brigadier general, and commanded the second brigade of General Solomon's division at the Battle of Marks Mills, in which he was seriously wounded.

General Drake had read law before entering the military, and after the war he resumed his study and was admitted to the Centerville bar. He practiced law for many years, amassed a fortune in the railroad business, and in 1895 was elected the governor of Iowa.

Drake's contributions to the war were matched by equally dedicated, if more humble, contributions by other Iowa lawyers and judges. Their private lives and law practices were put aside while they took up arms, and, if they were lucky, they returned to resume their legal careers after the war. Many discovered that even then their professional lives were touched by the effects of war, as shown in the following extract.

H. H. Trimble was born in 1827 on a farm in Dearborn county, Indiana. His parents were pioneer farmers. ... In February, 1850, he moved to Bloomfield, Davis county, Iowa. On the 29th day of April, 1850, he was admitted to the practice of law by Hon. J. F. Kinney, judge of the supreme court. In August of that year he was elected county attorney, and in August of 1852 was re-elected, serving four years. In 1856 he was elected state senator, and he attended the last session of the general assembly at Iowa City, and the first session at Des Moines. ...

In the summer of 1861 he took a leading part in organizing the Third Iowa cavalry, and was made Lieutenant-colonel of that regiment. The regiment had its rendezvous at Keokuk. In August, 1861, Mr. Trimble immediately commenced a course of military instruction, and was the sole teacher of the regiment as long as he remained a member of the regiment. It had the reputation of being one of the best drilled regiments in the service.

On March 7, 1862, while leading his regiment in a charge in the opening of the great battle of Pea Ridge, he was severely wounded in the face, and by reason of his wounds was afterwards compelled to leave the service. The character of this charge which he led was described by the war correspondent of the Missouri Democrat, now "The Globe Democrat," in the following language:

Return to Davenport of the Iowa First Volunteers. (*Harper's Weekly,* September 21, 1861)

"The cavalry charged forward along a narrow road, an old rail fence and field on their left and brush on their right. They were gallantly lead forward by Lieutenant-colonel Trimble. The men cheered. After going 300 yards in rear of and beyond a battery, a galling fire was poured in on them by a large body of McCullough's infantry, concealed in the brush to the right and in front. The latter wheeled and fired on the enemy, who were only a few yards distant. At the same time a large body of Rebel cavalry made a charge over the fence and into the field and were pursued by the Third Iowa cavalry. A running fight ensued in which the Rebel cavalry suffered heavy loss. ... "

In October, 1862, Mr. Trimble was discharged from the service on account of disability and wounds received in this battle. On his return home in the fall of 1862, he was elected judge of the district court of the Second judicial district, and served four years. The district extended one hundred miles along the Missouri border. ... Public feeling, embittered by the war, frequently invaded the court-room. On one occasion a company of militia marched into the courtroom with guns in hand to rescue their captain and one of their lieutenants then being held in custody upon an indictment for murder. On another occasion, a citizen who had been arrested by a self-appointed provo-marshal for alleged disloyal conduct, sued out a writ of habeas corpus before Judge Trimble in order to secure his release from this arrest. On the morning the case was to be heard, the large courtroom was crowded with excited men, most of them with guns in their possession, determined to take revenge on the court if the prisoner was released. He was released. No blood was shed. In these and all other similar cases, Judge Trimble was successful in administering the law and in sustaining the authority of the court by an appeal to the patriotism of the people, their love of peace, justice, and regard for law.

Chester C. Cole & E. C. Ebersole (ed.), *The Courts and Legal Profession of Iowa* (Chicago: H. C. Cooper, Jr., & Co., 1907), vol. II, pp. 764-67.

One of the many fallen in battle was thirty-six-year-old Brigadier General Samuel A. Rice. Rice had practiced law in Fairfield and Oskaloosa, and was serving as Iowa's Attorney General when he resigned to help organize the volunteer Thirty-third Iowa Regiment. In April 1864, he was wounded at the battle of Jenkins' Ferry in Arkansas and died in July after "severe and protracted suffering," leaving a wife and five children. General Rice was remembered in a moving tribute before the Iowa Supreme Court.

Supreme Court Room, Des Moines,)
December 20th, 1864.   )
                    The court met pursuant to adjournment.
                    JEFFERSON S. POLK addressed the court as follows:

MAY IT PLEASE THE COURT: It becomes my sad and painful duty to announce to this court the death of General SAMUEL A. RICE, a member of this bar. ... I have been directed by my brother members of this bar, in a meeting assembled here on yesterday, to present for your consideration the following

RESOLUTIONS:
    WHEREAS, General SAMUEL A. RICE, formerly a member of the bar of this court, and for four years Attorney-General of the State, died at his home in Oskaloosa, on the 6th day of July, 1864, from a wound received in battle at Jenkins' Ferry on the 30th day of April, 1864; and whereas, the high standing of the deceased as a member of the profession, as well as his exalted patriotism and many personal virtues, demand a special notice of his memory upon our part; therefore, be it
    Resolved, By the members of the bar now in attendance upon the Supreme Court:
    1. That we deeply deplore this dispensation of Divine Providence, in thus removing from our midst one who adorned his profession, and endeared himself to us by his uniform courtesy and upright conduct.
    2. That by his death, a brave and true soldier and officer has fallen in defense of his government, a kind father and true husband has

Brigadier General Samuel A. Rice died from wounds suffered in the Civil War. (Courtesy, State Historical Society of Iowa, Iowa City)

expression of his flashing eyes, as, taking me by the hand, he said: "I shall not die. I know that I shall survive. I shall yet live to return to the field and assist in crushing this most accursed rebellion." These hopes, these high resolves, were doomed to disappointment. In a few days or weeks, after the most patient suffering, he surrendered to the last, remorseless enemy. And yet he did not die; he does survive. He left this earth with the christian patriot's hope, and he has the patriot christian's reward. Though gone from earth, he survives in the many good deeds which live after him; in his labors, spread out abundantly upon the records of this court; in the strong hold which his many excellencies have given him in the affections of the bar, and the people of the State; in the enduring fame achieved in the field, battling and dying for the noblest government on earth.

It is directed that your merited and appropriate resolutions be spread upon the records, and that this court now adjourn.

Whereupon the court adjourned.

"Memorial," 17 Withrow 595-96, 600-02 (Iowa 1864).

been lost to his family, a valued citizen has been lost to the State, and an honorable and able advocate has been lost to the profession.

3. That we will cherish in affectionate remembrance his many virtues, and request the members of the bar to wear the usual badge of mourning during the term.

4. That we tender to the bereaved family our sincere testimony of the worth of the deceased, and assure them of our sympathy and condolence in their affliction.

5. That the court be requested to have these proceedings and resolutions spread upon the records of the court, and to furnish a certified copy of the same to the family of the deceased.
. . . .

Chief Justice WRIGHT then said:

GENTLEMEN OF THE BAR: With mournful pleasure, it is ordered that the resolutions presented be spread upon the minutes of this court. ...

I parted with [General Rice] in May last, as, nearing his home, with his family and friends around him, he was reclining on what proved to be his deathbed. I shall ever remember his face, and the speaking

Even those who did not serve in the military found that their lives and careers were irretrievably altered by the Civil War. One lawyer who gave distinguished non-military service was Chester Cicero Cole—later to become an Iowa Supreme Court judge, a professor in Iowa's first law school, and the founder of Drake Law School. Cole took time from his successful law practice to make "patriotic addresses" in those Iowa counties that had Southern leanings, an assignment that brought about Cole's estrangement from the Democratic Party.

My name is Chester Cicero Cole. I was born in Oxford, Chenango County, New York, in 1824. ...
Upon arriving in Des Moines, I secured an office over the bank of Cook, Sargent & Cook, on Walnut Street, and after continuing there a little time, I formed a partnership with J. E. Jewett ...

and continued the practice with Mr. Jewett for about two years .... I opened an office myself in the Sherman block on the corner of Third and Court Avenue; I continued in that office until I went upon the bench of the Supreme Court early in 1864. ...

Upon the receipt of the news of the firing upon Sumter in April, 1861, I was waited upon by F. W. Palmer, S. B. White, and another, and asked, since I had been the candidate of the Democratic party for Judge of the Supreme Court and the succeeding year for Congress, and was a representative man, to sign and lead the signers in a call for a public meeting in Sherman Hall that evening, pledging the support of the people to Mr. Lincoln and the Government against the rebels; and also to appear at the meeting and make the leading speech. ... I found myself supported by the young Democracy of my city and the State, but opposed by Dennis Mahoney and the older and old-time Democrats, who afterwards came to be known as Southern sympathizers. ...

President Lincoln, in September, 1862, issued a proclamation of his determination that unless the rebels should lay down their arms and cease their efforts to destroy the Government, he would on January 1, 1863, as a necessary war measure, issue his Proclamation emancipating all persons held in slavery within the Government of the United States. This proclamation of his intentions was made the occasion by many persons living in the counties of Iowa bordering on the State of Missouri and also those counties bordering the Missouri river as far north as and including Harrison County to threaten an uprising against the Government, in aid of the rebellion. This condition of affairs led Governor Kirkwood, the state officers, and many citizens of Des Moines to ask and urge me to go into most of these counties, every one of which had given majorities for me in the two previous elections, and make patriotic addresses and to exert every influence possible to quiet and dissuade the people from giving any support whatever to those in arms against the Government. The District Court of Polk County was in session, wherein I had engagements in many causes on the docket, and I presented my obligations to my clients, as precluding me from complying with their requests. Thereupon the Judge of the Court and the patriotic members of the bar agreed and placed their agreement in writing that the causes in which I was engaged should be continued or otherwise so disposed of as not to operate prej-

udicially in any way to my clients. I then went into those counties and by addresses pursuant to previous appointments did the best possible work to secure the ends desired, and spent between three and four weeks in such efforts with most satisfactory results.

All these matters inevitably brought about my separation from the Democratic party, and brought to me from many of the official and leading members of the Republican party multiplied expressions of thankfulness.

Chester Cicero Cole, quoted in Edward H. Stiles, *Recollections and Sketches of Notable Lawyers and Public Men of Early Iowa* (Des Moines: Homestead Publishing Co., 1916), pp. 474, 476–78.

A steadfast presence during the Civil War years was Iowa's Republican Governor Samuel J. Kirkwood. Kirkwood governed during the critical period 1860-1864, went on to fill James Harlan's unexpired U.S. Senate term in 1866-1867 after Harlan joined the Cabinet, and served again as governor of Iowa in 1876-1877. This term as governor was cut short when the legislature selected him as U.S. Senator in 1877, in which capacity he served until his appointment in 1881 as Secretary of the Interior under President Garfield.

In numerous special messages, Governor Kirkwood reported his emergency war measures and exhorted the legislators to pass necessary appropriation and relief legislation.

When the telegraphic despatch from the Secretary of War informing me of the requisition for the First Regiment reached me, I did not anticipate the uniforming [of] the men at the expense of the State .... Judging from the fact that other States were preparing for uniforming their Volunteers, that it would be desirable to have the same done here, I sent an Agent to Chicago to purchase material for uniforms, but the sudden and great demand for that kind of goods had exhausted the supplies in that city. On learning this ... I immediately instructed the persons

Iowa's Civil War governor, Samuel Kirkwood. (Courtesy, State Historical Society of Iowa, Iowa City)

acting as Commissaries, to purchase materials and make uniforms at the points where the several Companies had been raised. ... All that could be done was to have the men of each Company clothed alike, but differing from those of other Companies. ... Much of the clothing was made by the ladies which has to that extent lessened the cost. The amount of Clothing furnished, so far as the means now in my possession enable me to state, are as follows:

Capt. Herron's Company, Dubuque; each man, hat, frock coat, pants, two flannel shirts, two pairs of socks, and one pair of shoes.

Capt. Gottschalk's Company, Dubuque; blouse instead of coat, and other articles same as Capt. Herron's.

Capt. Cook's Company, Cedar Rapids; hat, two flannel shirts, pants, socks, and shoes, no jacket or coat.

Capt. Mahana's Company, Iowa City; hat, jacket, pants, two flannel shirts, socks and shoes.

Capt. Wentz's Company, Davenport; hat, blouse, pants, two flannel shirts, socks and shoes.

Capt. Cummins' Company, Muscatine; cap, jacket, pants, two flannel shirts, socks and shoes.

Capt. Mason's Company, Muscatine; same as Capt. Cummins.

Capt. Matthies' Company, Burlington; hat, blouse, pants, two flannel shirts, socks and shoes.

Capt. Streaper's Company, Burlington; same as Capt. Matthies.

Capt. Wise's Company, Mount Pleasant; same as Capt. Matthies.

... The entire amount expended for Clothing, so far as I can give it from the data in my possession, is about $12,000 or $13,000 .... If it be desirable in your judgment to have the Companies of this Regiment uniformed alike, it will be necessary to furnish all with coats of the same make, as also with pants, and to furnish an additional number of hats or caps. ...

... As the Second and Third Regiments will be clothed throughout alike, it would, no doubt, be very gratifying to the First Regiment to be placed in the same position, and it will afford me much pleasure to carry out whatever may be your wishes in that regard.
SAMUEL J. KIRKWOOD

Governor Samuel Kirkwood, Special Message to the House of Representatives, May 23, 1861, reprinted in Benjamin F. Shambaugh (ed.), *The Messages and Proclamations of the Governors of Iowa* (Iowa City: State Historical Society, 1903), vol. II, pp. 412-15.

Although he unstintingly supported Iowa's war effort and disdained the enemies of the Union cause, Governor Kirkwood was sensitive to those individuals (in particular, the Quakers) whose religious beliefs forbade them to carry arms. Kirkwood therefore urged an exemption for "persons who cannot conscientiously render military duty."

There are in this State some religious bodies who entertain peculiar views upon the subject of bearing arms, and whose religious opinions conscientiously entertained, preclude their so doing. Their members are generally among our most quiet, orderly, industrious and peaceful citizens, and their sympathies are wholly with the Government in this struggle now going on for its preservation, yet they cannot conscientiously bear arms in its support. It appears to me it would be unjust and wholly useless to force such men into the army as soldiers, and yet it would not be just to the Government or to other citizens that they should be wholly relieved from the burdens that others have to bear. I suggest, therefore, that these persons who cannot conscientiously render military duty, be exempted therefrom in case of draft, upon the payment of a fixed sum of money to be paid to the State.

Governor Samuel Kirkwood, Special Session Message, September 3, 1862, reprinted in Benjamin F. Shambaugh (ed.), *The Messages and Proclamations of the Governors of Iowa* (Iowa City: State Historical Society, 1903), vol. II, pp. 311, 316-17.

One of the measures passed by the Iowa legislature in its first special session of the Civil War—at the urging of Governor Kirkwood—was an act authorizing the issuance of up to $800,000 in state bonds to arm and equip the Iowa troops. A controversy soon arose concerning the constitutional validity of the war defense bonds, and a campaign to discredit the bonds was waged by a New York newspaper. Objectors urged that Article VII of the Constitution of 1857 prohibited the state from contracting aggregate debts exceeding $250,000, unless "to repel invasion, suppress insurrection, or defend the State in war .... " (Article VII, §§ 2, 4). The Chief Justice of the Iowa Supreme Court entered the fray with an opinion letter to the State Treasurer.

Keokuk, Iowa, July 8, 1861
Hon. J. W. Jones, *State Treasurer*—
The constitutional validity of the State bonds upon which the war loan is being made having been questioned in some quarters, his Excellency Gov. Kirkwood has requested an opinion upon the subject from the supreme tribunal of the State. The constitution limits the State indebtedness to $250,000, with an exception in the following words:

"In addition to the above limited power to contract debts, the State may contract debts to repel in-vasion, suppress insurrection, or defend the State in war."

We are not at liberty to entertain a doubt that a state or condition of things exists in this country, which fully brings the power of the State, to contract a debt beyond this constitutional limit, within the true meaning and sense of the above exception. The doubt, if any is honestly cherished, must have had its origin in the idea, that the invasion or rebellion referred to must be local and confined to our own borders and not extra territorial.—This restricted interpretation of the constitution overlooks the true theory of our political system, the connection and dependencies subsisting between the State and Federal Governments, that the former is a member incorporate of the latter, deriving its limited sovereignty—its legal status—its rights and powers—its independence and liberty from the *Union*, the overthrow of which by a rebellion, could not occur without in an important sense affecting the political status of the State.

Whether, however, this be true or not, one thing is clear, that it is the exclusive province of the law-making power to judge of the necessity, and to determine whether a state of things exists, making it important for the safety of the State, that a loan of money should be effected, and inasmuch as the act authorizing the issue and sale of State Bonds to procure such loan, declares that it is to enable the State to repel invasion and defend itself in war, that that absolutely concludes the question, and that no court in this country, laying the slightest claim to respectability would undertake to determine that the facts were otherwise than as found by the General Assembly. I need not say, perhaps, that my associates, Judges Wright and Baldwin, concur substantially in the above opinion.
[Signed] R. P. LOWE, Chief Justice

Chief Justice R. P. Lowe, letter to J. W. Jones, State Treasurer, July 8, 1861, reprinted in *Iowa State Register*, July 17, 1861.

The Iowa General Assembly responded quickly and repeatedly to Governor Kirkwood's calls for remedial legislation during its two regular and two special sessions of the Civil War years. A number of social and charitable provisions grew out of the measures enacted for the relief of Civil War soldiers and their dependents. Among its many acts and resolutions, the legislature voted to organize and equip the militia, exempt soldiers from the rigors of lawsuits, provide for the spiritual needs of the troops, and establish the work of Iowa's first named "Sanitary Agent"—Annie Wittenmyer of Keokuk.

A state law directed the governor to appoint Annie Wittenmyer of Keokuk as one of Iowa's "Sanitary Agents" during the Civil War. (Courtesy, State Historical Society of Iowa, Iowa City)

CLOTHING, MUNITIONS OF WAR, & C.

Be it enacted by the General Assembly of the State of Iowa,

Section 1. [T]he governor of the state of Iowa is hereby directed to procure for the use of the state, as soon as possible, twenty-five hundred approved arms and their proper accoutrements and equipments for military purposes, and he is further hereby invested with authority to purchase twenty-five hundred arms, with their proper accoutrements and equipments in addition to the twenty-five hundred first mentioned.

. . . .

Sec. 3. The governor of the state is hereby authorized to purchase such quantities of powder and other munitions of war, as he may deem necessary to make effective the arms aforesaid.

Sec. 4. The governor of the state is hereby authorized to purchase such clothing, tents, arms and camp equipage, for the use of, and all articles necessary for the subsistence of Iowa regiments now organized and accepted or that may hereafter be organized and accepted into the service of the United States government as he may deem necessary ....
Approved May 28th, 1861.

Acts of the Eighth General Assembly Extra Session, 1861, ch. 4, §§ 1,3,4.

VOLUNTEER SOLDIERS.

Be it enacted by the General Assembly of the State of Iowa,

Section 1. That in all actions now pending, or hereafter pending in any of the courts of this state or before any justice of the peace, it shall be a sufficient cause for a continuance, on motion of the defendant, his agent or attorney, if it shall be shown to the satisfaction of the court or justice of the peace, that the defendant is absent from home in the actual military service of the United States or of this state, and that the defendant's presence is in any degree necessary for a full and fair defense of the suit.

. . . .

Approved May 28th, 1861.

Acts of the Eighth General Assembly Extra Session, 1861, ch. 7, §1.

SUPPORT OF FAMILIES OF VOLUNTEERS.

Be it enacted by the General Assembly of the State of Iowa,

Section 1. That the board of supervisors of any county of this state shall have power to appropriate out of the county funds of their county, such sums as they may decide to be necessary for the support of the families of those persons who have volunteered, and are in the actual military service of either the United States or of the state of Iowa, who are in destitute circumstances, and whose families resided in the county making the appropriation at the time of the enlistment of said volunteers, and whose families still continue to reside in said county.

. . . .

Approved May 29th, 1861

Acts of the Eighth General Assembly Extra Session, 1861, ch. 23, § 1.

ROMAN CATHOLIC CLERGYMAN.

WHEREAS, It is understood that a considerable number of Soldiers of the Roman Catholic faith belong to the Iowa Regiments of volunteers, now in the service of the United States, and they wish the ministration of a Clergyman of that faith, therefore,

Resolved by the Senate and House of Representatives, That the Governor be requested to ask the War Department to permit a Roman Catholic Clergyman, to be named by him, to visit and remain with the Iowa Regiments of Volunteers in the service of the United States, and to minister to the spiritual wants of such soldiers thereof as may desire it, and that the War Department cause him to be paid the same pay and have the same allowances as the Chaplains of the said Regiments.

Approved, March 21st, 1862.

Acts of the Ninth General Assembly, 1862, Joint Resolution No. 13.

SANITARY AGENTS.

Section 1. *Be it enacted by the General Assembly of the State of Iowa,* That the Governor be and he is authorized and required to appoint two or more agents, (one of whom shall be Mrs. Annie Wittenmyer) as Sanitary Agents for the State of Iowa.

Sec. 2. It shall be the duty of said Sanitary Agents to visit the Iowa troops in the field, to ascer-

tain their condition and their wants; to report to the Governor at least once in three months; and said Agents shall from time to time inform the Governor of the condition of Iowa troops in the field, and their wants; and they may make such recommendations as to them may seem proper.

. . . .

Approved September 11, 1862.

Acts of the Ninth General Assembly Extra Session, 1862, ch. 36, §§ 1-2.

RELIEF OF SOLDIERS' FAMILIES.

Section 1. *Be it enacted by the General Assembly of the State of Iowa,* That for the relief of the families of privates and non-commissioned officers and musicians who have heretofore been, now are, or may hereafter be in the military or naval service of the United States from this State, there shall be levied in each county not less than two (2) mills on the dollar, in the years 1864 and 1865, on all taxable property in each county, and the amount so levied shall be collected in the same manner as other county taxes.

. . . .

Sec. 8. The word family, as used in this Act, shall be construed to mean only a wife, dependent children under the age of twelve years, brothers and sisters under the age of twelve years, and aged and infirm dependent parents.

. . . .

Approved March 28th, 1864.

Acts of the Tenth General Assembly, 1864, ch. 89, § 1, 8.

AFRICAN SOLDIERS.

Resolved by the House of Representatives, the Senate concurring, That we heartily endorse the policy of paying soldiers and seamen of African descent, in the service of the United States, the same pay as is paid to other soldiers and seamen of the same grade.

Resolved, That we recognize the right of soldiers and seamen of African descent, in the service of the United States, the same protection that other soldiers and seamen are entitled to by the laws of War.

. . . .

Approved February 27th, 1864.

Acts of the Tenth General Assembly, 1864, Joint Resolution No. 10.

Not all Iowans supported the Union cause. In Iowa, as in other northern states, some followers of the Democratic Party—known as the "Peace Democrats"—opposed the war policy of President Lincoln. Individuals who, in addition to opposing the war, were active southern sympathizers were known as "Copperheads" or "Butternuts." The difference between a Peace Democrat and a Copperhead often was lost on the average unionist, who classified all dissenters as traitors. In this climate of suspicion, numerous arbitrary arrests were made of individuals charged as deserters or war resisters.

One of the more controversial Iowa figures of the Civil War years was Henry Clay Dean, circuit Methodist minister and trial lawyer. Dean was a renowned orator and an ardent Democrat. During the war he spoke out forcefully against the policies of President Lincoln and his administration, which earned him the antipathy of many Iowans. In May 1863, while traveling to Keosauqua to attend a Democratic Party meeting, Dean was seized by a group of soldiers and citizens in Keokuk, nearly lynched, and held without trial as a military prisoner. He described his ordeal in a book, Crimes of the Civil War, *published in 1869.*

To the American People:

I have a personal reason for the publication of this book. I suffered under the reign of Mr. Lincoln, which was a vibration between anarchy and despotism. Why arrested? I cannot tell. Have never seen anything like charges, and suppose there were none in such form as would be recognized in any court of justice under the sun; and yet I am quite sure there was a cause for it, which is this: *I am a Democrat; a devoted friend of the Constitution of the United States; a sincere lover of the Government and the Union of the States; am anxious for a reunion, and believe it the right and duty of a freeman, in a calm, candid manner, to discuss in a temperate spirit, the best modes of effecting this purpose. I have dared to participate in these discussions freely, which I have done from convictions of duty. This was the cause of my arrest. ...*

I was on my way from Quincy, Illinois, to Keosauqua, Iowa, to attend a meeting of the Democratic party. Mobocracy had run riot in Keokuk for many months under the auspices of the officers commanding the post, and having in charge the Medical Department. I had to pass through Keokuk to reach the cars. Before I landed at the wharf, I learned that the *"Gate City,"* the only paper published in Keokuk, had demanded my arrest. Nearly every Puritan paper in the State had joined in the general howl. ...

My arrest had been agreed upon as soon as my name was registered at the Billings House. I could see the Puritans and Roundheads gathering in squads of four or five, talking in a low excited whisper. ... I called to see Hon. T. W. Clagett on business, and whilst sitting upon the porch with the Judge, I saw a crowd approaching near his gate, who inquired for me, calling out my name. ...

... A young man of the name of Ball, whilst in the office of the Provost Marshal, informed me, with the grin ... that he "wanted the boys to take their satisfaction out of me," and that he now arrested me in due form, and handed me over to the Sergeant of the Provost Guard. ...

After my arrest, I was placed in the front of the crowd, with a low-bred, insolent man, who commenced asking me offensive questions, of which I of course took no notice. After hurrying me through several streets, at length a hollow square was formed, where I was taunted, threatened and insulted for a full half hour. I was first informed that death was entirely too mild a punishment to be administered to a "Copperhead," who, in the choice language of their newspaper, was foolhardy and demented enough to venture through Keokuk.

... On the outside of the crowd there stood a merchant of thin visage, sharp nose, red head, and exceedingly thin lips, who cried out at the top of his voice, "He ought to be drowned, seeing the Mississippi so close at hand," when there went up a yell, *"drown him,"* "DROWN HIM," "DROWN HIM." Near by another of the malignants spoke up and said, "Drowning was entirely too easy and speedy a death for a Copperhead," and cried out, *"hang him,"* "HANG HIM," "HANG HIM." Still another commenced, and the cry went up *"shoot him,"* "SHOOT HIM," "SHOOT HIM."

... After much parleying, whooping, yelling and coarse insult, I was marched down to the office of the Provost Marshal, and there commanded by this young man, Ball, to strip myself stark naked, which I had to do in the presence of a large crowd, and remaining in that condition for fifteen minutes .... After I had been allowed to put on my clothes, my carpet sack was sent for to the hotel, carefully searched, and my private letters and papers read aloud in the presence of the crowd, open to the inspection of everybody.

After all this was over, Mr. Ball sent some one of the crowd to inform the soldiers that he would assure them that I would be severely dealt with, and they were permitted to retire. I was soon lodged in the Guard House ....

I was informed upon my first entrance into the place, that the central idea of a military prison was to make it as nearly the very essence of hell as was possible. In this they made a capital success. The room was about sixteen feet wide by forty-five feet long, with enough taken off of the side to make room for a flight of stairs. In this room there were fifty men lying side by side. They were of almost every conceivable grade, gathered from every rank in society, and charged with every manner of offence known to the laws of God and man. Some of them, even in sickness, lawless and ungovernable, had been sent in from the hospital, breathing the deadly malaria of all the diseases generated by the vices of the army. The stench of venereal taint issuing from their putrid breath, would nauseate the stomach of the oldest Bacchanalian. ...

For fourteen long and loathesome dreary days and nights, feverish with loss of sleep and gasping for breath, I was confined in this nameless place. ...

Weighing two hundred and thirty pounds, suffocation had well nigh exhausted my strength. At the end of fourteen days, my wife, who is a lady of feeble health and was sick, stopped at the Billings House. I obtained a parole of honor to be confined to that hotel, where I had permission to remain. During this time the United States Circuit Court was in session in Des Moines, for the purpose of finding indictments. ... Every effort was used—personal spite, political malice, private conversation, newspaper scraps, written speeches, political associations, and party antecedents, were all thoroughly examined for treason, sedition, or anything which would disparage my love of country or prove my sympathies with its enemies. But no indictment could be found ....

It was unfortunate for the safety of the country

Henry Clay Dean, trial lawyer, circuit minister, and anti-war activist. (Courtesy, State Historical Society of Iowa, Iowa City)

that my own is not the only instance of wrong suffered, nor this the only act of violence done in the city of Keokuk. They have been frequent and outrageous.

The *Constitution* newspaper office was destroyed. Mr. Hooker's store was destroyed in the same way. The private dwellings of a number of Democrats were assailed in the dead hour of night by the same persons. Houses were ransacked in the same way; and a note was sent by this young man, Ball, to an officer, not to attack a private family until the husband returned.

... Every demonstration against any one was instigated by the malignant citizens and the imbecile and corrupt officers. This was a part of the machinery for making war on the Copperheads of the North.

Henry Clay Dean, *Crimes of the Civil War* (Baltimore: J. Wesley Smith & Bro., 1869), pp. 11, 14-19, 21-23.

Henry Clay Dean emerged from his ordeal angry, shaken—but alive. Less fortunate was George Cyphert Tally, an outspoken Baptist Minister, southern sympathizer, and defender of slavery. On August 1, 1863, Tally addressed a political meeting near the town of South English in Keokuk County, where a Republican Party meeting also was gathered. Tally and some of his followers entered the town, shots were fired, and Tally fell dead in his wagon.

Fearing further violence between the well-armed Copperheads and their Union nemeses, Governor Kirkwood sent militia to the area and himself journeyed to Sigourney, where he addressed a crowd from the courthouse steps. Further violence was avoided, and "Tally's War" (also known as the "Skunk River War") passed into legend. A first-hand account of the incident later was recorded by R.B. Sears of North English, who as a boy of thirteen witnessed the killing of George Cyphert Tally.

I was born in Henry County, Indiana, in 1850. The next year my parents brought me to Iowa, and I have lived in the North English neighborhood ever since.

My sister Susan was fifteen years my senior. During the war she was married to Edward Cabler, a private in Co. F, 5th Iowa Inf[antry]. ...

On the morning of the Democratic Rally at South English, which as I recall it was on August 1st, 1863, I went with Ed to the grove where it was being held. ... We found plank seats arranged for the audience, but Cyphert Tally spoke from a wagon. ...

Excitement ran high at the grove, and there were many wordy altercations. I saw one Mrs. Starkweather, a loyalist, become engaged in a quarrel with a woman wearing a Butternut badge who was sitting next to her. During this quarrel Mrs. Starkweather tore off the other woman's badge, and in return Mrs. Starkweather's dress was torn to strips. ...

At the conclusion of this dispute Ed said to me that there would certainly be serious trouble before the day was over and that we had better go to his home for our rifles, and we started immediately. When we reached his home we discovered that we had not enough bullets and Ed and I molded a supply

and loaded our rifles, while my sister Susan tied the patching on the bullets. We then hurried back to South English. ... A Republican speaker was addressing a small group of people near the Phelps hotel, and Ed and I mingled with the people in the hotel bar room and on the street until the two loads of Copperheads from the grove appeared.

. . . .

Eighteen loyalist men had concealed their rifles in the hotel barroom, and seeing the Copperhead forces approach we hurried to secure them. ...

As the wagons approached our station some one in the wagons shouted "Cowards." A loyalist in the crowd answered "Copperheads." Then came "Abolitionists" and its reply, "Traitors." Tom Moorman came running up from his store in the block east of the hotel, carrying a revolver. This revolver was accidently discharged and I saw the bullet strike the ground. Cyphert Tally rode in the first wagon in a standing position armed with a gun in one hand and a knife in the other. When Moorman's revolver was discharged he immediately opened fire, apparently shooting at Ed Cabler and Tom Moorman, they being in uniform. One of Tally's shots took effect in the neck of a horse ridden by Dr. Arthur of North English. Tally was then about forty feet from us. I saw Ed Cabler take careful aim, saw the flash of his gun and heard the roar of its discharge, and for good or for bad, the soul of Cyphert Tally stood before his maker. The gun and knife fell from his nerveless grasp and his body fell with blood trickling from a wound in his forehead and down over his beard. ...

Of course firing became general immediately upon the discharge of Moorman's revolver. The crowd upon the street contained many persons wearing the Butternut badge. This perhaps prevented a general fire from the men in the wagons as they might be shooting down their own friends, wives and children, if they fired broadcast into the street. We believed that more than Tally had been killed or wounded in the wagons, for they immediately drove to the farm home of Dr. Miller, one-fourth of a mile away to the south, and an hour later might have been followed by the trail of blood spilled from the wagons.

One Wes Funk acted as a marshal for the Copperhead forces. He wore a large red sash, draped over one shoulder and under the other arm, and on his breast was pinned the hated Butternut. After the wagons had left he attempted to rally the Copperhead forces remaining in South English. Jim Moorman, crippled as he was, grabbed the horse's bit and shouted "G__D____ you, give me that badge." Funk started to obey but was not fast enough and Moorman tore the badge from his clothes. After this there was apparently no further effort to re-organize those men in town, but it was feared that the wagons might return from the Dr. Miller home. ...

Before the Copperhead Army had been dispersed by Governor Kirkwood, it sent word to South English demanding the surrender of the men who had killed Tally under threat of burning the town. But the town was then well guarded by recruits from the surrounding country and no attention was paid to the demand.

. . . .

I do not think [Ed Cabler] ever regretted his part in the affair. The country was in a highly inflamed state and under the eloquent appeals of Tally the disafection was spreading. Rewards had been offered for traitors, dead or alive, and I am satisfied that Ed felt he had performed as high a patriotic duty as ever he had on the field of battle. And I think he always believed, as did I, that a general riot was avoided and many innocent lives were saved by his prompt action.

Statement of R. B. Sears, reprinted in J. L. Swift, "The Death of Cyphert Tally," *Annals of Iowa* 3rd Series, vol. 41 (Winter 1972): 834, 836-41.

W*hile Iowans were fighting and dying for the Union cause—whose platform after the Emancipation Proclamation included the abolition of slavery—a war between the races was being fought in an Iowa courtroom.*

In 1851, the General Assembly had passed "An Act to Prohibit the Immigration of Free Negroes Into This State," which gave local authorities the power to order free black immigrants to leave the state within three days or be arrested and fined. On January 20, 1863, plaintiff Archie P. Webb filed a petition for a writ of habeas corpus, alleging that he was unlawfully restrained in the Polk County jail for violation of the statute. Webb, a black laborer, stated that he had been imprisoned without trial, the production of wit-nesses, or counsel, in purported violation of the "Act to Prohibit the Immigration of Free Negroes"—which he challenged as unconstitutional and invalid.

The case was tried before Judge John H. Gray of the fifth judicial district court, who, on February 2, 1863, ordered Archie Webb released. (The following year, the legislature repealed the act so repugnant to Judge Gray.) In a lengthy and impassioned opinion, the judge ruled the act unconstitutional and void.

T he plaintiff herein was notified by one of the trustees of Delaware township, in Polk county, to leave the State within three days. He refused. An order was made by Stephen Harvey, a justice of the peace, in and for said township, for the plaintiff's arrest. The sheriff arrested him, took him before the said justice, and he was then tried and fined in the sum of twelve dollars and costs and sent to jail until he should pay the fine and costs or consent to leave the State. In vacation a writ was issued to the sheriff to bring the plaintiff before me to inquire into the legality of his imprisonment. On the trial it was agreed that plaintiff is a free negro, born in the United States, and that he came from the State of Arkansas to this State since the passage of the law of 1851 excluding free negroes from this State. Upon these facts this cause is submitted to this court. This action arises under that which purports to be a law enacted by the Third General Assembly of the State of Iowa, held in January, 1851, and entitled, "An Act to prohibit the immigration of Free Negroes into this State," and approved February 5, 1851. ...

Was this Act of the Legislature a violation of the second clause of the fourth Article of the Constitution of the United States, which says: "That the citizens of *each State* shall be entitled to all the privileges and immunities of the citizens of the several States"? ...

The reasons urged for the support of the doctrine that free native born persons of color are not citizens of the United States are: 1st—They are a degraded race; 2d—They are not in any of the States admitted to all the privileges and immunities of white citizens; 3d—That they were not represented in that body which formed our National Constitution and therefore are not embraced in the words, "We, the people." &c., which are the first words of our Constitution. As to the first of these reasons: It is more a question of history than of law, and I propose to leave to history that which in my judgement can in no wise affect the law. It may be submitted to the enlightened conscience and the determination of a Christian world whether a race of men forced from home to foreign shores, which they never sought, and sold into bondage, should be more despised than pitied. The second reason urged is: That they are not in any of the States admitted to all the rights and immunities of white *citizens*. Suppose that be true. Does it follow that they are not citizens? ... After an examination of the authorities upon this question, together with the reasons upon which they are founded, it appears that a native-born free man of color, whether born free or a slave and manumitted, is a citizen within the meaning of the National Constitution.

If therefore they be citizens of the United States, they are entitled to all the rights guaranteed to, and privileges conferred upon, citizens of the same description in this State. ... The Constitution of this State is in perfect harmony with the Constitution of the United States in denying to free negroes the privilege of voting, of holding office and being militiamen. But the Legislature had no right to pass a law denying them the right to live in the State when the Constitution guarantees this right to all such citizens in this State at its adoption. ...

Was this law a violation of the old Constitution of this State under which it was enacted? Article 1st of the Bill of Rights says that "All *men* are by nature free and independent and have certain inalienable rights, among which are life and liberty—acquiring, possessing, and protecting property, and pursuing and obtaining safety and happiness." ... What is here meant by *all men*? The term defines itself—it can mean nothing less than all the human race, and when used in this clause means such of the human race as may be within the bounds of the State of Iowa. ...

[T]he judgment of the Court is that the law under which the plaintiff was arrested is inoperative and void; that the proceedings thereunder were therefore unauthorized, that the plaintiff herein is entitled to his liberty, and that he is hereby discharged from imprisonment.

[*Des Moines*] *Daily State Register*, February 3, 1863, reprinted in Coffin, "The Case of Archie P. Webb, A Free Negro," *Annals of Iowa* 3rd Series, no. XI (1913-15): 200, 204-05, 207-08, 210-11, 213.

The Iowa Supreme Court (which was increased from three to four judges in 1864) considered a number of cases related to the war. Among other decisions, it upheld a statute that allowed continuances of legal actions against defendants in military service, and asserted the freedom of the press to comment fairly on the acts and speech of public men in wartime.

When a father sought the release from military custody of his minor son charged with desertion, the Iowa Supreme Court considered the complicated question of whether it had concurrent jurisdiction with the federal courts to decide the controversy.

The relator, John H. Anderson, procured a writ of *habeas corpus* to be issued by me, directed to Lieutenant Peckenpaugh, in command of Post McClellan.

The object of the proceeding was to procure the discharge of his minor son from the military custody, in which he is held. ... It was admitted by the pleadings that the relator's son was a minor when he enlisted, and that his enlistment was without his father's consent. It may be further remarked, that acting under orders from the War Department, the respondent refused to produce the body of the person, and sought to be released because, 1st, of the alleged want of jurisdiction of a State court or judge in cases of this sort; and, 2d, because the crime of desertion is a military offense, and as such is exclusively cognizable before a military tribunal. ...

Whether the State courts have jurisdiction by *habeas corpus*, when the return shows that the prisoner is detained by an officer of the United States, by color, or under authority of the United States, has been very much discussed, and the result of my examination of cases like the present shows that the question is far from being settled. ...

... The writ of *habeas corpus* is intended for the protection of all the inhabitants residing within the territorial limits of the State. It is needless to enlarge upon its importance. As a judge or as a citizen, I shall make no complaint if it is found necessary to suspend it in Iowa, in order the more speedily to subdue the rebellion. But while the civil law is in full force, and the writ is not suspended, it is the duty of the judges, than which no duty can be more weighty and more

THE CIVIL WAR YEARS, 1860–1865

responsible, faithfully to guard the personal liberty and security of the citizen.

... I conclude my observations on this part of the case by saying, that my hasty examination since the argument on yesterday has failed to satisfy me, that the State courts have not jurisdiction concurrently with the federal courts to inquire into the *validity of an enlistment into the army of the United States.* As at present advised, I should exercise such a jurisdiction; and I have every reason to believe that the military authorities would not incur the odium or take the responsibility, in the loyal State of Iowa, of forcibly interrupting its exercise. ... But the return to the writ raises another and different question. The return states that the prisoner is held for the military crime of desertion for trial before a court martial. Both on principle and authority, this is a sufficient reason why he should not be set at liberty by the civil courts prior to his trial for his alleged military offense. Under the Constitution of the United States, Congress has exclusive power "to raise and support armies" and "to provide for the government and regulation of the land and naval forces." Under this power, Congress has acted. It has made desertion a high military offense. It has provided for the institution and regulation of courts martial.

These courts are governed by well settled rules; and if a person is charged with a military offense, the military authorities have a right to detain him for trial, and if found guilty, for punishment. ...

But it is answered, that because of minority there was no valid enlistment, and if no valid enlistment there could be no desertion. The reply to this is, that this is a question for the military court. On a charge of desertion, infancy is no defense. ... I therefore hold that the return of the respondent in this case, that he holds the prisoner for the crime of desertion, and that he is now awaiting his trial before a court martial, is sufficient, and that he must abide by the decision of the latter court, before the question of the validity of his enlistment can be determined in the civil courts on *habeas corpus.*

NOTE.—The above decision was made prior to the proclamation of the President suspending the right of *habeas corpus* in certain cases.

Ex Parte Anderson, 16 Withrow 595, 596, 598-99, (Iowa 1864).

In April 1865, two events that would change the course of the nation's history took place within the space of a week. On April 9, General Robert E. Lee surrendered to the Union forces at Appomattox courthouse. On April 14, President Abraham Lincoln was shot by the actor John Wilkes Booth while attending a play at Ford's Theatre in Washington, D.C.; he died from his wounds the next day.

Iowans went from a state of great rejoicing to a state of deep mourning. The emotions of the period were reflected in a special memorial before the Iowa Supreme Court.

Wednesday, 19th April, 1865
JOHN N. ROGERS, Esq., addressed the Court as follows:
. . . .

The term which to-day closes, must ever be a memorable one in the annals of the court, and in the recollections of all connected with it. Twice in one short week have your honors been called on to suspend your judicial labors, that you might unite with your fellow citizens in giving expression to the feelings excited by events of great national import; now; to "rejoice with them that did rejoice;" and, again, alas! to "weep with them that wept." It seems but yesterday that the booming cannon, the flags floating from every housetop, the illuminated city, the huzzas of the citizens, told us the joyful news of a hostile army laying down its arms, and a long and bloody war against treason virtually ended in triumph. And, now, the same buildings draped with the emblems of woe, the same flags half-masted and shrouded in crape, the saddened faces, the marks of grief everywhere and on everything, tell us of a revered and beloved President suddenly struck down in bloody death by a murderer's and traitor's hand, in the very bosom of the nation's capital, and in the midst of the nation's rejoicings over its redemption, under God so largely due to his counsels and labors. ...

In the universal execration of the crime, let it not be forgotten who are its real perpetrators. Not against the wretch who fired the fatal bullet, would I direct your horror and detestation. No! In the murderer of ABRAHAM LINCOLN, I behold not the form of the miserable player, who was but the instrument, though the conscious and guilty instrument of the deed. I behold rather the malignant and hateful form of Treason, gnashing its teeth in fury at its impotence to overthrow the government and constitution which are the objects of its rancorous hate, and aiming its expiring blow at the life of the nation, through the devoted head of its Chief Magistrate. The murderers of the President are the same men whose hands are red with countless former murders; the same who have murdered our gallant countrymen by tens of thousands on the battle-field, with shot and shell; who have murdered them in camps and hospitals by disease; who have murdered them in the horrible slaughter-pens of the South by starvation; who have murdered them in every form and mode in which loyal lives have been sacrificed in the struggle to crush this internal rebellion. ...

[L]et the whole loyal population of this land, clasping hands to-day over the body of their martyred President, swear a solemn oath that, so far as the power of the nation shall avail to do it, the extreme penalty of the law shall be rigorously meted out to these atrocious criminals.

But I am recalled to the melancholy duties of the hour. To-day we pay the last tribute of respect and affection to the noble, the honored dead. I behold the funeral procession move from the executive mansion, bearing to its earthly resting place the mortal remains of ABRAHAM LINCOLN:

> "Hush, the Dead March wails in the people's
> ears:
> The dark crowd moves, and there are sobs and
> tears:
> The black earth yawns: the mortal disappears:
> Ashes to ashes, dust to dust;
> He is gone who seemed so great.—
> Gone; but nothing can bereave him
> Of the force he made his own
> Being here, and we believe him
> Something far advanced in State,
> And that he wears a truer crown
> Than any wreath that man can weave him"

"Memorial," 18 Withrow 582-86 (Iowa 1865).

CHAPTER FOUR

A Nation Rebuilds

1865-1880

"[E]qual rights and equal protection shall be secured to all regardless of color or nationality."

— The Iowa Supreme Court

1865-1880

WHEN THE CIVIL WAR ENDED, THE nation turned its attention to the rights of former slaves and the reconstruction of the South. The reconstruction policy of President Lincoln's successor, Andrew Johnson, was strongly opposed by radical Republicans in Congress, who believed the policy to be too lenient toward the rebellious states.

In 1867, Congress passed Reconstruction Acts over President Johnson's veto and adopted measures to limit the powers of the President. The Tenure of Office Act required the President to seek Senate approval before removing an official who had been appointed with the advice and consent of the Senate. When in defiance of the act the President sought to remove the radical Republican Secretary of War, Edwin Stanton, the House of Representatives voted a bill of impeachment for "high crimes and misdemeanors." All of Iowa's congressmen voted in favor of impeachment.

With Chief Justice Salmon P. Chase presiding, President Johnson was tried in the Senate. Two votes were taken in May 1868 on the articles of impeachment and fell short by a single vote of the two-thirds necessary to convict. Iowa's Senator James W. Grimes (the former governor), despite an attack of paralysis, was present to cast his vote of "not guilty." Grimes resigned from office in 1869 due to ill health, widely criticized in his own Republican Party for having supported the President.

While the victorious Union imposed its reconstruction policies on the South, Iowa was undergoing its own kind of social reconstruction—this one voluntary. In June 1865, the state Republican convention passed a resolution urging that the Iowa constitution be amended to remove the bar to non-white voting. The General Assembly in 1866 and 1868 proposed amendments to the Iowa constitution that would strike the word "white" from the sections on suffrage, census enumeration, apportionment, and the militia.

In the 1868 general election, voters by a margin of 66.5% to 33.5% approved these constitutional changes (an amendment to remove the word "white" from the qualifications to serve in the legislature was adopted in 1880). Iowa became one of the first states to allow black male suffrage, and its action antedated the ratification in 1870 of the Fifteenth Amendment to the U.S. Constitution, which provided that voting rights could not be denied "on account of race, color, or previous condition of servitude."

Another disenfranchised group fared less well in the quest for suffrage. A proposal to delete the word "male" from the suffrage provision of the Iowa constitution passed both houses of the General Assembly in 1870, but did not receive the required second approval by the legislature in 1872. Nonetheless, women were heartened by measures to strengthen women's property rights passed by the General Assembly in its Code Revision of 1873.

Railroads, the economy, and the agrarian movement also dominated the public consciousness in the years after the Civil War. The growth of railroads west of the Mississippi encroached on river shipping, and led to pressure from shippers and the new Granger movement for regulation. In response, Iowa passed (and then repealed) regulatory legislation that withstood court challenge from the railroads.

The farmers' organization known as "The Grange" had been founded in 1867 to promote social, cultural, and educational activities for farmers, but it soon became a vehicle for airing economic grievances. Spurred by concern over rapid drops in farm prices, local Grange organizations grew rapidly in Iowa and the Midwest during the 1870s. The wild expansion of economic speculation—especially in railroad enterprises—led to the Panic of 1873, which was followed by an economic depression that lasted through most of the decade. Iowa's problems were compounded by great hordes of grasshoppers that descended on the state in 1873 and in subsequent years.

The economic crisis and charges of political corruption in the administration of President Ulysses S. Grant improved the prospects of the Democratic Party. In 1874, the Democrats won a majority of seats in the United States House of Representatives, with the Republicans losing nearly 90 seats. Iowa, however, remained steadfastly Republican in its state and national offices.

By the end of the 1870s, the formal Reconstruction of the South had ended, and the nation looked forward to greater stability in politics and the economy. With over 1,600,000 residents (making it tenth in population among the states) and a growing non-rural population, Iowa prepared to enter the final decades of the nineteenth century.

One of the most important legal developments in the years after the Civil War was the trial of President Andrew Johnson in the U.S. Senate for "high crimes and misdemeanors." The Senate failed to convict by only a single vote, and one of the few Republicans to cast his vote against impeachment was Iowa's Senator James W. Grimes. For his courageous vote, Grimes was vilified in the radical Republican press—and he responded vigorously to his critics.

THE TEST VOTE

Yesterday noon, while the country was holding its breath in anxious suspense, the news came flashing across the wires from Washington, that the High Court of Impeachment had rendered a verdict on the XIth clause of the articles preferred against President Johnson for high crimes and misdemeanors, and that thirty-five Senators had answered yea to his guiltiness, and nineteen has responded nay. On this vote the great Betrayer of his country saved his official head by the voice of one lone Senator. Had either of the seven Judases—Grimes, Fessenden, Fowler, Trumbull, Henderson, Ross or Van Winkle—but proven true to the right and their constituents, the momentous question would have been settled, and the scepter would have departed from the hands of the Tennessee autocrat. As it was, seven Republican Senators, in the face of everything sacred and just, and in wilful disobedience to the wishes and demands of the States they represent, cast their first votes with the Democracy, voted an endorsement of the American Nero, and with their base hands pulled from the scabbard a sword to deliver into the hands of Southern Thugs and Kukluxers for the slaughter of Unionism at the South. That Radical Iowa should be betrayed into the support of Johnson is painfully, terribly humiliating to every loyal citizen of the State. The false son of Iowa who has brought this shame upon us, has no longer a home, heritage or friend in this loyal commonwealth. Democrats may and do fawn upon him in the moment of his triumphant treachery, as did the English over Arnold; but in their inmost hearts, they despise the man and loathe his baseness, as severely as do Republicans. We utter no ponderous words against him. Neither his betrayed State nor death can consign him to a worse punishment than the hell of his own conscience.

[Des Moines] Daily State Register, May 17, 1868.

A Card to the Chicago Tribune. Washington, May 26, 1868.
. . . .
It is not true that Chief-Justice Chase sought to influence my judgment in the impeachment trial. I never had a word of conversation with the Chief-Justice on that subject, nor on the subject of a new party or of any political party; nor did he ever mention the subject of the presidency to me. I have not been in the house of the Chief-Justice for more than two years.

It is not true that I have ever been dissatisfied with the reconstruction plan of Congress. So far from it, I was one of the seven Senators who were members of the Joint Committee on Reconstruction, and signed the report. I was chairman of the sub-committee on the State of Tennessee, and it was upon my recommendation that that State was so early restored to the Union.
. . . .

It is not true that I ever had the slightest sympathy with the general policy of Mr. Johnson's Administration. I have had no personal intercourse with Mr. Johnson for two years; never asked him for a favor, and never received one from him.

It is true that, when I took an oath that "in all things appertaining to the trial of the impeachment of Andrew Johnson I would render impartial justice according to the Constitution and the laws" I ceased to act in a representative capacity. I became a judge, acting on my own responsibility and accountable only to my own conscience and my Maker; and no power could force me to decide in such a case, contrary to my convictions, to suit the requirements of a party, whether that party were composed of my friends or my enemies.

James W. Grimes.

Senator James Grimes, letter to the *Chicago Tribune*, May 26, 1868, reprinted in William Salter, *The Life of James W. Grimes* (New York: D. Appleton & Co., 1876), pp. 359-60.

The legal status of the former slaves was uppermost in the national consciousness as Congress and the President wrestled over reconstruction policies. The battle for social and political rights was fought in the courts as well as in the legislatures.

The Iowa Supreme Court (which in 1876 was increased to five judges) addressed racial issues in several cases. The most prominent were Clark v. The Board of Directors, etc. *(1868), in which the court held that children of color could not be refused admission to district schools, and* Coger v. The North West Union Packet Co. *(1873), in which it disapproved of racial distinctions on common carriers. In both cases, the Iowa Supreme Court showed itself to be in the vanguard of decisions affirming racial equality.*

Alexander Clark, Sr., of Muscatine brought a lawsuit on behalf of his daughter in 1868 that established rights of equal education in Iowa. (Courtesy, University of Iowa College of Law)

The petition sets forth, that plaintiff, Susan B. Clark, was born in the city of Muscatine, and has continued to reside therein up to the present time; that she is now twelve years of age, and sues by her next friend, her father, Alexander Clark, who is a resident freeholder and tax payer in the said city of Muscatine, and has been for many years past; that said city of Muscatine is an independent school-district, and the defendants, the board of directors, have established and maintained schools in said independent district; that one of said schools is designated as "Grammar School No. 2," and plaintiff resides in the neighborhood thereof ... that, on the 10th day of September, 1867, said school being in session, she presented herself, and demanded to be received therein as a scholar under the common school law; that said defendants refused to admit or receive her as a pupil, but illegally excluded her therefrom. She asks for a mandamus to compel the defendants to so admit her.

... The defendants then aver, that the plaintiff is of negro extraction and belongs to the "colored race;" that since the organization of said school-district there has been, and they have now, therein, and had, when plaintiff applied for admission, a separate school for colored children ....

COLE, J.—In view of the principle of equal rights to all, upon which our government is founded, it would seem necessary, in order to justify a denial

of such equality of right to any one, that some express sovereign authority for such denial should be shown. ...

Our first State Constitution was adopted in 1846. At the first session of the general assembly of the State, a law on the subject of common schools was passed, in which it was enacted that the "school shall be open and free alike to all *white* persons in the district between the ages of five and twenty-one years." ...

By the new Constitution, which was adopted in 1857, the educational interests of the State, including common schools, were placed under the management of a board of education. ... It was also provided by the new Constitution, article 9. "§ 12. The board of education shall provide for the education of *all the youths of the State,* through a system of common schools."
. . . .

Now, under our Constitution, which declares that provision shall be made "for the education of *all the youths of the State* through a system of common schools," ... is it not equally clear that all discretion is denied to the board of school directors as to what *youths* shall be admitted? It seems to us that the proposition is too clear to admit of question.

. . . .

That the board of directors is clothed with certain discretionary powers as to the establishment, maintenance and management of schools within its district cannot be denied. ...

But this discretion is limited by the line which fixes the *equality of right* in all the youths between the ages of five and twenty-one years. ...

The term "colored race" is but another designation, and in this country but a synonym for African. Now, it is very clear, that, if the board of directors are clothed with a discretion to exclude African children from our common schools, and require them to attend (if at all) a school composed wholly of children of that nationality, they would have the same power and right to exclude German children from our common schools, require them to attend (if at all) a school composed wholly of children of that nationality, and so of Irish, French, English and other nationalities, which together constitute the *American,* and which it is the tendency of our institutions and policy of the government to organize into one harmonious *people,* with a common country and stimulated with the common purpose to perpetuate and spread our free institutions for the development, elevation and happiness of *mankind.*

... For the courts to sustain a board of school directors or other subordinate board or officer in limiting the rights and privileges of persons by reason of their nationality, would be to sanction a plain violation of the spirit of our laws not only, but would tend to perpetuate the national differences of our people and stimulate a constant strife, if not a war of races.

... It was the clear legal duty of the board of directors, resulting from their said office, to admit the plaintiff to said school, and to equal privileges with the other pupils therein.

Clark v. The Board of Directors, 24 Iowa 266, 267-71, 274-77 (1868).

The plaintiff, being in the city of Keokuk, went upon the steamer S. S. Merrill, one of defendant's line of packets navigating the Mississippi river, for the purpose of conveying freight and passengers, to be transported to her home at the city of Quincy, in the State of Illinois. She is a quadroon, being partly of African descent, and was employed as the teacher of a school for colored children in the city where she resided. She applied at the office of the vessel for a ticket and was given one entitling her to transportation, but not to a state-room nor to meals, such as those which, under the custom and regulations of defendant's steamers, are given to colored persons. ... After this she requested a gentleman to buy her a ticket for dinner, who bought her one without any indorsements or conditions. ... When dinner was announced she seated herself at the ladies' table in the cabin at a place designated for certain ladies traveling on the boat .... The request was for her to leave the table and take her meal on the guards or in the pantry, not to leave the reserved seat and take another. She refused, and thereupon the captain of the boat was sent for, who repeated the request, and, being denied compliance, he proceeded by force to remove her from the table and the cabin of the boat. She resisted so that considerable violence was necessary to drag her out of the cabin, and, in the struggle, the covering of the table was torn off and dishes broken, and the officer received a slight injury. ...

In our opinion the plaintiff was entitled to the same rights and privileges while upon defendant's boat, notwithstanding the negro blood, be it more or less, admitted to flow in her veins, which were possessed and exercised by white passengers.

These rights and privileges rest upon the equality of all before the law, the very foundation principle of our government. If the negro must submit to different treatment, to accommodations inferior to those given to the white man, when transported by public carriers, he is deprived of the benefits of this very principle of equality. His contract with a carrier would not secure him the same privileges and the same rights that a like contract, made with the same party by his white fellow citizen, would bestow upon the latter. ...

The doctrines of natural law and of christianity forbid that rights be denied on the ground of race or color; and this principle has become incorporated into the paramount law of the Union. ...

It cannot be doubted that she was excluded from the table and cabin, not because others would have been degraded and she elevated in society, but because of prejudice entertained against her race, growing out of its former condition of servitude—a prejudice, be it proclaimed to the honor of our people, that is fast giving way to nobler sentiments, and, it is hoped, will soon be entombed with its parent, slavery. The object of the [recent] amendments of the federal constitution and of the statutes ... is to relieve citizens of the black race from the effects of this prejudice, to protect them in person and property from its spirit. ... We are disposed to construe these laws according to their very spirit and intent, so that equal rights and equal protection shall be secured to all regardless of color or nationality.

Coger v. The North West. Union Packet Co., 37 Iowa 145, 147-49, 153-54, 158 (1873).

Among other firsts, Iowa is credited as the first state to admit a woman to the practice of law. In 1869, Arabella Mansfield and her husband John were admitted to the Iowa bar. Arabella had studied law in her brother's Mount Pleasant law office, and although she and her husband would spend their lives as educators rather than practicing lawyers, this dramatic first was in great contrast to the position taken in other states.

Indeed, in 1872, the U.S. Supreme Court—in an opinion written by Iowa's own Justice Samuel Freeman Miller—declined on federal constitutional grounds to overturn the Illinois Supreme Court's refusal to grant a woman a license to practice law. By the time of this decision, the state of Iowa had taken the even more dramatic step of removing the words "white male" from its statute concerning the qualifications to practice law. The General Assembly's vote—in March 1870—was lauded in the [Des Moines] Daily Iowa State Register.

THE WORD "MALE" GOING!
    In the Senate yesterday action was taken to strike the word "white" from the law prescribing the qualifications of persons admitted to the practice of law. The people of

Arabella Mansfield was admitted to the Iowa bar in 1869, the first woman in the United States to be formally admitted to the practice of law. (Courtesy, State Historical Society of Iowa, Des Moines)

Iowa by thirty thousand majority, having decided that the question of cuticle has nothing to do with the qualifications of a voter, the Senate promptly arrived at the decision that neither has it properly anything to do with a lawyer. Not, only this. The Senate has taken another step forward, and with the word "white" also expunged the word "male." The woman of Iowa soon can be a lawyer, if she cannot be a voter. And the sign is now seen in the sky that the good day is coming fast when she will vote. The people of Iowa will not be long in declaring that an intelligent woman has as much right to the ballot as an ignorant man. So all you folks who won't live in Iowa when the women vote, may as well leave now with the other nice people who said they would not live in Iowa one minute "after the niggers voted."

[Des Moines] *Daily Iowa State Register*, March 5, 1870.

With the abolition of slavery and advances in black civil rights, reformers could again turn their attention to the subject of women's personal and property rights. Proponents of women's rights could take some comfort in an 1867 decision of the Iowa Supreme Court, which alleviated the harsh common law rule that a father was entitled to absolute custody of his children in the event of a divorce. In the case of Cole v. Cole, the Court awarded custody of the couple's thirteen-year-old son to a severely disabled mother, where the evidence showed that the father was often drunk and violent and the best interests of the child would be served in his mother's care.

But one question remains and this is the order in relation to the custody of the child. Our duty is to make such an order as shall be right and proper. This is the command of our law ....

Whether the effect of the statute is to abrogate the superior common law right the father has over the mother to the custody of their children ... this much is clear, that the tendency of all the modern decisions is to deny that this is an absolute right, and to regard what humanity, common reason and the best interests of society demands, that they should consult the welfare and future well being of their mutual offspring. ...

We have endeavored to consult the rights and feelings of both parents, and yet keep steadily in view the welfare of the child. We could not forget that he is of the age to demand the care, discipline and instruction of the father. Nor have we overlooked the feeble condition of the mother, nor yet her need of the society and assistance of the son in her affliction. Both are pecuniarily liable to secure an education and proper training, and both express an earnest willingness for his custody. Keeping in view all these considerations, and others readily suggesting themselves, and which we cannot stop to specify, the question remains, what does the best interest of this child require? Not without great doubt and hesitation we have concluded to leave him with the mother.

Cole v. Cole, 23 Iowa 433, 446-48 (1867).

The year 1870 was a notable one for women in the Iowa legislature. Miss Mary E. Spencer of Clinton (the daughter of State Representative Benjamin Spencer) was selected as the engrossing clerk in the House of Representatives, the first woman to be so employed. And the Thirteenth General Assembly—emboldened by the 1868 approval of black male suffrage—passed a joint resolution proposing a constitutional amendment to grant suffrage to women. (The resolution failed, however, to obtain the required second vote in the Fourteenth General Assembly.)

A convention of the Iowa Woman Suffrage Association met in Des Moines on October 19, 1871; an earlier meeting had been held in June 1870 in Mt. Pleasant. The formal efforts inaugurated at these meetings would continue for nearly fifty years, until the Nineteenth Amendment to the U.S. Constitution in 1920 at last gave women the vote. At the 1871 state convention, Annie Savery of Des Moines—who, four years later, would become one of Iowa's first women law graduates—gave a powerful address in favor of woman suffrage.

If I were to stand up before an audience of men and women, and undertake to show by a line of argument, that man has a right to the ballot, and to exercise all the functions and privileges of a free citizen, I would probably be regarded as a fool, or insane. And if I should undertake to show that because a negro was a man, and for this reason alone therefore entitled to the ballot, I would doubtless be regarded as having just awakened from a Rip Van Winkle sleep, of, well, only four years. And the time is not far distant, when to question the right and duty of woman, to vote, will be regarded with like absurdity.

... For there is not a reason in favor of man's voting that does not apply with equal force in favor of woman's voting. ...

And, oh, what a power, there is in that little piece of paper, which falls as quietly into the box as a snow flake descends upon the earth! How many millions of men and women, in all nations and climes, have struggle[d] and died for the privilege!

For they know that it is the sacred gift of liberty. It is more powerful than President or Congress, for these are its creatures. It is greater than the government, for it makes the government and controls its destinies. It makes war, and concludes peace. ... It ordains laws to protect the weak against the strong, the just against the unjust. It makes and unmakes the marriage bond. It chooses good or bad men to rule over us. All must suffer alike from its abuses, and all should participate alike in its advantages.

And yet, this sacred inheritance, in which centers the most important relations of life, is withheld from one half of the people of this government, not because they are any the less patriotic or intelligent, not because they are any the less industrious or honest, but simply because they are women. Suppose we should reverse the rule and say men are not entitled to the ballot, simply because they are men. Why, in this respect, we are, with all our boasted democracy, far behind frigid Russia.

. . . .

In that folded leaf, the grandeur of History is represented, Men have wrought with pen and tongue, and died on scaffolds, to obtain this symbol of freedom, and enjoy this consciousness of individuality. To the ballot have been transmitted—as it were—the dignity of the sceptre and the potency of the sword, and we feel confident that when this talisman of power is placed in the hands of woman ... it will become a tongue of justice, a voice of order, securing rights, abolishing abuses, and erecting new institutions of truth and love.

Annie Savery of Des Moines, suffragist and one of Iowa's first women law graduates. (Courtesy, State Historical Society of Iowa, Des Moines)

Address of Mrs. James C. [Annie] Savery before the Iowa Woman's Suffrage Association, Des Moines, Iowa, October 19, 1871, reprinted in [*Des Moines*] *Daily Iowa State Register,* October 21, 1871.

The disappointment of woman suffrage proponents at the defeat of the suffrage resolution in 1872 was assuaged in part by the provisions on married women's property rights in the Code of 1873. The Revision of 1860 had compiled statutes passed since the last code revision. The Code of 1873, in contrast, undertook the more substantive task of revising and re-arranging the laws, thus becoming—in addition to "The Old Blue Book" of 1838-1839 and the Code of 1851—Iowa's third major codification.

The Code of 1873 included many provisions adopted for the relief of needy, dependent, and impaired Iowans. This code recorded the establishment of such institutions as the hospital for the insane in Independence, the college for the blind in Vinton, the institution for the deaf and dumb in Council Bluffs, the penitentiary in Anamosa, and the reform school in Eldora. But it was the provisions regarding women's property rights—the fundamental principles of which remain entrenched in Iowa's law today—that won for the code the special praise of reformers.

SECTION 2202. A married woman may own in her own right, real and personal property acquired by descent, gift, or purchase, and manage, sell, convey, and devise the same by will, to the same extent and in the same manner that the husband can property belonging to him.

· · · ·

SEC. 2207. In case the husband or wife abandons the other and leaves the state, and is absent therefrom for one year without providing for the maintenance and support of his or her family, or is confined in jail or the penitentiary for the period of one year or upward, the district or circuit court of the county where the husband or wife so abandoned or not confined resides, may ... authorize him or her to manage, control, sell, and encumber the property of the husband or wife for the support and maintenance of the family, and for the purpose of paying debts. ...

SEC. 2211. A wife may receive the wages of her personal labor and maintain an action therefor in her own name, and hold the same in her own right; and she may prosecute and defend all actions at law or in equity for the preservation and protection of her rights and property, as if unmarried.

· · · ·

SEC. 2213. Contracts may be made by a wife and liabilities incurred, and the same enforced by or against her to the same extent and in the same manner as if she were unmarried.

· · · ·

SEC 2215. Neither husband nor wife can remove the other, nor their children, from their homestead without his or her consent, and if he abandons her she is entitled to the custody of their minor children, unless the district or circuit court, upon application for the purpose, shall, for good cause otherwise, direct.

Code of 1873, ch. 2, §§ 2202, 2207, 2211, 2213, 2215.

In addition to the rights of former slaves and women, another great liberal cause in the post-Civil War years was death penalty reform. In the same year of the great setback to women's suffrage in the Iowa legislature—1872—a vigorous campaign resulted in the abolition of capital punishment. The reform was short-lived, however, as the death penalty was restored just six years later, and remained part of Iowa law until it was re-abolished in 1965. The arguments for and against the death penalty raised in the emotional nineteenth century debates would reverberate in Iowa's second abolition campaign nearly a century later.

Iowa's method of execution was by hanging. The state abolished the death penalty from 1872-1878, and for a second time in 1965. (*Leslie's Illustrated Weekly Newspaper,* July 7, 1877)

The Death Penalty in Early Iowa: Abolition and Restoration, 1872-1878

IOWA'S FIRST TERRITORIAL LEGISLATURE passed a criminal code in 1839 that specified hanging as the punishment for murder.[1] Early efforts to abolish the death penalty reached a climax in 1851, when reformers nearly succeeded and the Iowa Senate voted for abolition. In the code passed that year, only premeditated murder in the first degree and treason would henceforth be punished with death. Second-degree murder would be penalized by a minimum of ten years imprisonment.[2]

During the next twenty years, periodic attempts to abolish the death penalty were made in the House of Representatives or Senate. Although the reformers always achieved a substantial vote, they never came near success. In 1870, the House voted by forty-six to thirty-eight and the Senate by twenty-seven to seventeen to retain capital punishment, which seemed firmly entrenched. No one could have foreseen that, within two years, a dramatic campaign would result in massive majorities in both houses voting to abolish the death penalty.

A murder in June 1870 started the train of events that led to abolition. William Patterson was found shot dead near Ames, and the following day a former railway worker named George Stanley was arrested for the murder. There was overwhelming circumstantial evidence against Stanley; he was tried in April 1871, convicted of murder in the first degree, and sentenced to hang. The Iowa Supreme Court upheld the conviction on February 24, 1872. After reviewing the case, Governor Cyrus C. Carpenter set April 12 as the date for Stanley's execution.

During his incarceration at Boone, Stanley was converted to Catholicism by Father P.M. Delaney. Father Delaney and his successor as the Boone parish priest begged Governor Carpenter to reprieve Stanley. Two major Quaker petitions were submitted to the governor. Governor Carpenter wrote to Father Delaney that he could not justify a reprieve, but he proclaimed himself an abolitionist who believed that life imprisonment was an adequate deterrent. To a leading Quaker, the governor wrote: "The legislature is now in session, and if as you seem to think, the public sentiment is opposed to the death penalty, this General Assembly, which is supposed to represent the average public will, has had every opportunity to wipe out the death penalty."[3]

The [*Des Moines*] *Daily Iowa State Register* published the governor's letters, treating them as calls to abolish the death penalty. The *Register* demanded the end of "this last relic of a long gone barbarism" and the saving of Stanley and Iowa from hanging—"the first within its borders for twelve years."[4] (Apparently the writer did not know about a hanging in Ottumwa in 1865.)

At the time the governor had set Stanley's execution date, the House of Representatives had resolved to grant to Marvin Bovee of Wisconsin the use of its Assembly Hall on April 4, 1872, for a lecture on capital punishment. The *Register* introduced Bovee to Iowa: "Mr. Marvin H. Bovee distinguished in this country and in Europe, as an earnest and successful laborer in the field of penal reform, intends visiting Iowa. ... The gentleman is the author of the most telling work ever published in the interest of this special reform."[5] Subsequently the *Register* wrote that Bovee "has been very successful in all his attempts in the good cause."[6]

Marvin Henry Bovee, whose campaign for death penalty reform persuaded the Iowa legislature to abolish the death penalty in 1872. (From an undated ambrotype in possession of Bovee's grandson, Kenneth B. Halvorson; Courtesy, State Historical Society of Wisconsin)

This last was an exaggeration. Bovee, a farmer and America's leading opponent of the death penalty, had successfully led the abolition campaign in Wisconsin in 1853. He had taken his one-man crusade into Illinois, New York, Massachusetts, Minnesota, and Pennsylvania. He had addressed many legislatures and hundreds of public meetings. He had vast experience in lobbying, drafting bills, and wooing editors to his cause. He was the campaigner par excellence. However, Bovee had nowhere repeated his abolition triumph in Wisconsin.

Bovee arrived in Des Moines on April 4 and hurled himself into a whirlwind campaign to abolish the death penalty and save George Stanley. He went straight to the governor, who described him as "an earnest sincere man."[7] Bovee gave his major speech that evening in the hall of the House of Representatives "largely attended by members of the Legislature, State officers and citizens of Des Moines."[8] The speaker was introduced by Governor Carpenter.

In his speech, Bovee argued that state cruelty led to individual cruelty. No one had a right to kill; still less could one delegate such a right to the state. Capital punishment was irremedial—too many people later proved innocent had been executed. "If an individual kill his fellow man, shall the State of Iowa commit a greater outrage by deliberately killing him?" Bovee claimed that capital crimes decreased when the death penalty was abolished, because juries were more likely to convict when their decisions could not lead to hanging. He read letters from prison wardens, governors, judges, and attorney generals in the three states that had abolished capital punishment—Michigan, Rhode Island, and Wisconsin—which testified to the beneficial effects of this reform.

Urging that mercy and reformation were the trend of the age, Bovee decried the established clergy for standing in the way of abolition. In refuting the Old Testament arguments of vengeance that "whoso sheddeth man's blood, by man shall his blood be shed," Bovee said: "The entire record of Christ's life was in opposition to this doctrine of retaliation." He closed with "an eloquent appeal to the General Assembly to repeal the brutal statute in Iowa."[9]

Bovee's speech had a marked effect. House Democratic leader John P. Irish wrote his reaction to Bovee in his [Iowa City] Press: "I expected … to see a face sicklied with the sallowness and drawn down to the longitude of the professional philanthropist; but instead he is one of the most manly of men, and delivers his views with a simplicity and directness that have no trace of cant."[10]

Both Des Moines newspapers carried lengthy reports of Bovee's speech. The State Leader commented: "For over two hours the speaker enchained his audience with his eloquent exposition of his subject,"[11] while the Register echoed Bovee's ideas in a powerful editorial.

Many newspapers across the state joined the Register's campaign, emphasizing the barbarism of the gallows and the disgrace to Iowa of hanging Stanley after so many years without an execution. A few newspapers urged retention of the death penalty, citing the need for deterrence and for consultation with the people. The Dubuque Herald campaigned for retention with special vigor, declaring that if legal hanging were abolished "mobs will frequently step in and do it."[12]

The retentionist press may have influenced some legislators, but in Des Moines the abolitionist Register and Leader held sway. Following Bovee's speech, both newspapers mounted major abolition campaigns, publishing the names of other pro-reform newspapers and excerpts from their editorials. Readers learned of the opposition to the death penalty of Bishop Lee of the Protestant Episcopal Church. An editorial reprinted from the *St. Louis Dispatch* and a letter from Ohio showed that other states were looking to Iowa to lead on the issue.

A lengthy and dignified interview with George Stanley printed in the *Register* was reprinted throughout the state a few days before his execution was due. The *Leader* published Bovee's long list of innocent people who had been executed. Notices of another public lecture by Bovee appeared with anti-gallows quotations by Benjamin Franklin and the reformer Theodore Parker. Bovee was busy in the lobbies as well as in the press. The *Dubuque Times*'s Des Moines correspondent reported that Bovee was "seconding the efforts of the *Register* ably and efficiently. The near execution of Stanley, at Nevada has been found a good lobby argument."[13]

Four days before Stanley's scheduled execution, the legislature reacted. The House unanimously passed a resolution asking the governor to delay the hanging until the General Assembly had acted on a bill to abolish the death penalty, and the next day the Senate concurred with only one dissenting vote. Governor Carpenter immediately postponed Stanley's execution for a month. The same day, a bill drafted by Bovee passed the House with the impressive majority of sixty-eight to twenty-two.

The following day, April 10, the Senate took up the matter of capital punishment. Dubuque Senator Benjamin B. Richards attacked abolitionism as "sickly weakly sentimentalism."[14] Senator John E. Burke of Bremer County cited "all that could be found in history" as evidence that "the gallows was one of society's strong props."[15] The stern Senator Moses A. McCoid quoted retaliatory Old Testament scriptures. Future governor William Larrabee urged his fellow senators not to be influenced by the case of Stanley, "nor by the teaching of the itinerant preacher (Mr. Bovee), who had been entertaining them with lectures for the few evenings past, but to act cooly and let the law take its course in this case (Stanley's) unfortunate as it was."[16]

On the reform side, Quaker Senator John C. Chambers emphasized that the prospect of hanging made juries reluctant to convict. Furthermore, "the death penalty did not prevent mob law, as facts showed it, even in this State."[17] Another Quaker senator relied on quotations from the New Testament. But despite their impassioned arguments, the retentionists won the day. Senator Larrabee proposed an amendment to give the jury the option of death or life imprisonment. The amended bill passed by a vote of twenty-five to twenty. The *Muscatine Journal* pithily commented: "The action of the Senate on the bill hangs Stanley but modifies the law."[18]

The next day, April 11, the abolitionists introduced a motion to reconsider the Senate vote. In opposition, Presbyterian Senator Samuel McNutt argued against hasty change, maintaining that the death penalty was an essential deterrent. Presbyterian Senator John McKean declared that public opinion opposed abolition, which he insisted would lead to lynch law. He claimed that Michigan since abolition had a far greater murder and general crime rate than Iowa. The retentionists won this test vote, defeating the motion to reconsider by twenty-five votes to twenty-three.

The two houses were now deadlocked. Bovee plunged straight back into the fray, giving another successful public lecture that evening. For the next nine days he worked to change the Senate vote, and two groups of Quakers petitioned the Senate. On April 19, Bovee's abolition bill was reintroduced in the House and passed by fifty-four votes to twenty-one. The next day, the Senate reversed itself and passed the bill by the remarkable majority of thirty-one to fourteen.

The victory belonged to Bovee. Both Des Moines newspapers wrote extensive eulogies of his campaign. The *Keokuk Constitution* aptly assessed Bovee's effectiveness: "The pressure was too heavy upon some of those who had been voting nay heretofore, and they 'slopped over'. Mr. Bovee, who has been lecturing and working in season and out of season for this result, was astonished as much as any one at his complete success. He had no full conception of the facility with which an Iowa legislator can change his vote on an important measure."[19]

The change in votes on abolition between the 1870 and 1872 legislatures had been dramatic. In the House, the reformers had increased their share of the vote from forty-five percent in 1870 to seventy-two percent in 1872; similarly, in the Senate, their numbers had risen from thirty-nine percent to sixty-nine percent. Of the eleven senators who had voted to retain in 1870 and were re-elected, four switched sides in 1872 and voted to abolish. The remarkable shift in votes during the course of the 1872 legislative session itself underscored Bovee's extraordinary influence—no less than eight of the twenty-five senators who voted to retain capital punishment on April 11 changed sides just nine days later.

Graph that shows the fluctuating votes against the death penalty in the Iowa legislature, 1851-1878.

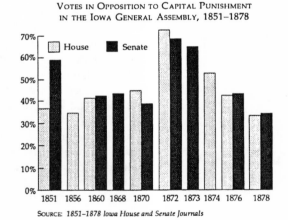

VOTES IN OPPOSITION TO CAPITAL PUNISHMENT
IN THE IOWA GENERAL ASSEMBLY, 1851–1878

SOURCE: *1851–1878 Iowa House and Senate Journals*

The abolition of the death penalty by Iowa in 1872 was sui generis. No other state had abolished capital punishment since 1853. There is no evidence that Iowa voters in general made their views known to the legislators or played any part in the abolition of the death penalty. A unique combination of a legislature confronted by the awesome decision of whether George Stanley should live or die, an abolitionist governor, an anti-gallows press campaign, the petitions of Quakers, the pleas of Stanley's Catholic priests, and—above all—Marvin Bovee's remarkable crusade, achieved the abolition of the death penalty in Iowa.

It would last for only six years.

The General Assembly sat in adjourned session in 1873 to revise the Code of Iowa. When the Senate considered the penalty for murder, Senator McCoid introduced an amendment to restore capital punishment, declaring that abolition had opened the floodgates of crime. Senator Larrabee concurred that murders were increasing. Although the restoration amendment was defeated by twenty-four votes to thirteen, three senators who had voted for abolition in 1872 now changed sides. The trend toward restoration continued in 1874, when the new House voted to instruct the Judiciary Committee to report a bill to reinstate the death penalty. The resolution's defeat, by a vote of forty-six to forty-one, was a narrow escape for the anti-gallows forces.

After a dramatic lynching in Des Moines in December 1874, however, opinion swung decisively in favor of restoration. In June, a murdered man had been found outside a brothel in Des Moines. Newspapers vividly reported the three-week long trial of bartender Charles Howard. The trial caused tremendous excitement, not least because there had been six murders in Des Moines in the previous four years. Several were unsolved, and Howard was the first person charged to be tried. While the jury deliberated for four days, the *Leader*—in a thinly veiled article—advocated lynching. The juror who held out for acquittal received a death threat.

Leaders of the Des Moines bar advised presiding Judge Hugh Maxwell to dismiss the jury. Instead, he ordered them to reach a verdict. The jury convicted Howard of murder in the second degree. Judge Maxwell then passed sentence on Howard in a thronged courtroom. Calling him "a fiend" and lynch mobs "our best citizens," he declared that Howard was "guilty of murder in the first degree, and ought to be punished accordingly." After proclaiming "most firmly that capital punishment ought to be sustained," Judge Maxwell sentenced Howard to life imprisonment.[20] That night a hundred masked men stormed the Des Moines jail and hanged Howard from a lamppost in the courthouse yard.

Newspapers across the state overwhelmingly blamed the lynching on abolition, reasoning that Howard should have been legally hanged. According to the *Keokuk Constitution*, the lynching was "the natural result of the abolishment of hanging by law by the damphool radicals."[21] There were numerous calls for restoration. The *Warren County Record* commented, "it is hard to find a man or woman in [Des Moines] that would not vote for capital punishment."[22]

A few newspapers continued to support abolition. The *Dubuque Times*—recalling that there was just as much lynching when capital punishment was the law—placed much of the blame for the lynching on Judge Maxwell's speech.

Howard's lynching crystallized Iowa opinion in favor of restoration of the death penalty. There was a terrible irony in this. As the anti-gallows *Davenport Gazette* pointed out, Howard had been convicted of second degree murder and so would not have hanged under the old law anyway. Furthermore, many people thought Howard innocent. Even the prosecutor (who was to become an Iowa Supreme Court judge) later said: "I did not believe then, and do not believe now, that [Howard] was guilty."[23]

A few days after Howard's death, the newspapers carried an incorrect report of another lynching, and the public came to believe in the myth that a plague of lynchings had struck the state. After a second bona fide lynching in Ottumwa in June 1875, the local press called for restoration of capital punishment.[24]

The failure of financier Jay Cooke in September 1873 triggered a national depression and a subsequent crime wave. In Iowa, murder, rape, and crime in general soared. The climate for restoration was favorable.

In early 1876, bills to restore capital punishment were introduced in both houses. The *Register*, which itself had remained abolitionist, reported: "The sentiment of the press is strongly and overwhelmingly in favor of the restoration of the old law. We only know some dozen papers which oppose it, and undoubtedly public sentiment is largely in favor of it."[25]

Even the *Dubuque Times* and *Davenport Gazette* had moved into the gallows lobby since the Howard lynching. The *Times* did so because "more murders have been committed in Iowa since the repeal of the death penalty than had occurred in a dozen years theretofore."[26] The *Gazette* observed that Iowans had never wanted abolition. "Then came a series of murders, and of lynch-law executions such as had never before disgraced the State, and the existing demand followed."[27]

Petitions on both sides flooded into the legislature, while reports of lurid crimes continued. In the House, the anti-gallows legislators argued familiar propositions: the reluctance of juries to convict when the penalty was death; life imprisonment as a sufficient deterrent; the risk of executing the innocent; and the teachings of Christianity. If the public had the same responsibility as the General Assembly, "they who favor the reenactment of the death penalty would pause and reflect."[28] Crime had decreased after the reform in states that had abolished capital punishment. Moreover, murder had increased in hanging states just as much as in Iowa.

On the restorationist side, speaker after speaker referred to the increase in crime in Iowa since abolition. Citing Howard's case, they urged that the state's abdication of its responsibilities had led to lynching. They emphasized that the people had never asked for abolition, and now the people demanded restoration. After a three-day debate, the restoration bill passed the House by fifty-five votes to forty-two.

The real drama came in the Senate. Dubuque Senator Dennis N. Cooley introduced the restoration bill, arguing that "there was a vast increase of crime ... that the present law was never the real sentiment of a majority of the state." Moreover, "abolishment has had the effect to increase mob law."[29]

Quaker Senator Elias Jessup dominated the anti-gallows side of the debate. Calling the bill "a step backwards towards barbarism,"[30] he used statistics to show that, allowing for population change, convictions in Iowa for first degree murder had actually decreased in the four years since abolition compared with the four prior years.

On the third reading of the bill, the restorers won the vote, twenty-five to twenty. They claimed that the bill therefore passed because they had obtained a majority of the forty-nine sitting senators (one member having just resigned). However, the president of the Senate ruled that the constitution required twenty-six votes for passage—a majority of those elected. Thus, by a hair's breadth, the restoration bill failed. But the crime wave and lynching had transformed opinion in the four years since abolition. In the House, the pro-hanging share of the vote had risen from twenty-eight percent in 1872 to fifty-seven percent in 1876; in the Senate from thirty-one percent to fifty-six percent. It was particularly telling that of the six senators who had voted to abolish in 1872 and who voted again in 1876, four changed sides and supported restoration.

	Murder					
	First Degree	Second Degree	Unclassified*	Total Murders	Rape	Total Convictions
1868	1	2	0	3	2	421
1869	0	3	0	3	2	439
1870	3	1	0	4	0	537
1871	0	3	1*	4	1	739
1872	0	1	2	3	1	616
1873	0	0	7	7	0	896
1874	0	1	1*	2	1	1,330
1875	1	10	4	15	8	1,317
1876	1	5	5	11	6	1,568
1877	3	11	0	14	2	1,672

Table that shows the soaring number of criminal convictions in Iowa that contributed to the restoration of the death penalty in 1878.

SOURCE: *Report of the Secretary of State in Relation to the Criminal Returns of the State of Iowa for the Years 1876 and 1877*, 157–58.

* NOTE: Some counties reported murder convictions without classifying them. For example, the one unclassified murder in 1871 was the conviction of George Stanley, a murder in the first degree; the one unclassified murder in 1874 was the conviction of Charles Howard, a murder in the second degree.

The crime statistics continued to rise. First degree murders increased from one in 1871 (Stanley's) to three in 1877, and second degree murders increased from three to eleven. Total criminal convictions more than doubled, from 739 in 1871 to 1,672 in 1877. Then, in November 1877, the third lynching since abolition took place. An attempted robbery in Warren County resulted in the shooting of a young woman, who identified a man named Reuben Proctor as one of her assailants. After Proctor was arrested, forty armed men overpowered his guards and hanged him from a scale beam.

A chorus of newspapers called for restoration. The *Webster County Gazette* said: "Let our next Legislature consider this matter in the light of experience, and the rapid increase of crime in our State, and restore the death penalty."[31]

The change in opinion since abolition was vividly demonstrated by the *Iowa State Register*. Edited since 1870 by James S. "Ret" Clarkson, who had made it into the state's dominant newspaper, the *Register* had played a large part in abolition. But an editorial in November 1877 announced: "[T]here is a rising tide in this State in favor of the restoration of the death penalty .... " The article reported that capital punishment had been an election issue in several districts where pro-death penalty candidates recently had been elected. The editorial concluded: "As to the murderer, if he is guilty, and absolutely known to be, we would say kill him, and the sooner the better."[32]

In 1878, the Senate debated a bill that would restore the death penalty for first degree murder but postpone execution for a year. The event attracted large crowds to Des Moines, and capital punishment was discussed all over the city. Representatives and spectators filled the gallery as fifteen senators engaged in an emotional three-day debate.

Senator McCoid argued that the exceptional heinousness of murder called for the death penalty. After appeal, a murderer's case "is one of unquestioned conclusive guilt. ... It is the high duty of government ... to administer punishment equal to the crime." He concluded that the death penalty "is founded upon the plainly expressed will of God."[33] Senator Larrabee and other death penalty supporters emphasized the great increase in crime and lynching since abolition. A family tragedy had caused Senator James M. Shelley to cast aside his Quaker upbringing. "He had ... lost a married niece, the mother of two lovely children, and the little ones themselves were killed with her, and the murderer had never been adequately punished."[34]

On the reformers' side, Senator William A. Foster—an outstanding defense lawyer—emphasized the risk of executing the innocent. Senator John S. Woolson said the death penalty violated the constitutional provision forbidding cruel and unusual punishment. Senator Joshua Miller supported abolition "from a personal knowledge, having been a shooter himself and tried for the offense."[35] Senator John Rumple asked: "Did not Christ abrogate the death penalty in his Sermon on the Mount?"[36]

But the author of the bill, Senator Samuel D. Nichols of Guthrie County, insisted that "the people of the state demand that something should be done, because crime is on the increase."[37] Heeding that demand, the Senate passed the restoration bill on its third reading, by twenty-eight votes to nineteen.

The House considered a separate restoration bill that gave the jury the option of deciding on hanging or life imprisonment. In a half-day debate, Representative Edward Taylor argued that mob law did not result from abolition. Twenty years earlier—when there was capital punishment—there had been many lynchings. Hard times, not abolition, was the cause of the current crime wave. Further, there had been six first degree murder convictions in Iowa in the six years before abolition, and only five in the six years since. Taylor was supported by Representative Henry Rickel, who mourned: "There is something melancholy in the fact that ministers of our Christian churches are placing their printed sermons on our desks, in which a clamorous appeal is made for blood!"[38]

Three restorers spoke briefly, once again emphasizing the Old Testament arguments, the deterrent effect of the death penalty, and the increase in crime. Representative Moses Bloom referred graphically to incidents of rape and murder, urging legislators to "[l]et all the wicked and depraved men in the State know that there is a law ... that will require their own lives as a penalty for the commission of murder."[39]

The vote in the House on the third reading was an overwhelming sixty-one to thirty-two to restore capital punishment. This bill reached the Senate on the final day of the session. The Senate passed the House bill by an equally crushing majority of thirty to sixteen. Thus, Iowa became the first American state and the first jurisdiction in the English-speaking world to have abolished and subsequently restored the death penalty.

Nothing highlights the change of attitudes since 1872 more than the *Register*'s reaction to the news. In 1872 that newspaper had greeted abolition joyfully, proclaiming: "The Register's arm and ax were early raised for the chopping down of the Gibbet in Iowa, and our work has been a labor of love. ... [We are] confident we have been in the Right, and that Time will so approve it."[40] On restoration, the *Register* said: "Now when a man commits murder in Iowa the jury trying him can hang him if he deserves it, or send him to the penitentiary for life, as they choose. ... Under this law the veriest villain can get his just deserts."[41]

Lynchings, murders, and public opinion were mainly responsible for bringing capital punishment back to Iowa. The lynching of Howard gave maximum publicity to the belief that, if the state would not hang murderers, mobs would. Proctor's lynching in late 1877 kept mob "justice" in the forefront of legislators' minds. Also, incidents of murder increased dramatically during the six years without the gallows. Legislators and most of the press attributed this increase to the abolition of capital punishment. In 1877, voters actually elected some legislators committed to bringing back the death penalty. The cumulative result in 1878 was the massive reversal of the 1872 vote and the restoration of capital punishment, which was to remain until Iowa re-abolished the death penalty in 1965.

The reasons underlying the decisions to abolish the death penalty in 1872 and to restore it six years later were very different. The 1878 legislature had theorized that capital punishment would deter murder and prevent lynching, and hence voted to restore it.

But the 1872 legislature had considered more than just a theoretical argument—it had had to decide whether George Stanley should hang. As a leading member of the House wrote four days before the scheduled execution: "This brings home to every legislator the responsibility of saying whether a fellow being shall be killed by the State."[42] Faced with the actual decision of whether a man should live or die, the legislature voted overwhelmingly that he should live.

*T*he debate over the death penalty was driven, in part, by the public's concern about crime and lawlessness. Lynchings and incidents of frontier violence continued into the last half of the nineteenth century. On July 21, 1873, a train was derailed and robbed west of Adair, Iowa; the bandits escaped with about $3,000. When the Des Moines newspaper reported the robbery the following morning, it wasn't yet known that the robbers were none other than the notorious Jesse James and his gang.

Jesse James and his gang robbed a train near Adair, Iowa, in July 1873.

The C., R. I. & P. R. R. train, due here [Des Moines] from the west last night at 10:30 o'clock, did not arrive on time, and about 11 o'clock the news spread over the city that it had been attacked, ditched and sacked by a masked gang of robbers, half-way between Anita and Adair, 64 miles west of Des Moines. The first dispatch received was about 10-1/2 o'clock, from Superintendent Royce, (who fortunately happened to be on the train) sent from Casey:

Casey, July 21.

Four miles west of Adair train No. 2 was ditched by robbers, and the express safe gone through. There was some kind of an obstruction put on the track on a sharp curve, and as Rafferty, the engineer, saw it, they shot him dead from the bank. The engine is on her side in the ditch, and one of the baggage cars is up on the bank. The other upset on the side. The passenger coaches are nearly all right. The track is some torn up. Several persons on the train are slightly hurt; don't think any of them are dangerously injured. There was at least seven of the robbers, all masked, and they went off south on horseback.

    H. F. R.

    . . . .

John Rafferty, the murdered engineer was a resident of East Des Moines. He was aged about 35; was married, and his wife and three children had the dreadful news sent them at midnight last night. His comrades speak of the dead man as a man of bravery and noble heart.

No other person besides the engineer was killed. Comparatively few of the passengers are injured; none, it is reported, seriously. ...

The robbers took two thousand dollars in money from the express safe. This was all they took. It is probable they thought there was bullion on the train. They cut open the mail sacks, but took none of the letters.

At 1-1/2 o'clock all the cars had been got back on the track, except one baggage car and the locomotive.

All accounts agree that the number of the robbers was seven or eight. They were closely masked, and kept their masks firmly clear through.

[*Des Moines*] *Iowa Daily State Register*, July 22, 1873.

A *nother crime that bestirred the residents of western Iowa and inflamed public passion occurred in Le Mars, Iowa, where a sizable English settlement—replete with fox hunting and country estates—grew up in the late 1870s and 1880s. A prominent Le Mars doctor was accused of drugging his fiancée and indecently assaulting her. While awaiting an appeal from his conviction, the doctor was shot by one of the prosecuting attorneys outside of a saloon called the "House of Lords" (nearby were the*

"House of Commons" and "Windsor Castle"). The doctor recovered from his wound; charges against the prosecuting attorney were dropped. The lurid details of these crimes were avidly reported by local newspapers.

D r. Porter, a well known doctor of physic at LeMars, was arrested in that place last Tuesday on a charge of committing a rape on the person of Miss Lina Ottaway. The young lady says that she was out riding with Porter one day last May and he persuaded her to stop at his office when he forced her to drink a glass of wine which she alleges was drugged, as it made her unconscious. When she recovered her senses she found out the terrible truth, but by threats and promises of marriage he kept her quiet for a time. He had just got back from Colorado and intended to return there again, so the young lady thought she would bring him to time or to sorrow, and had him arrested. He has been released, as the story goes, on only $250 bail, which of course will not hold him if there is any danger of being convicted on trial.

Sioux City Tribune, July 3, 1879.

The preliminary examination of Dr. Porter, of LeMars, charged with raping Miss Ottaway, began Wednesday, the 9th, and was terminated last Monday. The excitement continued unabated to the end. ...

Porter was put on the stand and admitted the improper intercourse but denied that it was against the girl's will, and denied also that she drank any wine at all.

There is little doubt from the girl's testimony and the circumstances that Porter at least deliberately planned her ruin. Whether he did it by force, so as to make the act a rape in the eyes of the law, is quite another question; and there are some circumstances which make it seem quite doubtful that he did. The letter she wrote to him after the occurrence tends to give such an impression, though coming from a weak and infatuated girl, as she evidently was, it is not absolutely incompatible with the charge of rape. But however this question may be decided by the courts, the public sense of justice and morality will recognize no difference or degree in the enormity of the crime whether it was accomplished by brute force alone or by brutal cunning alone.

The girl was a mere baby so far as experience and knowledge of the world are concerned, and Porter was ripe in experience and, according to common report, ripe in the most atrocious species of villainy.

Sioux City Tribune, July 17, 1879.

At LeMars Sunday evening, about 6 o'clock, Maj. C. J. C. Ball [a prosecuting attorney] shot Dr. Wm. B. Porter. The ball entered the neck about an inch and a half below the ear on the right side and is supposed to have lodged in the bones of the neck on the opposite side. From the peculiar nature of the wound the physicians had not dared to probe for the ball at last accounts. The wound bled very little, and it is remarkable that the jugular vein was not severed, as the ball entered the neck directly beneath the lobe of the ear. ... [Porter] suffers great pain, and at first it was thought the wound would be fatal, but a dispatch from LeMars last evening, says the wound is not considered dangerous, and that Porter was in as good condition as could possibly be hoped for under the circumstances.

Immediately after the shooting Ball went and gave himself up to the officers, but was allowed his liberty under the charge of the sheriff, and yesterday in company with that officer came to this city and attended Barnum's show. When he fell Porter laid on the sidewalk several minutes before persons came and carried him into his office. There are conflicting reports about the circumstances which led to the shooting. Ball says that as he was passing along the street Porter came out of an alley which runs by a saloon called the House of Lords, and pointing at Ball said, "There's the son of a bitch." Ball told him to stop that sort of talk, when Porter repeated the offensive remark, and at the same time put his hand to his hip pocket as if to draw a pistol, when Ball drew his revolver and fired with the result stated above. On the other hand, Porter says he had just come in from the country; that he met Ball on the street, and that, just as they passed each other Ball made some remark which he did not fully understand, and that as he turned to ask him what he said, that Ball fired. Porter says he was not armed and we hear this corroborated by the men who carried him up-stairs and disrobed

him, they finding no weapon upon him, even so much as a pocket knife.

. . . .

There had been bad blood between the two men for some time. It will be remembered by those who were readers of THE JOURNAL about a year ago that Dr. Porter was defendant in the highly sensational case at LeMars, in which he was charged by a Miss Ottaway, a school teacher, with having committed a rape upon her person after having first drugged her. The affair caused intense excitement at the time, and public sentiment ran so strong against Porter that he narrowly escaped being lynched. When the case came to trial Maj. Ball assisted the state's attorney in the prosecution of the case, and was very active in his efforts to convict Porter. Ever since then the two men have felt bitterly toward each other, and a personal encounter at some time was not wholly unexpected.

Sioux City Journal, July 13, 1880.

E*ven as problems of crime and punishment occupied public thought, the outward symbols of law and government continued their growth in Iowa. In 1868, legislators voted to authorize plans for a permanent state capitol building in Des Moines, a long and controversial process that finally gave Iowans their gold-domed state capitol in the year 1884.*

Des Moines became the site for another important symbol of law when, in May 1874, Iowa lawyers met at the Polk County courthouse to organize the Iowa State Bar Association. The Iowa Association is believed to be the first such organization in the country to maintain its existence for a lengthy duration. (The association evidently ceased meeting after 1881, to be resumed in 1895.)

Excerpts from the early proceedings of the Iowa State Bar Association show that the legal profession was growing in strength and coherence in the post-Civil War years—and that it now sought as an organized entity to address such important issues as attorney discipline and legal fees.

PROCEEDINGS OF THE ORGANIZATION MEETING OF THE IOWA STATE BAR ASSOCIATION

At eleven o'clock yesterday, (May 27, 1874) Col. C. H. Gatch, of Des Moines, called the legal gentlemen assembled in the County Court House to order, for the purpose of organizing a State Society, reading the call for the meeting, and nominating Judge James Grant, of Davenport, for temporary chairman. On assuming the chair Judge Grant spoke briefly on the purpose of the meeting, urging greater social intercourse between the members of the profession.

. . . .

AFTERNOON SESSION

Judge Hammond, from the Committee on Constitution and By-laws, presented their report, the constitution being adopted.

CONSTITUTION

ARTICLE I. This association shall be styled the IOWA STATE BAR ASSOCIATION, and its objects shall be to promote mutual acquaintance and harmony among the members of the Iowa Bar; to maintain a high standard of professional integrity, honor, and courtesy among them; to encourage a thorough and liberal legal education; to give expression to the deliberate and well-considered opinion of the legal profession upon all matters wherein its members are properly expected to act as a body; and to assist in the improvement of the laws and the better administration of justice to all classes of society, without distinction.

. . . .

ART. VIII. The admission fee shall be three dollars for members of the bar admitted more than five years before they join the society, and two dollars for members who join the society within five years after their first admission to the bar,—said fee to be paid in all cases before or at the time of signing the constitution.

. . . .

ART. XVI. Whenever five or more members of this association actually engaged in the practice of law, reside in the same county, they may form a county association, auxiliary to this body, and having the same objects, with such constitution and by-laws as they may adopt, not inconsistent with those of the state association.

PROCEEDINGS, SESSION 1876

Prof. Hammond, president of the association, called the meeting to order.

(In regard to the question of disbarment) Mr. Cook, of Newton, thought there should be something of this kind done. We have had two men in our profession in our town who have been sent to the penitentiary, and others that ought to be there. One man has literally stolen $2,000 from his clients, who reposed confidence in him because he was regularly admitted to practice, yet he cannot be disbarred.

Mr. McHenry thought there were other evils, especially in the judges. He complained of the post office Supreme Court where you sent your printed argument by mail and receive a postal card saying "you're beat".

PROCEEDINGS, SESSION 1877

The association then entered upon the discussion of two questions proposed by the Executive Council; the first of which was:

Shall the association as a body petition the next General Assembly to enact a reasonable fee-bill, or system of costs, to be taxed against the losing party in civil actions?

. . . .

Judge C. C. Nourse opposed the proposition. He said brains were worth more than muscle, and as the average legislator could not be made to understand that fact, he thought it unwise and unsafe to allow them to fix a fee-bill for the poor, honest, overworked lawyer. He preferred to make his own contracts for himself and collect his own fees.

Judge William Phillips thought some wise, judicious legislation on this subject desirable, particularly if it would tend to equalize the burdens of litigants and dispense with "cut-throat" contracts about fees, etc.

Mr. J. D. Campbell, of Davenport, the city famous for its modesty, thought it would be immodest and out of taste for lawyers to ask the legislature to help them get their fees out of clients.

Mr. J. M. St. John, of Des Moines, moved to adopt the proposition for the purpose of testing the sense of the meeting.

Mr. Seward Smith, of Des Moines, moved to postpone the subject indefinitely, which motion carried.

Proceedings of the Early Iowa State Bar Association Held at Des Moines, Iowa 1874-1881 (Des Moines: Iowa State Bar Assoc., 1912), pp. 12, 14-16, 36, 41-42.

*T**he formal organization of lawyers into the Iowa State Bar Association was a tribute to the advances in legal education and training made during the previous decade. Iowa's first law school—the oldest law school in continuous operation west of the Mississippi River—traces its roots to the year 1865. Today considered one of the top twenty law schools in America, the University of Iowa College of Law began in the post–Civil War years with the vision of Judge George G. Wright and a class of two law students.*

Judge George G. Wright, Iowa Supreme Court judge and founder of Iowa's first law school. (Courtesy, University of Iowa College of Law)

Judge Wright's Vision: The Founding of Iowa's First Law School

WHEN IOWA SUPREME COURT JUDGE George G. Wright arrived in Iowa City one memorable day in the late 1800s to lecture at the State University's law school, he was greeted at the railroad station by his entire class lined up in a double column on either side of the train platform. As Wright stepped down from his Des Moines train and walked through this corridor of young men, they suddenly broke forth in a yell:

Rah! Rah! Rah!
Law! Law! Law!
Who's All Right?
George G. Wright! George G. Wright!
Judge Wright![1]

When the judge reached the foot of the column, the young men, still yelling, rushed forward and lifted him into a closed vehicle from which the horses had been removed. The students carried their professor through the muddy streets of Iowa City to the St. James Hotel, yelling all the way. Years later, Wright's son, George G. Wright, Jr., said his father told the story with tears in his eyes, and always regarded the episode as one of the most gratifying in a career that included six years as a United States senator and fifteen years as a judge of the Iowa Supreme Court, seven of those as chief justice.

So began another day of classes in the early life of the State University of Iowa law department. After a year of study, the students in Wright's class would receive their Bachelor of Law degrees and be eligible for admission to the Iowa Bar—a far cry from the three years of preparation required of today's law students, but a considerable advance over the practice existing in 1865.

Before Wright opened his school, the only way to "learn law" in Iowa was to serve as an apprentice in the office of a practicing attorney. This system left much to be desired—a good lawyer often was too busy to instruct a student; a bad lawyer was a poor teacher. To correct this problem, in June 1865 a committee of the judges of the Iowa Supreme Court, including Wright, enthusiastically recommended to the State University of Iowa that the legislature establish a university law department.

While waiting for the university and the legislature to act on the proposal, Wright was confronted with the immediate problem of his eldest son, Thomas. Thomas had graduated from the state university in 1863 and had gone straight to the Civil War, during which he was captured and held in the Andersonville prison camp. When he returned to Iowa at the end of the war, Thomas Wright was determined to study law properly—not just pick up what he could learn in a lawyer's office.

So, in November 1865, with two pupils—Thomas Wright and George Peet (who did not graduate)—Judge Wright began teaching in his Des Moines office. Within a few weeks, the class had grown to include twelve young men, who assembled in Wright's office for two hours, three evenings a week. The young scholars listened to lectures from Wright and Supreme Court Judge Chester C. Cole, and earnestly discussed their reading assignments. These discussions probably waxed on far into the night. One of Wright's Des Moines students observed: "In class, he was always intensely earnest and not infrequently became so absorbed in the recitations that the hour sometimes lengthened indefinitely, and himself absorbed in the subject his class was none the less so."[2]

As Wright's first class continued their studies, the question of starting a law school at the state university came before the Iowa legislature. The Senate approved it by a huge majority, but, despite petitions from members of the bar throughout the state, the bill got blocked in a House of Representatives committee.

On May 24, 1866, a disappointed Judge Wright placed an advertisement in the [Des Moines] *Daily Iowa State Register* announcing that he and Cole had opened their own "Iowa Law School." The advertisement stated that the two judges had intended only a temporary school, but in view of the legislature's failure to establish a law department at the state university, they had decided to make it permanent. For $80, students could enroll in a one-year course consisting of "the various and usual branches of the Common and a thorough course of instruction on Commercial and Constitutional Law—as also Equity Jurisprudence, Code Pleading and Practice."

New Advertisements.

IOWA LAW SCHOOL.

To meet a want long felt in the State, the undersigned have opened a School in the City of Des Moines for the purpose of instructing those desirous of pursuing the Law as a study.

To accommodate a few young men we commenced these instructions in November last. Our hope and expectation were that the General Assembly just adjourned, would make some provison for a *Law Department in the State University*. Influenced by this thought we preferred to postpone any permanent arrangements until this question was determined. The measure failed, and we have therefore concluded to extend our labor. We are aware that many young men every year attend schools in other States, for want of facilities at home; and that having them they would prefer to remain here, thus avoiding expense, and at the same time have better opportunities of providing themselves with our own system of Pleading and Practice. This latter consideration every lawyer knows is of great importance to a student designing to establish himself in this State.

The school year will begin on the first Monday in January, and close on the first Monday in December.—The first term of each year will close on the third Monday in June. There will be vacations in April and October. Students will be received at any time, but it is better they should enter at the commencement of the term.

Our design is to afford a course of instruction to those who intend to practice the law as a profession. But we will, if desired, give instruction in *Commercial Jurisprudence* to those who design to devote themselves to *mercantile pursuits*.

The course will embrace the various and usual branches of the Common and a thorough course of Instruction on Commercial and Constitutional Law,—as also Equity Jurisprudence, Code Pleading and Practice. The students will be required to prepare and read synoptical reviews of the text books they study, and also attend to cases in moot court.

The tuition will be eighty dollars for the year, or fifty dollars for half or any smaller fraction thereof, in each case to be paid by the middle of the term; but under special circumstances further time may be arranged for.

At this place we have large and well selected public and private Law Libraries. The State and Federal Courts meet here also, and are in session from five to six months in each year. Students will thus have advantages, not surpassed certainly, by any other point in the State.

Unpretending in our efforts and promises, our hope is to contribute somewhat in advancing the student in his studies, and at the same time benefit ourselves by the undertaking. Any effort on the part of the Bar or our other friends throughout the State, in bringing this matter to the attention of the people, will be duly appreciated. Any further information we will give cheerfully and promptly, by letter if desired.

G. G. WRIGHT.
C. C. COLE.

May 15, 1866.—may24—dtf.

First advertisement for the "Iowa Law School" in Des Moines. (*[Des Moines] Daily Iowa State Register,* May 24, 1866)

An additional feature of special interest was that students would be required to "attend to cases in moot court"; in other words, they would have to argue mock cases among themselves.

The judges' prospectus ended with humility: "Unpretending in our efforts and promises, our hope is to contribute somewhat in advancing the student in his studies, and at the same time benefit ourselves by the undertaking." Thus, improbably, the law school was launched as a tiny commercial venture in Des Moines.

The law school was formally incorporated at the end of November 1866, when the first group of students completed their course of study. The commencement exercise was held on December 4. As families and friends looked on, eleven young men filed into the courthouse to receive their degrees and join the Iowa State Bar, having previously been examined by a committee designated by the Iowa Supreme Court.

Before the degrees were conferred, the graduates listened patiently to five of their fellows address the group. Thomas Wright's presentation swayed at least one female member of the audience, who wrote in her diary: "The next speaker, T.S. Wright—'Defense of the Guilty' … had a splendid voice. This young man is a son of Judge G.G. Wright. … He is a young man with a character—I like his looks."[3] Lacking the diarist's spirit of romance, the *Register* complained about "the inexcusable length of most of the orations," some of which "extended to thirty minutes. …"[4]

Finally, the speeches over, the young lawyers filed solemnly forward to take the State Bar oath and receive their Bachelor of Law degrees from Chief Justice

The law school graduation class, 1866. Pictured in the front row, left, is Thomas Wright, the son of Judge George G. Wright. (Courtesy, University of Iowa College of Law)

Ralph P. Lowe. Then the new barristers were off to Schaeffer's Restaurant, where an oyster supper awaited them.

Shortly before that first commencement, Professor William G. Hammond, an Anamosa attorney, joined the law school. Hammond would play the greatest part in shaping the school's future when it moved to the State University of Iowa. But first, two more classes would graduate and take their oaths in Des Moines.

In early 1868, the forceful Representative John Irish of Iowa City succeeded in persuading the legislature to appropriate funds to establish a law department at the university. After a great deal of negotiation, Wright's law school merged with the university's and moved to Iowa City on September 17, 1868. Graduates of the Des Moines law school were regarded as graduates of the university law department. Thus, the University of Iowa College of Law can claim an unbroken existence since 1865, making it the oldest law school in continuous operation west of the Mississippi.

Professor Hammond became chancellor of the law school and took up residence in Iowa City. Wright and Cole remained in Des Moines as Supreme Court judges and served as visiting professors. It fell to Wright to open the lectures in Iowa City, while Hammond was away in Chicago buying books for the law library. The [*Iowa City*] *State Democratic Press* reported: "The opening course of lectures before this Department by Judge Wright of the Supreme Court, is spoken of in terms of highest praise by all who were fortunate enough to hear them."[5]

The other law school faculty appear to have been equally gifted. Wright himself referred to Hammond as possessing "almost unequalled aptitude as a lecturer and teacher,"[6] and Cole received equally high praise from one of his former students: "Our instruction was Socratic and so far as I know, Socrates and Judge Cole are the only teachers of note who always taught by asking questions."[7]

Instructors met their students in the Old Capitol in what had been the assembly chamber. The largest room was a lecture and recitation room, one room was set aside for the law faculty, and a third room was a law library. This last was of special interest to Chancellor Hammond, who loaned his large personal library for the use of his students, and at his own expense donated "all the American law periodicals."[8] He spent much of his time in his thirteen years as chancellor trying to obtain money to develop the library and other law school facilities.

As the eighteen members of the first Iowa City law class neared graduation in June 1869, the *University Reporter*, a campus newspaper, gave their social profile: "The oldest member of the graduating class of the Law Department is thirty; youngest twenty; members of churches seven; Republicans fifteen; Democrats three; the number that use tobacco three; whisky three; beer eight; married three; engaged six; that want to be engaged nine; served in army twelve; held commissions as officers three; non-commissioned and privates nine; residents of Iowa sixteen; of Mo. two."[9]

The numbers of students enrolled in the law classes grew rapidly. From two students in Wright's Des Moines office in 1865 the numbers rose to thirty-four in 1870, and 101 in 1875. The fame of the law school spread, and in 1875 twenty of the students were from other states.

Professor William G. Hammond became chancellor of the law school when it moved to Iowa City in 1868. (Courtesy, University of Iowa College of Law)

The influx of new students also created the need for new faculty. A second resident faculty position was added in 1873, and several other Iowa judges and attorneys became part-time lecturers. L.W. Ross joined the law school as a third resident professor in 1880 and succeeded Hammond as chancellor in 1881.

The law school lost a faculty member in 1875, when Judge Cole resigned his visiting professorship—largely over salary—and started another law school in Des Moines. Although there were angry exchanges between Chancellor Hammond and Cole, ultimately, the split would benefit Iowa—Cole's law school later became the Drake University Law School in Des Moines.

While the Iowa law school was the oldest professional department in the university, it soon was followed by the medical school in 1870. A rivalry existed between the two from the outset. According to the *University Reporter* in November 1875: "The Laws and Meds attempted a game of football, a week ago Saturday, on the University grounds. A large crowd was present to enjoy the fun, which opened quite auspiciously, but in the progress of the second innings, *a little misunderstanding* arose, and the Laws left the grounds, refusing, under the circumstances, to finish the game."[10]

The following month the law students gave up on football entirely. The *University Reporter* stated: "The Laws have indignantly repudiated foot-ball. They suddenly discovered—that is to say, just after the Academics beat them five successive innings—that kicking is not their forte. Their stronghold, they claim, lies in some other direction than chasing a poor inanimate ball over a vacant block, kicking it as frequently as possible, and receiving themselves between fifty and one hundred impressions of players' boots."[11]

If football was not the law school's strength, diversity was. In 1870, the Iowa legislature voted to allow blacks and women to practice law. By 1873, Hammond and his faculty were able to record: "Among those who have ... completed the course this year will be found for the first time the name of a lady, Miss Mary B. Hickey of Newton, Iowa. It is simple justice to say that Miss Hickey has been one of the best scholars in the class." Moreover, "her selection as one of the speakers at commencement is not a mere compliment to her sex, but a testimony to which her work in the class fully entitled her." And she was popular: "Her demeanor through the year (in a position which to a lady of less tact and good judgment might have been embarrassing) has been such as to win the highest esteem from the Faculty and her classmates."[12]

Two years later, the law school produced two more prominent female graduates. Iowa City resident Mary Humphrey Haddock became the first female attorney in the country admitted to practice in the United States circuit and district courts, while Annie Nowling Savery gained fame both as a suffragist and as the co-founder, with her husband, of Des Moines' Hotel Savery.

In 1878, Moung Edwin of Burmaha, India, came to Iowa. Edwin already had completed theological degrees in the United States and decided to complete the one-year law course at Iowa before returning to India to be a minister of religion. That same year, Alexander Clark, Jr., became the first African-American student at the law school and, according to the *University Reporter*, was the first black student to enter the State University in Iowa City. He was the son of Alexander Clark, Sr., a Muscatine businessman and Iowa's most distinguished black politician of the day.

Mary Beth Hickey was the first female graduate of the Iowa law school, receiving her degree in 1873. (Courtesy, University of Iowa College of Law)

Alexander Clark, Jr., was the first African-American to graduate from the Iowa law school, receiving his degree in 1879. (Courtesy, University of Iowa College of Law)

The year 1883 saw perhaps the most remarkable student yet to attend the Iowa law school. Four years after Alexander Clark, Jr., graduated from Iowa, the chance remark by a white lawyer that he should study law and join the bar inspired Alexander Clark, Sr., to follow in his son's footsteps.

Clark, Sr., had settled in Muscatine in 1842 and subsequently opened a barber shop, which he ran until 1868. Careful investment in timberland and downtown property provided security for his family and eventually gave him the leisure to become active in Republican party politics. Clark was a "conductor" on the underground railroad that helped slaves reach freedom in the North, and after the Civil War he worked to secure equal benefits and pensions for black Union soldiers and equal access to public education for black children. (In 1868, Clark as "next friend" successfully brought suit to compel a Muscatine school to admit his daughter. The case became a landmark decision of the Iowa Supreme Court.)

Although in August 1883 Clark was fifty-six years old and a man of some means, he decided to go to law school—partly to fulfill his own ambition, and partly (he reportedly said) "as an example to young men of his own race."[13] His distin-

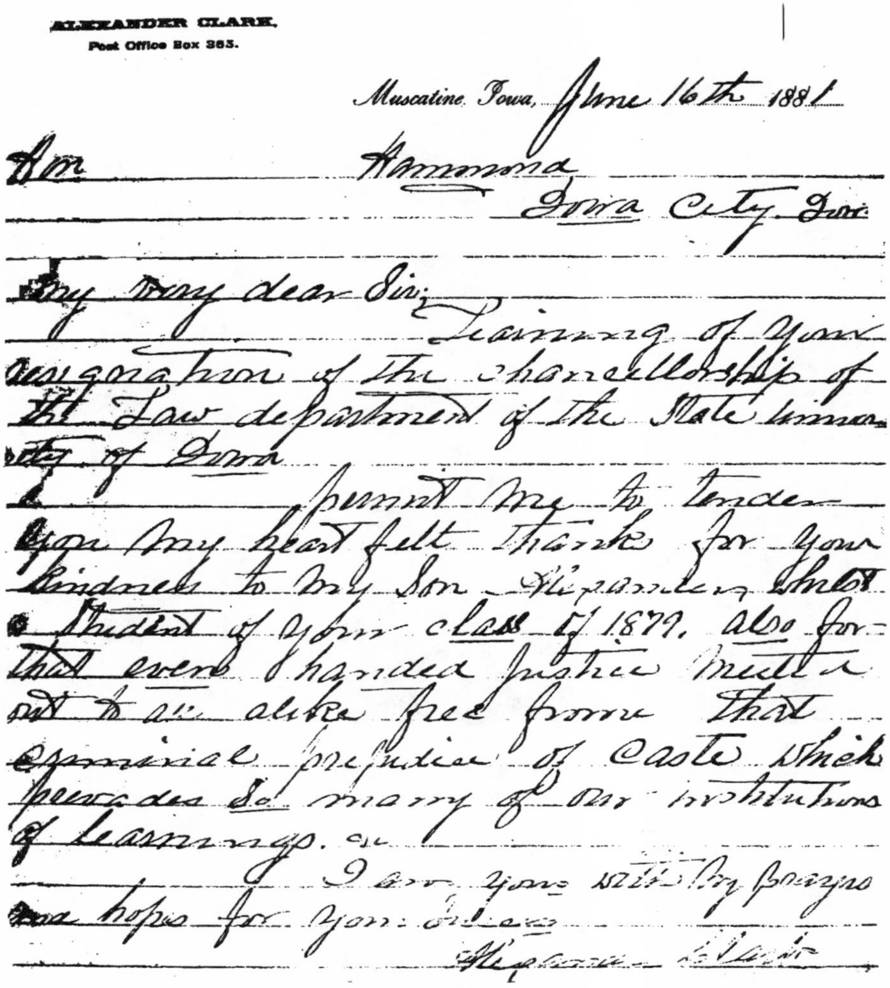

ALEXANDER CLARK.
Post Office Box 365.

[handwritten letter]

Muscatine, Iowa, June 16th 1881

Mr   Hammond
                    Iowa City, Iowa

My very dear Sir;
                    Learning of your
resignation of the chancellorship of
the Law department of the State University of Iowa

    permit me to tender
you my heart felt thanks for your
kindness to my son Alexander who was
a student of your class of 1879. Also for
that even handed justice meted
out to all alike free from that
sperminial prejudice of caste which
pervades so many of our institutions
of learnings. &c

        I am yours with my prayers
and hopes for you; &c.
                    Alexander Clark

A letter from Alexander Clark, Sr., to Chancellor Hammond in 1881 expressed his gratitude for his son's fine education in law. Clark Sr. himself entered law school in 1883
and received his degree the next year. (Courtesy, University of Iowa College of Law,
Special Collections, Hammond Papers)

guished career continued after his graduation from law school, when he became editor and publisher of a weekly Chicago newspaper and, in 1890, was appointed Min-
ister-Resident and Counsul-General to the Republic of Liberia.

Clark was immensely popular at law school. He was elected class treasurer on
the first day, and his speeches, writings, and activities generally were a subject for
comment throughout his law school career. His legendary powers as an orator spell-
bound his fellow students. As the new campus newspaper, the *Vidette-Reporter*,

said: "We can announce to Aleck's friends that he made a display of his oratorical abilities in a case in moot court the past week that captivated the members of the court by storm."[14]

When Alexander Clark, Sr., took his degree in June 1884, the University of Iowa law school had reached the end of its formative period. A full two-year course of study would be introduced the following year, and the student body had risen to 132 in 1883, making Iowa fourth in enrollment among the nation's forty-three law schools.

It was most fitting that the graduation speakers in 1884 included Judge Wright and Chancellor Hammond, the latter having returned to Iowa City from his new post as chancellor of the law school in St. Louis. Before leaving for Missouri in 1881, Hammond had worked continuously to persuade the legislature to require a two-year course of study before candidates were allowed to take the Iowa bar examination. Together, Wright and Hammond had steered the Iowa law school through its early history. Begun with a vision and two law students, the law school had become a large and distinguished institution—and a source of great pride to Iowa.

A decade after the founding of Iowa's first law school, a second law school opened its doors. The first became part of a state-sponsored university in Iowa City; the second was a private institution in Des Moines. The two schools were linked by the contribution of Iowa Supreme Court Judge Chester Cicero Cole, who had helped to establish the University of Iowa's first law department, and in 1875 founded a new law school at Des Moines. At first a department of Simpson College, in 1881 the school became affiliated with Drake University. Judge Cole gave an account of the reasons he decided to establish a competing law school in Iowa's state capital.

Iowa Supreme Court Judge Chester C. Cole was the founder of what would become Drake University Law School. (Courtesy, University of Iowa College of Law)

Without any purpose to disparage the University or Iowa City, let us look fairly at the causes [contributing to the desirability for a second law school].

Des Moines is the capital of the state; there, the Legislature convenes and the laws of the state are enacted; there the Supreme Court holds its principal sessions, occupying substantially the months of June and December; there, the United States Circuit and District courts are held, occupying nearly three months of the year, May and October, and a part of the months succeeding each; there, the District and Circuit Courts of the state are also held, occupying nearly eight months of the year; so that during the entire school year, one of the courts, and much of the time two of them, are in actual, open session and engaged in the trial of important causes. The opportunity for observation and the gaining of valuable information, not otherwise attainable, is as complete and entire as is possible. ... At Des Moines also, the Bar is large and the lawyers' offices are numerous which contain good law libraries, to which the students can have free access; and the books of the course can readily be obtained for use without money and for a trifling service which the student can profitably render. ... [T]he Iowa State Library which is said to be the largest and most complete Law Library west of the Alleghany mountains is open daily to the free use of the students. Other and numerous advantages connected with the location of a Law College at the capital, will readily occur to every one and need not be further mentioned in detail. At Iowa City none of these advantages are afforded—at most, there are only a few weeks' session each year of the Circuit and District Courts for the Eighth Judicial District of the State. ...

It is proper to state in concluding this article ... that The Iowa College of Law is not organized in any spirit of hostility or opposition to any other Law School in the state or elsewhere; but to supply a need which actually exists and has been felt and expressed by very many throughout the state, and which can not (for reasons, some of which have been stated) be met or supplied by the Law Department of the State University. Besides, there has been for the last two years and more a growing sentiment among the people, which has now apparently ripened into a settled conviction, that the people of the state ought not to, and shall not, further be taxed in order to afford a professional education to the few; and especially so, since they can obtain better advantages for such education elsewhere in the state, at a less cost to them and without any tax whatever upon the people or property of the state.

"The Iowa College of Law," *The Western Jurist* IX (August 1875): 451-53, 456.

The education of Iowa's youth was a continuing priority for lawmakers in the post-Civil War period. Local school boards and district superintendents were empowered to establish and enforce reasonable rules for school governance and student conduct. Occasionally, however, their actions were challenged before the state superintendent of public instruction or the courts. These cases give vivid glimpses of school life in the later part of the nineteenth century.

E. WATSON V. DISTRICT TOWNSHIP OF EXIRA
(Appeal from Audubon County)

Charges were preferred against E. Watson, a teacher in the schools of the district above named, for harsh and unreasonable punishment of a pupil; upon investigation the teacher was discharged; from this action of the board, he appealed to the county superintendent who reversed their action. The district appeals to the superintendent of public instruction.

From the evidence, it appears that the pupil, upon whom the punishment was inflicted, was a boy thirteen years of age, and that the offense was such that punishment was deserved. The instrument selected for inflicting punishment was a hickory stick, three-fourths of an inch in diameter at one end, and one-half inch at the other, and fifteen or eighteen inches long. The punishment was inflicted by striking upon the palm of the hand from eight to twelve strokes. It appears that the boy's hand was thereby disabled for some days.

... We consider the selection of such an instrument for the punishment of a pupil injudicious, unwarrantable, and dangerous, and that consequences might be fraught with the gravest results, and that such selection may serve in some degree, to indicate the animus of the teacher.
Reversed.
Alonzo Abernethy,
Superintendent of Public Instruction.
June 6, 1874.

MARY M. THOMPSON V. DISTRICT TOWNSHIP OF JASPER.
(Appeal from Adams County)

The board of directors discharged Miss Mary M.

Thompson for dereliction of duty as teacher in one of the public schools of the district. She appealed to the county superintendent, who reversed their decision; from this action, the board, through their president, John McDevon, appealed to the superintendent of public instruction. ...

The charges of dereliction were, want of promptness in commencing school in the morning, and an occasional refusal to hear the recitation of one or more of her pupils. For this dereliction there appear to have been some extenuating circumstances. Under the contract it was the sub-director's duty to have the fires built. The boy employed to do this work, often failed to have the school-house in comfortable condition at nine o'clock; the teacher usually made up lost time by teaching after four o'clock, and there is no evidence that the sub-director or board ever advised her with regard to the performance of her duties. ...

Affirmed.

Alonzo Abernethy,

Superintendent of Public Instruction.

May 8, 1876.

School Laws of Iowa, Edition of 1876 (Des Moines: State Printer, 1876), pp. 138-39, 164-65.

*L*ike education, railroad regulation was a growing concern for lawmakers as the Civil War receded in the public consciousness. Since railway building had begun in Iowa in the 1850s, the railroad industry had prospered, and rates within the state had soared. In 1874—upon the heels of the Panic of 1873—the Iowa legislature passed an act to set "reasonable maximum rates of charges" for freight and passenger trains. The act was popularly termed the "Granger Law," because of the Grange organization's efforts on behalf of farmers to achieve railroad regulation.

The Granger Law was opposed by those who feared it would deter railway building in Iowa, and a strong campaign in the press ensued for its repeal. On March 23, 1878—precisely four years after Governor Cyrus Carpenter had signed the act into law—a bill for its repeal was signed by Governor John Gear. The repealing legislation created a new railroad commission.

Ironically, before its repeal the Granger Law (and the state's power to regulate the railroads) had been upheld by the U.S. Supreme Court. The

Railroad rate regulation occupied the Iowa legislature in the 1870s, and was challenged in the courts by the powerful railroad industry. Shown here, a Rock Island train in Indianola, 1881.(Courtesy, State Historical Society of Iowa, Iowa City)

Court affirmed an 1875 decision of the Circuit Court for the District of Iowa in the case of Chicago, Burlington & Quincy Railroad Co. v. Attorney General. *The circuit court case was presided over by the eminent John F. Dillon, and the lawyer for the railroads was David Rorer, who had represented the former slave Ralph in Iowa's first reported territorial Supreme Court decision. Rorer gave a suitably impassioned plea—to no avail—against regulation of railroad rates.*

If a natural person has not the right to fix the price of his labor or services, this such person is not a free man—but is simply a slave. He may be made to serve for nothing, or for a price at which he will starve. Hence the free citizens of Iowa may fix their own price upon which they will labor for others; and railroad corporations being clothed with all the rights and powers of such citizens in that respect, may do the same. Inability to claim pay for services, or make contracts for, and to enjoy the price of one's own labor is prominently one of the great distinguishing features that constitute the difference of status betwixt a free person and a slave.

Argument of David Rorer, January 5, 1875, reprinted in George H. Miller, "Chicago, Burlington and Quincy Railroad Company v. Iowa," *Iowa Journal of History* 54 (October 1956): 289, 301-02.

Dillon, C. J. ...

In all civilized countries the duty of providing and preserving safe and convenient highways to facilitate trade and communication between different parts of the state or community, is considered a governmental duty. ... As to ordinary high-ways these propositions are unquestioned. But it is denied that they apply to railways built by private capital and owned by private corporations, created for the purpose of building them. [S]uch railways possess a two-fold character. Such a railway is in part public, and in part private. Because of its public character, relations and uses, the judicial tribunals of this country, state and national, have at length settled the law to be that the state, to secure their construction, may exert in favor of the corporation authorized by it to build the road both its power of eminent domain and of taxation. ... In its public character a railroad is an improved highway or means of more rapid and commodious communication, and its public character is not divested by the fact that its ownership is private. ... The power which the state may legitimately exercise over railways within it is subject to such further restrictions as it may have consented to by express grants in charters in respect of which no power of repeal or alteration is reserved ....

[T]he legislature has not expressly conferred upon railway corporations in this state the exclusive power to fix their own charges; ... such a power cannot be deduced by implication from the constituent act of the corporations, and ... whatever powers are conferred in this respect, are subject to an implied condition that they shall not be oppressively or unreasonably exercised, and also subject to the future exercise of the police regulations of the state, or any other power possessed by the state, properly legislative in its nature, which includes the power to regulate, consistently with the charter, all of the franchises granted, and to prescribe and limit the amount of toll or charges which it shall be lawful to take.

Chicago, Burlington & Quincy Railroad Co. v. Attorney General, 5 F. Cas. 594, 596-97 (Cir. Ct. D. Iowa 1875), *aff'd,* 94 U.S. 155 (1876).

CHAPTER FIVE

The Close of a Century

1880-1900

"The question . . . is not between prohibition and license, but whether law or lawlessness shall rule."

— GOVERNOR William Larrabee

1880-1900

T HE FINAL TWO DECADES OF THE NINE-
teenth century represented the last great era of unrestrained freedom for business enterprises. During this time, the railroad industry in Iowa—as in the nation—reached the zenith of its influence
and power. Total railroad mileage in Iowa grew from 4,157 miles in 1878 to 7,249 miles in 1884,
and to 8,263 miles in 1888.

The nationwide momentum for regulation of the railroads culminated in 1887 with the passage of the Interstate Commerce Act, which created the first federal independent regulatory
agency—the Interstate Commerce Commission. The Iowa legislature, strongly encouraged by
Governor Larrabee, also responded to pressure for state regulation of railroads. In 1888, Governor
Larrabee signed into law the Railroad Commissioner Law, strengthening the powers of the Board
of Railroad Commissioners and requiring reasonable, non-discriminatory rates.

Aided by a vast system of railway transportation, the greatest part of Iowa's tillable land was
under cultivation by the end of the nineteenth century, and the state's frontier receded into history.
The rapid spurt in Iowa's population began to slow. Still, the state grew from 1,624,615 residents
in 1880 to 2,231,853 in 1900. Although the federal census of 1880 showed that nearly ninety percent of Iowans lived in rural areas, the most important demographic trend was the development of
the state's urban centers.

In July 1881, Republican President James A. Garfield (whose Secretary of the Interior was
the former Iowa governor, Samuel J. Kirkwood) was felled by an assassin's bullets. He died in
September and was succeeded by Vice-President Chester Arthur. In 1884, Democrat Grover
Cleveland won the presidency, only to lose in 1888—despite a popular vote majority—to Republican Benjamin Harrison, who won a majority in the electoral college (including Iowa's votes). In
1892, Cleveland regained the presidency from Harrison.

Iowans, meanwhile, were occupied with the controversial issue of prohibition. Encouraged
by a strong temperance movement, the General Assembly in 1880 and 1882 approved the passage

163

of a prohibition amendment to the Iowa constitution, and the measure was ratified by a majority of voters. However, the Iowa Supreme Court in 1883 invalidated the constitutional amendment on technical legal grounds.

During the next few years, the Republican legislature passed statutory measures to enforce prohibition. A split in the Republican Party over the prohibition question contributed to the election in 1889 of Horace Boies as governor, the first Democrat to hold that office in over three decades. Then, in 1894 (following an anti-temperance reaction), the "Mulct law" was enacted. This act—while stating that its provisions did not legalize the business of selling intoxicants— nonetheless permitted certain communities to bar the enforcement of prohibitory laws with the consent of residents and the payment of a $600 yearly "tax" by liquor sellers. Although this strange law seemed perilously close to the county license scheme law invalidated by the Iowa Supreme Court in 1858, the Court subsequently upheld its validity.

The rise of the farmers' Grange movement in the 1870s—an important factor in the pressure for railroad regulation—was followed by the formation of other grass-roots organizations concerned with agrarian issues. The 1880s saw the growth of the Farmers Alliance; the 1890s witnessed the rise of Populism and the People's Party. General James B. Weaver, an Iowa resident and an attorney, was the People's Party candidate for president in 1892.

The People's Party was influential in the presidential elections of 1892 and 1896 and supported a number of positions that later would become law, including the popular election of United States Senators and a graduated income tax. The Panic of 1893 added impetus to the reform movement.

The closing years of the nineteenth century witnessed the Spanish-American War and Pacific expansionism. On February 15, 1898, the United States battleship *Maine* exploded and sank in Havana harbor. President William McKinley asked Congress for authority to use military force in the Cuban struggle for independence. Congress responded in April 1898 with a declaration of war. Commodore George Dewey destroyed Spain's Pacific fleet in Manila Bay, and American troops took possession of the Philippines. A cease fire soon was declared, and the Paris Peace Treaty was signed in December 1898.

As the new century approached, a revolution in technology was on the horizon, which would transform the business of the nation. The steam power that had fueled steamboats and railroads would be eclipsed in the twentieth century by gasoline and diesel-fueled machines. In the decades after statehood, Iowans had settled and tilled the land using manpower, horsepower, and steampower. In future decades, their quest for economic prosperity would be driven by tractors, automobiles, and airplanes.

The Iowa prohibitory law of 1855 had not satisfied adherents of a growing temperance movement. An 1858 amendment had exempted from the prohibition "beer, cider from apples or wine from grapes, currants or other fruits grown in this state." In addition to selling wine and beer, many establishments continued illegally to dispense whiskey and other hard liquor.

This state of affairs spurred the growth and vigor of temperance organizations. Among the groups that urged the Iowa legislature to pass a prohibitory constitutional amendment was the Woman's Christian Temperance Union (W.C.T.U.), led by J. Ellen Foster, a lawyer from Clinton. In a book written as superintendent of the Department of Legislation for the national W.C.T.U., Foster offered practical advice to aid the passage of state and federal prohibition amendments.

The first requisite of successful work along the line of constitutional prohibition, is a conviction that something must be done to stay the tide of intemperance that is sweeping over our beloved land. Not an impression that something ought to be attempted and might be successful, but a conviction deep enough to impel to action, and to hold the individual to long continued, steady endeavor. ...

... Let a town be districted and a dozen women start out to get signatures to a petition for prohibition, and there can not fail to be a *general stirring* of dry bones, which shall cause some to rise and breathe and walk forth. Let the persons who carry the petitions be sensible, earnest men or women, not children; let them go to every building—be it house or shop or store; let every individual over the required age be asked to sign. Let a few petitions be left in places of common resort, such as the post-office or barber-shop, to catch the signatures of those who might otherwise be overlooked. ... While this work is going on let temperance men look well to the making up of the Legislature before whom the petition is to come. Let the primaries and caucuses of all political parties be attended by temperance men in these parties, and let none but men who will submit the desired amendment, receive nominations for members of the Legislature. ...

The proceedings of the Legislature should be carefully watched, judicious men or women, or both, should be at the capital, and by personal interviews inform the members of both bodies in the Legislature of the people's will. This work is wearisome and sometimes disagreeable, but somebody must do it.

If the Legislature does not heed the prayer of your petition, you must do the work over again; not feeling that the agitation has been lost. ... Let temperance men and women see to it that every legislator who voted against the resolution to submit is *elected to stay at home* in the future.

If the Legislature does vote to submit, and it goes directly to the people for their vote—or even if the Constitution requires that a second Legislature should ratify the action of the first, in either instance the hand-to-hand work of securing the popular vote in favor of the amendment should be rigorously carried on. ...

... Let every newspaper available be pressed into the service. If the editor will not himself take up the weapons of war, he will perhaps give space to a Woman's Christian Temperance Union, or a Good Templars' Lodge, or an Amendment Association, to set forth the discussion. ...

... Let the women go the polls; let them have the right tickets for distribution, let them spread lunches, that, so the common table with the home look of mother and sister and child, may keep this home constituency in hourly remembrance. Let decorations of mottoes in print and in evergreens assist the eye and speak to the heart. ... And do not forget the prayer-meetings, let the bells ring hourly the calls, and from the opening to the closing of the polls let the fire on the altars of religion be kept burning.

J. Ellen Foster, *Constitutional Amendment Manual: Containing Argument, Appeal, Petitions, Forms of Constitution, Catechism and General Directions for Organized Work for Constitutional Prohibition* (New York: National Temperance Society and Publication House, 1882), pp. 52, 56-57, 59, 61, 63.

Pressed by temperance groups and sanctioned by the Republican Party platform, the Iowa General Assembly in 1880 and again in 1882 approved a constitutional amendment prohibiting the manufacture and sale of intoxicating liquors as a beverage, "including ale, *wine and beer." The proposed amendment was submitted to a popular vote in June 1882 and was ratified by a majority of nearly 30,000 votes.*

The campaign for approval and ratification of the constitutional amendment was loud and enthusiastic. The Iowa State Bar Association joined in the general fervor by hotly debating the issue at its eighth annual meeting in Des Moines in May 1881.

The president then submitted to the association the first topic for discussion, viz: Prohibitory Amendment

"What is the true construction of the proposed prohibitory amendment to the state constitution?"

. . . .

George E. Hubbell, of Davenport ... said that [a] constitutional amendment can not enforce itself, but must be vitalized by statutory measures. He asked if the friends of prohibition intended to weaken the present laws? He believed not, and the besetment by the women of Iowa 'round the legislative bodies was to open the door to more stringent enactments. ...

C. C. Nourse, of Des Moines ... said the laws of 1855 declared wine and beer to be intoxicating liquors, and afterwards the words "wine and beer" were stricken out by the legislature. This move tended to bring the republican party into favor with the Germans, and as a consequence, this party carried Scott county. ... The only justification for putting the prohibition in the organic law would be to give notice to immigrants that they have no right to come here and pauperize themselves and families—that there was no such constitutional right for them.

The next speaker was John C. Bills, of Davenport. He thought the proper course to pursue was, if one man used intoxicating liquors to an undue extent, to punish him, but don't prevent the ninety-nine who want these drinks and will use them temperately, from having their rights. He said that prohibitionists were not concerned about their own individual morality but were eternally hunting for a job of cleaning up some one else. Prohibitory legislation was like abolishing horses to prevent horse stealing, or deporting all the women to extirpate prostitution. ...

... Judge Rogers said that the proposed constitutional amendment was at variance with the spirit of our institutions. ... He did not believe in hampering the state constitution with a measure that was sure to be violated, and thus whenever a man took a drink he would be trampling under foot the constitution of the state. He wondered if there was an intelligent lawyer who believed that a measure on the statute today, violated, would strike terror to evil doers tomorrow, simply because embodied in the constitution. He would oppose the idea of putting mere penal police regulations in the constitution. He repudiated any sympathy with beer sellers and drinkers, and spoke as a lawyer on a constitutional question.

. . . .

Mr. Bills here asked, if the public sentiment of Iowa and Des Moines was so strong against the selling of liquor, why in the world did not Judge Nourse and the prohibition people of this city stop the saloons which were so numerous on all of the principal streets? The speaker went on to show that prohibition had not nor ever could be enforced against the sentiment of the people. Prohibition is a failure everywhere but among the Mohammedans. It was no more of a crime for him to sit down and drink two or three glasses of beer when he had ought to drink but one (each glass containing a less per cent of alcohol than a strong cup of coffee) than for Judge Nourse to go home and stuff his stomach with two or three dinners when he should eat but one. It was the same thing. The stomach suffered in both cases the same.

Proceedings of the Early Iowa State Bar Association, Held at Des Moines, Iowa 1874-1881 (Des Moines: Iowa State Bar Assoc., 1912), Session of May 10-11, 1881, pp. 72-75, 79-81.

No sooner had Iowans ratified the prohibition amendment to the state constitution than its validity was challenged in court. In April 1883, the Iowa Supreme Court heard an appeal from a case filed in the Scott County district court. In a ruling greeted with delight by the foes of prohibition, the Court held that the amendment had not been constitutionally enacted. The fatal flaw was that the House and Senate in the first legislative vote had not approved identical wording—the Senate version of the amendment had included the seemingly innocuous words, "or to be used."

Constables for the Des Moines Searchers and Advance Guard of the Fighting Prohibition Army, 1889. (Courtesy, State Historical Society of Iowa, Des Moines)

At a special election held on the 27th day of June, 1882, the electors of the State, by a majority of about thirty thousand, ratified an amendment to the Constitution, which, it is claimed, had been previously agreed to by the Eighteenth and Nineteenth General Assemblies, prohibiting the manufacture and use of intoxicating liquors as a beverage, including ale, wine, and beer, as therein provided.

The question is fairly presented in the record in this case, whether or not the amendment aforesaid has been constitutionally agreed to and adopted ....

When the Constitution was adopted, it was wisely therein provided ... that "any amendment or amendments to this Constitution may be proposed in either house of the General Assembly; and if the same shall be agreed to by a majority of the members elected to each of the two houses, such proposed amendment shall be entered on their journals ... and if, in the General Assembly so next chosen ... such proposed amendment or amendments shall be agreed to by a majority of all the members elected to each house, then it shall be the duty of the General Assembly to submit such proposed amendment to the people .... Art. 10, § 1.

This is the only way the Constitution can be

amended or changed except by a convention called for that purpose.

In compliance with the foregoing provision, there was introduced into the House of Representatives of the Eighteenth General Assembly a joint resolution ....

This resolution was agreed to by the House, sent to the Senate, and referred to the appropriate committee. ... Various amendments were offered, and finally it was moved to adopt a substitute for the House resolution. The substitute was as follows:

"No person shall manufacture for sale, or sell, or keep for sale, as a beverage, *or to be used* for such purpose, any intoxicating liquors whatever."

The substitute was amended by adding after the word "whatever" the words "including ale, wine, and beer." It was further amended by striking out the words "for such purposes." Thereupon the substitute, as amended, was adopted. ...

[T]he House concurred in the "Senate amendments."

The House journal shows that the ... joint resolution thus signed and approved was as follows: "No person shall manufacture for sale, or sell, or keep for sale, as a beverage, any intoxicating liquor whatever, including ale, wine and beer." This proposed amendment to the Constitution was agreed to by the Nineteenth General Assembly, and ratified by the electors .... The plaintiff contends that it is made clear and certain by an examination of the Senate journal that the words *"or to be used"* were in the resolution when it passed the Senate, and that the journal is the best evidence of such fact. ...

We deem it sufficient to say that, if there is any provision of the Constitution which should be regarded as mandatory, it is where the Constitution provides for its own amendment otherwise than by means of a convention called for that purpose. ... The object of the provision cannot be doubted or misunderstood. It is to preserve in the manner indicated the identical amendment proposed, and in an authentic form, which, under the Constitution, is to come before the succeeding General Assembly. ...

[A] statute should not be declared unconstitutional unless it clearly appears to be so. It follows, this rule should be applied to amendments of the Constitution. Mindful of this rule, and feeling its full force, it is possibly to be regretted that we have felt forced to declare that the amendment in question, which was ratified by so large a majority of the electors, has not been constitutionally adopted. But we cannot ignore another rule, which also universally obtains, which is that it is not only the province, but the duty of the judiciary, to fearlessly declare a statute or amendment to the Constitution to be unconstitutional, when such is clearly the case.

Koehler & Lange v. Hill, 60 Iowa 543, 545-49, 555-56, 568 (1883) (emphasis added).

A mong the strongest opponents of prohibition were Iowa's German communities. By the end of the nineteenth century, German-Americans formed the largest single ethnic group in the state, and they vigorously defended their right to consume beer and wine.

The novel legal theory that led to the downfall in 1883 of the prohibitory amendment is believed to have originated with an elderly and eminent member of Davenport's German community—Hans Reimer Claussen. Claussen had come to Iowa in the wave of German immigration following the 1848 revolutions in Europe. His remarkable career in Iowa law and politics exemplifies the contributions made by immigrants to the growing state.

Hans Reimer Claussen:
The Story of an Immigrant Lawyer

A YOUNG LAW STUDENT FROM DAVENPORT, Iowa, toured Europe in 1877. A highlight of his trip came in his ancestral Germany. Years later he recalled: "In Frankfurt I visited St. Paul's church, in which in Germany's revolutionary days the Frankfurt Parliament held its sessions. Here I found the seat, and for a few moments occupied the seat, which my venerable friend H.R. Claussen had occupied while a member of that important and historic body."[1]

The youth's action symbolized the respect many Davenport German-Americans had for Hans Reimer Claussen, who lived a remarkable life in Europe and America. During the 1840s, Claussen was a leading politician in his native Schleswig-Holstein and became a member of the all-German Frankfurt Parliament. Forced to flee after the collapse of the 1848 revolution, Claussen immigrated to Davenport, where he lived until his death in 1894. His long and productive life in Iowa was spent as a distinguished lawyer and political leader of the local German-American community. Few immigrants to Iowa have played such a vital part on two continents as Hans Reimer Claussen.

Claussen was born in February 1804 in the German-speaking duchy of Holstein. He studied law at the University of Kiel and, after admission to the bar in 1830, practiced law near Heide in Holstein. Two years later he married Annina Rahbek, and the couple had two children who survived infancy—a daughter Elfriede and a son, Ernst.

In 1834, the Claussens moved to Kiel, the main city of Holstein. There Claussen practiced as a lawyer in the supreme court and taught law at the university. He wrote many legal articles, and his treatise on an aspect of Roman law excited much discussion among German university professors. Eventually he turned to politics at a time of great political unrest in Schleswig-Holstein.

The twin duchies of Schleswig-Holstein were at the extreme north of Germany. Although most of the population was German-speaking, the duchies had been ruled since 1460 by the King of Denmark. Germany in the 1830s and 1840s was a loose confederation of many states with absolute monarchs. A rising tide of German nationalism marked those decades. Claussen, who throughout the 1840s was a member of the Holstein Estates (or legislature), belonged to the German Party, which sought to join the German Confederation.

In 1848, after Paris broke out in revolt against the French king, revolution spread across Europe. The revolutionary atmosphere pervaded Schleswig-Holstein, and their combined legislatures drew up demands of the King of Denmark for a separate constitution and freedom of assembly and the press. Claussen and four other delegates were sent to Copenhagen to put their grievances before the king. The king rejected the duchies' demands. Upon their return to Schleswig-Holstein, Claussen and his colleagues found that a full-scale revolution had broken out against Denmark. With the approval of the provisional government of Schleswig-Holstein, Claussen journeyed to Prussia and other German states, where he succeeded in obtaining armed assistance for the revolt.

Meanwhile revolution had spread throughout the German Confederation, and a Parliament from all the German states met at Frankfurt. Holstein elected Claussen to the Frankfurt Parliament, where he was one of the radical members. The Parliament drew up a constitution for a united Germany based on universal male suffrage; it then offered the crown to the King of Prussia, who turned it down.

The Frankfurt Parliament collapsed, the tide of revolution receded, and the Danes regained control of Schleswig-Holstein. In 1852, the King of Denmark published a general amnesty for the rebels. However, he issued a decree that banished the twenty-one most important revolutionary leaders—including Hans Reimer Claussen.

But Claussen, realizing he had no future in his homeland, had already departed for a new life. In 1851, he set off with his family for America. His destination was a haven for many Schleswig-Holsteiners—Davenport, Iowa.

German immigration to Davenport had begun in 1836. After the failure of the 1848 revolution, a flood of German refugees known as the "Forty-eighters"—many from Schleswig-Holstein—fled to Davenport. One German immigrant, writing in 1851 about Davenport and its estimated 4,000 inhabitants, enthused: "One-third of the people are Germans, and in the country perhaps one half of the people are Germans. One hardly realizes that he is in America because everywhere you hear German spoken."[2]

Davenport's German language newspaper *Der Demokrat* was begun in 1852, and the following year the Turnverein—the Forty-eighters' quintessential organization—was founded. This gymnastic society believed in "a sound mind in a sound body" and "freedom, education and welfare for all."[3] Claussen was a frequent lecturer to the Turnverein.

The Forty-eighters set up their own literary society, theatre, schools, singing societies, and rifle club. They started breweries and beer gardens. One historian has described Davenport and Scott County as "the new Schleswig-Holstein."[4]

After arriving in Davenport in August 1851, Claussen—then forty-seven years old—set himself the herculean task of learning English and taking the Iowa bar examination. In just two years he achieved both goals and began to practice as a lawyer. He was soon writing legal articles for *Der Demokrat*.

From his earliest days in Davenport, Claussen encouraged other Germans to

German immigrant Hans Reimer Claussen, an attorney and state senator, lived in Davenport from 1851 until his death in 1894. (Courtesy, State Historical Society of Iowa, Iowa City)

A pharmacy in Davenport, displaying German song lyrics in the left window. German-Americans in Davenport openly displayed their heritage until the anti-German bias of World War I. (Courtesy, Putnam Museum of History and Natural Science, Davenport)

immigrate to Iowa and contributed articles to newspapers in Schleswig-Holstein extolling the virtues of his adopted state. He also wrote a chapter on Iowa law in a German booklet for would-be immigrants to Iowa.

In 1855, Claussen built a grist mill at Lyons near Clinton. When grain prices collapsed at the end of the Crimean War, Claussen lost virtually all his money. He returned to Davenport in 1858 to start again.

Now, at the age of fifty-four, Claussen hurled himself into his law practice. He proved most successful at finding clients among the German-Americans of Scott County. A fellow lawyer recalled: "In a few years he had acquired both the practice and the reputation of an able lawyer. Many times I saw him in the court. He was stockily built, not above medium height, and very quiet in demeanor. ... His deep learning and high character gave him an excellent standing not only with members of the bar and courts, but with the community in general."[5]

Throughout the nineteenth and early twentieth centuries, prohibition threatened the whole culture of Iowans of German descent. During his many years in Iowa, Claussen struggled politically for German-Americans' freedom to drink alcohol and to enjoy dancing and other entertainment on Sundays. Claussen gave a fiery speech at the first recorded anti-temperance meeting in Iowa, held at Davenport in 1852.

Claussen originally supported the anti-slavery Free Soil Party (he considered slavery "a sin and a crime"),[6] and inevitably he became a member of the Republican Party upon its formation in 1856. He was elected a justice of the peace for Davenport on the Republican ticket in 1858 and again two years later.

As president of the German Republican Club of Scott County, Claussen in 1858 wrote an open letter to the Republican candidate for Congress, William Vandeveer. He demanded to know if Vandeveer supported a longer probation for foreigners as a precondition to citizenship and an extended period before naturalized citizens could vote. Claussen's letter forced Vandeveer publicly to disown these nativist policies.

On March 7, 1860, Claussen called a meeting of the German Republican Club in Davenport to condemn Edward Bates of Missouri—then a prominent contender for the Republican presidential nomination (which ultimately went to Abraham Lincoln). The club endorsed lengthy resolutions drawn up by Claussen, stressing that Bates had revealed anti-immigrant tendencies, and had supported a pro-slavery candidate for Congress and the fugitive slave law. Therefore, Bates was an opponent of fundamental Republican principles.

Claussen sent the resolutions to every prominent German in the country, and they received general approbation. Many prominent newspapers reprinted and commented on the resolutions. Claussen's efforts played a major part in destroying the Bates candidacy.

During the Civil War, Claussen continued his legal practice, expanding it in 1862 by taking his son Ernst into partnership. After the war, he entered state politics. In 1867, he unsuccessfully stood as a Republican candidate for state senator in Scott County. Two years later, Claussen won a four-year Senate term with a majority of 523 votes.

Claussen made a powerful impression in the Iowa Senate. "One of the most remarkable men of this Assembly is Senator Claussen," a fellow senator later wrote.

"He is now seventy years old, with hair as white as the snowflake, and step and movement as elastic and quick as a young man of twenty. ... He is a man of high literary culture, a profound scholar ... and although his speech is broken ... there are but few who speak or write the English language with more purity."[7]

In the Senate, Claussen battled over causes held dear by the German-American community, beginning with a bill that sought to increase the penalty for breaking the 1857 "Act for the Observance of the Sabbath."[8] This law forbade dancing, shooting, hunting, fishing, buying, selling, or doing any but essential work on Sundays. Claussen as a member of the Senate Judiciary Committee introduced a minority report opposing the increased penalty.

In his minority report, Claussen argued that the Sabbath Law was unconstitutional as a law respecting the establishment of religion. He further argued that the Sabbath Law was "impracticable, inoperative and contrary to the notions of a greater portion of Christians." Nearly all European Christians enjoyed dancing and other amusements after church on Sundays, and "there is nowhere any good reason for a provision that an act, innocent in itself, shall become criminal by every seventh revolution of the earth around its axis."[9] The Senate voted that Claussen's report be printed, and took no further action on the bill.

During the same legislative session, Claussen also opposed a bill that prohibited the sale of wine and beer, but left to each county the decision whether to enforce the law locally. In a minority report of the Committee on Suppression of Intemperance, he argued powerfully that the bill was unconstitutional, citing as a precedent an Iowa Supreme Court decision on a similar law of 1857.[10] (He was proved right—in 1871, the Supreme Court of Iowa struck down the new law.)[11]

In a notable speech on the bill, Claussen stressed that 300 million Europeans and thirty million Americans approved of alcohol; the error lay with the four million Americans who supported prohibition. Prohibition was unenforceable, and had been a complete failure in Massachusetts. He ended: "[T]he advocates of a strict prohibitory law ... want to make the State more moral and extricate vice ... [W]e are not here to legislate in order to make the people moral by our laws. We are here to protect life and liberty and to advance the educational interests of our State."[12]

In May 1871, Claussen retired from his legal practice, and the Scott County bar gave a fine banquet in his honor at which a letter from former Iowa Supreme Court Judge John F. Dillon was read. Judge Dillon wrote that Claussen had a "natural keen unperverted and ever active sense of Justice and Right ... His great knowledge of the civil law is a fountain to which, as he knows, I have often resorted ...."[13]

The next day, Claussen and his wife departed for a six-month visit to Europe. Bismarck had just united Germany, and Claussen heard Bismarck speak in the Berlin Parliament. Then he visited Schleswig-Holstein, from which he had been banished in 1852. He returned to Davenport in time for the 1872 legislative session.

Although he was liberal in most causes, Claussen opposed woman suffrage, as did the Davenport Turners generally. Claussen had unsuccessfully voted against an 1870 Senate resolution to give the vote to women and, in January 1872, was reported as "working and writing letters in opposition to female suffrage."[14] The Senate by a majority of two opposed the passage of this second resolution, thus preventing a constitutional amendment being put to a public referendum.

In the Senate debate on the subject, Claussen gave a major speech. He listed three broad reasons for denying women the vote: "The particular interest of the females does not require Female Suffrage. ... There is no natural right to Female Suffrage [and] ... The same is against public welfare."

Claussen developed his theme: "The women, generally, have deeper feelings, more intensive tenderness, a finer taste, and a nicer sense of propriety, than the rougher male sex. All these qualities make them excellent wives and mothers ...." He concluded: "We should leave the government ... in the hands of men. The women have their sphere in domestic life .... Would it not satisfy the highest ambition of an American lady to be the mother of a second Washington?"[15]

Like many German-Americans, Claussen probably feared that if women received the vote, the temperance movement—long supported by women reformers—would triumph. Certainly on every aspect of women's rights other than the vote, Claussen was a progressive. During the 1873 special session of the legislature, he voted with the majority on measures to reform married women's property, inheritance, and other legal rights. Moreover, despite his public words, a glimpse of Claussen's home life suggests that his own wife Annina was far from kitchen-bound and enjoyed intellectual discussion. A student whom Claussen helped with his law studies in 1872 recalled: "[H]e would talk to me on a variety of other subjects most interestingly .... Often Mrs. Claussen would join us in these conversations."[16]

Now in his sixty-ninth year, Claussen was on the Senate Judiciary Committee, which had a crucial role in drafting the 1873 Code of Iowa. When the Senate in its 1873 special session decided to hold two sessions a day to consider the code, Claussen asked to be excused from further service on the committee, citing his age. Two days later, the Senate unanimously requested that he rejoin the Judiciary Committee. Claussen, "visibly affected,"[17] once more took his place on the committee and by all accounts made a major contribution to the revision of the Iowa code.

Shocked by the corruption of President Grant's administration, Claussen in 1872 joined the break-away Liberal Republican movement and chaired a Davenport meeting supporting Horace Greeley for President. After Greeley's defeat, Claussen played no further part in national politics. He retired from the state senate in 1873.

During his years in the legislature, Claussen had concentrated primarily on opposing prohibition, Sabbath observance, and woman suffrage. But he also promoted causes such as immigration and education, continuing to serve on Davenport's board of education after retirement. He voted consistently for the abolition of capital punishment and remained a staunch champion of freedom of the press.

Always of a philosophical bent, Claussen was a keen student of Locke, Hume, Kant, Hegel, and others. He delivered many lectures to the Davenport Turnverein on topics such as "The Moral System of Grecian Philosophers" and "Communism in Contradiction to Morality, Law, and Sound Politics."

In 1879, Claussen gave his last Turnverein lecture to a large audience at the German Theatre in Davenport. He strongly criticized Bismarck's policies in Germany and looked to his adopted country for the future. The *Davenport Gazette* reported: "Mr. Claussen concluded with an eloquent reference to the United States as embodying the hopes of freedom loving people."[18]

Claussen's life upon retirement from politics belonged to honored old age: honored at the twenty-fifth anniversary of the Schleswig-Holstein revolt; honored on his golden wedding anniversary in 1882 by the Turners hoisting the flag over their hall; honored on that day, too, by a large party, speeches, telegrams, a poem recited in German by his granddaughter, and the gift of a painting of Heide in Schleswig-Holstein, where the Claussens had married. A newspaper account of the occasion said: "The Doctor [Claussen] was very much touched by these many evidences of kind regard, and addressed the company, giving expression to the feelings of himself and his wife."[19]

With the advancing years, Claussen showed his legal mind was as sharp as ever. In 1882, a state constitutional amendment of prohibition was ratified. Claussen's fellow Forty-eighter, Theodor Gülich, now a Burlington editor and lawyer, wrote in an open letter to the governor: "It is the opinion of able jurists that the amendment will not stand a legal test."[20]

Claussen—a fine constitutional lawyer who shared with Gülich a hatred of prohibition—was undoubtedly one of these "able jurists." A history of Scott County recorded: "It was [Claussen] that discovered the legal flaw in the prohibition constitutional amendment, which rendered that amendment illegal and unconstitutional."[21] The critical flaw was a difference in language between the resolutions of prohibition in the House and the Senate of the Eighteenth General Assembly. The Nineteenth General Assembly had agreed to the wording of the amendment passed by the previous House, but not that of the Senate. Accordingly, to the great glee of the German-Americans, the Iowa Supreme Court in 1883 ruled that the prohibition amendment was unconstitutional.

The last years of Claussen's life were marked by bereavement. His daughter, wife, and son all died between 1883 and 1892. Claussen lived on another two years. In 1894, at ninety years of age, he died at the home of his son-in-law.

Claussen had always had a Turner's attitude to life. He exercised regularly and had an iron constitution. One obituary described how "[t]he remarkable manner in which he preserved his youthful vigor [had] enabled him to be about and greet his acquaintances upon the streets until recently."[22] Claussen showed a streak of radicalism to the last: he had taken the unusual step of arranging to have his body cremated.

Few immigrants, in just over two decades of arriving in a new country and learning a new language, could play a leading part in drafting the legal code of an American state. But Hans Reimer Claussen was an exceptional man. In Europe, Claussen had fought for Schleswig-Holstein and united Germany. In Iowa, as a prominent lawyer, legislator, and civic leader, he fought for the rights of individual clients and of an entire immigrant group.

On his death, the *Davenport Democrat* saluted Claussen with the title bestowed on him by the local German community— "the patriarch of Davenport."[23]

The cause of woman suffrage took a back seat to the debate over prohibition in the last two decades of the nineteenth century. The Iowa General Assembly in 1882 proposed a constitutional amendment for equal suffrage, but it failed to obtain the necessary approval in the next succeeding legislature. During the following decade, the suffrage measure foundered. However, in 1894 the legislature did pass a tiny concession to the cause of woman suffrage.

AN ACT conferring upon women the right to vote in certain cases.
Be it enacted by the General Assembly of the State of Iowa:
Section 1. That in any election hereafter held in any city, incorporated town or school district for the purpose of issuing any bonds for municipal or school purposes, or for the purpose of borrowing money, or for the purpose of increasing the tax levy, the right of any citizen to vote shall not be denied or abridged on account of sex, and women may vote at such elections the same as men, under the same restrictions and qualifications.
Approved April 13th, 1894.

Acts of the Twenty-fifth General Assembly, 1894, ch. 39, § 1.

Do Dubuque Women Want To Vote?

"NO!"

was the emphatic reply Monday, April third, when LESS THAN 100 WOMEN in all Dubuque voted on the bond issue for a swimming pool---a question of taxation!

Men, by your vote June 5th, please do not force the ballot upon women who do not want it and who have just shown you so.

Women were given a limited vote on city bond issues in 1894. In this Dubuque handbill, used in a 1916 referendum on woman suffrage, opponents claimed that few women exercised their limited bond issue vote. (Courtesy, State Historical Society of Iowa, Iowa City)

Iowa Woman Suffrage Association convention, Oskaloosa, 1889. Carrie Chapman Catt sits in the front row, center, wearing cape. (Courtesy, State Historical Society of Iowa, Des Moines)

Iowa's most famous contribution to the cause of woman suffrage was Carrie Chapman Catt, who moved from Wisconsin to Iowa as a child and spent her young adult years in Mason City. Active in the Iowa Woman Suffrage Association, she entered the national movement with a speech at the 1890 convention of the National Woman Suffrage Association in Washington, D.C. After her second marriage in 1890, Catt moved to the West Coast, but she remained active in the Iowa suffrage movement. In 1900, she succeeded Susan B. Anthony as president of the National Woman Suffrage Association. She assumed that position a second time in 1915, and led the successful national suffrage campaign that, in 1920, culminated in the ratification of the Nineteenth Amendment to the U.S. Constitution.

In January 1897, the National Association held its annual convention in Des Moines. The Iowa Senate, meeting in special session, invited the delegates to appear before the Senate. The [Des Moines] Iowa State Register called the occasion "one of the most memorable gatherings ever assembled in the state house," and reported that "Susan B. Anthony presided over the Senate for the space of one hour …." One of the featured speakers was Carrie Chapman Catt.

Suffragist Carrie Chapman Catt, as she appeared in 1890. (Courtesy, State Historical Society of Iowa, Iowa City)

Mrs. Carrie Lane-Chapman-Catt made one of the brightest and most interesting talks of the hour. She said "Gentlemen of the Senate: We are not here to convert you to our cause, but to induce you to submit it to a vote of the people that they may decide for themselves whether they want women to vote. Iowa has always taken the stand that the people shall rule. If not a single member of this body believed in our cause I would yet deem it your duty to submit the question to a vote of the people.

For years the women have striven to get it before the people but it has never been granted to them. Nine years ago in this state a member of the general assembly stated he would favor woman suffrage if the women wanted to vote. We circulated a petition in this town and got every woman in the town save ten to sign it, asking him to vote for equal suffrage. …
. . . .

Believe in democracy whether you believe in woman suffrage or not and give to the men of Iowa an opportunity of saying whether your state shall have woman suffrage."

[Des Moines] Iowa State Register, January 30, 1897.

The rights of former slaves continued to attract political support in Iowa, although—like woman suffrage—this cause aroused less fervor than the prohibition debate in the late nineteenth century. After the U.S. Supreme Court had declared unconstitutional a federal equal accommodations provision, the Iowa legislature in 1884 passed a law to guarantee equal access to public accommodations—Iowa's first Civil Rights Act.

AN ACT to Protect all Citizens in their Civil and Legal Rights.
Be it enacted by the General Assembly of the State of Iowa:

Section 1. That all persons within this state shall be entitled to the full and equal enjoyment of the accommodations, advantages, facilities and privileges of inns, public conveyances, barber shops, theaters and other places of amusement; subject only to the conditions and limitations established by law, and applicable alike to every person.

Sec. 2. That any person who shall violate the foregoing section by denying to any person, except for reasons by law applicable to all persons, the full enjoyment of any of the accommodations, advantages, facilities or privileges enumerated in said section or by aiding or inciting such denial, shall for each offense, be deemed guilty of a misdemeanor. Approved, March 29, 1884.

Acts of the Twentieth General Assembly, 1884, ch. 105, §§ 1-2.

The legislature also had occasion to consider the legal rights and status of the residents of the Meskwaki settlement in Tama County. In 1896, the General Assembly passed an act that purported to cede title and control of the settlement to the U.S. government, while reserving jurisdiction for certain limited purposes. The meaning of this law was tested in federal court when the parents of an Indian girl resisted her compulsory attendance at the recently created Indian training school in Toledo.

The first matter for determination is the position or relation which the Indians settled upon the reservation in Tama county hold with reference to the state and federal governments. It appears that under date of October 11, 1842, the United States entered into a treaty with the Sac and Fox Indians whereby the latter ceded to the United States all their lands west of the Mississippi river .... [I]n accordance with the terms of this treaty a reservation was set apart for the Indians, which is now included within the boundaries of the state of Kansas, and the tribes removed thereto. Subsequently a few of the number returned to Iowa, and, uniting with some scattered remnants that had not gone to the new reservation, they established themselves in Tama and the adjoining counties. The government of the United States endeavored to induce these members to join the confederated tribes, and for years refused to pay them any portion of the tribal annuity, but these efforts were of no avail. Finally, in 1856, the state of Iowa, by an act of the general assembly, recognized their right to remain in the state; and in 1857 the Indians bought an 80-acre tract of land in Tama county, making it the nucleus of their proposed permanent settlement, which has increased, through the bounty of the state and national governments, until it now in-

An 1899 photo shows children at the Indian training school in Toledo. The Iowa Supreme Court held that Indian children could not be compelled to attend the school contrary to their parents' wishes. (Courtesy, State Historical Society of Iowa, Iowa City)

cludes nearly 3,000 acres in extent, with an Indian population of about 400 souls. In 1895 there was organized what is known as "The Indian Rights Association of Iowa," the main purpose of which was to labor for the advancement of the Indians on the Tama reservation; and to that end the general assembly of Iowa was induced to pass in 1896 an act ceding to the United States jurisdiction over the reservation in question, which cession was accepted by congress .... [T]here was secured from congress, under date of June 10, 1896, an appropriation of the sum of $35,000 for the purchase of a site and the erection of the necessary buildings for an industrial school at or near the reservation in Tama county; and the money thus appropriated was used in the construction of the buildings now constituting the Indian training school, which adjoins the town of Toledo, and is some four or five miles from the reservation. From this brief statement it sufficiently appears that the reservation in Tama county and the Indians living thereon are now committed to the care and control of the United States government, and the source of the authority of the Indian agent and superintendent of the school over the Indians must be sought in the legislation of congress, and the regulations of the department in charge of Indian affairs. ...

The next question for consideration is whether the Indian agent has the right to compel the attendance of the Indian children at the training school, regardless of the wishes of the parents or of the children themselves. My attention has not been called to any act of congress making attendance upon this school compulsory upon the children of the reservation, or conferring upon the agent the power to take the children from their homes and place them in the school, and to enforce their remaining at the school by measures restrictive of their personal liberty ....

... Owing to the inherent nature of the Indians, and to the conflict that has existed between them and the whites since the advent of the latter upon this continent, it must be expected that their suspicions of the motives of the whites will be easily aroused, and cannot be readily allayed. It would seem clear that the success of the training school at Tama City, as now constituted, cannot be assured unless it is so conducted as to win the confidence and good will of the tribe as a whole, or at least of a large portion of the more progressive element; and surely this cannot be accomplished by the use of force or other means whereby the will of the Indian is overcome, leaving his judgment unconvinced. ...

The conclusion reached upon the questions submitted to the court is that the respondents, as the agent and school superintendent at the Tama county reservation, cannot by force or compulsion take the Indian children from the reservation proper, and keep them at the Indian training school, without the consent of the parents ....

In re Lelah-Puc-Ka-Chee, 98 F. 429, 431-33, 435-36 (N. D. Iowa 1899).

During the final decades of the nineteenth century, the Iowa General Assembly turned its attention to laws promoting the health, safety, and welfare of workers and the public. Air purity in mine shafts, the regulation of imitation butter and cheese, the treatment of female factory workers, and railroad safety were among the concerns singled out for special consideration by the legislature.

The Code of 1873 had stood for many years as Iowa's official compilation of laws. But as the legislature churned out laws with ever greater frequency, some private codes were published to fill the gap. In 1894, the legislature authorized the compilation of a new official code, which it finally approved in a special session three years later. The Code of 1897—all 2,362 pages of it—contained extensive annotations and sold for $5 a copy.

The laws embodied in the new code displayed an admirable range of concern for the physical and moral well-being of Iowa's citizens.

Sec. 2784. Water-closets. [The Board of Directors of a school township] shall give special attention to the matter of convenient water-closets or privies, and provide one [for every] school-house site, not within an independent city or town district, two separate buildings located at the farthest point from the main entrance to the school-house, and as far from each other as may be, and keep them in wholesome condition and good repair. In independent city or town districts, where it is inconvenient or undesirable to erect two separate out-houses, several closets may be included under one roof ... and the approaches to the outside doors for the two sexes shall be separated by a substantial close fence not less than seven feet high and thirty feet in length.

. . . .

Sec. 4958. Obscene productions by phonograph. If any person exhibit through a phonograph, or any other instrument for receiving and reproducing the human voice, any story, song or any other matter containing any obscene, indecent or immoral language, he shall be imprisoned in the penitentiary not more than one year, or be fined not exceeding one thousand dollars.

. . . .

Sec. 4977. Spreading infectious disease. If any person inoculate himself or any other person or suffer himself to be inoculated with the smallpox within the state, or come within the state with the intent to cause the prevalence or spread of this infectious disease, he shall be imprisoned in the penitentiary not more than three years, or be fined not exceeding one thousand dollars and imprisoned in the county jail not exceeding one year.

. . . .

Sec. 4999. Seats for female employes. All employers of females in any mercantile or manufacturing business or occupation shall provide and maintain suitable seats, when practicable, for the use of such female employes, at or beside the counter or work-bench where employed, and permit the use thereof by such employes to such extent as the work engaged in may reasonably admit of. Any neglect or refusal to comply with the provisions of this section by any employer shall be punished by a fine not exceeding ten dollars.

. . . .

Sec. 5003. Opium smoking. Any person who shall keep and maintain any shop, house, room or other place to be resorted to by other persons, in which opium or any of its preparations or compounds is sold or given away to be smoked or used in such place ... and every person who resorts to such shop, house, room or other place for the purpose of smoking opium or its preparations and compounds, shall be deemed guilty of a misdemeanor and upon conviction thereof shall be fined not exceeding five hun-

dred dollars, or imprisoned in the county jail not exceeding six months, or both. ...

Sec. 5004. Selling firearms to minors. No person shall knowingly sell, present or give any pistol, revolver or toy pistol to any minor. Any violation of this section shall be punished by a fine of not less than twenty-five nor more than one hundred dollars, or by imprisonment in the county jail not less than ten nor more than thirty days.

Code of 1897, §§ 2784, 4958, 4977, 4999, 5003-04.

The *Iowa court system continued its growth and development. In July 1882, Congress approved an act dividing the state into two federal judicial districts—the single District of Iowa became the Northern and Southern Districts. The Iowa Supreme Court, as well, experienced change. In June 1886, the Court moved into its present courtroom in the newly built capitol building in Des Moines, and in 1894 the number of judges was increased to six.*

Among the many issues considered by the Iowa Supreme Court in this period was one that would resonate a century later—prayer in the public schools and the constitutional separation of church and state.

The record shows that the teachers of the school are accustomed to occupy a few minutes each morning in reading selections from the Bible, in repeating the Lord's prayer, and singing religious songs; that the plaintiff has two children in the school, but that they are not required to be present during the time thus occupied. The record further shows that the plaintiff objected to such exercises, and requested that they be discontinued; but that the teachers refused to discontinue them, and the directors refused to take any action in the matter.

The plaintiff concedes that under a statute of Iowa, section 1764 of the Code, if constitutional, neither the school directors nor courts have power to exclude the Bible from public schools. The provision of the statute is in these words: "The Bible shall not be excluded from any school or institution in this state, nor shall any pupil be required to read it contrary to the wishes of his parent or guardian."

. . . .

The plaintiff insists, however, that it is unconstitutional. The provision of the constitution with which it is said to conflict is article 1, section 3, bill of rights. The provision is in these words: "The general assembly shall make no law respecting an establishment of religion, or prohibiting the free exercise thereof; nor shall any person be compelled to attend any place of worship, pay tithes, taxes, or other rates, for building or repairing places of worship, or the maintenance of any minister or ministry."

The plaintiff's position is that, by the use of the school house as a place for reading the Bible, repeating the Lord's prayer and singing religious songs, it is made a place of worship; and so his children are compelled to attend a place of worship, and he, as a taxpayer, is compelled to pay taxes for building and repairing a place of worship.

… For the purposes of the opinion it may be

The Iowa State Capitol building under construction in Des Moines, 1884. (Courtesy, State Historical Society of Iowa, Des Moines)

The Iowa State Capitol building about 1890. (Courtesy, State Historical Society of Iowa, Des Moines)

conceded that the teachers do not intend to wholly exclude the idea of worship. It would follow from such concession that the school house is, in some sense, for the time being, made a place of worship. But it seems to us that, if we should hold that it is made a place of worship within the meaning of the constitution, we should put a very strained construction upon it. The object of the provision, we think, is, not to prevent the casual use of a public building as a place for offering prayer or doing other acts of religious worship, but to prevent the enactment of a law whereby any person can be compelled to pay taxes for building or repairing any place designed to be used distinctively as a place of worship. ... We do not think ... that the plaintiff's real objection grows out of the matter of taxation. We infer from his argument that his real objection is that the religious exercises are made a part of the educational system into which his children must be drawn, or made to appear singular, and perhaps be subjected to some inconvenience. But, so long as the plaintiff's children are not required to be in attendance at the exercises, we cannot regard the objection as one of great weight. ...

Possibly the plaintiff is a propagandist, and regards himself charged with a mission to destroy the influence of the Bible. Whether this be so or not, it is sufficient to say that the courts are charged with no such mission. We think that the injunction was properly denied.

Moore v. Monroe, 64 Iowa 367, 368-70 (1884).

An early photograph of the chamber of the Iowa Supreme Court in the State Capitol building. The chamber was first occupied in 1886. (Courtesy, State Historical Society of Iowa, Des Moines)

Iowa's Samuel Freeman Miller, associate justice of the United States Supreme Court, died in October 1890 at the age of seventy-four. He had served on the Court since his appointment by President Abraham Lincoln in 1862, had participated in over 5,000 Supreme Court decisions, and had written over 600 majority opinions. Justice Miller's long and distinguished career was lauded in a memorial tribute by United States Chief Justice Melville Fuller.

The loss so universally felt in the death of Mr. Justice Miller comes home in an especial degree to his brethren, participants in his toil and sharers of his intimate friendship.

When he became a member of the Court its deliberations were presided over by Chief Justice Taney, and Catron and Nelson and Grier and Clifford were among his associates, together with the venerable Wayne, the last survivor of the Bench as constituted under John Marshall. Of the forty-five Associate Justices up to the time of his death, only Catron equaled, and Washington, William Johnson, Story, McLean, and Wayne exceeded, him in length of service. ...

When he took his seat the country was in the throes of internecine conflict; when his eyes closed it was upon a happy, prosperous, and united people, living under the form of government devised by the fathers, the wisdom of whose fabric the event had vindicated. Great problems crowded for solution. The suspension of the habeas corpus; the jurisdiction of military tribunals; the closing of the ports of the insurrectionary States; the legislation to uphold the two main nerves, iron and gold, by which war moves in all her equipage; the restoration of the predominance of the civil over the military authority; the reconstruction measures; the amendments to the Constitution, involving the consolidation of the Union, with the preservation of the just and equal rights of the States—all these passed in various phases under the jurisdiction of the Court; and he dealt with them with the hand of a master.

While he took his full share in the consideration of every subject of judicial investigation, notably in reference to some, as, for instance, those pertaining to the public lands, yet he chiefly distinguished him-

Much courthouse building occurred in the last years of the nineteenth century. The old octagonal courthouse in Grundy County, built in 1857 (*top*); and Grundy County's second courthouse, built in 1891–1893 (*bottom*). (Courtesy, State Historical Society of Iowa, Des Moines)

Iowan Samuel Freeman Miller served on the U.S. Supreme Court from 1862 until his death in 1890. (Courtesy, State Historical Society of Iowa, Iowa City)

self in the treatment of grave constitutional questions .... His opinions, from his first, in the Second of Black's Reports, to his last, in the One hundred and thirty-sixth United States, some seven hundred in number (including dissents), running through seventy volumes, were marked by strength of diction, keen sense of justice, and undoubting firmness of conclusion.

. . . .

His last years were suffused with the glow of the evening time of a life spent in the achievement of worthy ends and expectations, and he has left a memory dear to his associates, precious to his country, and more enduring than the books in which his judgments are recorded.

Memorials of the Justices of the Supreme Court of the United States (Littleton, Colorado: Fred B. Rothman & Co., 1981), vol. IV, pp. 36-39.

Now that Iowa was widely settled and a more sophisticated transportation system linked its cities and towns, the practice of law demanded less physical fortitude than in the early years of statehood. Still, the legal profession retained a colorful aspect, captured in this reminiscence of an 1890s lawyer.

I was admitted to the [Appanoose County] bar in May, 1894. ...

In the 90s the terms of court were usually nine weeks four times each year. Jury trials followed one after the other. In that respect we have much less court practice than we had then. One reason was that we seldom compromised a case, but fought it out to the end of the law. People would spend more on a law suit than they ever expected to get back, but vindication seemed to be the motive.

There were no bankruptcy laws until 1898, and no Workman's Compensation laws, and after those laws were enacted it took away a lot of the lawyer's business.

In those days we had all-men juries and it was not until about 1920 that women came on the jury. ...

In the old days we had a large Justice of the Peace practice, which has almost disappeared. Seldom a week went by in those days that we did not have one or more J.P. cases. Trying a lawsuit in the J.P. court was the hardest work a lawyer ever had. The J.P.'s were not familiar with the law, and anything that we lawyers could put over by argument, getting mad, pounding the table and threatening to fight one another impressed the J.P.

We had one old fellow at Moulton who was strictly honest. Although he had his office in with my chief opposing lawyer, I found out before my opponent did, that the old fellow was trying to give the decisions about even, and he would give me one ruling and then the next one would go to my opposing lawyer. I took advantage of this knowledge, and when it was my time to win, I would try the case before his honor, and when I thought it was my time to lose I would take a jury. ...

Another source of legislation in the early courts was the "blind tigers" where they dispensed liquor illegally. They furnished a considerable amount of business for the lawyers. ...In the old days you had to sneak into a blind tiger, reach through a hole in the wall, deposit your money and the liquor would be put in your hand without seeing the seller. The bars where liquors were sold legally had saw dust on the floors and no chairs. [The patrons] had to stand up, and did not stay so long. ...

Knowing hundreds of preachers, teachers, professional lecturers, students as well as lawyers I have as high a regard for the lawyer as any other profession including the ministry. I have met and associated with lawyers in my travels as well as in my practice, and there are no more democratic or agreeable body of men, than the lawyers.

State Senator J. R. Barkley, *Old Time Lawyers and Law Suits of Fifty Years Ago* (privately printed), pp. 1-3, 5, 7 (reprinted from the *Centerville Daily Iowegian and Citizen*, September 20, 1945).

Few lawsuits in Iowa history have achieved the status of legend. However, a series of cases in the late nineteenth century—known collectively as the Jones County Calf Case—undoubtedly can claim this distinction. No reckoning of the legal history of the period 1880-1900 would be complete without recounting the story of this utterly remarkable case.

The Legendary Jones County Calf Case

THE THEFT IN 1874 OF FOUR CHEAP CALVES, valued at twenty-four dollars, sounds like the pettiest of criminal cases. Soon dealt with, of no significance, and soon forgotten. Yet that theft was the basis of more than fifteen major court proceedings in five Iowa counties, including four appeals to the Iowa Supreme Court. In 1894—twenty years, countless lawyers, and a reputed $75,000 in litigation costs later—the last of the proceedings was disposed of by the courts. And today, a century after the series of cases ended, people still speak of them as one case—the Jones County Calf Case.

Robert (Bob) Johnson, the hero of the saga, was a farmer in Jones County. One fateful day in June 1874, a man named S.D. Potter, of Greene County, came to visit him. Potter wanted to buy some calves, and he asked Johnson to look out for likely prospects. Johnson and Potter were old friends—they had been raised together in Ohio before moving to Iowa—and so Johnson promised to help.

The following day, Johnson and his brother, Newt, went into Olin to buy some hardware at Coppes & Derr's general store. Bob Johnson inquired of the storekeepers if they knew anyone who had calves for sale. They did not, but at that moment a stranger who was sitting in the store said that he had four calves for sale. He gave

Robert (Bob) Johnson, the dogged litigant in the Jones County Calf Case. (Courtesy, State Historical Society of Iowa, Iowa City)

Charles E. Wheeler, attorney for Robert Johnson in the legendary Jones County Calf Case. (Courtesy, State Historical Society of Iowa, Iowa City)

his name as "John Smith," and said he was the son-in-law of a man named Clem Lane.

Smith and the Johnsons went down to the common by the river. They found three of the calves that Smith said were his, but could not find the fourth. Bob Johnson told Smith that when he had found the fourth calf, he should put all four in a pasture near Johnson's house. Smith explained that he must have the money right away, because he was being sued. Newt Johnson had the necessary money, and Bob Johnson paid the man off. In court, Smith was to be referred to as "mythical" Smith, for no one ever saw him again.

The next day, Bob Johnson got word that Potter was returning with other calves he had bought. Johnson went to the pasture near his house, and there he found the three calves Smith had offered him the previous day, and a fourth one with them. The four calves were all dark colored—this is the crux of the case. They were *dark*.

Before Johnson met up with Potter, a man called Pete Onstott saw Potter. For twenty years in court, he swore that he noticed four light-colored calves in the herd Potter had with him. He asked Potter where he had got the calves, and Potter gave somebody's name. Then Johnson arrived and delivered his four dark-colored calves to Potter, and Potter went on back to Greene County.

Now at the same time, a man named John Foreman, who lived in Jones County, lost four *light*-colored calves. Upon hearing that Potter had been buying calves in Jones County, Foreman sought him out in Greene County. There he identified his four light-colored calves, and he asked Potter where he got them. Potter replied that he had bought them from Bob Johnson.

Potter and Foreman came to see Johnson, and the three men went to a young lawyer in Mechanicsville named Charles Wheeler. Johnson explained that Foreman had lost four calves and found them in Potter's herd. Potter said he had bought them from Johnson. Johnson explained he had bought the calves from "mythical" Smith. The lawyer advised Johnson that he must pay for the calves and look to Smith for reimbursement.

The three men went to Coppes & Derr's store in Olin, and the two merchants confirmed Johnson's story of how he had bought the calves from Smith. But they added significantly that Smith was a complete stranger to them. Johnson gave a promissory note to Foreman for twenty-four dollars—six dollars apiece for the four calves—and the three men had a drink on it.

Then Johnson went after Smith. He filed an information against Smith and got a warrant from a justice of the peace. Johnson and a constable went to see Clem Lane, and told him that Smith had said he was Lane's son-in-law. Lane said he did not have a son-in-law called Smith. Johnson tracked men named "John Smith" all over Iowa and neighboring states, but he never could find the man from whom he bought the four dark-colored calves.

Bob Johnson was indicted for stealing the four Foreman calves in the December 1874 term of court. After the indictment, he heard that the Foreman calves were all light-colored. So he and his brother went to Greene County to interview Potter about the matter. Potter pointed out the four Foreman light-colored calves, and said that they were the calves he'd bought from Johnson. Johnson insisted he had sold Potter dark-colored calves, and a fight began. Newt Johnson stopped the fight.

Thus it was that Bob Johnson realized he had never handled Foreman's light-colored calves at all. So he refused to pay the twenty-four dollar note he had signed in favor of Foreman. The note subsequently had been acquired by a bank as an innocent purchaser, and suit was brought—the first of the Jones County Calf cases.

Attorney Wheeler later recalled that the note case "was litigated about every full of the moon for several years."[1] (One judgment entry on September 25, 1875, shows a judgment of $49.10 and $677.30 costs entered in favor of John Foreman against Robert Johnson.) Johnson ultimately lost the case, and Wheeler estimated that the entire proceedings cost Johnson about $1,400, an enormous sum in those days.

The criminal indictment against Johnson had been instigated by members of the Iowa branch of the Northern Missouri Anti-Horse Thief Association. Johnson was not a member of the Association, but many of his neighbors were, and they persuaded both Foreman and Potter to join. The organization had talked to the Jones County district attorney about the theft, and members testified before the grand jury.

Johnson's lawyers (the young Wheeler having been joined by a seasoned Linn County attorney, Colonel Isaac Preston) moved for the indictment to be quashed because of an error in drawing and impaneling the grand jury. While the motion was pending, Johnson's house, and later his barn, were burned down. One morning Johnson found a rope with a hangman's knot on his horse block, with a note that

An entry from the Appearance Docket of the Jones County district court showing the malicious prosecution lawsuit filed by Robert Johnson.

A jury room at the Jones County courthouse as it would have appeared at the time of the Jones County Calf Case. The amenities included several spitoons. (*Anamosa Eureka,* September 2, 1937)

read: "We advise you to appear and be tried under the indictment ... or take the lamented Greeley's advice and go west, or take this."[2]

The first indictment was quashed, and a second indictment was returned in May 1875. Johnson's father-in-law posted bond for his freedom pending the trial. Feelings were running so high in the community, that Colonel Preston told Wheeler to discuss with their client whether he should jump bond and leave the country. Wheeler reluctantly complied, but Johnson would have none of it: "Boy, I never stole the John Foreman calves, and, by God, I will go to the penitentiary off my doorstep before I will ever jump my bond!"[3]

Johnson's attorneys moved for a change of venue, fearing that the notoriety of the case in Jones County would prejudice a jury. A change of venue was ordered, and the trial was held in Cedar County. The trial resulted in a hung jury—eleven for acquittal and one for conviction. A retrial was ordered, and this time Johnson was triumphantly acquitted. Thus ended the second phase of the Jones County Calf Case.

Now Bob Johnson was determined to vindicate his reputation and honor by suing those who had instigated the criminal prosecution against him. On April 14, 1877, he filed a petition for "malicious prosecution" in the Jones County district court against seven defendants, including Foreman and Potter, claiming that the de-

fendants had conspired without probable cause to have him convicted of grand larceny.

This third legal proceeding—*Johnson v. Miller et al.*—was the true "Jones
County Calf Case." The case was tried, retried, and appealed repeatedly over the
next sixteen years, during which Johnson proved himself unbelievably dogged.
Again and again he said to his lawyer, Charles Wheeler: "*I am going to have my
character back!*"[4]

The first trial of the lawsuit in 1878 was held in Benton County, but the jury
was unable to reach a verdict. Later the same year in the same county, the case was
retried, and the jury awarded Johnson $3,000 damages. However, the judge set the
verdict aside as not being warranted by the evidence. The case was tried for a third
time in Clinton County, and Johnson received a verdict of $7,500. This verdict, too,
was set aside, because a defendant was wrongly included.

The case was tried for a fourth time in Black Hawk County. Much testimony
was offered about the Anti-Horse Thief Association. Among the evidence was one
of the defendants' statements that "if they could not get rid of [Johnson] no other
way, they would burn him out." A similar statement imputed to a defendant was:
"[W]e will convict Johnson sure, or, if we do not convict him, we will drive him out
of the county."[5] Another witness gave evidence that he was present when a vote was
taken at an Anti-Horse Thief Association meeting to prosecute Johnson and money
was raised for the purpose. At the close of the evidence, the jury again found for
Johnson and awarded $5,000 damages.

The defendants appealed to the Iowa Supreme Court.[6] Representing the defendants before the Court was Horace Boies, who five years hence would be elected
Democratic governor of Iowa. On April 25, 1884, the Court reversed the judgment
in Johnson's favor, finding that key evidence admitted at the malicious prosecution
trial was inadmissible, indefinite or uncertain. Among other errors, the court should
not have allowed evidence about the burning of Johnson's barn or the threatening
letter, in the absence of a showing that these incidents were connected to the individual defendants. In addition, evidence should not have been excluded concerning
the first hung jury, since it showed that some jurors believed Johnson was guilty, and
thus tended to establish probable cause for the prosecution.

The case was retried in the Black Hawk County district court. This time a witness testified that one of the defendants had said: "If we had our way we would
make short work of him, as they did of Hi Roberts."[7] Hiram Roberts in 1857 had
been lynched in the Walnut Grove community by members of an anti-horse thief association, and the witness testified that he supposed this statement to mean they
would hang Johnson by the neck, as they had Roberts. Johnson again won a jury
verdict, this time for damages of $6,000.

Once more the defendants appealed to the Iowa Supreme Court.[8] On October
15, 1886, the Court again reversed the judgment, holding that it was error to submit
to the jury the question of whether the defendants knew Johnson was laboring under a mistake of fact when he admitted selling Foreman's calves to Potter, there being no evidence that—except as to Potter—the mistake was known at the time of the
instigation of the alleged malicious prosecution. Further, the witness had improperly
been allowed to give his opinion as to the meaning of the reference to "Hi Roberts."
The case again was remanded to the district court.

Back the case went to Black Hawk County. The judge directed the jury to find in favor of one defendant, Herman Keller, based on the failure to prove his connection with the Anti-Horse Thief Association. However, the jury returned a verdict against the remaining six defendants, awarding Johnson $1,000 in damages. Once again, the defendants appealed to the Iowa Supreme Court.[9]

This time, in an opinion handed down on January 27, 1891, the Court affirmed the judgment of the district court. The Court reasoned that it was no defense to an action for malicious prosecution that the criminal proceedings against Johnson were instituted on the advice of counsel, if the defendants did not act in good faith believing Johnson guilty. The jury's special and general verdicts were consistent with a finding that the defendants did not, in fact, believe Johnson to be guilty. Accordingly, the Court upheld the jury's verdict.

But still the proceedings were not finished. A matter of costs had to be dealt with. The Black Hawk County district court ruled that the six defendants—other than Keller, who had since died—should bear the full burden of the costs at trial, in the amount of $2,886. 84. The defendants appealed to the Iowa Supreme Court, contending that they should bear only six-sevenths of the costs. On December 20, 1894, the Iowa Supreme Court upheld the cost judgment against the six defendants, reasoning that the lawsuit had been a joint action against all defendants, who had raised a joint defense.[10]

And so—twenty years after Bob Johnson was indicted for stealing John Foreman's calves—he was vindicated. Johnson was thirty-seven years old when he purchased four dark-colored calves; he was fifty-seven when the litigation finally ended. He had established his good name, but the lawsuit had bankrupted him many times over. Still, even after the statute of limitations had run on the debts, he insisted on repaying every dollar he owed to his friends and neighbors. He later went into the real estate business in Anamosa with his son, and his standing in the community was confirmed when he was twice elected mayor of Anamosa. The local newspapers reported the celebration of his fiftieth wedding anniversary in 1911, and his sudden death in 1914 at the age of seventy-seven.

Johnson never regretted his lifetime of litigation. He said: "I know I was right in this case. ...My honor and integrity were questioned. It pays to fight under such circumstances. I lost my farm of one hundred and sixty acres and all my property but I feel well repaid. My wife, my children and my friends know now I was innocent, and I can look any man in the face without a blush."[11]

Charles Wheeler, who stood by his client during all those years, had grown from a young, inexperienced lawyer to a lawyer of some renown throughout the state. Johnson had occasionally borrowed money from Wheeler during the litigation, which at the end totaled about $1,500. He gave Wheeler all that he had—a spavined horse and $130—but Wheeler declined the rest: "I said, 'Bob, I have been a thousand times repaid. I didn't have any clients; I didn't have anything to do when you came to me twenty-five years ago, and I have made an acquaintanceship, and that has done me good, and you don't owe me another dollar.' And so we shook hands and looked the other way .... "[12]

Thus Bob Johnson "got his character back," and in the process made Iowa legal history. And no one will ever know who really stole John Foreman's calves.

CHAPTER SIX

The Progressive Era

1900-1917

*"When any society ceases to grow better,
it has begun to grow worse."*

— GOVERNOR Albert Baird Cummins

1900-1917

AT THE DAWN OF A NEW CENTURY, Republican William McKinley was the twenty-fifth President of the United States. In the year 1900 there were forty-five states with a combined population of nearly seventy-five million. Iowa, with a population of 2,231,853, ranked tenth in size. For the first time since achieving statehood, Iowa's population experienced a slight decline, decreasing 0.3 percent between 1900 and 1910.

On September 6, 1901, President McKinley was shot by an assassin and died a week later. He was succeeded by Vice-President Theodore Roosevelt, who had distinguished himself as the commander of the Rough Riders in the Spanish-American War. During Roosevelt's administration, the United States obtained the right in perpetuity to construct and operate a major canal across Panama, linking the Atlantic and Pacific oceans. The Panama Canal was completed in 1914 and was controlled by the United States until transferred to Panamanian control in 1979.

Theodore Roosevelt was elected President in his own right in 1904 and became the champion of the progressive movement. The Progressive Party became a third-party vehicle for Roosevelt when, in 1912, he challenged his hand-picked successor, conservative William Howard Taft. Like much of the country, Iowa split its traditional Republican votes between Roosevelt and Taft, casting a plurality for Democrat Woodrow Wilson. Not since Franklin Pierce in 1852 had a Democratic presidential candidate won the Iowa popular vote.

The defeat of Roosevelt by Woodrow Wilson marked the downturn in the fortunes of the Progressive Party, but it left in its wake a raft of Congressional regulatory and consumer legislation. The national reform mood continued, as reflected in the passage of populist-inspired amendments to the United States Constitution. The Sixteenth Amendment, ratified in 1913, gave Congress power to levy and collect income taxes. The Seventeenth Amendment, ratified the same year, provided for the popular election of United States senators.

The progressive movement was strongly mirrored in Iowa with the 1902 election of Republican Governor Albert Baird Cummins. During Cummins's three terms as governor, the Iowa General Assembly passed numerous reform measures, including a direct primary law, regulation of the insurance industry, the creation of a juvenile court system, elimination of free railroad passes, and compulsory education. After Cummins moved to national politics as a U.S. Senator in 1908, voters elected a series of conservative or "standpat" Republican governors.

The Iowa General Assembly in 1913 and 1915 approved an amendment to the state constitution to extend the vote to women. However, the measure was defeated in a 1916 referendum by a vote of 172,990 to 162,849. The defeat was especially welcomed in those counties with large immigrant populations (particularly German), who feared that woman suffrage would lead to prohibition. This fear of prohibition soon was realized at the national level, when the Eighteenth Amendment to the U.S. Constitution establishing prohibition of alcoholic beverages was ratified in 1919. The Nineteenth Amendment granting woman suffrage was ratified the following year; Iowa became the tenth state to ratify the federal suffrage amendment.

Even as Americans enjoyed a period of progressive reform and economic revival, storm clouds were gathering in Europe. The storm broke in June 1914 with the assassination of Archduke Franz Ferdinand by a Serbian nationalist. Soon much of Europe was at war, with the Central Powers of Germany, Austria-Hungary, Turkey, and Bulgaria fighting the Allied Powers of Great Britain, France, Russia, Italy, and other countries. The United States watched anxiously and resisted efforts to be drawn into the war. President Wilson announced a policy of neutrality, and was elected to a second term in 1916 on the platform: "He kept us out of war."

The war extended a period of agricultural prosperity, known as the "Golden Age of Agriculture," that had begun shortly before the turn of the century. Iowa and other states experienced large increases in exports. The government loaned money to the Allies to purchase food and later established guaranteed minimum prices for certain crops needed in the war effort. Farmers borrowed money and mortgaged their farms to expand their operations—buying more land and equipment, and raising more crops. The bubble of expansion would burst dramatically in the years following the war, but in the meantime, Iowans basked in the wartime slogan, "Food will win the war!"

In 1915, the British liner *Lusitania* was sunk by a German submarine off the coast of Ireland, and about one-tenth of the 1,200 killed were Americans. Pressure grew for United States involvement in the war, as Americans realized the growing menace of German submarine power. Patriotic and anti-German sentiments took root. After Germany resumed unrestricted submarine warfare in February 1917, the United States severed diplomatic relations. In April 1917, President Wilson asked Congress for a declaration of war to make the world "safe for democracy." America plunged headlong into The War to End All Wars.

The progressive era in Iowa was marked by the enactment of many laws concerning pure food and drugs, sanitation, and the prevention and treatment of infectious diseases. The publication in 1906 of The Jungle by Upton Sinclair focused national attention on conditions in the meat-packing industry. This concern was mirrored in Iowa with the passage in 1913 of an Act for the Sanitation of Food Producing Establishments.

SANITATION OF FOOD PRODUCING ESTABLISHMENTS.
Be it enacted by the General Assembly of the State of Iowa:
Section 1. [E]very building, room, basement or cellar occupied or used as a bakery, confectionery, cannery, packing house, slaughter-house, dairy, creamery, cheese factory, restaurant, hotel, grocery, [or] meat market ... shall be properly lighted, drained, plumbed and ventilated and conducted with strict regard to the influence of such conditions upon the purity and wholesomeness of the food therein produced ....

Sec. 4. The doors, windows and other openings of every food-producing or distributing establishment during the fly season shall be fitted with self-closing screen doors and wire window screens of not coarser than 14 mesh wire gauze, provided that this section shall not apply to sheds used for husking corn ....

Sec. 5. Every building, room, basement or cellar occupied or used for the preparation, manufacture, packing, canning, sale or distribution of food, shall have convenient toilet, or toilet rooms separate and apart from the room or rooms where the process of production, manufacture, packing, canning, selling or distribution is conducted. ...

Sec. 6. Cuspidors for the use of operatives, employees, clerks or other persons shall be provided whenever necessary, and each cuspidor shall be thoroughly emptied and washed daily with disinfectant solution .... No operative, employee, or other person shall expectorate ... except in cuspidors as provided for herein.

. . . .

Sec. 10. The sidewalk or street display of food products is prohibited unless such products are en-

Governor Albert B. Cummins, during whose three terms in office (1902-1908) much progressive legislation was enacted in Iowa. (Courtesy, State Historical Society of Iowa, Iowa City)

closed in a showcase or similar device which shall protect the same from flies, dust or other contamination; ... but the sidewalk or street display of meat or meat products is prohibited. ...
Approved April 14, 1913.

Acts of the Thirty-Fifth General Assembly, 1913, ch. 201, §§ 1, 4-6, 10.

By the turn of the century, the automobile had begun to appear alongside the horse and buggy on Iowa's streets and highways. The Iowa legislature soon decided it was time to regulate (and derive revenue from) this new contraption. The first state law "Requiring Registration of Motor Vehicles and Regulating Their Use or Operation Upon Highways or Streets" was passed in 1904.

MOTOR VEHICLES.
Be it enacted by the General Assembly of the State of Iowa:
. . . .

Sec. 2. Every owner of a motor vehicle shall, for every such vehicle owned by him, file in the office of the secretary of state a statement of his name and address, with a brief description of the vehicle to be registered, on a blank to be prepared and furnished by

FROM "THE BOGGES AND THEIR AUTO"

Cartoons of the period commented on the hazards wrought by "the machine," which led to many lawsuits. Here, a cartoon by J.N. "Ding" Darling as it appeared in the *[Des Moines] Register and Leader* in 1910. (Courtesy, J.N. "Ding" Darling Foundation)

HIS FIRST LESSON IN RUNNING THE MACHINE.

such secretary for that purpose. The filing fee shall be one (1) dollar.

. . . .

Sec. 8. No person shall operate a motor vehicle on a public highway at a rate of speed greater than is reasonable and proper, having regard to the traffic and use of the highway, or so as to endanger the life or limb of any person, or in any event in the closely built up portions of a city, town or village, at a greater rate than one (1) mile in six (6) minutes, or elsewhere in a city, town or village at a greater rate than one (1) mile in four (4) minutes, or elsewhere outside of a city town or village at a greater average rate than twenty (20) miles per hour ....

Sec. 9. Any person operating a motor vehicle shall, at request or on signal by putting up the hand, from a person riding or driving a restive horse or other draft or domestic animals, bring such motor vehicle immediately to a stop, and, if traveling in the opposite direction, remain stationery so long as may be reasonable to allow such horse or animals to pass ....

Approved April 12, 1904.

Acts of the Thirtieth General Assembly, 1904, ch. 53, §§ 2, 8-9.

As the number and speed of the horseless carriages increased, the clash between the old and the new featured in many lawsuits. The following trial excerpt in a case alleging the defendant's negligence in operating his automobile illustrates the novel hazard posed on Iowa's roadways by "the machine."

Plaintiff gave the following version of the affair:

When first the machine [the automobile] turned towards me I pulled out to my side of the road about as close as I dared get. Q. How did that machine seem to be coming towards you? A. It seemed to be coming fast—extra fast. It was on the east side of the road and seemed to be coming direct to me. Q. What happened when the machine came to you? Did it change its speed in any manner that you observed? A. As the machine got direct to me,

seemed to be in front of me, the two coming together, my horse whirled off, went over the embankment. Q. What happened to you and to the buggy and to the horse? A. The horse turned and went down the embankment and the buggy went over, and the buggy turned over and laid on its two right-hand wheels. The horse headed north with the one thill on its back and the other on its side. Mr. Truax and Mr. Netcott and I picked the buggy up, then investigated as to where the wheel tracks of the automobile were. Q. Where was the left wheel of the automobile with reference to the center of the traveled way? A. It was nearer the east side than it was to the west side. I was driving the horse and single buggy. I have driven the horse before, and had met automobiles before when I had been driving her single. I met automobiles a number of different times. I met one that morning right here on Main street. It ran across the bridge right behind me, and when I got on the other side of the bridge it went by me. The horse is an extra gentle animal. When I met the automobile I had my lines one in each hand, and had my whip in the right hand. When I had met automobiles before the animal seemed to be quiet, and I had passed them without difficulty. Q. As the automobile approached closely to you, it turned to the right of the road, Mr. Needy? A. No, sir. Q. It didn't turn out to the right on the road at all? A. Not that I saw. ... I mean that it come direct to me—come direct to me; then when it, just as my horse flew, it veered over a little to the right, but was not over half of the road. ... Q. Didn't touch you, did it? A. I don't know as it did, because the horse cleared herself away from there.

Needy v. Littlejohn, 137 Iowa 704, 706-07 (1908).

Another hazard reflected in the litigation of this period was coal mining, which reached its zenith of production in southern and central Iowa during the years of World War I. Laws to ensure worker safety had been enacted in the 1870s and had grown in number and complexity, with extensive legislation being passed in the progressive era. Still, there were frequent injuries and deaths from coal mining accidents, including Iowa's worst coal mining dis-

aster at Lost Creek in 1902, in which twenty miners lost their lives. The dangers of coal mining were borne out in many decisions of the Iowa Supreme Court.

There was evidence tending to show that decedent, an experienced coal miner, was employed on the day of the accident in question as a [mule] driver in defendant's mine, and that it was usual for the driver to crouch between the mule and the loaded car, his left hand on the back of the mule, his left foot on the draw chain, his right foot on the bumper of the car, and his right hand on the car itself; it being necessary for him to ride in this position because the entries [passageways] through which the cars must be hauled were little higher than the back of the mule. The evidence also tended to show that, after the accident, decedent was found at what is called the "parting" in an entry, complaining of having been injured by getting squeezed coming out of a room with a car of coal, and that the mule got caught on a cap piece of the timbering and the car squeezed him. A witness who heard deceased make this statement was directed by the pit boss to go back along the entry and find the mule and car which he did, and ... a tie, similar to the ties used in laying the track was found hanging by a projecting spike from the hames of the mule. ... The jury might have found from this evidence, including the declarations of deceased that a tie with a spike projecting from its lower side had been used as a cap piece on top of a prop in room seven; that, as the mule driven by decedent passed under it, the spike caught in the hames of the mule, causing him to be suddenly stopped, so that the loaded car ran against him, squeezing decedent, who was riding in the usual position between the mule and the car .... As a result of the injury received by decedent he died the next day at the hospital; it being discovered by *post mortem* examination that his intestines had been ruptured by the injury. The negligence alleged was in failure to provide decedent with a safe place in which to work ....

... The jury might well have found that there was negligence on the part of defendant in allowing this cap piece with projecting spikes to remain in position over the track at this place with the danger that the harness of a mule passing under it might be caught, with the natural result that the mule should be checked and the loaded coal car following him should run against the driver crouching between the mule and the car.

As we think the court erred in striking out the evidence as to custom and usage and in directing a verdict for defendant, the judgment is reversed.

Spevak v. Coaldale Fuel Co., 152 Iowa 90, 91-92, 98 (1911).

The hazard of driving mules that pulled pit cars in coal mines was borne out in Iowa court decisions. (Courtesy, State Historical Society of Iowa, Iowa City)

Among those killed or injured in the Lost Creek tragedy were young boys, who were still widely employed in the mines. The Iowa legislature in 1874 had enacted a law that no boy under ten years of age and no female could be employed in the mines. In 1880, the legislature substituted a provision that no boy under twelve years could work in a mine, but the act applied only to mines employing more than fifteen people. In 1906, the legislature passed a child labor law that prohibited any child under fourteen from working in the mines. The act also applied to other Iowa industries and establishments.

Boys were often employed in Iowa coal mines, as shown in this 1908 photo, until Iowa law raised the age of child labor. (Courtesy, State Historical Society of Iowa, Iowa City)

EMPLOYMENT OF CHILD LABOR.
Be it enacted by the General Assembly of the State of Iowa:
        Section 1. No person under fourteen years of age shall be employed with or without wages or compensation in any mine, manufacturing establishment, factory, mill, shop, laundry, slaughter house or packing house, or in any store or mercantile establishment where more than eight persons are employed, or in the operation of any freight or passenger elevator.

Sec. 2. No person under sixteen years of age shall be employed at any work or occupation by which, by reason of its nature or the place of employment, the health of such person may be injured, or his morals depraved, or at any work in which the handling or use of gun powder, dynamite or other like explosive is required, and no female under sixteen years of age shall be employed in any capacity where the duties of such employment compel her to remain constantly standing.

Sec. 3. No person under sixteen years of age shall be employed at any of the places or in any of the occupations recited in section 1 hereof before the hour of six o'clock in the morning or after the hour of nine o'clock in the evening, and if such person is employed exceeding five hours of each day, a noon intermission of not less than thirty minutes shall be given between the hours of eleven and one o'clock, and such person shall not be employed more than ten hours in any one day, exclusive of the noon intermission, but the provisions of this section shall not apply to persons employed in husking sheds or other places connected with canning factories where vegetables or grain are prepared for canning and in which no machinery is operated.
    · · · ·

Approved April 10, 1906.

Acts of the Thirty-First General Assembly, 1906, ch. 103 §§ 1-3.

In 1913 the number of Iowa Supreme Court judges was increased from six to seven—the first such increase since 1894. The work of the Court continued to grow, with the number of filed cases nearly doubling between 1892 and 1902.

One of the most important cases decided by the Court in the early years of the new century was a challenge to the corporate existence of the Amana Society. The state claimed that the Society's business and property interests exceeded its non-profit corporate powers, and therefore the corporation should be dissolved. The Iowa Supreme Court rejected this contention, and in so doing gave a rousing defense of the Amana Society's communal ideals.

The defendant is an organization of a religious character. The charitable and benevolent objects included are such only as are enjoined as duties in the exercise of that Christian faith for the promotion of which the corporation was created. The preamble to the Constitution, which is the foundation of all the articles of incorporation, recites the emigration of the "community of True Inspiration" from Germany to this country in 1843 "for the sake of civil and religious liberty," its settlement at Ebenezer, near Buffalo, N. Y., and removal therefrom to Iowa county "according to the known will of God." The purposes of incorporating may be gathered from this constitution.

 . . . .

It is manifest from these extracts from the articles and constitution that the corporation was organized to aid in effectuating certain ideals in religious life, especially those relating to communistic ownership of property; and the State insists that such ownership and the management of the property for the maintenance of the community cannot be other than purely secular and is inappropriate to religious purposes. Possibly a majority of Christians have concluded that community ownership of property apparently ordained by the Apostles was merely temporary but this opinion has not been shared by all. The Moravians, Shakers, the Oneida Community, and more recently the Zionists, have thought otherwise. No one will claim that the doctrine is entirely without support in the Scriptures. Those who became believers on the day of Pentecost, we are told, not only continued "steadfastly in the Apostles' doctrine," but "were together, and had all things in common ...."

The members of the defendant society regard the mode of life described in the Acts of the Apostles as an essential part of their religion. Their notion is that people are placed in this world for the one purpose of saving their souls, and that this requires the crucifixion of such desires and appetites as divert attention from God. Their aim is to live such a life as Christ lived. To attain this they believe it necessary that everything be held in common; that each individual be relieved from the cares and burdens of separate property ownership, to the end that selfishness may be eradicated; and that all may enjoy the better opportunity of knowing and serving God. ...

[I]t is argued that the organization and maintenance of such a society is obnoxious to sound public policy. Certain it is that the status of the individual members is not in accordance with prevailing American ideals. ... But in this country all opinions are tolerated and entire freedom of action allowed, unless this interferes in some way with the rights of others. ... Under the blessings of free government, every citizen should be permitted to pursue that mode of life which is dictated by his own conscience, and if this, also, be exacted by an essential dogma or doctrine of his religion, a corporation organized to enable him to meet the requirement of his faith is a religious corporation and as such may own property and carry on enterprises appropriate to the object of its creation.

State of Iowa v. Amana Society, 132 Iowa 304, 310, 312-14, 317, 319 (1906).

Iowa's Civil Rights Act was over twenty-five years old when Mrs. Susie Brown of Des Moines sued to enforce its provisions. Mrs. Brown alleged that she had attended a "Pure Food Show" held by the Des Moines Retail Grocers' Association, but was refused a sample of coffee at the defendants' booth because of her color. The defendants argued that the Civil Rights Act did not apply, because the booth itself was not the type of public accommodation covered by the act. The Court agreed with this contention, but not without a rousing dissent by Chief Justice Evans.

Evans, C. J.—I can not concur in the majority opinion. ...

The pure food show addressed itself to the public as a *quasi* public exhibition. It sets its dates and collected toll at its gates. It necessarily consisted of its many parts. ... Whatever may be said of the booth of J. H. Bell Company if it had been a separate and independent entity, it seems to me that the pure food show in its entirety partook of the character of a place of entertainment and amusement as well as of a place where refreshments were served. ...

In as much as the defendant was in charge of one of the booths of the pure food show, and in as much as he was confessedly serving its accommodations and privileges indiscriminately to white people, and yet refused the same accommodation and privilege to the plaintiff solely on the ground that she was colored, it seems to me that the case comes fairly within the letter of the statute, and clearly within its spirit. ... The statute is simple and direct, and its spirit is too manifest to be mistaken. The majority opinion is professedly "divorced from sentiment;" but the statute is a statute of sentiment. It had its origin in sentiment and draws all its life therefrom. It does not deal with ordinary property rights. It is a form of the chivalry of the older days. It is an embodiment in statutory form of the sympathy of the dominant race for the weaker race in its struggle for the higher levels of worthy citizenship. The struggle is strenuous at best. Perhaps no race that has aspired to the recognition of higher civilization has ever carried a heavier load of disadvantage. This was the situation that appealed to the framers of this statute. It was framed in language broad and comprehensive. Its manifest purpose was and is to protect this burdened race against the further burden of pubic discrimination and humiliation. It does not attempt to deal with social rights, nor is there any question of social rights involved in this case, nor was the humiliation of the plaintiff a mere "social humiliation," as indicated in the majority opinion.

Brown v. The J. H. Bell Company, 146 Iowa 89, 105-07 (1910).

Perhaps the most famous and colorful litigants in turn-of-the century Iowa were sisters from Marion, Iowa, forever enshrined in vaudevillian history as the Cherry sisters. The sisters began performing in Iowa in 1893, and eventually moved to the national stage. Whether deliberately or by accident, their act was ludicrously bad, and audiences responded enthusiastically with jeers, tomatoes, and other projectiles.

But while the sisters could tolerate any manner of object thrown from the audience, they could not tolerate criticism from the press. So when a leading state newspaper reprinted a particularly nasty review, the Cherry sisters took their act to court.

The Cherry Sisters: A Case of Libel

THE CHERRY SISTERS WERE LEGENDARY FOR being the worst performers in the history of American vaudeville. In 1898, the *Des Moines Leader* reprinted a criticism of their act, which must rank as one of the most scathing reviews written about any performer in any newspaper. The sisters promptly took the newspaper to court, claiming they had been libeled. After a colorful and much-publicized trial, one sister's case was appealed to the Iowa Supreme Court. In 1901, the Court handed down a classic opinion on the limits of fair comment in libel actions, and the Cherry sisters passed from stage legend to legal legend.

The sisters were raised on a farm in Linn County. Ella was born in 1854, followed by Lizzie, Addie, Effie, and, in 1871, Jessie. In 1888 their father died and, as Effie wrote, "we five girls were left orphans to battle our way through life alone."[1] The young women started a dairy business with six cows in Marion, Iowa.

Effie claimed that the idea of going on the stage was hers. In any event, in January 1893, Effie, Jessie, and Ella gave a concert in Marion. The house was crowded with curious onlookers. A member of the audience recalled: "[We] didn't throw things but [we] whistled and stumped and sang. Effie played the harmonica—there was absolutely no tune. One of them read an essay ... there was not a word heard. It was the audience you got the fun from ...."[2]

The Cherrys were nonetheless encouraged, and on they went to Cedar Rapids. The *Cedar Rapids Gazette* review gives the true flavor of their performance: "Such unlimited gall as was exhibited last night at Greene's opera house by the Cherry sisters is past understanding .... If some indefinable instinct of modesty could not have warned them that they were acting the part of monkeys, it does seem like the overshoes thrown at them would convey the idea. ... Cigars, cigarettes, rubbers everything was thrown at them, yet they stood there, awkwardly bowing their acknowledgements and singing on."[3]

Effie, Jessie, and Addie Cherry—the famous Cherry sisters. (Courtesy, State Historical Society of Iowa, Iowa City)

The sisters filed an information for criminal libel against the city editor of the *Gazette*—and this plus the review made the Cherrys famous throughout Iowa. Their lawyer persuaded them to do a second performance, withdraw the libel charge, and instead have a mock trial at Greene's Opera House.

The *Gazette* reported: "[O]f all the crazy experiences Cedar Rapids was ever treated to the one last night was the worst." The paper prayed that such "pitiable simpering gawks (never again) be permitted to away themselves on a stage for a frenzied audience to hoot at, to yell at, and to throw at." The "jury" in the audience sentenced the city editor of the *Gazette* to work on the Cherry's farm and to "submit himself to the choice of the said sisters, beginning with the eldest, and the first one who shall consent to such an alliance to that one shall he then and there be joined in the holy bonds of matrimony."[4]

After their Cedar Rapids performances, the sisters also performed in Davenport and Vinton, and then went on to Dubuque. They were beginning to make money. Cedar Rapids had given them fame throughout the state of Iowa; Dubuque would bring them national attention.

At the Cherrys' Dubuque performance, tin horns, cowbells, rattles, and roars from the audience drowned out the opening song. The Cherrys withdrew from the stage, then tried again. According to the *Dubuque Herald*, they then became the targets for "a perfect fusilade of garden trash, decayed fruit, tin cans and other noxious missiles."[5] The audience squirted the Cherrys with fire extinguishers and seltzer siphons, striking one sister full in the face. Down went the curtain.

The Cherrys tried yet again. More "garden truck and hen fruit and streams from the fire extinguisher and several seltzer siphons" descended on the sisters. One sister came on with a shotgun, but was forced to retreat by a volley of turnips. Along with the turnips, cabbages, and ancient eggs, somebody had thrown a washboiler at the stage. The manager called an end.

When the sisters drove to their hotel after the performance, rowdies pelted their carriage with sticks and stones. As the Cherrys alighted, the rowdies hurled eggs at them.

Newspapers throughout Iowa reported the event, some of them very critical of the behavior of the Dubuque audience. Within three months, the widely circulated *National Police Gazette* had printed a huge story on the sisters and the debacle at Dubuque. Thus the Cherrys became celebrities even in New York.

"Played the hose on her. A wild and disgraceful scene in the Grand Opera House, Dubuque, Ia., during a recent performance given by the Cherry Sisters." (*The National Police Gazette*, June 17, 1893)

The sisters fled back to Marion, $150 the richer from their Dubuque performance. The experience had taken its toll, and Effie suffered a nervous reaction. But rested by a summer on their farm, Addie, Effie, and Jessie toured Iowa and Illinois during the next two winter seasons.

The newspapers and the Cherrys were always at war. For example, in the summer of 1895, the *Center Point Tribune* wrote that the Cherrys had arrived at the right time, as "the vegetables are about the right size to toss on the stage very handily." Another newspaper reported that the sisters had gone after the *Tribune's* editor, and "proceeded to give him a good flogging with whips."[6] They were arrested and fined.

In La Porte in August 1895, Jessie Cherry showed that the sisters could also take on the audience. A newspaper reported: "The Cherry sisters' entertainment ended in a riot Saturday night. A gang threw onions, etc. on the stage, when one of the Sisters came down and struck Frank Fritz on the head with a club."[7]

Then the famous impresario Oscar Hammerstein invited the sisters to perform in New York. Hammerstein, in financial difficulties, is reported to have said: "I've tried the best now I'll try the worst."[8] His agent convinced Addie, Effie, Jessie, and even Lizzie to accept the engagement.

Their opening night at the Olympia Theater was vegetable free. But the next night, the New Yorkers took up where the Iowans left off, and threw vegetables. The *New York Times* wrote: "Never before did New Yorkers see anything … like the Cherry sisters from … Iowa. It is to be sincerely hoped that nothing like them will ever been seen again."[9] The Cherrys stayed for four weeks, and it was reported that the price of vegetables skyrocketed in the vicinity of the Olympia Theater.

From New York the sisters went to Chicago, St. Louis, and Cincinnati. Next they toured in the east, from Brooklyn to Washington, D.C. This was the peak of their extraordinary career, and they were reputed to have earned considerable money.

The Cherrys were in constant legal battles. An unpublished biography recorded: "The string of lawsuits growing out of the concert tours had been endless. Every season had produced its quota of arrests and counter arrests, actions for damages for property, actions for personal assault with and without weapons. They had seen Effie dragged by her hair down the aisle of a theatre, Jessie belaboring a heckler with a cudgel, all three sisters combining to horsewhip an editor, rows, routs, and riots innumerable."[10] Their most famous legal battle lay ahead.

In February 1898, Addie, Effie, and Jessie Cherry were touring in western Iowa. On Wednesday, February 9, they performed in Odebolt. The *Odebolt Chronicle* gave a vitriolic review. Under the heading "The Cherries (sic) Were Here," the report by editor William Hamilton began: "When the curtain went up on Wednesday evening of last week … [t]he audience saw three creatures surpassing the witches in Macbeth in general hideousness."

The next passage was to be the subject of the great libel case:

> Effie is an old jade of 50 summers, Jessie a frisky filly of 40, and Addie, the flower of the family, a capering monstrosity of 35. Their long, skinny arms, equipped with talons at the extremities, swung mechanically, and anon were waved frantically at the suffering audience. The mouths of their rancid features

opened like caverns, and sounds like the wailing of damned souls issued there-from. They pranced around the stage with a motion that suggested a cross be-tween the danse du ventre and a fox trot, strange creatures with painted faces and a hideous mein. Effie is spavined, Addie is knock-kneed and string-halt, and Jessie, the only one who showed her stockings, has legs without calves, as classic in their outlines as the curves of a broomhandle.[11]

On February 23, the *Des Moines Leader* reprinted the infamous passage. All three sisters sued the *Des Moines Leader* for libel, each claiming damages of $15,000. The case was dismissed for technical legal reasons. Then Addie Cherry—whom the review had described as "knock-kneed and string-halt"—brought a sepa-rate suit against the *Leader* for libel, claiming $15,000 damages.

Addie Cherry's petition, filed July 12, 1898, alleged that the defendants pub-lished the review "maliciously intending to injure your petitioner in her said good name, fame and credit … and exposing her to public hatred, contempt and ridicule. … "[12] In its answer, the *Leader* denied malice, stating that "the said article was writ-ten in a facetious, humorous and satirical style, and was so meant by the said de-fendants, and that it was by all persons so regarded …."[13]

On April 20-21, 1899, the case was tried in the Polk County district court, Judge C.A. Bishop presiding. The *Des Moines Daily News* reported that the court-room was crowded with spectators, "anxious for a glimpse of the famous people." The Cherry sisters "were very talkative, and gave their attorneys a great deal of ad-vice as to the manner to conduct the case." The newspaper added: "[T]he girls have all improved both in looks and wealth. Effie is the only one who shows any age. Jessie is a young girl and was very prettily dressed this morning."[14]

Addie—who seriously understated her age as thirty-one—was the first witness. She testified that people in many towns had mocked her about the *Leader* review. Young men in the audience would say: "Addie is knock-kneed, and I wonder if she is." While on the streets of Des Moines, she heard: "There goes Effie, the Leader says she has got spavins, and Addie, she is knock-kneed and got string-halt." The article had led to difficulty in making theatrical engagements and had kept people away from their performances. Addie testified that the review had been the cause of great anxiety, affecting her health and nervous system.[15]

During cross-examination, Addie described a typical Cherry sisters perfor-mance:

> I don't sing much, the others do. … I recite essays and events that have happened I have written up of my own. … I sing … a eulogy on ourselves. It is a kind of a ballad composed by ourselves. I help the others sing it. …
>
> "When the Cherry Sisters come to town, they are the cry both up and down, I want to see that modern show, and will ask Dad if I can't go."
>
> Then the chorus is Ta, ra, ra, ra, ra, Boom de ay, repeated four times. We beat the bass drum. The orchestra generally accompanies us. We kick a little with our feet.

The defendants' counsel asked Addie to show the jury how she kicked her feet, and she demonstrated. She described her movements in another song: "In the chorus I walked a little around the stage, kind of a fast walk or a little run." Addie strongly denied that spectators at any time had thrown "cabbages at us, nor sticks, nor a dead cat, nor pieces of meat, nor old turnips."

Effie Cherry testified next—like Addie giving an optimistic view of her age. She stated that several members of the Iowa legislature had drawn her attention to the *Leader* article, and people on the street repeated its epithets. Addie had indeed suffered a nervous reaction to the review, was unable to sleep, and sometimes walked the floor until midnight.

Jessie Cherry—who had shed a decade to give her age as seventeen—was the third and last witness for the plaintiff. She confirmed Addie's sleeplessness, and told how she had heard Addie described as "knock-kneed."

The sole defense witness was William E. Hamilton, editor of the *Oldebolt Chronicle* and the author of the original review. He testified:

> It was the most ridiculous performance I ever saw. There was no orchestra there, the pianist left after the thing was half over. She could not stand the racket and left .... They read essays and sung choruses and gave recitations, interspersed with the remarks that if the boys didn't stop the curtain would go down. One young man brought a pair of beer bottles which he used as a pair of glasses. They threatened to stop the performance unless he was put out, but he was not put out and they didn't stop.

> When the curtain went up the audience shrieked, and indulged in cat calls, and from that time one could hardly hear very much to know what was going on to give a recital of it. ... I am not qualified to pass an opinion upon the merits of the singing. The discord was something that grated on one's nerves.

Hamilton described the Cherrys' movements: "They went around the stage ... sort of a mincing gait, shaking their bodies and making little steps, that is what made me describe it as a cross between the *danse du ventre* and a fox trot." The act had closed with a tableau: "Jessie was the central figure in that piece with her eyes uplifted, red lights, and so on; there was a 'Rock of Ages.' The audience was talking to the women, and they, the Cherry sisters, would talk back. They would say: 'You don't know anything. You have not been raised well or you would not interrupt a nice, respectable show.'"

When asked during cross-examination what he had meant in his review by "spavined," Hamilton said: "I mean a deformity of the limbs or legs, which was apparent. I could not see, but I would judge from the gait. The terms, string halt and knock-kneed, was from the same standpoint, their appearance, walk, etc., on the stage." The defense rested.

The defendants then asked the court to instruct the jury to find in the defendants' favor, on the grounds that the article contained nothing libelous *per se* and was without express malice, no special damages had been proved, and the publication was "conditionally privileged." Judge Bishop sustained the motion, and the jury duly entered a verdict for the defendants.

The *Leader* reported that in so ruling, the judge said that "persons taking part in public entertainments subject themselves to criticism and ... cannot recover so long as no personal reflection is made on their character and no malice is shown."

When Judge Bishop gave his ruling, Addie Cherry became very excited and, rising to her feet, announced that she wanted to say something about the case. Her attorney pushed her back into her chair, and the judge gave her "a significant nod" which subdued her.[16]

Addie Cherry appealed to the Iowa Supreme Court which, on May 28, 1901, affirmed the judgment for the defendants. The Court found that the review was "qualifiedly privileged," reasoning that it "was published of and concerning plaintiff in her role as a public performer ... and it is well settled that the editor of a newspaper has the right to freely criticize any and every kind of public performance, provided in so doing he is not actuated by malice." The Court defined actual malice as "personal spite or ill will, or culpable recklessness or negligence," and found that no extrinsic evidence or evidence from the publication itself indicated that the review was actuated by malice.[17]

The Court gave broad scope to the right of comment on a public performance: "One who goes upon the stage to exhibit himself to the public ... may be freely criticized. He may be held up to ridicule, and entire freedom of expression is guarantied dramatic critics, provided they are not actuated by malice or evil purpose in what they write. ... Mere exaggeration, or even gross exaggeration, does not of itself make the comment unfair."[18]

The Court affirmed the district court's ruling, concluding: "If there ever was a case justifying ridicule and sarcasm,—aye, even gross exaggeration,—it is the one now before us. According to the record, the performance given by the plaintiff and the company of which she was a member was not only childish, but ridiculous in the extreme. A dramatic critic should be allowed considerable license in such a case."[19]

The case of *Cherry v. Des Moines Leader* has since been regarded as having established important principles of libel law. One authority has described it as "[t]he case that is so often cited in judicial rulings on fair comment and criticism."[20]

The Cherry sisters continued their tours until 1903, when Jessie Cherry suddenly died in Hot Springs, Arkansas, from typhoid and malaria. The other sisters retired from the stage, but over the years attempted periodic comebacks. However, their legendary days were behind them.

Addie and Effie both died in the 1940s, and on the death of the latter in August 1944, the *New York Times* published an obituary describing their act as "artistically the worst on any stage." But the *Times* concluded with what may have been the Cherry sisters' best review:

> Maybe the laugh was on their side. Maybe the Cherry sisters knew better than the public did what was really going on. Be this as it may, they left behind an imperishable memory. And they gave more pleasure to their audiences than did many a performer who was merely almost good.[21]

Social reform in progressive-era Iowa did not include the long-sought-for woman suffrage. The popular defeat in a 1916 referendum of a proposed suffrage amendment to the state's constitution was a grave disappointment to those reformers who had rejoiced when the General Assembly passed a suffrage resolution in the two previous legislative sessions. The Iowa campaign had been bolstered by a visit from the English suffragette Sylvia Pankhurst, who—like her famous mother, Emmeline—was imprisoned and force-fed for the cause of woman suffrage. On February 1, 1911, Sylvia Pankhurst addressed a joint session of the Iowa General Assembly.

Arriving after an all-night journey at Desmoines [sic], Iowa, having entirely lost my voice, I was met by a group of women, who told me that at noon I must address the Senate and the House of Representatives in joint convention. The only woman who had previously done so was Susan B. Anthony .... I whispered that my voice was gone, but Dr. Dewey, an osteopath, assured me that she would put it right for me, and she absolutely fulfilled her promise in a miraculous manner. A Bill to enfranchise the women of Iowa was then pending, and in view of this I felt very deeply the responsibility laid upon me. The Speaker bowed low and led me to the dais to speak; the legislators were cordial. The women assured me I had helped them.

E. Sylvia Pankhurst, *The Suffragette Movement: An Intimate Account of Persons and Ideals* (London: Longmans, Green and Co., 1931), p. 347.

A militant suffragette is not necessarily a circus, nor a bold female person with a loud voice and a forward manner.

Somehow a contrary impression had come out of England, where the militant suffragette moves and has her being. But when the eminent Miss Sylvia Pankhurst walked down the aisle of the house of representatives at the state house shortly after noon yesterday to address the assembled legis-

A parade staged by the Iowa Equal Suffrage Association, Boone, Iowa, October 27, 1908. (Courtesy, State Historical Society of Iowa, Des Moines)

lature and the crowds in the galleries, this impression was quickly dispelled.

. . . .

After her introduction by Speaker Stillman, Miss Pankhurst expressed her deep sense of gratitude and of responsibility for the privilege extended to her by the legislature. It gave her, she said, opportunity to bring to Iowa the message of Englishwomen and also to speak for the suffrage measure now before the legislature.

"For me this is a most auspicious occasion," she continued, "and this opportunity to speak to a legislative body an extraordinary privilege. For six years we women of England have sought to speak face to face with our legislature and the officers of our government upon matters of vital concern to us, and again and again we have been thrown into prison for trying to do this."

. . . .

When she had finished with this portion of her address, she made her argument for woman suffrage in America. Women here are taxed without representation, she declared, which is unamerican. ...

Women need a voice in the government of the United States because they have become workers in the industrial and commercial fields, millions of them. Their voice is needed to shape industrial legislation properly. Their voice is important to secure proper adjustment of social conditions and in many other matters of which women have knowledge and in which they have special interest.

"Your women will press forward and demand the vote much as we have had to do in England," said Miss Pankhurst with a prophetic ring in her voice. "They are determined. They cannot be checked. Do not press them to militancy."

"We women want the vote not so much for its political effect, but more to develop our character and give us larger and broader interests in life. We want to be complete human beings."

The [Des Moines] Register and Leader, February 2, 1911.

This sign urged Iowa voters to approve the woman suffrage amendment to the Iowa constitution at the polls on June 5, 1916. The amendment was defeated. (Courtesy, State Historical Society of Iowa, Iowa City)

Not until 1920 would Iowa women obtain general rights of suffrage—and this due to a federal, rather than a state, constitutional amendment. Still, women continued to make inroads in the legal profession. In 1905, at the Eleventh Annual Meeting of the Iowa State Bar Association, Grace Ballantyne of Des Moines became the first woman to formally address a bar association convention, on the fitting subject, "The Woman Lawyer."

The Toastmaster: There are eleven hundred woman lawyers in the United States, and these lawyers probably are not physically as strong as the rest of us, but as to culture they are quite our equal; as to mentality they are quite our equal. Against opposition and against prejudice these eleven hundred lawyers have picked out of their path the rubbish that was in their way, and they have rolled away the stones of opposition; they have entered the greatest profession in the world, and they are in to stay, and are making a splendid success. We have with us one of those eleven hundred lawyers tonight, who will represent this class of lawyers, and she will speak on "The Woman Lawyer."

I take great pleasure in introducing Miss Grace H. Ballantyne, of Des Moines. (Applause.)

Miss Ballantyne: ... So far as I know, none of the State Bar Associations have extended to women the courtesy of representation on any of their programs, and we greatly appreciate this honor. In Massachusetts and New York the women have their separate organizations, but here we have the broader spirit, and both men and women are more liberal sharers in the good things at hand. We have a motto to the effect that "In all that is good Iowa affords the best." We cordially endorse this sentiment in its application to the Iowa State Bar Association. It is a pleasure also to recall the fact that Iowa was the first of the states to admit the regular woman lawyer of America, back in 1869.

The evolution of the woman lawyer has been along perfectly natural lines. We have not yet come to regard her as necessary as steam engines, for instance; but the steam engine was not considered a necessity until some time after it had been in general use. Both are the result of social development, of changed methods of doing things, of social energy handed down or passed on to us from others. We are borne onward by the imperative forces of evolution which bring to us constant change of standards and requirements, of mental attitudes and ideals. ...

Though doubtless the profession exacting the most for the laurels of success, its more liberal spirit is shown by its cordial reception of women into its ranks, and we are in the work to stay. We feel that with your friendly aid we shall prove ourselves a part of the legal fraternity of which some day, not far distant, you may be justly proud.

Proceedings of the Eleventh Annual Meeting of the Iowa State Bar Association (Iowa City: Press of Economy Advertising Co., 1905), Session of July 13, 1905, pp. 81-83, 85-86.

During the hot summer of 1912, southwest Iowa experienced one of the state's most horrific episodes of mass murder, in a case that garnered nationwide headlines. Eight people—a family of six and two neighbor children—were found in the tiny town of Villisca, brutally axed to death as they slept.

Despite vigorous public and private investigations and a $2,000 reward (later increased to $3,500), not until 1917 was a suspect brought to trial. The Reverend George Kelly, an eccentric, itinerant preacher, confessed to the crime, saying God had told him to "slay utterly." He later recanted his confession. Kelly's first trial resulted in a hung jury; after a second trial in November 1917, a "not guilty" verdict was returned. The Villisca ax murders remain Iowa's most famous unsolved mystery.

EIGHT PEOPLE MURDERED IN THEIR BEDS IN VILLISCA SUNDAY NIGHT

Sunday night, or early on the morning of Monday, June 10, 1912, Villisca was the scene of one of the most vicious crimes in all the history of the world. While the city was sleeping, following a peaceful night, some fiend incarnate entered the home of Mr. and Mrs. J. B. Moore on East Third street, and, using an ax, murdered eight people while they slept in their beds.

The dead are:

Josiah B. Moore, age 43.

Mrs. Moore, age 39.

Herman Moore, age 11

Katherine Moore, age 10

Boyd Moore, age 7

Paul Moore, age 5

Lena Stillinger, age 12

Ina Stillinger, age 8 ...

The discovery of the crime threw the city into the wildest state of excitement, and hundreds hurried to the scene of the tragedy. Few there were who were permitted to enter the house of carnage, and few, indeed, were there who cared to. The sight was one to make the stoutest hearts quail. Down stairs, in a bed in the northwest room, lay the bodies of the two Stillinger girls, their heads chopped open with an ax, and their blood and brains presenting a spectacle so re-

$2,000 REWARD

For the arrest and conviction of the murderer or murderers of J. B. Moore and family and Lena and Ina Stillinger at Villisca on the night of Sunday, June 9, 1912, the state of Iowa, Montgomery county, citizens of the city of Villisca, and the adjoining community offer a reward approximating $2,000.

By authority of the governor the state of Iowa has offered $300 for each murderer taken dead or alive, the county has offered $500, and citizens of Villisca have increased the amount by over $500. The John Deere Implement company of Omaha telegraphed their willingness to subscribe any amount for this purpose, and citizens of Clarinda and other neighboring towns have sent word of a reward fund being raised. It is likely that by the end of the week the reward will total over $2,000.

STANDING REWARD

There is also a reward of $1200 standing for the apprehension of the Monmouth murderers.

Reward offered for the arrest and conviction of the Villisca ax murderer. (*The Villisca Review,* June 13, 1912)

pulsive that it was almost beyond comprehension that six more victims, murdered in identically the same fashion, lay in the two bedrooms up stairs. ... There were no signs of a struggle on the part of any of the victims, except perhaps in the case of one of the girls downstairs, on whose arms a slight cut appeared. The bodies were not mutilated below the heads, and their faces had been covered up after the crime, either with part of the bedding or some discarded wearing apparel. . . .

Nothing that has happened since Mr. Thiele murdered his wife in Villisca twelve years ago has served to attract the attention and to hold the morbidly curious crowd as has this unparalleled crime. It is estimated that fully five thousand people gathered on the streets of the city Monday, hundreds coming from out of town ....

Company F under Capt. C. J. Casey was ordered out by Sheriff O. E. Jackson, and a patrol was sta-

tioned around the J. B. Moore home at six o'clock Monday evening to keep the curious crowds away until the dogs came to do their work. The city has been under martial law since.

The Villisca Review, June 13, 1912.

When Republican Governor Beryl Carroll took office in 1909, Iowa had a penitentiary at Fort Madison, a reformatory at Anamosa, and "industrial schools" for boys and girls at Eldora and Mitchellville, respectively, under the administration of the Board of Control of State Institutions. In addition, there were city or county jails in each of the 99 counties.

Due to public interest in the subject of prison conditions, Governor Carroll requested Attorney General George Cosson to head an investigative committee. The committee's report, printed on May 25, 1912, carried the shocking conclusion that Iowa's jail system was "a disgrace to the state." The legislature soon acted to implement a recommendation that a custodial farm be established for less serious offenders. The Cosson Report stands as one of the most comprehensive and constructive proposals of the progressive era.

Our jail system is a disgrace to the state, and except as a place of detention for persons awaiting trial, there is not a single excuse or justification for its existence. ...

In one county we find the jail to be "small, poor and dirty." In another county it is reported that "The jail is in a basement and damp, although the sheriff does the best he can." In another county it is reported that the jail is not even a safe place for keeping prisoners, and in a very large number of counties it is reported that there is no separate apartment for women and no means of segregation between first offenders and the most hardened criminals except such as is afforded by confinement in the cell, and this admits of

Prisoners in the prison yard of the penitentiary at Fort Madison, taken on a Sunday, circa 1909. (Courtesy, State Historical Society of Iowa, Des Moines)

course of constant communication. ...

In addition to the evidence that a number of jails are dirty, unsanitary, unsafe, and that there is no proper means of segregation of minors, first offenders and even women, this committee has convincing evidence that in some counties intoxicating liquors and various forms of dope are permitted to be passed to the prisoners.

. . . .

All of the reasons urged in support of the necessity of the elimination of the county jail as a means of punishment for men committing misdemeanors makes it equally necessary to provide some isolated colony for the purpose of caring for women offenders who are arrested and convicted of offenses less than a felony; the keeping and being an inmate of a disorderly house, vagrancy, petty larceny and intoxication comprising the largest part of these offenses.

Reports of chiefs of police from ten of the

The State Reformatory at Anamosa, from a postcard, circa 1905. (Courtesy, State Historical Society of Iowa, Des Moines)

"The Three Grades," prison uniforms worn at the Fort Madison penitentiary, circa 1915. (Courtesy, State Historical Society of Iowa, Iowa City)

largest cities in Iowa show that over 1,000 women were arrested and convicted of immorality and other misdemeanors during the year 1911. ...

Chiefs of police and police officials advise the committee that there is no proper way of dealing with these offenders. A woman convicted of a misdemeanor must either be discharged, committed to the county jail or fined. ... If a fine is assessed against her it is usually paid by some one who has participated in her crime, and who therefore feels that he has a mortgage on her body, or a right to share in her nefarious business until he is repaid, and hence one wrong is added to another.

. . . .

In view of these conditions and the general defects in our penal system previously referred to, the question confronting our state is whether we will continue to cling to a false economy and blindly fol-

low precedent in our method of dealing with the large number of persons annually convicted of crime, or whether we will have the larger vision and adopt a plan both humane and scientific, in consonance with the heart, the character and the culture of our people. Respectfully submitted,
George Cosson;
M. A. Roberts,
Parley Sheldon,
Committee.

The Report of the Committee Appointed to Investigate the Character of the Warden and the General Management of the Iowa Penitentiary at Fort Madison Together With a Report Concerning the Jail System of Iowa With Recommendations (Des Moines: State Printer, 1912), pp. 79-81, 92-93, 95.

George Cosson, Attorney General of Iowa from 1911-1917, wrote a report critical of Iowa's county and city jail system. (Courtesy, State Historical Society of Iowa, Iowa City)

CHAPTER SEVEN

World War I and Its Aftermath

1917-1929

"The time has come, even in Iowa ... when we must decide whether we are going to be American or foreign."

—GOVERNOR William L. Harding

1917-1929

THE UNITED STATES DECLARED WAR against Germany on April 6, 1917, and America began an enormous effort to marshall its work force and material supplies. In May, Congress passed the Selective Service Act, and by the end of November troops of the 42d Division, U.S. Army—the "Rainbow Division"—had begun arriving in France. In December, America declared war against Austria-Hungary. Iowa's native son, Herbert Clark Hoover, was named Food Administrator, in charge of conserving and supplying the nation's food resources.

Germany concluded an Armistice with the Allies on November 11, 1918. The 1919 Treaty of Versailles imposed harsh conditions on Germany and established the League of Nations. President Woodrow Wilson led the American delegation to the Paris Peace Conference, but despite Wilson's personal campaign on behalf of the League (for which he won the 1919 Nobel Peace Prize), the Senate failed to ratify the treaty. Not until July 1921 did Congress pass a joint resolution formally declaring an end to war.

In the short period of brutal warfare, United States casualties exceeded 320,000. There were over 116,000 war-related deaths, including 53,000 killed in battle. Over half a million Iowans registered for the Selective Service and nearly 115,000 served in the armed forces. Over 2,100 Iowans were killed or died from disease or accident. One of the first three Americans killed in World War I was an Iowan, Merle Hay of Glidden.

Iowa farmers had enjoyed unparalleled prosperity during World War I, with rising prices and a needy European market. The end of war meant a change of fortune. In 1920, the government announced the withdrawal of price supports on crops and the end of loans to the Allied powers in Europe. Farmers had borrowed widely to buy more land and expand their crop production; now the loans became due and, with tight money, many farm mortgages were foreclosed. This marked the beginning of a period of drastically falling farm prices and business failures that were particularly felt in Iowa and the Midwest.

In 1920, Republican Warren Harding was elected President. Harding chose Henry C. Wallace, publisher of *Wallaces' Farmer*, as his Secretary of Agriculture, the third Iowan to serve in this cabinet position. Wallace and his son, Henry A. Wallace (who later served as Secretary of Agriculture under President Franklin Roosevelt) were both strong advocates for farmers. During the difficult 1920s, Secretary Wallace worked closely with the farm bloc in Congress—which, until 1922, included Iowa's progressive Republican senator William Kenyon—to advance legislation alleviating the farmers' plight.

Wallace's views on the need for federal government intervention in agricultural affairs increasingly were in conflict with the other Iowan in the Harding cabinet, Secretary of Commerce Herbert Hoover. Hoover—who favored farmer cooperatives rather than federal intervention in the marketplace—opposed the tariff equivalent plan for agriculture supported by Wallace.

In August 1923, President Harding died after a brief illness and was succeeded by his Vice-President, Calvin Coolidge. Coolidge was elected in his own right the following year, but chose not to run again in 1928, and the Republican nomination fell to Herbert Hoover. In November 1928, Hoover became the only native-born Iowan to win election as President of the United States, defeating Democrat Alfred Smith.

Hoover carried Iowa in the 1928 election, but he faced opposition from many farmers who disagreed with his agricultural policies and viewed him suspiciously as an unsympathetic Californian. It was left to later generations of Iowans to take more pride in Herbert Hoover and his accomplishments.

President Hoover entered his term with optimism, confident that his laissez-faire views of the economy could provide the panacea for economic recovery. In 1929, he signed the Agriculture Marketing Act, creating a Federal Farm Board to encourage the formation of farm cooperatives and control surpluses of farm products. Then late in October 1929 came a heavy slide in stock prices and frantic selling. The Great Stock Market Crash on October 29 resulted in billions of dollars in stock losses. Thousands of investors were financially ruined.

The President and his advisors at first failed to acknowledge (or perhaps to realize) the enormity of the economic depression, and Hoover wrongly predicted that the worst effects of the stock market crash would soon be alleviated. The recovery failed to materialize, and the remainder of Hoover's term would prove increasingly difficult for the new President—and for the nation.

*S*oon after the United States entered the war, the Iowa legislature responded to a growing patriotic sentiment by passing an expanded statute against the desecration of the American and state flags. The legislature also reacted to growing fears about the activities of foreign sympathizers by passing a law to punish the crimes of "insurrection or sedition" against the state.

DESECRATION OF THE FLAG OF THE UNITED STATES.

Be it enacted by The General Assembly of the State of Iowa:

Section 1. ... Any person who ... shall publicly mutilate, deface, defile or defy, trample upon, cast contempt upon, satirize, deride or burlesque, either by words or act, such flag, standard, color, ensign, shield or other insignia of the United States, or flag, ensign, great seal or other insignia of this state, or who shall, for any purpose, place such flag, standard, color, ensign, shield or other insignia of the United States, or flag, ensign, great seal or other insignia of this state, upon the ground or where the same may be tread upon, shall be deemed guilty of a misdemeanor and shall be punished by a fine not exceeding one hundred dollars ($100.00) or by imprisonment for not more than thirty (30) days and shall also forfeit a penalty of fifty dollars ($50.00) for each such offense, to be recovered, with costs, in a civil action or suit in any court having jurisdiction, and such action or suit may be brought by and in the name of the state, on the relation of any citizen thereof ....
Approved April 25, 1917.

Acts of the Thirty-Seventh General Assembly, 1917, ch. 411, § 1.

INSURRECTION OR SEDITION.

Be it enacted by the General Assembly of the State of Iowa:
. . . .

Sec. 2. Any person who shall in public or private, by speech, writing, printing or by any other mode or means advocate the subversion and destruction by force of the government of the state of Iowa or of the United States, or attempt ... to incite or abet, promote or encourage hostility or opposition to the government of the state of Iowa or of the United States shall be guilty of a misdemeanor and upon conviction shall be punished by imprisonment in the county jail not less than six months nor more than one year and shall be fined not less than three hundred nor more than one thousand dollars.

Sec. 3. Any person who shall become a member of any organization, society or order organized or formed, or attend any meeting or council, or solicit others so to do, for the purpose of inciting, abetting, promoting or encouraging hostility or opposition to the government of the state of Iowa or to the United States, or who shall in any manner aid, abet or encourage any such organization, society, order or meeting in the propagation or advocacy of such a purpose shall be guilty of a misdemeanor and upon conviction shall be imprisoned in the county jail not less than six months nor more than one year and shall be fined not less than three hundred nor more than one thousand dollars.
. . . .

Approved April 24, 1917.

Acts of the Thirty-Seventh General Assembly, 1917, ch. 372, §§ 2-3.

*T*he Iowa State Bar Association, meeting during the height of America's involvement in World War I, abandoned its usual business for talks relating to the war effort, including a prominent address by Governor William Harding. But despite fervent calls to patriotism, there were mingled words of caution against the excesses of suspicion and fear. In his address to the Bar Association, Judge J.W. Kintzinger of Dubuque warned against the "poison" of excessive zeal.

*T*he State Bar Association meets this year under circumstances that are most peculiar. At our last meeting, this great war had just begun, and, at that time, little or no preparation had been made for meeting it. Much has been accomplished since then; but much more remains to be

Newspaper advertisements for liberty bonds urged Iowans to show their patriotism. Individuals who failed to contribute to wartime causes sometimes found themselves before self-constituted "courts." (*[Bloomfield] Davis County Republican,* September 26, 1918)

done, and the Bar of this State will do its share. ...

[L]awyers are already on the battle front. Some are in training in the different cantonments, and all will do their share. ... I believe the main object of this session will be to assist the Government. There are many ways in which this can be done. [M]ob rule has manifested itself in different sections of our State. This should not be countenanced.

Poison gas is being used to kill soldiers on the battle front. Another form of poison gas is being used in this State, and all over the country, and has all the effect of German propaganda. For instance, in our community, and these instances may occur in different parts of the country, a committee on the Third Liberty Loan drive, in calling at one house, were told that a neighbor across the way was not loyal, and hadn't purchased, and refused to purchase, any Liberty Bonds, and that he should be made "to come across". Upon investigation, the committee found that the neighbor thus accused was an ordinary wage-worker, but his family already had three sons in the service; and I believe if that family had not contributed one cent, they would have done their share, and have made sufficient sacrifice for their country; but the committee found that, in addition to the three sons already in the service, that little family had also purchased nine Liberty Bonds. Another instance has reference to the Local Exemption Boards. As a member of the Legal Advisory Board, I had occasion to see an anonymous letter to our local board, complaining of a young man not being in the service, while others, not so well-to-do, had been taken away. This complaint was unsigned, and the writer could not be called in. The same complaint may have been made to a lot of neighbors. The facts in that case were that the young man thus complained about had been placed in Class 1, by the Local Exemption Board, and had also made several efforts to enlist, but was not accepted because of physical disabilities. Such reports are poison gas, and ought to be stamped out. What we all need to do is to boost the war along, and stand unitedly behind our government. This is the surest and quickest way to a victorious peace.

J. W. Kintzinger, "Response to Address of Welcome," *Proceedings of the Twenty-Fourth Annual Session of the Iowa State Bar Association* (Iowa City: Iowa State Bar Assoc., 1918), Session of June 27, 1918, pp. 10-11.

Judge Kintzinger's caution against excessive patriotic zeal was challenged by another speaker at the 1918 annual meeting of the Iowa State Bar Association. A member from Council Bluffs explained the work of a self-constituted and extralegal "Military Court" in his home city, before which people suspected of disloyalty were summoned to appear.

I have been asked to tell the story of the Military Court at Council Bluffs. Ten men, believing disloyalty should be extinguished, enlisted for that service. It seemed clear to us, whenever the law imposes a duty, a sufficient power can always be found to enforce the duty. ... For the enforcement of this self-evident, indisputable and incontestable law of social order we simply organized a Court, assuming the power of compelling that duty which the conscience of every one should enforce unaided. ...

The complaints coming to us generally related to disloyal utterances, or disloyal conduct, or the failure of duty to purchase bonds, or subscribe to war charities, or aid in war service. It did not appear to us to be practicable nor fully compatible with the dignity of our Court to consider ourselves as a visiting committee. We therefore prepared a form of summons inviting the derelict to appear before us at a particular hour on a particular day. He was admonished to bring with him a detailed statement of all his property and all his debts. When you remember that the person cited to appear is charged with disloyalty to his Country, you will not be surprised when I say to you that out of nearly four hundred cases, not a single one failed to appear. ...

A learned District Judge asks how we reconcile our procedure with the "due process" clause of the Constitution. A fair answer, one as fair at least as the culprit's position, is that process in the instant case is past due before we commence. ... It does not constitute a deprivation of life, to require a German sympathizer to spend his life, enjoy it, or endure it in a land other than free America. It does not constitute a deprivation of liberty to forcibly withdraw the license of preaching sedition in the language of our Country's enemy. It is unthinkable that the Huns' implements of sabotage and treason can be treated as property under the Fifth Amendment of the Constitution. ...

Skeptics may quibble, the timid may hesitate and the disloyal may express doubts, nevertheless the American people have a power—a God-given power, a power higher and greater than their Constitution or law, the power from which the law derives its being, and the patriotic people of America have the courage to exercise that power to save the Government, to save the Flag, and to save the law itself from destruction at home as well as abroad.

Emmet Tinley, "Recruiting," *Proceedings of the Twenty-Fourth Annual Session of the Iowa State Bar Association* (Iowa City: Iowa State Bar Assoc., 1918), Session of June 27, 1918, pp. 129-31, 134.

In the wartime fervor, even those who refused to contribute to war relief funds were suspect, as a prominent Davis County farmer learned. E.G. Dickson's reluctance to contribute and his alleged "disloyal utterances" led to years of litigation, and his eventual prosecution (and acquittal) under the federal Espionage Act. Dickson sued his accusers for malicious prosecution, losing after three appeals to the Iowa Supreme Court. His earlier lawsuit for assault and trespass illustrates the atmosphere of suspicion and fear that set neighbor against neighbor.

This cause of action is a local echo of the world war. The causative facts have to do with certain quasi governmental agencies in the county of plaintiff's residence for the raising of funds to assist in the successful prosecution of the war, which movement apparently did not enlist the sympathy of the plaintiff, a well-to-do Iowa farmer of Davis County. ...

The plaintiff instituted this action to recover damages for an assault alleged to have been committed on and against his person and also for a trespass upon and damages to his real property. ...

The plaintiff alleged in his petition that the defendants "jointly and severally conspired, confederated and associated themselves together as a mob for the purpose of threatening, assaulting, and coercing this plaintiff ... shaking fists in his face and threatening to commit battery upon his person.

That further the said defendants and all of them did jointly and severally and in pursuance of said conspiracy, confederacy and association and as a mob then and on the same day maliciously, willfully and for the purpose of damaging and injuring the plaintiff and his property, paint a building on plaintiff's premises with yellow paint."

[The defendants] alleged that they were acting as solicitors for funds for the war activities of the United States government in the world war and, without any force or show of force, properly and politely solicited the plaintiff.

... The plaintiff Dickson himself ... testified: "I don't know who put the paint on my house on the farm west of town. I don't know that any of the defendants put paint on it that night. I delayed bringing this action until I thought the Federal authorities had

"MY COUNTRY, 'TIS OF THEE"
(*German-American Version*)
My country over sea,
Deutschland, is sweet to me;
To thee I cling.
For thee my honor died,
For thee I spied and lied,
So that from every side
Kultur might ring.

A cartoon showing the bias against German-Americans during World War I. (*Life* magazine, June 13, 1918)

dropped the criminal charges against me for violating the espionage act. After I had made my donation to the Red Cross part of the crowd around there left and went in the direction of my farm. I don't know which ones of the defendants went there. No one struck me there that night. Someone did jostle me that night but I don't know who it was and I don't know whether it was accidental or intentional. It didn't hurt me any though."

Each and every one of the defendants testified in substance that there was no plan, arrangement, understanding or suggestion made by anyone to their knowledge that E. G. Dickson or his brother Cowp was to be solicited for a donation on the night in question ... that none of them took any part in the solicitation of the donation except Harper and Gleason, the regularly appointed Red Cross solicitors ... that Harper who was in company with Gleason stated to the plaintiff that he hadn't given anything to the Red Cross drive to which Dickson replied, "No;" and he said that he ought to give something and shortly thereafter made the donation by a subscription of $100.

... There is no evidence of physical abuse and there is no evidence tending to prove that by concert of action that the defendants or any of them jointly committed the alleged torts.

Dickson v. Yates, 194 Iowa 910, 911-12, 914-15 (1922).

The war aroused intense anti-German feelings throughout the nation. German-Americans were the largest single ethnic group in Iowa at the time of World War I, and this posed a particular dilemma. On the one hand, some of the state's best, brightest, and most loyal citizens were of German origin. On the other hand, the speaking of the German language seemed an uncomfortable reminder of the antagonist.

In May 1918, Iowa's Governor Harding issued a proclamation requiring English to be used in school teaching, church services, public places, trains, and telephone calls. The story of this edict—which was aimed at all foreign language speakers—sheds light on the balance between the rule of law and the exigencies of wartime.

Governor Harding's Proclamation and the School Language Law, 1918-1923

DURING WORLD WAR I, MANY STATES passed laws restricting the public use of the German language. In Iowa—where about 41 percent of the population was either foreign born or born of foreign parents—Governor William Harding sought to go much further. In May 1918, he issued a proclamation that purported to ban the public use not just of German, but of all foreign languages, including those of America's allies in the war. Harding's proclamation followed a lengthy campaign to Americanize the language of Iowa.

In May 1917, Governor Harding appointed a non-statutory State Council of Defense to assist in all patriotic endeavor. The chairman was a former United States Senator named Lafayette Young. Young was the editor of the *Des Moines Capital*, who, as a war correspondent in Europe in 1915, had been held as a spy by the Austrian government. For two years prior to America entering the war, his newspaper had denounced the evils of speaking too many languages in the United States.

An editorial in June 1917 exemplified Young's views. Complaining of communities where English was not spoken, he wrote: "To make [America] what it ought to be, we must have a harmonious people: therefore we must have one language."[1] In August, Young wrote that differences in language had caused wars throughout the world. "We must have real unity in this big free republic and we can't have it without we all speak the same language."[2] He was to return to this theme again and again.

On September 10, at a large "Loyalty Conference" held by the Council of Defense, Governor Harding concurred. Emphasizing the number of foreign settlements in America with their own customs, language, and ideals, Harding said: "The trouble has been that the pot has not melted." As a remedy, he called for language assimilation: "In every community there should be a strong sentiment created for the use of the American language in school, in pulpit and in press." Although there was

Governor William L. Harding issued a controversial proclamation in
May 1918 that sought to ban teaching and public speaking in foreign
languages. (Courtesy, State Historical Society of Iowa, Des Moines)

no statutory authority for enforcing the use of the "American" language, Harding
urged the assembled sheriffs, county attorneys, and city officials "to create the
moral sentiment" for its use.[3]

In late November, the Council of Defense urged the abolition of teaching German in the public schools. At the same time, Lafayette Young was railing in the *Des
Moines Capital* against foreign preachers, complaining that "the majority of them
are traitors."[4] The next month he wrote: "It is high time that preaching in the German language in Iowa be discontinued."[5]

Not long after, the sheriff at Audubon had to stop a mob that had thrown a rope
around the neck of a German preacher for alleged pro-German activity; immediately
afterwards, a German pastor from Yorktown in Page County received a death threat
for teaching the German language. In January 1918, the Page County Council of
Defense closed three German-speaking parochial schools and insisted that "American" be used in the German language churches. Signs such as "German language
strictly forbidden on the streets and in all public places in Sutherland,"[6] began to appear in Iowa.

On consecutive days in early April, two major Americanization conferences
were held in Washington, D.C., attended by eighteen state governors and representatives of state Councils of Defense. The conferences advocated that elementary
school subjects be taught in English, and that all preaching and teaching in German
be stopped. Lafayette Young, representing Iowa at the conferences, gained national
attention for his views. He claimed that thousands of midwestern schools sang

Two Tons of German Text Books, Ousted From Des Moines Schools, Junked--Bring About $27

"Junking the Kaiser" shows German school books removed from Des Moines schools being mutilated by employees of the school board. (*Des Moines Capital,* April 24, 1918)

"Deutschland Über Alles"[7] every day. Blaming the German press and language, he announced at the second conference: "There are 5,000 persons in Iowa who ought to be in the stockade this very minute."[8]

Back in Iowa, the State Superintendent of Schools directed that the teaching of German cease, and by the end of April, the schools had complied. German textbooks were removed from schools and burned. In several places the German language was banned on the telephone. The *Des Moines Capital* crusaded against the use of all foreign languages in Iowa churches. In early May at Ocheyedan, a crowd beat up a Dutch speaker who asserted his rights to use the Dutch language. Signs went up in Sibley, Iowa: "Speak the American Language Only."[9]

In Le Mars in April and May, signs were painted all over the town:

> If you Are An American at Heart
> Speak OUR Language
> If you Don't Know It
> LEARN IT
> If you Don't Like It
> MOVE[10]

On May 23, 1918, after lengthy consultation with the State Council of Defense, Governor Harding issued his foreign language proclamation. Four rules lay at its heart: "*FIRST*. English should and must be the only medium of instruction in public, private, denominational or other similar schools. *SECOND*. Conversation in public places, on trains and over the telephone should be in the English language. *THIRD*. All public addresses should be in the English languages. *FOURTH*. Let those who cannot speak or understand the English language conduct their religious worship in their homes."[11]

There was uproar among the Czechs of Cedar Rapids, who deluged the Governor with furious telegrams and letters. One Czech summed them all up: "[T]o say that the language of [our] people should be placed in the same category and under the same ban as the German language, it seems to me is going beyond the limits of reason and seriously reflects upon the loyalty, patriotism and sacrifices of the Bohemian people."[12]

So strong was the Czech reaction that the governor sent a representative to Cedar Rapids, who reached agreement with the protestors. The Cedar Rapids press published a clarification of the proclamation, explaining that English had to be the medium of instruction in schools, but other languages could be taught. Moreover, the governor "has no intention to say that people who do not speak English should be barred from conducting their religious worship, or business in their own language."[13]

Apart from this concession to the Cedar Rapids Czech community, the proclamation continued in full force, and most Iowans appeared to support it. The *Council Bluffs Nonpareil*, which opposed Harding politically, on May 31 wrote: "The governor may have no law in support of his position but he does have public sentiment .... 'Speak the language of your country' is a slogan now which is very popular."[14]

However, foreign language speakers in general disagreed with the governor's action. Like the Czechs, the Danes were openly angry. On the Sunday following the proclamation, three Danish churches in Cedar Falls closed as a protest, and several Danes wrote letters of complaint to the *Des Moines Register*. At the dedication of the service flag at Grand View College, the Reverend S.D. Rodholm made a passionate speech in favor of the Danish language, declaring: "I believe this proclamation to be unjust, unlawful, unconstitutional ...." He ended: "[A]s I do not believe that any power on earth has a right to dictate what language a man must speak to the living God, I shall lead you in a brief prayer in the Danish language."[15]

On the day of Reverend Rodholm's defiant speech, Governor Harding spoke at the Chamber of Commerce in Des Moines. "I am also telling those who insist upon praying in some other language that they are wasting their time for the good Lord up above is now listening for the voice in English."[16]

The pastor of the Danish Nazareth Church in Cedar Falls wrote an incensed letter to the governor: "To me it appears incredible that the honored chief executive of our state could or would publicly and in such a fashion, mock the thousands of praying men and women of foreign extraction ... within the state of Iowa."[17] Harding replied that he had been misquoted but ended his letter: "I cannot see how any loyal American citizen able to speak English could desire to use another language in voicing his supplications to the Almighty."[18]

Letters protesting against the proclamation poured into the governor's office and the State Council of Defense. The *Des Moines Register* and other newspapers published critical editorials. In response to all the criticism, Harding wrote a letter on June 12, 1918, which the State Council of Defense sent to its county councils and to all Iowa's newspapers.

The letter explained that the proclamation was needed because German propaganda was being spread in foreign languages. Harding insisted he had "plenty of authority" to issue the proclamation, and warned: "[t]hose who stiffen their necks and assume a defiant attitude will injure themselves and our country's best interests." However, the governor made a major concession by quoting with approval a foreign minister who conducted the main service in English, but afterwards gave the sermon again "in the language of our former country" for the benefit of those who did not understand English.[19]

Later that month, Governor Harding proposed the same arrangement to a delegation of Norwegian Lutheran pastors from Winnebago County. He told them they might first deliver a sermon in English, and immediately afterwards in Norwegian.

Disobedience to the proclamation resulted in a deplorable incident in Mahaska County. On June 13, a Dutch language church in Richland township was burned down—the *Des Moines Capital* blamed the event on the recalcitrance of a Dutch preacher. On the same day, the First Reformed Church at Pella voted to dispense with Dutch services and henceforth to use English.

The main burden of the proclamation inevitably fell on German-speaking people. The most notorious incident occurred on June 14, 1918, when four women of Le Claire were summoned before the chairman of the Scott County Defense Council for speaking German over a rural telephone line. During the "hearing," it developed that a German emblem adorned the barn of Herman Lippold, husband of the principal accused. The chairman ordered the emblem to be removed for fear of mob violence.

Mrs. Lippold stated at the hearing: "I just asked my daughter 'How are you' in German." Her daughter added that she only spoke German on the telephone when her mother failed to understand in English. Mrs. Lippold's daughter-in-law said she had used but a few words in German over the telephone when speaking to her mother-in-law. During the hearing, Mrs. Lippold could only compose herself for brief periods. At one point, she broke down completely and cried: "I would kill myself before I returned to Germany."

The chairman declared that 500 people in Scott County had reported violations of the governor's proclamation, and said he was determined to see it enforced. He imposed a fine of $100 on Mrs. Lippold and a total of $125 on the other three women, to be paid to the Red Cross. He also ordered them to sign pledge cards of membership in the Le Claire Community Defense Council. Mrs. Lippold, who had lived in America for thirty-six years, said: "It is hard for a person who is accustomed to speaking German most of the time to speak English all the time over the telephone. I'll never talk over the telephone again."[20]

Later that June, the *Des Moines Register* surveyed the foreign language churches in Des Moines and concluded that the proclamation generally was being obeyed. The only exception was a Danish church whose pastor spoke no English. The Des Moines Turnverein—the German gymnastic and cultural association—whose constitution insisted on the use of the German language, disbanded.

At the end of the month, the State Council of Defense reported to Governor Harding that Iowa's foreign language churches were invariably holding their main services in English, and many were taking advantage of his exception by repeating the sermon in a foreign language afterwards. Although the Defense Council had difficulty in stopping people from talking foreign languages on the telephone, for the most part the proclamation was being obeyed.

Even the Welsh language congregation in Williamsburg had locked up its church to comply with the proclamation. The *Marshalltown Times-Republican*—no friend of Harding's—said: "Quit arguing with the governor over the foreign language proposition. Law or no law he has four-fifths of all Iowa behind it."[21]

Nonetheless, the governor's office and the State Council of Defense received numerous reports about people talking in foreign languages on Iowa's streets and telephone lines. In early July, one complainant forwarded his niece's letter, which said of some Marshalltown Germans: "[F]our of the dirty creatures [were] all talking in their own language."[22]

Some local patriotic associations took disciplinary action. In Sac County, the Bureau of Military Affairs fined a man $25 (payable to the Red Cross) for repeatedly speaking German in Wall Lake. The Bureau of Military Affairs in Crawford County summoned a local postmaster for taking down a notice forbidding the use of foreign languages. The Scott County Council of Defense ordered the Davenport Symphony Orchestra to stop its musicians talking in German at rehearsals. The marshal in Waverly, discovering that the glee club had sung "The Blue Danube" in German, forbade any repetition.

Various clergyman were reprimanded. In Alta, the Board of Military Affairs instructed a German-speaking pastor to take a vacation and learn English. The Jasper County Council of Defense ordered a minister to cease holding services in Dutch, and the Page County National Defense Council did the same to two Swedish-speaking pastors. The Lyon County Council of Defense stopped a preacher conducting hymns in Norwegian, while the Scott County Council of Defense gave a pastor a good going over for preaching in German at a funeral.

Perhaps Governor Harding's doughtiest opponent was a German-speaking pastor of Denver, Iowa, the Reverend P. Blaufuss. At the outset he wrote to Harding that the proclamation was unconstitutional as interfering with freedom of religion, explaining that most of his congregation could only worship God in the German tongue.

Reverend Blaufuss continued his services in German. On June 18, 1918, one of Iowa's wartime secret service agents visited Blaufuss and ordered him to use English. His constant reply was: "I am standing on my constitutional rights, and you, the state or the nation cannot make me stop preaching in the German language."[23] The U.S. marshal at Denver summoned Blaufuss and leading members of his congregation, but they refused to abandon their use of German.

Next, two more secret service agents insisted to Blaufuss that he conform with the proclamation. He announced his agreement in church, and the congregation signed a resolution agreeing to the agents' demands. However, the agents considered the resolution inadequate.

On the evening of July 10, the two agents entered Reverend Blaufuss's house, declaring that he had not complied with the proclamation. Blaufuss wrote: "They forced me with violence out of my house into an auto and took me to Waterloo and through that city ...."[24] During the drive, the agents insisted that Blaufuss sign a statement that he would use English; eventually he gave in. Thereafter, he sent a furious letter to the governor, calling the episode "a blow into the face of American justice, truth, honesty and humanity."[25] He demanded an inquiry and the return of the piece of paper he had signed, which he did not consider binding.

In a further letter to the governor, Blaufuss stated that he was complying under protest with the proclamation, and ended: "I stand by the federal and state constitutions and laws and demand my rights as an American citizen."[26] Harding wrote back: "I decline to enter into any controversy with you."[27] Blaufuss's last word was in late September. "Now Governor, if you would come out before the people fair and square and admit, that you exceeded your power by issuing the language proclamation and revoke it, then to my judgment you would have the best show to be reelected this fall."[28]

Like Blaufuss, the *Des Moines Register* in its editorials repeatedly challenged the constitutionality of Governor Harding's proclamation. In an address to the Iowa State Bar Association at the end of June 1918, Harding—himself a Sioux City lawyer—attempted to defend the legality of his proclamation. He argued that freedom of speech was no constitutional guarantee to use any language other than English, and that freedom of religion did not guarantee either the right to use a foreign language when English could be used or to use a foreign language to create discord in time of war. Prior to the proclamation, fifty communities had erected signs insisting on the use of English, and the governor was duty-bound to act rather than allow the people to take the law into their own hands.

In a widely circulated letter written on August 2, Governor Harding admitted that the "violation of a proclamation issued by an Executive does not carry a penalty." However, "a proclamation, framed in harmony with existing statutes which do carry a violation penalty is susceptible of enforcement." Iowa's Insurrection or Sedition Act, "while not directly aimed at the use of a foreign language ... might very easily be, if a situation should arise where those who persisted in the use of a language ... would bring themselves under the provisions of this and other statutes."[29]

On July 4 at Sac City, Governor Harding directed his attack on foreign languages at the Danes of Audubon and Shelby Counties. He said: "Now think of a man who was brought from the filth of Denmark and placed on a farm for which he paid perhaps three dollars an acre. Ye Gods and fishes what Iowa has done for him he never can repay."[30]

Foreign language speakers did not mount a constitutional challenge to the proclamation in court—they saved their response for the ballot box. Harding's atti-

An editorial cartoon reacts to Governor Harding's foreign language proclamation.
(*Cedar Rapids Gazette,* May 27, 1918)

tude and actions lost him the foreign language vote in the November gubernatorial election. He squeaked into office again, but his share of the Democratic/Republican vote plummeted from 62.6 percent in 1916 to 51.3 percent in 1918. The first reason that Harding himself gave for the plunge in his popularity was that the Democrats "catered to the elements which were sore because of the foreign language proclamation."[31]

With the Armistice on November 11, 1918, the wartime proclamation lapsed—but the English language question did not. In his inaugural address in January 1919, Harding spoke to the legislature of America's need for English: "We are big enough, old enough, and good enough to have a language of our own, loved and used by all citizens." Accordingly, he recommended that "the least you do be to provide that each child be required to be taught in English and no other language up to the grade of high school. After that, they may be permitted to study foreign languages as they choose, but that all schools use English as the medium of instruction in all branches."[32]

Seven times during these remarks, the legislators burst into applause. H.E. Dean, a representative of Ocheyedan County, promptly introduced an English language school bill into the House, saying: "There's only one language that should be used in the United States and that's the English language."[33] The bill required that in every Iowa school English be the medium of instruction in all subjects, including religion.

The German Lutheran Church Missouri Synod (Iowa District) strongly opposed the Dean bill. The synod circulated the Iowa legislators with a powerful memorandum, urging them to permit religion to be taught in foreign languages. The synod wanted the word "secular" to be inserted in the first line of the bill, which would then read: "That the medium of instruction in all 'secular' subjects ... shall be the English language."[34]

When the House of Representatives debated the Dean bill on March 11, 1919, L.H. Mayne of Palo Alto County introduced an amendment along the lines the Missouri Synod had suggested—"in all 'secular' subjects"—thereby permitting religion to be taught in a foreign language.

The debate took two hours. Dean opposed the amendment, saying: "If my political future depends upon my vote in this matter I am willing to say good-bye to my future and stand on my Americanism." Will I. King of Hardin County concurred. He explained that both his parents were born in Germany, and that he himself could speak nothing but German until he attended a rural school in Iowa at the age of five. "I am going to stand for the original bill if I stand alone ...."

Representative Mayne, in support of his amendment, blamed American officials and politicians for the foreign language problems of the last few months. C.V. Findley of Webster County supported Mayne, urging that Scandinavian, German, and Jewish parochial schools should be allowed to teach religion in their own language. U.S. Alderman of Story County took a similar line on behalf of the Norwegians of his county. However, F.S. Finley of Henry County opposed the amendment, declaring: "This worry about religion is useless. Certainly we should think about God and citizenship in the same language."[35]

The House supported the Mayne amendment by a vote of sixty-three to forty, and adopted a further amendment that permitted foreign languages to be taught as cultural studies above the eighth grade. Then the House unanimously adopted the English language school bill. The Senate passed the bill by thirty-six votes to twelve, and it took effect in July 1919.

The Missouri Synod obtained a legal opinion on the bill, and at the end of August 1919 resolved "[t]hat decisive steps be taken legally to debilitate or remove the new school law, as Synod considers it unconstitutional."[36] Another German Lutheran synod—the Evangelical Lutheran Synod of Iowa and Other States—also concluded that the Dean bill was unconstitutional as contrary to the liberty guarantee in Article I, section 1 of the Iowa constitution and the Fourteenth Amendment to the U.S. Constitution. These two Lutheran synods combined to bring a case to test the constitutionality of the new law.

The case concerned the Reverend August Bartels, a minister and schoolmaster of the Iowa Synod who taught at Maxfield in Bremer County. When Governor Harding had issued his proclamation, Bartels had written a powerful letter to the Bremer County Council of Defense denouncing the proclamation as unconstitutional. He concluded: "If you force me to use the English language you will change a peaceful German minister to a man fighting for freedom of speech and religion."[37]

In January 1920, the president of the Iowa Synod, Reverend Emil H. Rausch, filed a "friendly" information in the Justice of the Peace court in Waverly, charging that Bartels had taught reading in a foreign language to pupils below the eighth grade at a Lutheran parochial school. The court found Bartels guilty and fined him $25. Bartels appealed to the district court, which, on March 1, 1920, upheld the conviction.

With the two Lutheran synods paying his legal costs, Bartels appealed to the Iowa Supreme Court. On February 12, 1921—by a four-to-three majority—the Court upheld the conviction. The Court held that teaching parochial school pupils under the eighth grade to read in German using German textbooks violated the English language school law. The Court reasoned that this was, indeed, the teaching of a secular subject, even though the purpose was to enable the pupils to read the German catechism and Bible and participate in religious worship.

The Court held that the prohibition against teaching secular subjects in foreign languages did not deny any rights or privileges guaranteed by the Iowa or U.S. constitutions. It reasoned: "There is, as we view it, no inherent right, no 'privilege,' to teach German to children of tender years that cannot lawfully be denied by the legislature when, in its judgment and discretion, the exercise of such right under existing conditions is inimical to the best interests of the state."[38]

Bartels appealed to the U.S. Supreme Court, which, on June 4, 1923, handed down separate decisions concerning statutes in Nebraska, Iowa, and Ohio. The first such case was *Meyer v. Nebraska*,[39] which concerned facts similar to those in Bartels' case. In *Meyer*, the U.S. Supreme Court, by a seven-to-two majority, ruled that a Nebraska statute that prohibited the teaching of any subject in a non-English language to pupils under the eighth grade in a public or private school, violated the liberty interest guaranteed by the Fourteenth Amendment to the U.S. Constitution.

Justice McReynolds, giving the majority opinion, stated: "Mere knowledge of the German language cannot reasonably be regarded as harmful. Heretofore it has been commonly looked upon as helpful and desirable. Plaintiff in error taught this language in school as part of his occupation. His right thus to teach and the right of parents to engage him so to instruct their children, we think are within the liberty of the [Fourteenth] Amendment. ... The protection of the Constitution extends to all, to those who speak other languages as well as to those born with English on the tongue."[40]

Then the Court delivered its opinion in *Bartels v. Iowa*.[41] Based upon its ruling in *Meyer*, the Court reversed the judgment of the Iowa Supreme Court, holding that the Iowa statute was subject to the same constitutional objections as the Nebraska statute. Justice Holmes, joined by Justice Sutherland, wrote a dissenting opinion in *Bartels*. He stated: "[I]f there are sections in the State where a child would hear only Polish or French or German spoken at home I am not prepared to say that it is unreasonable to provide that in his early years he shall hear and speak only English at school. But if it is reasonable it is not an undue restriction of the liberty either of teacher or scholar. ... [T]herefore I am unable to say that the Constitution of the United States prevents the experiment being tried."[42]

Lafayette Young's *Des Moines Capital* gave the U.S. Supreme Court decision banner headlines. The Reverend Rausch (who had initiated the *Bartels* test case) wrote in the *Lutheran Herald*: "We have every reason to rejoice that the highest tribunal of the country has again upheld the principle of religious and civil liberty all chauvinistic agitation to the contrary notwithstanding."[43]

In June 1918, August Bartels had written: "We Germans are rapidly adopting the English language ...."[44] The trend continued. In 1919, 57 percent of the Missouri Synod's services in the Iowa District were held in German. By 1929, the number had fallen to 41 percent. In 1931, the synod resolved to make English its official language. During the next fifteen years, the number of stations that held their services half in German and half in English declined dramatically, from sixty-five in 1930 to only ten in 1946. Governor Harding would have been pleased.

At a time when the American Bar Association still discouraged black lawyers from joining its ranks, the Iowa State Bar Association admitted black members. George H. Woodson, founder of the Iowa Negro Bar Association in 1901 and the National Negro Bar Association in 1925, was an active member of the Iowa bar.

George Woodson received his law degree from Howard University in Washington, D.C., and moved to Iowa in 1896, living first in the black mining communities of Muchakinock and Buxton, and later moving to Des Moines, where he died in 1933 at the age of sixty-seven. In 1919, Mr. Woodson addressed the Iowa State Bar Association's annual meeting, speaking about the contribution of black soldiers to the American war effort.

I want to take about three minutes of the time of this Association. I made the promise at Council Bluffs that from fifty thousand to one hundred thousand black men would join with the white men in this country for maintaining the honor of the country and the glory of its flag. I am here to say that in the last world war the Government estimate is that four hundred thousand negroes gave their service in this war.

… While the war preparedness movements were carried on, every single unit of our American citizenship was asked to join. Not one single effort was made by the white people to interest their colored brethren. When we applied to the administration, to the patriotic people of this country, to give us a training camp, they went so far as to say they did not think there was a State in the Union that would tolerate a colored training camp. I shall always feel proud for the State of my adoption, that in it a camp could be

George H. Woodson, an active member of the Iowa State Bar Association and the founder of the Iowa Negro Bar Association and the National Negro Bar Association. (Courtesy, Mrs. Marguerite Esthers Cothorn and Cleota Proctor Wilbekin, Ph.D., of the History Committee of the National Bar Association)

Gertrude Durden Rush of Des Moines in 1918 became the first African-American woman admitted to the Iowa State Bar Association. In 1921, she was elected president of the Iowa Negro Bar Association, the first black woman in the country to assume such a position. In 1925, she became a founding member of the National Negro Bar Association, whose first president was Iowan George H. Woodson. (Courtesy, Ruth Davis Wyatt and Cleota Proctor Wilbekin, Ph.D., of the History Committee of the National Bar Association)

carried out to success.

... We should cherish a more universal friendly relation with the black people in this country who have also done patriotic service and who have never raised their hand against the flag or honor of their country. I want to say here that broader consideration should be extended to these people ....

I want to thank this Association again for the courtesies extended the fifteen years or more of my membership, and for this privilege.

George Woodson, *Proceedings of the Twenty-Fifth Annual Session of the Iowa State Bar Association* (Iowa City: Iowa State Bar Assoc., 1919), Session of June 27, 1919, pp. 155-58.

*O*ne of the more unusual personal injury lawsuits to reach the Iowa Supreme Court in the post-war period grew out of the Armistice with Germany on November 11, 1918. The case involved a victory celebration that got slightly out of hand—and the popular practice of "anvil shooting."

*T*his action was commenced by plaintiff against the town of Portsmouth, Iowa and other defendants to recover damages for personal injuries caused by the alleged negligence of the defendants. ...

The facts disclose that on November 11, 1918 the town of Portsmouth gave public expression of rejoicing by reason of the suspension of hostilities between the combatants in the World's War. It was Armistice Day, and in common with other cities and towns of this country there was a general indulgence in the use of many noise-making devices that usually mark our popular celebrations of great events.

On prior patriotic occasions the defendant William Hammerand had fired anvils. The method adopted was to place one anvil face downwards in the street so as to expose a square hole in the bottom of the anvil and around and above this hole was placed an iron ring. The hole and ring were then filled with powder, some of which was scattered over the outside surface of the anvil. Another anvil was placed upon the right and the powder was then fired with an iron rod heated red hot at one end.

On the morning of this day two citizens named

An Armistice Day parade. Iowans' enthusiastic celebrations of the Armistice on November 11, 1918, led to an unusual personal injury lawsuit. (Courtesy, State Historical Society of Iowa, Des Moines)

Doyle and Olinger, who happened to be town councilmen, requested the assistance of Hammerand in "shooting anvils." ...

When the powder that Hammerand was using became exhausted he ceased operations leaving the noise-making instrument where it had been used. It was then that the defendants Smith and Clark appeared on the scene and on their own initiative undertook the shooting of the anvils. After a few explosions the iron ring was lost. Thereupon they procured an iron wagon burr and proceeded to use it until the happening of the accident giving rise to this action.

Powder of a different quality was used by Smith and Clark and after a few explosions, and about twenty minutes after Hammerand had left, the wagon burr burst into pieces one of which struck the plaintiff in the eye causing a serious injury.

Is the defendant town under these circumstances liable for the damages sought to be recovered by the plaintiff? This case does not involve the violation of a town ordinance nor does the evidence disclose that the injury and consequent damages was by virtue of any corporate act of the town. ...

The defendant town was not bound to anticipate the negligent act of a third party, and it was the improper handling of the anvil by strangers to the town that proximately caused the injury. If anyone was negligent it was the defendants Clark and Smith, and a jury has said they were not negligent.

Heller v. Town of Portsmouth, 196 Iowa 104, 105-07 (1923).

At the height of America's involvement in World War I, the Woodbury County courthouse in Sioux City was completed. Begun in 1916 amidst controversy due to its unusual design, it was occupied on March 1, 1918, and is now recognized as a historic example of the Prairie School architecture. (Courtesy, State Historical Society of Iowa, Des Moines)

Public fears about state and national security continued into the post-war period, fueled in part by reaction to the Bolshevik Revolution—the so-called "Red Scare." A nation that had grown accustomed to wartime suppression of dissent found it easy to transfer its suspicions to foreigners generally, suspected radicals, and the increasingly powerful and militant trade unions.

Governor Harding in his 1919 inaugural address urged the Iowa General Assembly to "pass laws against the red flag." The legislature responded accordingly, and also passed one of the nation's most stringent "criminal syndicalism" laws.

RED FLAG OR OTHER INSIGNIA.
Be it enacted by the General Assembly of the State of Iowa:

Section 1. Any person who displays, carries, or exhibits any red flag, or other flag, pennant, banner, ensign, or insignia, or who aids, encourages, or advises such display, carriage, or exhibition, with the intent thereby to himself, or to induce others, to advocate, encourage, or incite anarchy or treason or hostility to the government of the United States or of the state of Iowa, or to insult or disregard the flag of the United States, shall be guilty of a misdemeanor and upon conviction shall be fined not to exceed one thousand ($1,000) dollars or be imprisoned not to exceed six (6) months or both.

Sec. 2. If any person so violate the provisions of section one of this act, and be then and there armed with a dangerous weapon, he shall be guilty of a felony and upon conviction shall be imprisoned not to exceed five (5) years.

. . . .

Approved April 10, 1919.

Acts of the Thirty-Eighth General Assembly, 1919, ch. 199, §§ 1, 2.

CRIMINAL SYNDICALISM.
Be it enacted by the General Assembly of the State of Iowa:
Section 1. Criminal syndicalism is the doctrine which advocates crime, sabotage, violence or other unlawful methods of terrorism as a means of accomplishing industrial or political reform. The advocacy of such doctrine, whether by word of mouth or writing, is a felony punishable as in this act otherwise provided.

Sec. 2. Any person who:

A. By word of mouth or writing, advocates or teaches the duty, necessity or propriety of crime, sabotage, violence or other unlawful methods of terrorism as a means of accomplishing industrial or political reform; or

B. Prints, publishes, edits, issues or knowingly circulates, sells, distributes or publicly displays any book, paper, document or written matter in any form, containing or advocating, advising or teaching the doctrine that industrial or political reform should be brought about by crime, sabotage, violence or other unlawful methods of terrorism; or ...

D. Organizes or helps to organize, or becomes a member of or voluntarily assembles with any society, group or assemblage of persons formed to teach or advocate the doctrines of criminal syndicalism, is guilty of a felony and punishable by imprisonment in the state penitentiary or reformatory for not more than ten years (10) or by a fine of not more than five thousand dollars ($5,000.00) or both.

. . . .

Approved April 25, 1919.

Acts of the Thirty-Eighth General Assembly, 1919, ch. 382, §§ 1, 2.

A prime target of the criminal syndicalism laws enacted by many states was the Industrial Workers of the World (IWW), an advocate of industrial unions that had refused to support America's war effort. In 1919, Henry Tonn was arrested and charged under Iowa's criminal syndicalism act, based on IWW literature taken from his room without a search warrant. The Iowa Supreme Court allowed the evidence to be used, but reversed Tonn's conviction due to a prejudicial jury instruction. A dissenting opinion condemned the illegal search and questioned the continuing relevance of the Criminal Syndicalism Act.

Weaver, J.—(dissenting). I concur in the majority opinion in so far as it relates to the error found in the trial court's charge to the jury, but beg leave to dissent from the argument and conclusion therein expressed upon the admissibility of the evidence obtained by seizure and search of the defendant's property. ...

... In the face of our constitutional guaranties, I confess it is not a little disconcerting to find the Supreme Court of Iowa putting itself on record in quoting approvingly and giving its adherence to the proposition that evidence is admissible "however unfairly and illegally obtained," even when it is procured under the circumstances which "meet with the unqualified disapprobation of the courts," so long as the accused has not been "compelled to do some positive, affirmative act inculpating himself." ...

... The question of the constitutionality of the statute under which the appellant has been convicted is not discussed by the majority, and, for the purposes of this opinion, I shall assume its validity. It is the product of conditions created by the recent world war—an extraordinary piece of legislation which finds its moral justification, if any it has, in the exercise of the war power of the state for its protection against the machinations of its enemies from within its borders, as well as from without. Since it was devised for such commendable purposes, the average loyal citizen yielded cheerful obedience thereto, and few, if any, were disposed to object to its enforcement. With the return of peace, many have felt that the statute in at least some of its features has outlived its usefulness, and should be repealed or materially modified. ... The case seems to have been tried below on the theory (which the majority come dangerously near approving) that proof of membership in what is known as the "I.W.W." is all that is required to sustain the conviction. That such is not the law is not open to doubt. To hold that no crime is shown is not to approve or indorse the teachings or purposes of the society. These may be economically unsound or wild and sociologically impossible, without exposing their adherents to a charge of crime. Even the best of men are not all cast in one mold. Their theories of life, its duties and responsibilities, and their ideas of social order and the regulation of personal and property rights, may and do vary between wide extremes. It is the legitimate right of government to exact obedience to all constitutional legislation, but it is not within its authority to impose a penalty upon the operation of the citizen's mind or conscience or belief.

State of Iowa v. Tonn, 195 Iowa 94, 116, 118, 120-21 (1923) (Weaver, J., dissenting).

In 1921, an Iowa criminal defendant charged with breaking and entering appealed his conviction, contending, among other grounds, that women had improperly been included on the list of potential jurors. The Iowa Supreme Court was faced with the issue of whether the Nineteenth Amendment to the U.S. Constitution—ratified in 1920—gave women civic rights in addition to the vote.

The fourth ground of challenge presents a new question to this court: *Are women competent and eligible to act as jurors under the Constitution and statutes of Iowa?* ...

[The Nineteenth] amendment as adopted August 26, 1920 and as declared by the certification of the secretary of state reads as follows:

"The right of citizens of the United States to vote shall not be denied or abridged by the United States or by any state on account of sex. ..."

. . . .

By the inherent force of the language of the Nineteenth Amendment, as a part of the supreme law of the land, women are included and made a part of the electorate of this state, and no further legislation pursuant to this amendment is required by Congress or by the general assembly of the state of Iowa. The amendment is self-executing. ...

One further question is suggested: *Is Article 1, Section 9 of the Constitution of Iowa violated in permitting women, who are qualified electors and who possess the other qualifications defined by law, to serve as jurors in the courts of this state?* The article reads as follows:

"The right of trial by jury shall remain inviolate; but the general assembly may authorize trial by a jury of a less number than twelve men in inferior courts; but no person shall be deprived of life, liberty, or property, without due process of law."

Section 332 of the Code of Iowa provides:

"All qualified electors of the state, of good moral character, sound judgment, and in full possession of the senses of hearing and seeing, and who can speak, write and read the English language, are competent jurors in their respective counties."

. . . .

It is the *number* that is guaranteed by our Constitution, and nowhere therein are qualifications of jurors defined or limited. The essential elements for a trial by jury at common law are number, impartiality and unanimity. ...

We hold therefore that the Nineteenth Amendment perforce extended suffrage to women in the state of Iowa, and since jury service by statute is made dependent upon the right to vote, that with the extension of the franchise to a citizen class, *ipso facto* that class is made eligible to jury service and subject to the exemptions of the law, and that no inhibition exists in the state Constitution.

State of Iowa v. Walker, 192 Iowa 823, 828-29, 835-36 (1921).

Breaking up a still in Prohibition-era Iowa, Johnson County. (Courtesy, State Historical Society of Iowa, Iowa City)

During the decade of the 1920s, criminal arrests for bootlegging and other alcohol-related offenses were commonplace. The Eighteenth Amendment to the U.S. Constitution prohibiting the manufacture, sale, and transportation of intoxicating liquors had been ratified in 1919, and would not be repealed until 1933. The Iowa Supreme Court heard its share of such cases on appeal—some of which, like the 1926 appeal that follows, involved inventive methods of concealing the illegal brew.

On October 24, 1925, one Barney Berg, who had a search warrant in his possession, went with Sam Lang, a deputy sheriff, to appellant's place of business in LeMars, and made a search thereof for intoxicating liquors. ... The evidence introduced by the State tended to show that, when Lang entered the premises, he announced that he had a search warrant; that Berg

leaped over a counter and sought to obtain possession of a pitcher sitting on the ledge of an iron sink; that he was immediately grappled by appellant, who succeeded in emptying the contents of the pitcher into the sink; that Berg was able to soak some of the contents up in a towel lying in the sink; that the pitcher, towel, some glasses, and other utensils were seized and carried away by the searching party to the office of the local justice of the peace who issued the search warrant; that the towel was placed in the pitcher or vessel from which the contents were poured into the sink; that it was left for a brief time at the office of the justice, and then taken by the deputy sheriff to his office in the courthouse, and the contents of the towel wrung out into the pitcher. The liquid thus obtained was poured into a clean bottle, sealed, and later delivered to a chemist for analysis. The analysis disclosed the presence of 11.4 per cent alcohol. ...

... The testimony on behalf of appellant tended to show that the towel was used to wipe the bar and sink; that fruit juices contain more or less alcohol when they become sour. And, therefore, it is claimed that the evidence that the liquid in question was that dumped from the pitcher leaves too much to speculation; but we think that it was for the jury to say what the facts were.

The court instructed the jury that, if it appeared from the evidence that appellant dumped, or attempted to dump, the contents of the pitcher into the sink in the presence of the deputy sheriff during the time the premises were being searched, it would be presumed that the liquid was intoxicating. ... Whether appellant emptied the contents of the pitcher into the sink was a question of fact, and, if he did, the statutory presumption arose. ...

[T]he judgment of the court below [convicting appellant for maintaining a liquor nuisance] is affirmed.

State of Iowa v. Barton, 202 Iowa 530, 531-34 (1926).

In 1921, the legislature adopted the State Banner of Iowa, designed by the Iowa Society of the Daughters of the American Revolution—a blue, white, and red flag with a spreading eagle bearing in its beak the state motto, "Our liberties we prize and our rights we will maintain."

A major achievement of the Iowa legislature in the 1920s was the enactment of the Code of 1924, the first official code of laws since the Code of 1897. The Code of 1924 was described by its editors as "technically an extensively amended Code of 1897, compiled in one volume," but it was unique as the last official code adopted after a years-long process of code revision. The legislature voted that henceforth a new code edition would be prepared after each even-numbered regular session. A state senator who witnessed the process of adopting the Code of 1924 explained why this new scheme was better than the more cumbersome, old-fashioned way.

We have had four Codes or revisions [Code of 1851, Revision of 1860, Code of 1873, and Code of 1897] and the fifth will be issued in October, 1924. Each has been necessary, and each has been of great benefit to the people in presenting the law in a manner to be more easily understood. ... By reason of private publication of the laws in Miller's and Mc-Clain's codes and supplements, the next general revision was postponed a quarter of a century.

. . . .

The [code] commission qualified on the 19th day of March, 1919, and immediately organized and entered upon the discharge of its duties. ...

The Commission prepared and issued the compiled code as directed and, also, prepared in all about three hundred (300) bills, covering such parts of the compiled code as in the judgment of the Commission urgently needed codification and revision. ...

The 40th General Assembly convened in extra session on December 4, 1923, and immediately began consideration of the report of the code commission. ...

Certain professional lobbyists made strenuous efforts to secure the indefinite postponement of some of the bills, apparently because of fear that the general assembly would enact them with provisions which the lobbyists considered might be inimical to the interests which they were hired to represent. Two notable cases were the Workmen's Compensation Act and the Drainage Act.

. . . .

[U]nless conditions change or unless greater interest is taken in primaries and elections by more people who really believe in our system of government, it is probable that well organized, cohesive and militant minorities representing radicalism in varying degrees will be able to crystalize their ideas into legislation which will be extremely difficult to remove or to change. Therefore, I look with great favor upon the plan proposed by the 40th General Assembly for a continuous codification and revision of our laws. ...

Our general assembly is always composed mainly of farmers and business men, and there are few members who have ever made a study of code revision and who, either by experience or natural aptitude, are competent to draft bills. Each general assembly would save a great deal of time and money if it would employ persons thoroughly capable of drafting measures under consideration.

Senator J. H. Trewin, "Code Revision," *Proceedings of the Thirtieth Annual Session of the Iowa State Bar Association* (Des Moines: Iowa State Bar Assoc., 1924), Session of June 20, 1924, pp. 208-10, 212, 214-16.

CHAPTER EIGHT

The Great Depression
1929-1941

"The farmer's problem ... will be solved when the farmers of this nation raise sufficient hell .... "

— Milo Reno, FARMERS HOLIDAY ASSOCIATION

1929-1941

PRESIDENT HERBERT HOOVER'S SINGLE TERM
in office was dominated by the Great Depression. In the months following the stock market crash of October 29, 1929, industrial production decreased, and unemployment dramatically increased.

Pressed by farmers to protect them from foreign competition, Hoover in 1930 signed a tariff act; but instead of relief, trade suffered further under a worldwide tariff war. Bank failures in Europe led to bank failures in the United States. In June 1931, President Hoover arranged a one-year "Hoover Moratorium" on the repayment of war debts and reparations. The following year, he established the Reconstruction Finance Corporation to loan money to ailing banks and other businesses.

Despite the creation of a Federal Farm Board, farm production continued to outstrip demand, and farm prices continued well below the production costs. Momentum grew for price supports that guaranteed cost of production plus a reasonable return. In Iowa, the "cost of production" campaign was strongly advanced by the rapidly growing Iowa Farmers Union and its dynamic leader, Milo Reno.

In May 1932, the Farmers Holiday Association was formed in Des Moines with Milo Reno as its president. To draw attention to their plight, farmers were urged to withhold their products from the markets. The strike, begun in August, was marred by blockades, milk dumping, and acts of violence. On September 1, Reno called for an immediate "temporary truce." Although the strike had attracted little support among Iowa farmers, the Farmers Holiday Association later would be more successful in forcing "holidays" from farm foreclosures.

The nation continued to suffer the devastating effects of the Great Depression. To depression-weary Americans enduring widespread unemployment, tight money, and mortgage foreclosures, President Hoover's initiatives seemed too little, too late. Anti-Hoover sentiment grew. In the general election of 1932, Hoover was soundly defeated by his Democratic opponent, Governor Franklin Delano Roosevelt of New York.

Roosevelt swept into power with over 57 percent of the popular vote. Iowa deserted its

Republican tradition—and its native son, Herbert Hoover—to vote like the rest of the nation. The Iowa governorship, legislature, and most congressional seats and county offices were won by Democrats.

Upon taking office in March 1933 (presidential terms thereafter would begin in January, thanks to the "lame duck" constitutional amendment ratified in 1933), President Roosevelt acted decisively to install new programs for economic recovery. His New Deal gave special relief to farmers, under the guiding influence of the Secretary of Agriculture, Iowan Henry A. Wallace. Domestic allotment and farm credit programs, among others, helped to restore stability and direction to the agricultural sector. By the late 1930s, farmers were enjoying relative prosperity.

In 1936, President Roosevelt was elected to a second term in office. Roosevelt again carried Iowa, but by a smaller margin than in the last election. Concerned about the concentration of power in Washington and Roosevelt's "court-packing" plan, Iowans returned to the Republican fold in the 1938 state election. In 1940, Roosevelt was elected to a third term in office, but despite his choice of Iowan Henry A. Wallace as a running mate, Iowa cast a majority of votes for Republican Wendell Willkie.

While America was advancing toward economic recovery, storm clouds were gathering over Europe. When, in September 1939, Adolf Hitler invaded Poland, war broke out on the continent. A national sentiment in favor of neutrality postponed America's involvement in the war, but the fall of France and the Battle of Britain in 1940 brought the country closer to intervention.

On December 7, 1941, Japanese aircraft attacked the American base at Pearl Harbor, Hawaii, destroying much of the U.S. Pacific fleet anchored there and killing over 2,300 soldiers, sailors, and civilians. Declaring December 7 "a day which will live in infamy," President Roosevelt the next day asked Congress for a declaration of war. For the second time in twenty-five years, the nation prepared to enter a world war.

The farmers' growing frustration over economic conditions erupted in what is known as the "Iowa Cow War." A 1929 statute made compulsory the test for bovine tuberculosis. Many farmers disputed the reliability of the test and the adequacy of compensation for cattle destroyed. Opposition to the measure grew, and in March 1931, farmers marched in Des Moines. In August and September, farmers in Cedar and Muscatine counties actively (and sometimes physically) resisted the work of state veterinarians. Republican Governor Dan Turner—himself a farmer—sent the Iowa National Guard into several southeast Iowa counties to enforce the tests. The most famous "battle" of this unusual "war" occurred on September 21, 1931.

Governor Dan Turner sent the Iowa National Guard into some southeastern Iowa counties during the "Iowa Cow War" of 1931. (Courtesy, State Historical Society of Iowa, Des Moines)

County is Under Military Rule
Peaceable Settlement of Affairs is Hoped for in the Cedar County Bovine Test War

At noon, Tuesday, Cedar county was declared under military surveillance according to proclamation of Governor Dan W. Turner of Iowa and order of Brigadier General Park A. Findley in command of the state national guard units which have been mobilized here with headquarters established at the Cedar county fair grounds.

A deplorable condition of affairs has developed in the matter of testing of cattle in the community for bovine tuberculosis. Objectors to the test have persistently held that the test is inaccurate and that their stand is right and justified under present conditions. Appeals have been carried to highest courts of the land and the courts have upheld the statute.

Following a demonstration at the J. W. Lenker farm near Wilton last Monday afternoon in which more than sixty state deputies and the county sheriff were overpowered, a requisition for state military aid was sent to Governor Dan W. Turner, who at once issued a proclamation declaring the county under military law and directing the national guard mobilized for enforcement of the state law.

. . . .

The first contingent of the 2,000 to arrive in the city reached the war zone about 3:00 p.m. Special train brought four hundred fifty men from northern Iowa cities; 100 more came by bus from Iowa City. The second special train carrying Council Bluffs and Des Moines companies arrived shortly after three o'clock. The third special arrived about seven in the evening on Tuesday with guard units from Glenwood, Centerville, Burlington, Shenandoah, Red Oak, Washington, Corning, Fairfield and Villisca. Trucks arrived during the afternoon with supplies etc. from the Camp Dodge national guard arsenal.

. . . .

Plans for proceeding with testing of cattle today were reported practically complete Wednesday evening. A number of state veterinarians are present ready to go ahead with the work under military protection.

. . . .

The commanding officer of the camp yesterday circulated several thousand copies of the governor's

Iowa National Guard Troops at Tipton, Iowa, called out by Governor Turner to preserve order during the "Iowa Cow War." (Courtesy, State Historical Society of Iowa, Des Moines)

proclamation over the county in order that everyone might know what the facts of the affair really were. It is generally hoped by the citizenry that the proceedings will be of quiet nature and that the objector herd owners may be prevailed upon to have due regard for the military forces of the state.

Tipton Advertiser, September 24, 1931.

*D*espite the hope for economic recovery engendered by the election of President Franklin Roosevelt and his plans for federal relief, the depression grew worse before it grew better. In January 1933, the newly elected

Democratic governor of Iowa, Clyde L. Herring, urged the legislature to pass measures to address the crisis of farm foreclosures. In the interim, Governor Herring issued an emergency proclamation of doubtful legal validity.

*P*roclamation
To the citizens of the State of Iowa:
WHEREAS, an emergency exists in the State of Iowa with reference to mortgage foreclosures of both real and personal property and the enforcement of statutory liens caused in large measure by the financial and economic depression and conditions incidental thereto, and

WHEREAS, farmers, laborers, and citizens generally, of this great Commonwealth are in danger of

State of Iowa, to forthwith refrain from and discontinue the enforcement of said liens on real estate or personal property, or from taking possession of the personal property covered by said lien, and to discontinue and refrain from the prosecution of any suit or proceedings heretofore instituted for the foreclosure of such lien or liens, or the seizure or sale of any such property, save and until the respective legislative bodies having the power so to do, have reasonable opportunity to enact legislation to meet such emergency ....

WITNESS my signature and the great seal of the State of Iowa hereto attached, on this nineteenth day of January, in the year of our Lord, Nineteen Hundred Thirty-three, and of this Commonwealth, the Ninety-seventh year.

(Signed) Clyde L. Herring
Governor of the State of Iowa

"Proclamation," January 19, 1933, Clyde L. Herring Papers, University of Iowa Libraries, Special Collections, Iowa City, Iowa.

Governor Clyde Herring issued an emergency proclamation on farm foreclosures in January 1933. (Courtesy, State Historical Society of Iowa, Iowa City)

losing their farms, homes and means of earning a livelihood for themselves and members of their families because of present financial conditions, and

WHEREAS, these conditions are becoming more acute and more aggravated as time goes by, and

WHEREAS, the 45th General Assembly of the State of Iowa has just been recently convened and as yet has not had sufficient time or opportunity to pass remedial legislation correcting these difficulties ....

NOW THEREFORE, I, Clyde L. Herring, Governor of the State of Iowa, by and with the authority vested in me as Chief Executive of the State of Iowa, do hereby call upon all holders of mortgages or other liens upon real estate or personal property within the

The Forty-Fifth Iowa General Assembly, meeting in 1933, quickly responded to Governor Herring's call for remedial legislation by passing acts to delay the foreclosure of real estate mortgages and to extend unexpired redemption periods. The need for such relief was acute—the resistance to farm foreclosures in Iowa had begun to assume ominous forms, as shown by a shocking episode in Le Mars.

Judge Bradley Upholds
His Oath of Office

THE DESPERATION OF IOWA FARMERS OVER the worsening farm crisis during the Great Depression was especially acute in the northwestern part of the state. The most serious milk dumping and acts of violence during the Farmers Holiday Association strike in August 1932 had occurred at Sioux City. And it was in the northwestern town of Le Mars that farmers' anger over farm foreclosures and forced sales led to an appalling attack on Judge Charles C. Bradley, the most serious ever on an Iowa judge.

With the crash of 1929, farm prices had collapsed. The price of a bushel of wheat fell from $1.03 in 1929 to $.38 in 1932, while the price of corn fell from $.80 per bushel to $.32 in the same period. Hog prices per head fell from $11.36 in 1931 to $4.21 in 1933. About half of Iowa's farmers financed their land through mortgage debt, and with the collapse in the prices of produce, foreclosures became inevitable. From 1921 to 1933, thirteen percent of the state's farmland was foreclosed. Land values had slumped from $140 per acre in the late 1920s to $92 per acre in 1932. This meant that the proceeds from the sale of foreclosed property usually were insufficient to pay the mortgage debt, and the farmer was faced with the impossible burden of a deficiency judgment.

An anti-foreclosure movement intensified in January and February 1933, when at least seventy-six "penny auctions" took place in the Midwest. At penny auctions, a crowd sympathetic to the farmer being foreclosed dominated the proceedings. One very low bid would be made, which the auctioneer would be obliged to accept. An outsider who tried to bid would be firmly dissuaded by the farmer's friends. The "penny" would be paid by the friendly bidder, and the property returned to the farmer. At one chattel auction in Holstein, Iowa, in January 1933, the sum bid was only $11 on $1,500 worth of chattel.

Northwest Iowa was the most active area in the state's anti-foreclosure movement, and Le Mars was its center. On January 4, 1933, hundreds of farmers thronged the Plymouth County courthouse in Le Mars for the foreclosure sale of the farm of John Johnson. The insurance company that held the mortgage submitted a bid for $3,000 less than the mortgage debt. The infuriated crowd dragged the company's attorney from the courthouse steps, and slapped aside the sheriff who attempted to intervene. The mob threatened to lynch the attorney unless he raised the bid. He telegraphed for the company's permission, pleading: "Rush answer, my neck at risk!"[1] The company complied.

During the fracas, scores of farmers hurried into the courtroom, where Judge Chauncey W. Pitts was presiding. They insisted that he sign no more foreclosure decrees, and refused to allow him to leave the courtroom. The judge explained that he had to comply with his duties under the law. A farmer named Morris Cope exclaimed: "I would think you would be more worried about your neck than your oath of office."[2] The judge mollified the farmers by promising to write to Governor-elect Herring.

Due to the farmers' intense opposition to mortgage foreclosures, a group of insurance companies that held over forty percent of the farm mortgages in Iowa notified the governor they would suspend foreclosure actions until the General Assembly enacted debtor relief legislation. In February 1933, the legislature passed a moratorium law that allowed mortgage debtors to request continuances of pending and newly commenced foreclosure proceedings until March 1, 1935. This was followed by additional legislation to extend unexpired periods of redemption to the same date. Relief under both laws could be denied by the court for "good cause."[3] During the next year, about half of the farmers who qualified for this relief took advantage of the new laws.

In the wake of similar legislation in other states, demonstrations against farm foreclosures in the Midwest declined sharply between January and April 1933. But where there were demonstrations, the violence was sometimes alarming.

The motivation of the rebel farmers is illustrated by the experience of Morris Cope, the Plymouth County farmer who had threatened Judge Pitts and was to be a ringleader in the affair of Judge Bradley. Cope was a hog farmer in southeastern Plymouth County near Kingsley, where he owned eighty acres of land. For twenty-five years, Cope's father, Jacob, had been one of northwestern Iowa's leading farmers. He had a large house and 550 acres of first-class farmland.

In January 1932, 510 acres of Jacob Cope's land was foreclosed. Reduced to owning only forty acres, he was poor and embittered. Thus, in a few short months, Morris Cope had seen his father near ruin and his own hopes for the future destroyed. Small wonder that he was one of the leaders of the Iowan farmers who rebelled against foreclosure.

Judge Charles C. Bradley—the unfortunate object of the farmers' rage—was fifty-four years old in 1933. He had spent most of his early life in Audubon, Iowa, and then had moved to Council Bluffs. He attended the University of Iowa and graduated from the law department in 1901. Thereafter he practiced law in Le Mars, and became a district judge in 1918.

Although his career was conventional enough, many of the people of Plymouth County believed that Judge Bradley had a less conventional private life. According to one former resident of Le Mars: "His public personality was cold, stern, and forbidding; he was deaconlike in bearing. However, his secret home life scandalized the town, for he employed a housekeeper with whom he was also sleeping .... Salacious tales about his lively bachelorhood abounded .... "[4] This reputation may explain the sexual aspect of the attack on Judge Bradley.

April 27, 1933, was to be an unforgettable day at Le Mars. At nearby Primghar,

A crowd of farmers make a deputy sheriff kiss the flag on the courthouse lawn at Primghar, April 27, 1933. Part of the crowd then moved to Le Mars and took part in the attack on Judge C. C. Bradley.

county seat of O'Brien County, a crowd of farmers gathered for the sheriff's sale of John Shaffer's farm. Soon after 10:00 a.m., a deputy sheriff appeared on a second floor balcony to call for bids. Someone yelled "get him," and the crowd rushed into the courthouse.[5] Over twenty special deputies with clubs defended the staircase, and a general melee broke out. Morris Cope received a severe crack on the skull and went to have it bandaged by a doctor. The farmers were driven off, and the creditor's attorney and John Shaffer conferred.

Morris Cope returned and announced: "[W]e're going up now to get the judge." "No you're not," the sheriff replied. Cope asked the sheriff who was on the bench, and was told it was Judge Pitts. "Then," Cope said, "we'll go to Le Mars and get Judge Bradley." (Judge Bradley was known to have presided over the lengthy debt collection litigation that resulted in the execution sale of John Shaffer's property.) Then Cope went out on the balcony of the courthouse and urged the crowd to go on to Plymouth County. "We've showed you guys we are fighters," Cope shouted. "Now come on with us to Struble and Le Mars. We've got another job."[6]

Shaffer accepted his creditor's offer, and the settlement was announced to the crowd. The farmers insisted that the creditor's attorney, the sheriff, and his deputies kiss the flag at the front of the courthouse. A crowd of more than 100 men drove on to Le Mars. There they went to the home of Clarence Becker, who had recently been declared owner of a disputed property by the courts. While a "committee" of the men talked to Becker, others spoke to the crowd spread out over the lawn and the street.

One of the leaders then suggested that they go to the courthouse to look for Judge Bradley. At about 5:00 p.m., the crowd swept into the courtroom where the judge was sitting. Morris Cope, his head swathed in bandages from the fight in Primghar, demanded that the judge do justice to farmers. Judge Bradley asked his name. "I'm Morris Cope of Kingsley, Iowa," he said, and continued his harangue.[7] After a few moments, the judge attempted to silence Cope.

While Morris Cope spoke, the farmers filled the courtroom seats and stood along the walls. Judge Bradley said: "This is my courtroom. Take off your hats and stop smoking cigarettes."[8] The men shouted back: "It's not your courtroom. We built this courthouse with our tax money."[9] There were cries of "take him out" and "let's get him."[10] About half a dozen men rushed the judge. Clutching at his legs and throat, they brought him down from the bench.

An editorial cartoon in the *Des Moines Register,* April 29, 1933, reacts to the attack on Judge Bradley. (Courtesy, J.N. "Ding" Darling Foundation)

"Promise you won't sign any more foreclosure actions," the men demanded.[11] Judge Bradley refused, saying he had not had sufficient time to study the fifteen cases then before him. The men slapped and hit the judge, and dragged him along a corridor, down the steps, and into the courthouse square. Again they demanded that the judge swear he would sign no more foreclosure orders. Again the judge refused.

During the struggle in the courtroom, the court reporter was knocked out, while the bailiff was severely jostled. Outside the courthouse, five men with blue bandanas tied over their faces once more demanded that Judge Bradley take an oath not to sign another foreclosure order. When he refused, the men knocked him down. A group of about ten men put the judge into a truck and announced they were going to hang him. As they drove off, a man named Martin Rosburg offered the judge a bottle. He said: "Come on Judge, have a drink on us."[12] The judge clenched his teeth; Rosburg forced them open with a screwdriver and poured the alcohol down the judge's throat.

About sixty others followed the truck to a crossroads a mile and a half southeast of Le Mars. Here a seventy-five year old farmer named A.A. Mitchell blindfolded the judge, knotting a blue bandana with white dots around his head. The crowd again demanded that Judge Bradley sign no more foreclosure orders. Again he refused. Someone removed a grease-filled hubcap from the wheel of a truck and placed it on the judge's head. The grease oozed down over his face, and some of the mob smeared dirt from the road into the grease.

Mitchell produced a rope and pulled it taut around the judge's neck. Judge Bradley still would not swear the oath the farmers demanded. The mob lifted him off the ground by the rope, and he appeared to collapse.

Then the crowd took Judge Bradley to an electric light pole nearby, bearing a sign: "33,000 volts, danger." They tossed the rope over the sign and again tightened it around his neck, without lifting him from the ground.

Next the mob's leaders took Judge Bradley to the highway and asked him to kneel and pray for the farmers. "I'll do that gladly," he said. Still blindfolded and covered in dirt and grease, the judge knelt down. "Oh Lord, I Pray Thee do justice to all men."[13] Some of the men removed the judge's trousers, filling them with dirt and grease. They put grease on his testicles and threatened him with castration.

The editor of the *Le Mars Globe-Post*, who was present at the scene, warned Mitchell that the judge was in poor health and that they might have murder on their hands. With this, the masked men rushed to an automobile and drove off.

Judge Bradley—his neck chafed, his lips bloody, his hair and face filthy—refused the offer of a ride from others in the crowd. He started walking, and eventually was overtaken and given a lift back to Le Mars by the son of a Presbyterian minister.

The incident was a major news item across the nation. Iowa's Governor Herring declared martial law in Plymouth County. He described the events of the previous day as a "vicious and criminal conspiracy and assault upon a judge while in discharge of his official duties, endangering his life and threatening a breakdown of all law and order."[14] The next day, over 200 state militia were encamped at Le Mars, and martial law remained in force until May 11, 1933.

Judge Bradley was restrained in his statements to the press about the incident. The *Des Moines Register* reported his few comments: "I have sympathy for them.

Judge C. C. Bradley resigned the bench soon after the attack at Le Mars in April 1933; he died in 1939. (Courtesy, *Des Moines Register*)

... Of course I have considerable sympathy for these farmers." He continued: "I am something of a farmer in that I hold title to considerable farm property and I realize full well the problems farmers are up against."[15]

Ultimately thirteen men appeared before Judge Peters of Clarinda, charged in connection with the attack. The first three were given minor contempt citations. By the end of May, seven other men had pleaded guilty to a variety of charges. One of the ringleaders, Martin Rosburg, received a six-month sentence in the county jail on a charge of interference with justice, and a one-year suspended sentence in the penitentiary on a charge of assault to commit great bodily injury. Another leader received a similar sentence. Two men were given thirty days in the county jail and one-year suspended sentences in the penitentiary. Three others received suspended sentences in the county jail.

In July, A.A. Mitchell pleaded "not guilty" to charges of assault to commit great bodily injury. At his trial, witnesses testified that Mitchell had blindfolded the judge and put the rope around his neck. Judge Bradley himself took the witness stand and gave his account of that day.

In a calm, steady voice, the judge described those who had entered his courtroom: "I was unable to recognize Mitchell in the group but I did recognize [Morris] Cope .... He appeared nervous and agitated and I tried to cool him off." The judge testified what happened on arrival at the cross roads: "Taken from the truck, I was blindfolded from behind by someone I did not recognize. Someone threw grease from the hubcap of the truck on my hair and also tossed sand in my face and hair ...."

He ended his testimony: "While I was praying someone kept a continual tugging on the rope. Then, my prayer finished, someone took my trousers down and threw grease and sand in my trousers. There were some threats of mutilation. I didn't remember taking the blindfold off and I was unable to identify any of the group because they were leaving when I could see again."[16]

The jury was out for six and one-half hours and found Mitchell guilty of a lesser charge of assault and battery. The court sentenced Mitchell to thirty days in the county jail.

The last to appear in court were Morris Cope and Ed Casper, who had been in hiding. They gave themselves up just after Mitchell's trial, and pleaded guilty to charges of interfering with justice and assault. Judge Peters gave both men a one-year suspended penitentiary sentence on the charge of interference with justice. He gave Casper six months in the county jail for assault.

In passing sentence on Morris Cope for the charge of assault with intent to inflict bodily injury, Judge Peters said: "I have heard the evidence ... and I believe you were somewhat of a leader. Therefor I feel you should serve a longer sentence than the others. I sentence you on this charge to serve a year in the county jail."[17]

The sentencing of Morris Cope, a farmer so deeply embittered by foreclosure, brought an end to the court proceedings. As for Judge Bradley, he could scarcely have done more to uphold the honor of his office. Even in explaining his reluctance to comment on the episode to the press, the judge maintained a dignified reticence: "It is not ethical for the bar to get into the limelight."[18]

Judge Bradley retired from the district court bench in December 1933, eight months after the outrage. He went to live in Des Moines, where he was trustee of an insurance company receivership. Because of ill health, he resigned his position and left Des Moines a few weeks before his death. In July 1939—six years after the terrible attack—Charles C. Bradley, aged fifty-nine, died at his home in Le Mars.

Several Iowa county courthouses were constructed with the assistance of grants from the federal Public Works Administration or the Works Progress Administration (the W.P.A.). Pictured here is the Cass County courthouse in 1934. (Courtesy, State Historical Society of Iowa, Des Moines)

Unemployment and homelessness created heavy social burdens for Iowa's townships and counties. An Iowa statute permitted local authorities to issue a "warning to depart" to individuals wishing to settle in the county "who are county charges or are likely to become such." This statute was considered by the Iowa Supreme Court in an action to remove the defendants, a husband and wife, from Emmet County.

The defendants] were married in Hamilton county, Iowa, in 1920, and lived at Webster City for about five years. They then went to Jackson county, Minnesota, where they lived for about fourteen months. From there they moved to Dickinson county, Iowa, where they stayed about two months, and on or about September 1, 1926, moved to Emmet county. ... From Emmet county they went to Jackson county, Minnesota, and worked on a farm for a few months, and then moved to Martin county, Minnesota .... About March 15, 1930, they returned to Emmet county, and have lived there continuously since that time. On the 29th day of

December 1930, a certain alleged warning to depart was served upon [the defendants] and another such alleged warning to depart was served ... on December 2, 1931 ....

On May 12, 1931, [the defendant husband], as a person in destitute circumstances and unable to obtain work, applied to the overseer of the poor of Emmet county for aid, and relief was denied by the county because of the serving of the purported warnings to depart, and upon the grounds that said appellee had not acquired a settlement in Emmet county as by law provided.

. . . .

Code section 5315 is as follows:

"Persons coming into the state, or going from one county to another, who are county charges or are likely to become such, may be prevented from acquiring a settlement by the authorities of the county, township, or city in which such persons are found warning them to depart therefrom. After such warning, such persons cannot acquire a settlement except by the requisite residence of one year without further warning."

. . . .

This is a free country. People generally have the right to settle where they please, and where they can best pursue the serious business of making a living for themselves and families. To give to any officer or board the power to cause and require any one to move on by the service of a notice is to bestow upon them an arbitrary and a serious power and authority. It is the placing of an unusual power, the exercise of which might cause serious hardship, and it is because of this unusual power that the courts universally have held that the power, in order to be effective, must be exercised strictly according to the statute. The language of this statute is clear. The notice is to be served "upon the order of the trustees of the township, or of the board of supervisors." There is no showing in this record of strict compliance with the statutory requirements. ...

The order of the trial court dismissing the petition [to remove the defendants from Emmet County] is affirmed.

Emmet County, Iowa v. Dally, 216 Iowa 166, 167, 169-70 (1933).

The mortgage foreclosure and redemption moratorium laws were renewed by the legislature in its sessions of 1935 and 1937. The Iowa Supreme Court had upheld the constitutionality of the original statute extending the period of redemption. But when, several years later, the Court was again asked to determine the validity of the moratorium laws, it took a different view.

This is the first case presented to us questioning the constitutionality of the last Act of the Legislature re-enacting and extending the provisions of prior Moratorium Acts, in which a record was made upon which we could base a judgment or conclusion as to the constitutional questions involved. ...

We feel that the appeal should be determined directly upon the question that the Act is unconstitutional because it impairs the obligation of contracts in contravention of and repugnant to article 1, section 10 [and] the Fourteenth Amendment to the Constitution of the United States, and article 1, sections 9 and 21, and article 12, section 1, of the Constitution of the State of Iowa.

Briefly, moratorium legislation first occurred in this state during the session of the 45th G. A. and what is now generally known as the first Moratorium Act was passed by that assembly as chapter 182, on February 9, 1933. This act was re-enacted and extended ... effective February 8, 1935, and again was re-enacted and extended ... effective February 19, 1937. ...

We feel that we are foreclosed from considering these Moratorium Acts other than the last one enacted ... for the reason that in a very able and extended opinion former Justice Kindig, speaking for a majority of the court, held in Des Moines Joint Stock Land Bank v. Nordholm, 217 Iowa 1319, 253 N. W. 701, that the so-called first Act of February, 1933, was constitutional, basing such final determination upon the fact that an emergency existed in the state which called for an exercise of the reserve police power ....

In 1933, at the birth of the first Moratorium Act, the state, as well as the nation, was confronted with a great emergency: Banks were closed; home owners and farm owners were being ousted from their homes and farms through foreclosure proceedings; farm strikes existed; open, defiant and militant resistance to courts and court orders and decrees was in evidence; labor was unemployed; there was scarcely any price or market for farm products; and the health and social welfare of the people, as well as the sovereignty and perpetuity of organized government was seriously menaced and in the balance. In the presence of such conditions it is fair to conclude, as did the Legislature of this State, that a great temporary emergency existed ....

[T]he record shows, without controversy, that practically all of the depressed conditions existing in 1933, do not exist at this time. ... Farm values have been bettered; the price of farm produce has increased; the banking situation has been made stable and secure, and no orgy of bank failures and receiverships longer exists; thousands of Iowa farm homes that were under foreclosure proceedings have been refinanced through the government and other agencies.

[W]e are compelled to say that the law has ceased to operate, and restating the principle that moratorium legislation is not valid and cannot be sustained unless based upon an existing emergency, we must hold that no emergency now exists, and that it did not exist at the time of the enactment of Senate File 15, and that the trial court erred in sustaining the act ....

First Trust Joint Stock Land Bank v. Arp, 225 Iowa 1331, 1332-35 (1939).

The temperance movement continued to occupy the arena of public opinion, particularly following the repeal of the federal prohibition amendment in 1933. It fell again to the states to consider liquor legislation, and the Iowa legislature in 1934 passed the "Iowa Liquor Control Act," optimistically deemed "An Act to promote temperance in the state of Iowa." The law created the Iowa Liquor Control Commission to regulate liquor traffic through the establishment of state liquor stores. Individuals who did not have bottles bearing state liquor seals found themselves charged with illegal possession of alcohol.

The county attorney's information filed in this case charged the defendant with illegal possession of alcoholic liquor on the 12th day of December, 1935, in Page county, Iowa .... Upon trial of the case the State introduced evidence showing that on the 12th day of December, 1935, under a search warrant duly issued, the deputy sheriff, a constable and a police officer searched a gasoline station operated by the defendant and also the home of the defendant [and] in the filling station they found five bottles of alcohol; that they found eight gallons of whiskey in an upstairs room of the defendant's home, and also one bottle of whiskey in the basement thereof; ... that all of the liquor thus found in both the filling station and at the home of the defendant was intoxicating liquor; and that there were no state liquor seals on any of the bottles containing such intoxicating liquor. ...

It is the contention of the [defendant] that, under the liquor laws of the state of Iowa, as they existed at the time of the seizure of the liquor here involved, the mere possession of intoxicating liquor in this state, in bottles or containers which do not bear the liquor seals of the liquor commission of the state of Iowa, is not a violation of the law ....

We think it apparent [that the] "Iowa Liquor Control Act", intended to place the complete control of all traffic in intoxicating liquors in this state, except beer, under the Iowa liquor control commission; that, under the provisions of this act, all intoxicating liquors, except beer, manufactured, sold, kept for sale, possessed within this state, or transported into this state, are subject to the Iowa liquor control commission [and] before any such liquors legally can reach the hands of private individuals, they must be in containers bearing the seals of the Iowa liquor control commission.

It is undisputed that the defendant in this case had in his possession a large quantity of intoxicating liquors in containers which did not bear the seals of the Iowa liquor control commission. ... In fact, while it is not shown in the evidence, it is admitted in [the defendant's] argument that these liquors were bought in Missouri and brought into Iowa from Missouri. ...

... The evidence was amply sufficient to show that the possession was in violation of the plain provisions of the Iowa Liquor Control Act and to sustain the conviction of the defendant in this case.

State v. Johnson, 222 Iowa 1204, 1205-07, 1209 (1937).

I f the 1920s was the decade of bootleg liquor and organized crime, the 1930s belonged to the bank robber. Perhaps no gang of robbers has achieved more enduring notoriety than the Barrow gang. Clyde Barrow and his girlfriend Bonnie Parker were the best-known figures in the gang, which also included Clyde's brother, Buck, Buck's wife, Blanche, and a furtive figure known as W.D. Jones. Their lengthy and bloody crime spree included a fateful trip to Iowa during the summer of 1933.

"Enough Blood and Hell": Bonnie and Clyde in Iowa

"Some day they'll go down together;
And they'll bury them side by side;
To few it'll be grief—
To the law a relief—
But it's death for Bonnie and Clyde."[1]

—BONNIE PARKER, *The Story of Bonnie and Clyde,* 1934

IN THE EARLY 1930s, THE BARROW GANG PASSED into American folklore. The 1967 film, *Bonnie and Clyde,* with Warren Beatty and Faye Dunaway, enhanced their myth. But the junior member of the gang, W.D. Jones, stressed the horrible reality: "That Bonnie and Clyde movie made it all look sort of glamorous, but like I told them teenaged boys sitting near me at the drive-in showing: 'Take it from an old man who was there. It was hell."[2] The gang's most hellish episode took place in July 1933 near the little town of Dexter, Iowa.

Twenty-four-year-old Clyde Barrow dominated the gang. The 5'7", 125-pound son of a Texas tenant farmer, Clyde began stealing cars as a seventeen-year-old in Dallas. He later progressed to armed robbery—his targets were small stores, gasoline stations, and sometimes banks. During 1932 and early 1933, Clyde murdered seven men, bringing him nationwide notoriety.

From August 1932, twenty-two-year-old Bonnie Parker—a 4'10", 85-pound former waitress from Dallas—was Clyde's constant companion as they drove stolen cars throughout the Southwest. Obsessed by Clyde and his life of crime, Bonnie celebrated their lives in verse. Her best known poem, "The Story of Bonnie and Clyde," was widely published after her death.

W.D. Jones joined Clyde and Bonnie in December 1932. A seventeen-year-old petty criminal, Jones had known and hero-worshipped Clyde since their Dallas childhoods. On Christmas Day, Jones helped Clyde steal a car. Clyde murdered the owner and, as an accomplice, Jones became locked into the gang.

Clyde's elder brother, Buck, had received a five-year prison sentence for robbery in 1929. He escaped and, during 1931, married Blanche Caldwell, a tiny young woman whom his sister called "a splendid, gentle, good country girl."[3] When Blanche discovered that Buck was an escaped convict, she got him to surrender. Later, she persuaded the Texas governor to pardon her husband. When the twenty-eight-year-old Buck— an even smaller man than Clyde—left prison in March 1933, he arranged a "family reunion" with his brother. Although Buck's plan made Blanche cry for two days, she went with him.

This strangely assorted quintet rented an apartment in Joplin, Missouri. Police spotted and surrounded them, but they shot their way out. Clyde killed two officers, while Blanche ran away screaming. Buck had held a gun, and thereafter he and Blanche also were locked into the gang.

In June 1933, Clyde had a car crash; the car caught fire and Bonnie was trapped in the flames. Clyde and Jones pulled her free, but she was shockingly burned. Jones recalled: "The hide on her right leg was gone from her hip down to her ankle. I could see the bone at places."[4] It was months before she could walk again.

As Bonnie lay suffering, Buck and Jones robbed two Piggly-Wiggly grocery stores in Arkansas. While they were escaping, Buck killed a marshal. By mid-July Bonnie was able to travel, but she had to be lifted in and out of the car. Needing funds, the gang drove northwards to Fort Dodge, Iowa, where the women were left outside the city. Buck drove, while Clyde and Jones robbed three gas stations of $150. The gang escaped to a tavern in Platte City, Missouri.

Their movements aroused the suspicion of local authorities, and at 11:00 p.m. the next night, officers raided the Barrows' cabins. The gang again shot their way out, wounding the sheriff. Even Blanche was reported to have fired. Buck was shot, the bullet passing through his skull, and the others dragged him into the car. As Clyde drove off, a volley of bullets shattered the car's rear windows. The glass cut Blanche's face and permanently blinded her in one eye.

A maimed gang re-entered Iowa on Thursday, July 20. Blood oozed from Buck's awful head wound; Blanche was half blind; Bonnie was still crippled. A farmer at Caledonia, near Mount Ayr, watched Clyde, Blanche, and Jones burn bloody bandages and clothing. The gang bought food and gas in Caledonia and headed north.

Clyde decided to lie low until Buck's wound improved. He chose a spot next to Dexfield Park, a disused amusement park near Dexter, thirty miles from Des Moines. They drove up a side road and stopped in a small wooded area from which trees stretched down to the South Raccoon River.

Each day Clyde drove into Dexter to buy food at the Blohm Cafe. He got remedies and bandages from the Pohle and Stanley Drug Stores. When Mr. Stanley asked the purpose of all the gauze and bandages, Clyde pretended he was a veterinarian.

On Sunday, July 23, the gang drove to the nearby town of Perry, where Jones stole another car. During their absence, a farmer picking berries came upon their camp. Half-burned, bloody bandages made him suspicious, and he told the Dexter special deputy, John Love, what he had found. The latter, after watching the gang through binoculars, reported to the local county sheriff. Guessing they were the Barrow gang, the sheriff requested men with automatic guns from Des Moines.

That night, local armed men guarded Dexfield Park and the adjacent area. Later county officers arrived and, at midnight, state officers, deputies, and police from Des Moines joined the posse. By the morning of Monday, July 24, fifty armed men surrounded the Barrows' camp on three sides. The posse left the side leading to the river unguarded.

At 6:00 a.m., Jones was roasting some leftover wieners for breakfast on a small fire. Clyde and Bonnie were sitting on a car cushion, and Buck and Blanche were in the back of one of the cars. The posse was within fifty feet of the gang when Bonnie and Clyde saw them. The Barrows went for their automatic Browning rifles and automatic pistols. As they fired, the posse took refuge behind logs and trees and let loose a fusillade of bullets, badly wounding all the gang except Blanche. Only one of the posse, Rags Riley of Des Moines, was injured.

After a two-minute gun battle, the Barrows took to a car. Clyde drove onto a tree stump and got stuck. Jones tried to pry the car off with a rifle, but was unsuccessful. The posse's bullets had wrecked the other car, so the Barrows had to run. Jones carried the lame Bonnie. Blanche helped Buck, who was now wounded in the hip as well. The gang vanished into the woods.

Clyde realized that Buck could not keep up. Blanche would not leave him, so the others deserted them and made for the river. Jones waited with Bonnie, while Clyde went toward the road to steal a car. The editor of the *Dexter Sentinel* and another armed man were guarding the bridge. Clyde saw them and called: "Don't shoot."[5] Thinking him a colleague, they held their fire. Clyde ducked behind a large tree, began shooting, and another gun battle raged. When his ammunition ran out, Clyde hastened back to Bonnie and Jones.

The two men half swam, half stumbled across the river, with Bonnie on Jones's back. They came out wet and bloody. Clyde's right leg and shoulder were wounded, and a bullet had grazed his head. Jones, bleeding profusely, had been hit six times. Bonnie had been shot in the chest and stomach. They made their way into a cornfield.

The farm belonged to Valley Fellers. He, his son, and a hired man were feeding the livestock when Clyde appeared, brandishing a pistol—unknown to them empty. Clyde threatened to shoot their dog; then he whistled, and Jones emerged from the corn carrying Bonnie. Clyde ordered the Fellers to fetch their car.

Jones handed Bonnie over the fence to Valley Fellers, who remarked on her condition. Clyde said that he had given her a shot of morphine to deaden the pain. The two Fellers carried Bonnie to the back seat of their Plymouth. The son showed Clyde—who usually stole Fords—how to operate the gear lever. Then Clyde and Jones got in and drove off.

After the trio had a flat tire, they stole another car in Polk City. They abandoned the Fellers' car, its seats covered in blood, and disappeared.

Meanwhile the Fellers reported that only three of the gang had escaped. Cautiously the posse searched the woods and, at about 8:00 a.m., some deputies found Buck and Blanche hiding behind a log. Buck held a pistol threateningly, so Dr. H. W. Keller, a Des Moines dentist, shot him in the shoulder.

Buck stiffened as if dead, and Blanche screamed. Two men caught her by her arms. Blanche struggled, and then shrieked to Buck lying on the ground: "Don't die, don't die!"[6]

The men carried Buck into Dexfield Park, laid him down, and sent for a car. Buck asked for a cigarette, and Dr. Keller lit him one. Blanche, looking down at her wounded husband, cried: "Daddy, Daddy, are you all right?" Buck quietly an-

Two members of the Barrow gang are captured near Dexter. Blanche Barrow (in sunglasses) struggles; her wounded husband, Buck, is hidden behind the kneeling men on the right. (*Des Moines Tribune*, July 24, 1933)

swered, "Sure Baby, I'm all right."[7]

Police drove the Barrows to a doctor in Dexter, where 1,000 people thronged to glimpse the notorious gangsters. The doctor bandaged Blanche's blind eye and Buck's grievous wounds. Asked by police where he was wanted, Buck said: "Wherever I've been."[8] The police drove Buck to the hospital in Perry, and Blanche to the Polk County jail in Des Moines.

At the site of the gun battle, branches had been shot off the trees and souvenir hunters dug bullets out of the wood. Spectators gaped at the Barrows' cars riddled with bullet holes. Among the gang's effects, the police found thirty-two automatic pistols, two revolvers, two automatic rifles ... and a Bible.

In the jailhouse, Blanche—still dressed in a thin, once-pink blouse, blood-stained khaki trousers, and leather riding boots—answered questions. She said of the shoot-out: "I figured it was the end." She denied using a gun: "There was plenty of hell but I didn't contribute to it."[9]

Later Missouri authorities interviewed Blanche about the shoot-out at Platte City, and the next day removed her to the Platte City jail. Eventually Blanche

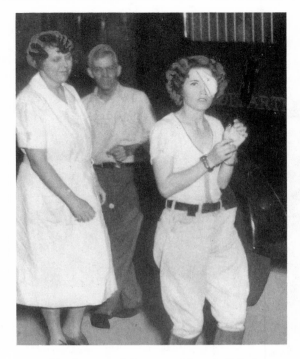

Blanche Barrow being escorted from the Polk County jail to face charges in Platte City, Missouri. (*Des Moines Register,* July 26, 1933)

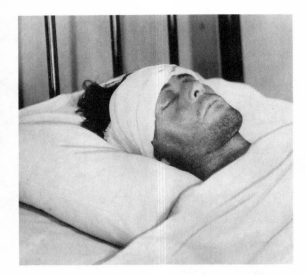

Buck Barrow, Clyde's brother, lies gravely wounded in a Perry hospital after his capture. (*Des Moines Tribune,* July 26, 1933)

pleaded guilty to assaulting the sheriff with intent to kill, and received a ten-year prison sentence, serving six years.

Meanwhile in the Perry hospital, Buck lay dying from the head wound received in Missouri. He admitted to the murder of the Arkansas marshal, and said to an Arkansas officer: "It was a good thing you got out of the way or you might have got yours."[10]

Soon Buck's mother arrived from Texas. She sat by his bedside, while he called for Blanche and Clyde. On Saturday, July 29, Buck died. He was buried in Texas.

Police in Broken Bow, Nebraska, found the car that Clyde and Jones had stolen in Polk City, Iowa. The inside was covered in blood and strewn with empty medicine bottles, press photos of the Barrows, and a Des Moines newspaper dated the day of the Iowa shoot-out.

The fugitives drove through state after state. For W.D. Jones, Dexfield Park was the end. At the first opportunity—in Mississippi—he escaped from Clyde and Bonnie. As Jones put it: "I'd had enough blood and hell."[11] He was arrested in Texas and received a fifteen-year sentence for murder, serving six years.

When they recovered, Clyde and Bonnie resumed their nomadic life—stealing and driving, forever driving. In early 1934, Clyde killed two or three more men, and Bonnie is said to have murdered a police officer. That year they returned to Iowa. The evidence is that on January 31 in Rockwell City, they stole a set of Iowa license plates numbered 13-1234. The next day, Clyde robbed $300 from a bank at nearby Knierim.

Apparently Clyde and Bonnie even came back to the Dexfield Park area. On April 16 in Stuart, near Dexter, a young woman waited outside a bank in a car—license plates number Iowa 13-1234—while two untidy men stole $1,500. Soon afterward, they roared through Dexter at over eighty miles per hour. Then, on May 3, robbers escaped with $700 from a bank in Everly in northwest Iowa—their license number was Iowa 13-1234.

In Louisiana three weeks later, on May 23, 1934, Texas and local lawmen ambushed Clyde and Bonnie in their Ford and riddled them with bullets. Among the license plates in their car was Iowa number 13-1234.

Five members of the Barrow gang had come to Dexfield Park. Ultimately, the three principals were killed by law officers, and the two lesser members spent years in prison.

W.D. Jones was right. The gang's story was not glamorous. It was hell.

Not to be outdone by Dexter's link to Bonnie and Clyde, the town of Mason City also laid dubious claim to the privilege of "hosting" a well-known crime figure in this era of lawlessness. The nation's Public Enemy No. 1, John Dillinger, and a gang that included the equally famous Baby Face Nelson, robbed the First National Bank of Mason City of over $50,000 during an otherwise quiet afternoon on Tuesday, March 13, 1934. The next day, the local newspaper published the gripping details.

Dillinger Blamed for Holdup
$52,000 Robbery Loot Here Sets New Recent High

That the sinister hand of "Whittling" John Dillinger, Indiana desperado, was seen in the $52,000 robbery of the First National bank of Mason City Tuesday afternoon was the growing belief among officers here Wednesday.

While two states were being combed for clews [sic] of the mobsters, with bridges guarded across the Mississippi, Sheriff J. M. Robertson was continuing his work of getting a complete description of the seven men who in the midst of a machine gun barrage robbed the bank and carried away the money surrounded by a wall of human hostages.

. . . .

At least three persons identified the guard who stood in front of the bank door as being John Dillinger.

. . . .

Dr. Charles V. Dietz, whose office window opens on to Federal avenue but a short distance to the north of the bank entrance said that he stood in the window and saw the bandit guard, whom he was satisfied was Dillinger. He said that he saw the guard shoot at Jim Buchanan, police officer, who was behind the monument in the park directly across the street.

The man believed Dillinger was of medium build, wore a light gray suit and dark overcoat and dark hat, according to Dr. Dietz. He had the bullets pinned on his vest and reloaded his automatic while he was in front of the bank. ...

The bandits entered the lobby of the bank about 20 minutes before closing time. Several of the raiders stood guard at the entrances. The 31 employes and approximately 25 customers were ordered to raise their hands.

Tom Walters, bank guard in a bullet proof cage, was unable to fire on the robbers because of the crowd in the lobby. He loosed one tear gas bomb and a hail of machine gun bullets splattered on his cage. None pierced it. Then his tear gun jammed on him and he was unable to fire more.

H. C. Fisher, assistant cashier, was forced to open the vault and pass out the money. In the tellers' cages, another bandit made a systematic collection of currency.

Willis G. C. Bagley, president, was fired at through the door of his private office. The bullet punctured his coat but did not strike him.

Outside Patrolman Buchanan and the leader of the gang exchanged shots. Neither was hit. A commercial motion picture cameraman was ordered to stop taking pictures.

"We'll do all the shooting around here," the bandits told him.

The robbery completed, the bandits ordered the hostages around them as a human shield, speeded away and released the men and women four miles outside the city limits. Shortly afterward the robbers' car was found wrecked in a ditch.

. . . .

Trailing the bandit car and serving as a target for the fusilade of shots which the robbers turned loose at intervals was the small sedan of Roger Grippen, commandeered by a deputy from the sheriff's office. Dick Brady was also a passenger in the car.

According to Grippen the gunmen drove at almost a leisurely rate of speed, even after they were out of the city traffic. They stopped from time to time to spread roofing nails across the highway, in every case asuring themselves that most of the points were sticking up; every action being done with the utmost nonchalance and studied carelessness.

On meeting oncoming cars the bandits would stop them and order them to remain there for five minutes, according to Grippen.

Mrs. William Clark and Mrs. Frank Graham, the last two hostages to be released by the gang, reported that the men handling the guns while they were leaving town were shooting more or less at random and once, in an apparent prank, they took a few pot shots at a signboard.

Mason City Globe-Gazette, March 14, 1934.

By the end of the 1930s, the devastating effects of the Great Depression had begun to wane. The Iowa Supreme Court—which had considered many cases involving depression-era relief legislation, foreclosures, and pauperism—returned to a more varied menu of human problems. Three such cases, excerpted below, involved breach of the Sabbath, buried treasure, and the classic "mouse in the Coke bottle."

Section 13227, Code of Iowa, 1939, provides in part as follows:

"Breach of Sabbath—exceptions. If any person be found on ... Sunday ... or in any manner disturbing a worship assembly or private family, or in buying or selling property of any kind, or in any labor except that of necessity or charity, he shall be fined .... "

. . . .

The record shows appellants are members of an organized religious order or group .... The acts charged in the information occurred between 10 a.m. and 1:30 p.m., on said Sunday. Appellants went singly to the doors of various homes in Clinton, at which they made known their presence by knocking or ringing doorbells. If granted admission, they sought, by word of mouth and printed booklets and, in some instances, by playing recorded transcriptions on a phonograph, to disseminate the doctrines and teachings of the order. ...

It is contended by the State that the calling upon householders after 10 a.m. on Sunday for the purpose of propagandizing appellants' religious views by spoken and printed words constituted "disturbing a private family." ... We are not prepared to hold that the calling at private homes in the middle of the Sabbath day, however unwelcome the caller may be, in itself, constitutes a desecration of the Sabbath.

The State also contends the distribution of the booklets and occasional receipt of the sum of ten cents constituted "selling property" within the prohibition of the act. However, appellants were not engaged in selling booklets. The alleged sales were merely incidental and collateral to appellants' main object which was to preach and publicize the doctrines of their order. ... We do not think the statute contemplates that the distribution of booklets of this nature and under these particular circumstances constitutes desecrating the Sabbath.

State of Iowa v. Mead, 230 Iowa 1217, 1218-20 (1941).

This case presents a rather novel legal question, and one concerning which our court has had little to say, but the law seems to be fairly well settled, both in England and in this country, that where money is found under circumstances such as the record in this case discloses, the finder is entitled to possession as against everyone except the true owner.

There is no dispute as to the material facts. The money was concealed beneath the floor of a closet adjacent to a bedroom. It was contained in three ordinary glass fruit jars, two of which had glass lids, and one a zinc lid, with rubber bands beneath the lids. These fruit jars were placed in an ordinary granite bucket or pail. Within the bucket above the jars was a tin lid. This pail was placed in a hole dug in the ground beneath the floor of this closet. Over the bucket was placed a cement slab. Entrance was gained to this place by means of a trap door which had been cut in the floor of the closet. ...

This money was found in June, 1933 .... It seems that the children in the neighborhood, including Ida Mae Zornes, were in the habit of hiding in this closet as they went about their play, and finally discovered this place in the floor where the boards were sawed in two, and pried up the same. The floor was up off the ground several inches, leaving room for the children to crawl in and hide under this trap door. This little eleven year old girl discovered this hole in which this bucket was concealed, and in digging around found the cement slab and removed it, discovered this old granite pail that the rust had eaten full of holes, and these jars wrapped in cloth. ... There was an inventory made of the contents of the jars, and the money consisted of $140 in silver dollars, $16.50 in 50-cent pieces, $4.75 in 25-cent pieces, $165 in $5 gold pieces, $340 in $10 gold pieces, $440 in $20 gold pieces, $13 in $1 currency, $4 in $2 currency, $50 in $5 currency, and one $10 bill, making a total of $1,183.25. ...

It was the finding of the trial court "that the money unearthed by the minor Ida Mae Zornes is treasure trove [and] that the right to the possession of said money ... should be established in the finder Ida Mae Zornes ...." This, we think as heretofore stated, is in accord with the great weight of authority.

Zornes v. Bowen, 223 Iowa 1141, 1142-45 (1937).

O n June 9, 1935, the country club had what was called an "open day," on which occasion devotees of golf were generally invited to be present and participate. Among those who resorted to the club was the plaintiff .... The plaintiff purchased a bottle of Coca-Cola at the stand maintained by the club. After drinking a part of the contents of the bottle and finding it distasteful he discovered a mouse in the bottle. ... After drinking,

plaintiff attempted to continue his golf game, but after a few minutes quit and went to Red Oak to consult a doctor. This physician treated him, and sealed the bottle containing the mouse. On Wednesday following the plaintiff developed sore throat, diarrhea, and other disabilities which need not be set out but which abundantly warranted the verdict returned by the jury. It became necessary for the plaintiff to leave his work, and he lost about twenty pounds in weight. Two doctors testified that in their opinion plaintiff's condition was the direct result of drinking the contaminated beverage.

. . . .

The defendants, in the trial of this case, offered testimony minutely describing the process and the precautions under which the Coca-Cola sold to the country club was bottled; and they claim a degree of care which made it appear absolutely impossible that the mouse found in this bottle could have been in it at the time it was sold to the country club. It must be admitted that if the jury believed this testimony they could have found that a high degree of care was exercised by the defendants in bottling this Coca-Cola; nevertheless, the evidence does establish that a mouse was found in the bottle, and that the plaintiff became sick as a result of drinking therefrom. Moreover the jury might have found from the testimony that it was not while the Coca-Cola was in the custody of the country club that this mouse could have gotten into the bottle. The caretaker testified that the cases of this beverage were kept under lock and key ... and it appears, too, that there was no interval of time from the moment of sale until plaintiff started to drink which would permit an inference that the bottle had been tampered with after the sale. ...

Finding no error in the action of the trial court, its judgment [for the plaintiff] should be and it is affirmed.

Anderson v. Tyler, 223 Iowa 1033, 1034-36, 1038 (1937).

B y the mid-1930s, a number of women had graduated from Iowa's law schools or been admitted to the Iowa bar by examination. (From 1866 through 1936, over fifty women graduated from the University of Iowa *law school.) However, few women had actually engaged in the private practice of law for an extended period. An early exception was Martha C. Hoffman, born in 1897, who practiced law in Leon, Iowa, from 1939 to 1983 and was one of Iowa's first women county attorneys. Ms. Hoffman left a memoir of her experience as a practicing woman lawyer in Iowa.*

I was the seventh child of a seventh child, but I wasn't born on the banks of the Nile, and they weren't all daughters.

However, Fate did nudge me gently on from one step to another until, willy-nilly, I was practicing law in the County seat town where my father's family had settled in the early 1850's in the office over a store where my father began the practice of law 59 years before me.

It wasn't that I had any ambition to be a lawyer, either, but on both sides of the family I come of a long line of lawyers and teachers—and I didn't want to teach school. It wasn't even my idea, as much as it was my family's, that after I graduated from High School I should attend college for two years, take enough liberal arts to enjoy the social life of the college, take enough shorthand and typing so I could qualify as a stenographer, and go into my father's office as his secretary. It never entered anyone's head, including my own, that I might go to law school. Girls didn't do that in my day, and besides, I had three older brothers, and one of them was going to be the lawyer.

. . . .

We children seized every opportunity to attend court, and we grew up in an atmosphere where legal terminology was a commonplace, and most of our Sunday afternoons were spent in hearing my father and his brother, who was also an attorney, fighting over old battles.

My father was a gentleman of the old school, and believed that the innocence of his unmarried daughters must be protected at all costs. ...

After I became his legal secretary I often wondered how he thought it was possible for me to preserve my girlish innocence in a law office, considering the confidences that were poured into my ears by women who had been abused by their husbands, and girls who had been sexually molested, sometimes even by their own father or brother or some other relative of the family. ...

At the time, in the late 1930's, when I was admitted to the practice of law, the requirements were two years of college education, and three years study in a lawyer's office and then passing the bar examination. These were, as I remember it, three days of written examinations, which counted as 90% of the grade, and the oral test was counted as the remaining 10%. There were only three women who took the examination when I did. One of them had already failed twice to pass and this was her last chance. The other was taking the examination so she could go into an abstract office with her father, and she did not intend to practice law. It was very difficult at the time for any woman to practice alone—all those I knew were going into firms where they had fathers, brothers, or other close relatives. ...

When my brother died I took into practice with me a young attorney just starting to practice law. The next year he was elected County Attorney. Then World War II came along, and he went into military service, and the Board of Supervisors appointed me to fill out his term, one of the first, if not the first woman to serve in this capacity in my state. ...

After the war was over, my partner returned, and we went back into private practice ....

Women still find it much harder than men to establish a practice of their own. Many women lawyers do as I did myself, join a family firm, confine themselves to office practice and leave the trial work to the men in the firm. ...

I am glad to say that this prejudice seems to be slowly fading away as it has been doing in the case of women doctors. However, a woman lawyer still starts out with one strike against her because she is a woman. Though I do not expect to practice many years longer, I am still actively engaged in the profession myself and find that many women like to have another woman to talk to about her troubles and advise her, and there are many men who respect a woman's judgment and knowledge if they know her, so I have both men and women as clients. ... I hope that before long all prejudice against women as lawyers or as doctors will have vanished completely, but I am afraid that time has not yet arrived.

"Woman Lawyer," Memoirs of Martha C. Hoffman (unpublished, 1976), pp. 1-2, 4-6, 12, University of Iowa Law Library, Manuscript Division, Iowa City, Iowa.

CHAPTER NINE

Years of Turmoil and Peace

1941-1970

"Say that they fought so there might be the sun over their land ...."

— "FOR THE IOWA DEAD," Paul Engle

1941-1970

THE THREE DECADES FROM 1941 TO 1970 witnessed the United States at war—in World War II, Korea, and Vietnam. The first of these began with the bombing of Pearl Harbor on December 7, 1941. Congress immediately declared war on Japan; within a few days, Germany and Italy had declared war on the United States. President Franklin Roosevelt signed a new Selective Service Act, and the nation mobilized for the war effort.

During the first half of 1942, Japan dominated southeast Asia and the Pacific islands. Japanese forces conquered the Philippines despite strong resistance from U.S. and Philippine troops, overwhelming the Bataan Peninsula in April and the island of Corregidor in May. However, in June the Japanese suffered a critical naval defeat at the Battle of Midway. Within the next few months, U.S. bombers made their first raids over Europe, and troops under General Dwight D. Eisenhower landed in North Africa. During 1943, the United States led successful offensive operations in North Africa and Sicily, and war continued in the Pacific.

On June 6, 1944—"D-Day"—General Eisenhower as Supreme Allied Commander landed troops in Normandy, France, and secured the beachheads, enabling American, British, Canadian, and Free French troops to drive inward. On August 25, Allied troops liberated Paris. In February 1945, President Roosevelt, Britain's Prime Minister Winston Churchill, and Russian leader Josef Stalin met at Yalta to discuss post-war plans. Roosevelt died soon afterward, less than three months into his fourth term of office. He was succeeded by Vice-President Harry S Truman.

Germany surrendered to the Allies in May 1945, but the war with Japan continued. On August 6, 1945, the United States dropped an atomic bomb on Hiroshima, and three days later, on Nagasaki. Japan formally surrendered on September 2, 1945. The previous April, delegates from fifty nations had met in San Francisco to draft the Charter of the United Nations. The United States ratified the charter in July 1945.

The wartime demand for food boosted Iowa's farm economy and advanced manufacturing and industrial production. The state had resumed its tradition of Republican governors with the election in 1938 of George Wilson, and not until Herschel Loveless's election in 1956 did the Democrats regain the governorship. Iowa's most prominent contribution to national government was the appointment in 1943 of Wiley B. Rutledge, Jr., to the U.S. Supreme Court. Rutledge had lived in the state for four years as Dean of the University of Iowa law school; he served as an Associate Justice until his death in 1949.

An "iron curtain" descended over post-war Europe as the Soviet Union installed communist regimes in eastern European countries. To combat this new threat, the United States and eleven other nations in 1949 formed a political and military alliance, the North Atlantic Treaty Organization (NATO). The United States also funneled massive economic aid to Europe through the Marshall Plan, launched in 1948.

In June 1950, North Korean communist forces invaded South Korea. U.S. General Douglas MacArthur led a counter-offensive of United Nations forces, consisting mostly of United States and South Korean troops. Republican Dwight Eisenhower was elected President in 1952, and an armistice with North Korea was signed in July 1953. Eisenhower was elected to a second term in 1956.

In 1959, Fidel Castro seized power in Cuba and increasingly fell under Soviet influence. That year Soviet Premier Nikita Khrushchev visited the United States—and made a notable stop in Iowa—but the "cold war" against Communism continued to grow in intensity. In the 1960 presidential election, Democrat John F. Kennedy, a senator from Massachusetts, defeated Vice-President Richard Nixon.

President Kennedy authorized the ill-fated Bay of Pigs invasion by CIA-trained Cuban exiles in April 1961, and presided over the Cuban missile crisis with the Soviet Union in October 1962. On November 22, 1963, Kennedy was assassinated in Dallas. Two days later, his accused assassin, Lee Harvey Oswald, was shot while in police custody by nightclub owner Jack Ruby. Vice-President Lyndon B. Johnson was sworn into office.

President Johnson won a landslide victory over Republican Senator Barry Goldwater in the 1964 presidential election. Johnson oversaw the enactment of the Civil Rights Act of 1964 and a number of federal programs for his "Great Society." The build-up of military advisors in Vietnam, begun under President Kennedy, escalated. Johnson ordered U.S. air strikes against North Vietnam in early 1965, and the first combat ground troops landed in March. By 1968, the number of U.S. troops in Vietnam exceeded half a million. Amidst growing anti-war sentiment, Johnson decided not to seek re-election.

In 1968, Richard M. Nixon was narrowly elected President over Vice-President Hubert H. Humphrey. The number of United States troops in Vietnam was reduced, but widespread anti-war demonstrations continued, particularly on American campuses.

The decade of the 1960s drew to a close on a positive note. On July 20, 1969, astronaut Neil Armstrong became the first man to set foot on the moon, announcing: "That's one small step for a man, one giant leap for mankind."

Bourke B. Hickenlooper (who later served as a U.S. senator from 1945-1969) was elected governor of Iowa in the 1942 general election. In his inaugural address—the first given since the Japanese attack on Pearl Harbor—Governor Hickenlooper spoke about Iowans' contribution to the war effort and the effect of the war on the business of state government.

Not since the second administration of Governor Kirkwood, in Civil War days, has an Iowa administration begun and a legislature convened, with our country at war. Because of this, the problems that confront us are peculiar. For more than a year the united effort of all has been absorbed by the war effort. The emergency, and its necessary demands, have changed our economic and social attitudes and these changes will increase daily as the fight goes on. Usual peacetime activities and commodities have been restricted, many thousands of our men and not a few of our women have joined the armed forces. Our money has been poured out in ever increasing millions to meet the cost, and our fertile fields have responded to the untiring work of our farmers by producing the greatest volume of food in our history. ...

The national government is demanding sacrifice, restriction and curtailment of our normal civilian goods and activities, as a necessary part of the war effort. Rationing of food and other commodities in support of our armed forces ... has been and will be gladly complied with by a willing public that has efficiently administered such programs locally as a patriotic duty.

. . . .

The curtailment of normal civilian activities, construction and venture means also that normal government activities and venture must be curtailed. This does not seem to be the time for experiment in public affairs. ...

With over 100,000 of our men now in service and before this emergency ends, if we raise an army of 8 to 10 millions, then no doubt over 200,000 in service, it would be unfair to experiment with or substantially alter functions of government in their absence. ...

... Guided by the faith and wisdom of our "Fa-

thers", inspired by their courage and our own appreciation of our heritage, led by the proven tenets of Divine mandate, we can discharge our debt to those who gave us freedom by preserving it for ourselves, by perfecting it as a greater heritage for posterity.

Governor Bourke B. Hickenlooper, Inaugural Address, January 14, 1943, reprinted in *Journal of the Senate of the Fiftieth General Assembly* (Des Moines: State Printer, 1943), pp. 49-50, 53, 55.

The most notable wartime legislation passed by the Iowa General Assembly was the Iowa Emergency War Act of 1943. This act gave emergency powers to the governor and to the Iowa Industrial and Defense Commission. The commission was charged with the task of preparing the Iowa citizenry for possible enemy attack. The act also imposed severe penalties for individuals committing certain crimes during "blackouts."

IOWA EMERGENCY WAR ACT OF 1943. *Be It Enacted by the General Assembly of the State of Iowa:*
[Sec. 7] The Iowa Industrial and Defense Commission shall have the following powers and duties:

. . . .

(g) To establish plans for the defense of the lives, health and welfare of the citizens of this State, and to safeguard them from attack, and for the protection of the property of the State and its citizens: including plans for the evacuation of residents from any area and to care for evacuees and other victims of disaster [and] to plan for the mobilization and interchange of police, fire and other protective services between communities of the State ....

(m) To promulgate such orders, rules and regulations in cooperation with the military authority of the Federal Government and with the Office of Civilian Defense, as may be deemed necessary to organize, maintain and operate complete protective services including aircraft warning, observation and listening posts, information and control centers, air raid warning facilities, the planning and execution of

3. PUT OUT LIGHTS

Whether or not black-out is ordered, don't show more light than is necessary. If planes come over, put out or cover all lights at once—don't wait for the black-out order. The light that can't be seen will never guide a Jap. Remember a candle light may be seen for miles from the air.

The U.S. Office of Civilian Defense issued air raid precautions and advised citizens to turn out lights during "black-outs," as in this notice in the *Des Moines Register,* December 14, 1941. The Iowa legislature increased the penalties for certain crimes committed during black-outs.

blackouts, practice blackouts, air raid drills and all precautionary and protective measures under actual conditions of enemy attack ....

Sec. 21. Penalties increased for certain crimes.

Whosoever shall be convicted of the crime of robbery, larceny from a building, larceny from the person, breaking and entering a building for the purpose of committing a crime, assault with a deadly weapon, grand larceny, arson, rape or assault with intent to commit a felony, when such crime has been committed in an area in which a blackout, or practice blackout is in effect, or during an actual air raid or enemy attack, shall be sentenced to penitentiary for life, or to a term of years at the discretion of the court. ... Approved March 18 1943.

Acts of the Fiftieth General Assembly, 1943, ch. 61, §§ 7, 21.

Like other professions and businesses during World War II, the business of law was disrupted when many of its members left their work to enter military service. The loss to the legal profession during the long years of war was reflected in regular news bulletins from the Iowa State Bar Association.

Lieut. Johon Sherman Greene
Killed by Japanese Bomb

In the attack on Hickam Field, Hawaii [at Pearl Harbor], Lieutenant Johon Sherman Greene, a prominent and respected attorney at Colfax, was killed. A graduate of the University, Lieut. Greene was called to the colors on August seventeenth, and reported for duty in Hawaii on October first. Lieut. Greene was serving his fourth term as city solicitor, was an officer of the Young Democrats and had twice been a candidate for the office of Jasper County Attorney. Lieut. Greene was a member of the Iowa State Bar Association. The bar of the entire state will deeply regret his death.

The News Bulletin of the Iowa State Bar Association, vol. II, no. 2 (January 1942):4.

Editorial Comment

The draft and the war have brought about a very serious situation in the law schools. A reduction in the enrollment in the law schools of as much as fifty per cent is anticipated. This means that the schools' revenues are diminished to a point where it will in some cases be a question of whether they can remain open. ...

It is clear that two things must be done. First, the faculties of our law schools must be maintained intact. ... In the second place, standards of admission cannot be undermined. Temporary adjustments in the timing of bar examinations and the conditions of admission will have to be worked out. ...

Fortunately, in this state, the Association's Committee on Legal Education is already formulating plans in cooperation with the Supreme Court and the law schools to insure that legal education, standards of admission and the standards of the Iowa bar will be protected.

Ibid., vol. II, no. 3 (February 1942):2.

Law Commons Occupied by Army Men

The University of Iowa has announced that The Commons, former home of the law students at the University, has been turned over to the United States Army Air Corps for the duration. The building will be used to house students in the new Air Corps pre-meteorological school, scheduled to begin on the campus on March 1st. The present occupants of the Commons, most of them freshmen students, will be relocated elsewhere on the campus.

Ibid., vol. III, no. 3 (February 1943):2.

Smallest Bar Class

The smallest bar class in Iowa's history took and passed the state examinations October 3 at the state house.

Candidates were Miss Ethel Nagel of Cedar Falls, Virgil Kittleman of Creston and Dewey M. Robinson of Des Moines. All three were admitted to the bar of Iowa.

In prewar years classes averaged from 60 to 90 persons.

Ibid., vol. IV, no. 12 (December 1944):3.

924 Iowa Lawyers in War

Out of approximately 3,000 attorneys in the state of Iowa, 924 served in the armed forces or in some war activity .... A total of 871 Iowa lawyers served in the armed forces; 19 were killed and one is reported missing in action. 34 joined the FBI, 4 the Red Cross and 15 entered other war-related tasks.

Ibid., vol. V, no. 10 (November 1945):7.

Special Law Exam

The Supreme Court has directed the Iowa Board of Law Examiners to hold a special examination for applicants for admission to the Bar on February 13, 14, and 15, 1946, at the State House in Des Moines, Iowa.

The purpose of holding a special examination at this time is to afford immediate opportunity of admission to the Bar to the many persons who have heretofore completed the course of study of law, but

In 1943, while the nation was at war, Wiley B. Rutledge, Jr., was appointed to the U.S. Supreme Court, where he served until his death in 1949. Rutledge had been dean of the University of Iowa law school from 1935 to 1939. (Courtesy, University of Iowa College of Law)

who have been prevented from taking one of the regular examinations by reason of military service or other reasons, and to avoid the necessity of such applicants waiting for the regular examination, which is to be held in June.

Ibid., vol. VI, no. 1 (January 1946):1.

During 1945, the Mutual Surety Company of Iowa published three editions of Barristers Abroad. *These booklets contained the names and addresses of all members of the Iowa bar serving in the armed forces, as well as many of their letters written for publication. Excerpts from these letters paint a remarkable picture of the conditions of war.*

[undated]
[from ship board]

I think [*Barristers Abroad*] is a capital idea, and

it will be good to receive the publication when it is off the press. After all we like to see where the various brothers in the bar are located, and to divine, in part, where their legal training has landed them in the service.

I am navigating officer on my ship, and really find it very interesting and enjoyable. Quite a far field from the law, in a sense, what with stars and all to worry about, but it is quite a nice thing to know, and I get a kick out of doing it.

Lt. (J.g.) Bailey C. Webber (Ottumwa)

[December 10, 1944]
[from a prisoner of war camp, Germany]

I've begun to attend an informal law review class—really a discussion group—taught and attended by officers who have about the same law experience I have. Class meets 0930-1130, Monday through Friday; and aside from being a pleasant reacquaintance of an old friend—though I'm dismayed at how rusty I am—it is a good time consumer.

[December 17, 1944]

Have attended law classes every day (really it's seminar rather than class) and I have started thinking about matters legal again. ... We are making plans to do all we can to make Christmas somewhat cheerful—homemade decorations, church services, a play, and there will even be the traditional vacation from 'school', though for the first time I wish it were not so.

Major Robert C. Christensen, letters to Mrs. Jean Christensen (Iowa City)

[January 1945]

I am sending certification of address. You will note, however, that the Cpl. has been changed to Sgt.

Will be looking forward to receiving your booklet listing the Iowa lawyers in service. Have been anxious to learn whether Clyde Herring has by any possible chance been released from the Prisoner of War Camp in this recent exchange of prisoners.

Sgt. Doris E. Mann (Lansing)

[January 26, 1945]
[from Luxembourg]

Since leaving the States (how I love them all), I have been in Scotland, England, France, Holland, Belgium, back in France again and now in the little Duchy of Luxembourg which—I imagine—could be very pretty if the damn Jerries weren't quite so close. All I can say about this war is that someone back there gave me the incorrect information, to-wit: that a Finance Officer was never in danger—I can certainly disprove that statement.

In any event—I am sure of one thing—I wouldn't trade one foot of good old Iowa ground for this whole daggone country and England thrown in for good measure.

Maj. Leonard J. Wegman (Anamosa)

[February 7, 1945]
[from Burma]

Have looked for the Burmese equivalent of a lawyer but so far the village headman appears the closest approximation. Evidently life this far up is too simple as yet to enjoy the luxury of a legal confidant. And by the way, enjoy those Iowa eggs. The villagers get $3 a dozen for them here.

Lt. Arnold H. Myhra (Colfax)

[April 3, 1945]
[from France]

At last I have time to write; in fact there is very little else to do in this hospital. March 23d a shell hit me so I have shrapnel wounds in the left foot, right leg and left hand. I've been operated on twice and will soon be out of bed. Perhaps in a month I'll be up front again if the war is still going on.

Capt. John E. Donahey (Panora)

[April 4, 1945]
[from Holland]

A few weeks ago I had occasion to visit an American Cemetary a few miles from where I am located. I there found the grave of Rudolph Bolte an Iowa lawyer who made the supreme sacrifice for his country. Rudolph finished at the University a couple of years before I did but I remember him very well. ... Iowa lawyers have and are giving their all that we

At the height of World War II, in October 1944, only three candidates took the Iowa bar exam. After the war, the law schools filled again. Pictured here, students at the University of Iowa law school in 1947 argue a mock case before members of the Iowa Supreme Court. (Courtesy, University of Iowa College of Law)

might someday return to a peaceful practice of the profession we all hold so dear.
Donald E. Moore, Captain C.E. (Chariton)

[April 15, 1945]

I have seen this war, at its best and worst. In the past twenty-six months I have seen the destruction, poverty, homelessness, heartaches, hunger, hopelessness and misery of those who were in the paths of advancing armies, in North Africa, Italy, France, Belgium and Germany. I have seen men die, others with mangled bodies, glassy eyes, clothing holding in their guts. I have seen human suffering at its worst.
Lt. Col. Robert J. Shaw (Sigourney)

[August 13, 1945]
[Service Command District,
Colorado/Wyoming]

One of the wonders of this war is the ability of the Army to transform lawyers into everything else from policemen to cooks.
Jesse E. Marshall, Lt. Col. Inf. (Sioux City)

[October 3, 1945]
[Marshall Islands]

So far I have seen Pearl Harbor, Marshall Islands, Carolines, Philippines, China Sea, Saipan, Guam and Tokio Bay and have operated near Iwo Jima and Okinawa. I have seen plenty of water and traveled thousands of miles but have seen nothing to compare with Iowa and when I get back it is going to take extradition procedure to get me out of the state again.
Carl B. Parks, SM 3/c (Des Moines)

Barristers Abroad (Des Moines: Mutual Surety Company of Iowa, 1945), 1st ed., p. 29; 2d ed., pp. 12, 14, 18-19; 3d. ed., pp. 31-32, 34, 45.

One group that found its views at odds with the wartime mentality was the Jehovah's Witnesses. Although this religious group courageously opposed Hitler in Germany—often suffering loss of life—their stand against saluting the flag and joining the armed forces made them the targets of harassment in the United States. Soon after the war, the Witnesses sought to use the city park in Lacona, Iowa, for religious meetings. When their meetings were obstructed, the Iowa Civil Liberties Union took their case to federal court, claiming the denial of the constitutional rights of free speech, assembly, and worship.

The controversy grows out of an attempt by what is known as the Des Moines company or congregation of Jehovah's witnesses to hold a series of religious meetings in the park of the Town of Lacona on four successive Sundays, commencing September 1, 1946. ...

On September 8, when the Jehovah's witnesses attempted to hold their meeting in the park, they found a large number of people—probably 700 or 800—in and around it. ... Benches in the park were turned over, so that old ladies who had come to attend the lecture to be given by the Jehovah's witnesses could not sit down. Children were encouraged to play baseball, thus to interfere with the meeting. The Jehovah's witnesses did not attempt to use the bandstand, but endeavored to set up their sound equipment in another part of the park. The men who were in the bandstand then rushed down to the group which had the sound equipment, "cursing and yelling there would be no talk held that Sunday or any other Sunday." ... There were numerous fist fights, with the usual results—bloody faces, black eyes, broken glasses and teeth, and torn clothing. ...

On Sunday, September 15, the Sheriff, with the assistance of about 100 special deputies and some State highway patrolmen, blockaded all the highways leading into the Town. Everyone approaching the Town on the highways was turned away, except a doctor and a few residents who were returning home. The Jehovah's witnesses from Des Moines reached the blockade, and were turned back after being told by the Mayor and the Sheriff that they could not hold their scheduled meeting.

. . . .

The theory that a group of individuals may be deprived of their constitutional rights of assembly, speech and worship if they have become so unpopular with, or offensive to, the people of a community that their presence in a public park to deliver a Bible lecture is likely to result in riot and bloodshed, is interesting but somewhat difficult to accept. Under such a doctrine, unpopular political, racial, and religious groups might find themselves virtually inarticulate. Certainly the fundamental rights to assemble, to speak, and to worship cannot be abridged merely because persons threaten to stage a riot or because peace officers believe or are afraid that breaches of the peace will occur if the rights are exercised.

. . . .

While we do not question the good faith of the Mayor or the Sheriff in concluding that the best and easiest way to maintain peace and order in Lacona on September 15 was to blockade the roads leading into the Town, we are convinced that evidence of unconfirmed rumors, talk, and fears cannot form the basis of a finding of the existence of such a clear and present danger to the State as to justify a deprivation of fundamental and essential constitutional rights.

Our conclusion is that the plaintiffs are entitled to a decree declaring: (1) That they and others of Jehovah's witnesses have the right to hold religious meetings in the public park in the Town of Lacona, Iowa, without molestation and without securing the permission of the Town Council; (2) that the resolutions of the Town Council purporting to require the plaintiffs and others of Jehovah's witnesses to obtain a permit to use the park for religious meetings, and purporting to deny them such a permit, are unconstitutional, void and unenforceable; (3) that the Jehovah's witnesses are entitled to be protected in the exercise of their constitutional rights of freedom of assembly, speech and worship; (4) that the action of the Sheriff, sponsored by the Mayor, in blockading public highways leading into the Town of Lacona, for the purpose of preventing the Jehovah's witnesses from holding a meeting in the public park on September 15, 1946, constituted an unlawful deprivation of the constitutional rights of the Jehovah's witnesses.

Sellers v. Johnson, 163 F.2d 877, 878-79, 881, 883 (8th Cir. 1947).

*A*s war-related issues receded, subjects like civil rights again came to the fore in public discourse and in the courts. In 1954, an Iowa federal court was asked to consider whether the Iowa Civil Rights Act—initially enacted in 1884—entitled a black woman to gain admission to a public ballroom in Clear Lake.

Some time prior to December 8, 1951, Lionel Hampton's Dance Band had played at the Surf [ballroom]. It is an all colored band. At that time a number of colored men and women, including the plaintiff and her husband, sought admittance to the Surf and were admitted. The defendant advertised in a Mason City newspaper that on December 8, 1951, the same band would again appear at the Surf. ... On the evening of December 8, 1951, a group of eight, consisting of the plaintiff, her husband, and six of their acquaintances, went to the Surf. All of the group were colored. Tickets were purchased by members of the group for the group and they entered into the large hallway. When the group sought to go from the large hallway into the ballroom proper they were refused admittance by a ticket taker stationed at one of the aisle entrances. ... The manager informed them that personally he had nothing against the members of the group or against colored people in general but that he had received word from the main office of the defendant at Chicago that it was against the policy of the defendant to admit colored people to its dances. ...

The Iowa Civil Rights Act ... provides as follows:

"Infringement of civil rights. All persons within this state shall be entitled to the full and equal enjoyment of the accommodations, advantages, facilities and privileges of inns, restaurants, chop houses, eating houses, lunch counters and all other places where refreshments are served, public conveyances, barber shops, bath houses, theaters and all other places of amusement. ... "

[D]efendant referred to the matter of "social acceptability" in connection with the matter of exclusion. As heretofore noted, the defendant under its rules denies the privileges of its dance hall to those who are improperly dressed, to those who are lacking in cleanliness, to those under the influence of liquor, and to those who are guilty of misconduct. ... To those grounds or reasons for exclusion the defendant has added exclusion because of color. ... Exclusion because of color is manifestly not a "reason applicable to all persons." ...

The Iowa Act includes within its scope (emphasis added) "*all* other places of amusement." ... It was and is the view of this Court that ... dance halls of the type and kind operated by the defendant are within the provisions of the Act.

Amos v. Prom, Inc., 117 F. Supp 615, 618-19, 629-30 (N.D. Iowa 1954).

*I*n 1956, the Iowa Supreme Court was asked for the first time to determine whether the state recognized a "right of privacy." The case was brought by the parents of a deceased boy, who sued a newspaper for publishing a front-page photograph of the murdered child. The Court agreed that Iowa recognized a right of privacy, but held that the newspaper was not liable because the public newsworthiness of the event outweighed the plaintiffs' privacy interest.

This is an action for damages brought by the parents of [an eight-year old boy] for invasion of their right of privacy. The petition alleges plaintiffs' son ... disappeared from his Sioux City home and remained missing for approximately one month until September 29, 1954, when his mutilated and decomposed body was discovered in a field near Sioux City; that on said date the evening edition of defendant newspaper carried on the front page a large picture of the site where the body was found, "that toward the bottom center of the photograph the mutilated and decomposed body ... lay exposed." ...

Defendant points out that neither the statutes of Iowa nor the decisions of this court recognize the right of privacy. Hence, it contends no action for the violation of such right may be maintained in Iowa. With this contention we do not agree.

. . . .

The modern doctrine of the right of privacy is a development of the common law to fill a need for the protection of the interest which a person has in living without unwarranted publicity. The doctrine is supported by the great weight of authority in this country and we are satisfied it is sound. Hence, we hold an action for interference with such right may be maintained in this jurisdiction.

. . . .

Plaintiffs state: "While it may be true that the public was interested in the fact that the missing ... boy was found and whether or not he was dead or alive, the public had no legitimate interest or concern in the condition of the body." That conclusion is without support. From a news standpoint the public is interested in the appearance of the body of such a local victim. Such appearance may be pictured by words or by photographs or both.

[T]he incident of the finding of the body of the missing local boy was one of proper public interest. In other words, the event was newsworthy. Under the decisions cited herein, it is clear the facts pleaded by plaintiffs were insufficient to state a cause of action against defendant. ...

Larson, Chief Justice (dissenting)

[T]he majority holds that once it appears the matter is of legitimate public interest, the privilege of the press is absolute—unless possibly the picture is alleged to be indecent—and the individuals' right of privacy is completely abrogated. With such a determination I cannot agree.

. . . .

I am not advocating that the courts or anyone else try to act as censors of the press, but who will protect the invaded rights of citizens if the courts do not? It is not censoring, as I view it, to provide a remedy for a wrong, once the wrong has been done.

It is my feeling that we should take this opportunity to clearly express a sound position on this important question. We should recognize the right of privacy by more than lip service. We should limit and define the privilege accorded the press and radio to invade this right of individual privacy here in Iowa.

Bremmer v. Journal-Tribune Publishing Co., 247 Iowa 817, 819, 821-22, 827-29 (1956).

The 1960s were a decade of bold legislative initiatives, both at the federal and state levels. President Johnson's "Great Society" included the passage of the Civil Rights Act of 1964. The Iowa legislature—which in the nineteenth century had enacted one of the nation's first civil rights laws—unanimously passed the Iowa Civil Rights Act of 1965. The act prohibited discriminatory practices in employment and job training, as well as public accommodations, and established the Iowa Civil Rights Commission to ensure compliance.

CIVIL RIGHTS COMMISSION.
Be It Enacted by the General Assembly of the State of Iowa:
. . . .

Sec. 6. 1. It shall be an unfair or discriminatory practice for any owner, lessee, sublessee, proprietor, manager, or superintendent of any public accommodation or any agent or employee thereof:

a. To refuse or deny to any person because of race, creed, color, national origin, or religion the accommodations, advantages, facilities, services, or privileges thereof, or otherwise to discriminate against any person because of race, creed, color, national origin, or religion in the furnishing of such accommodations, advantages, facilities, services, or privileges.

. . . .

Sec. 7. 1. It shall be an unfair or discriminatory practice for any:

a. Person to refuse to hire, accept, register, classify, or refer for employment, to discharge any employee, or to otherwise discriminate in employment against any applicant for employment or any employee because of the race, creed, color, national origin, or religion of such applicant or employee.

. . . .

Sec. 9. 1. Any person claiming to be aggrieved by a discriminatory or unfair practice may ... make, sign, and file with the [Civil Rights] commission a verified, written complaint ....

. . . .

12. If, upon taking into consideration all the evidence at a hearing, the [Civil Rights] commission shall find that a respondent has engaged in or is engaging in, any discriminatory or unfair practice as de-

fined in this Act, the commission shall state its findings of fact and shall issue and cause to be served upon such respondent an order requiring such respondent to cease and desist from such discriminatory or unfair practice and to take such affirmative action … as in the judgment of the commission shall effectuate the purpose of this Act.

. . . .

Approved April 29, 1965.

Acts of the Sixty-First General Assembly, 1965, ch. 121, §§ 6-7, 9.

In addition to the Iowa Civil Rights Act of 1965, other laws of major significance for the state's future were enacted in the mid-1960s. In 1963, at the urging of newly elected Democratic Governor Harold Hughes, the General Assembly authorized "liquor by the drink" in bars and restaurants. And in 1965, for the second time in the state's history—the first being the period 1872-1878—the legislature abolished capital punishment.

The abolition of the death penalty would have been welcomed by one of Iowa's most famous "lifers," Tom Runyon, who died in 1957 while a prisoner at the Fort Madison penitentiary. Runyon became nationally famous for a book about life behind bars, titled In For Life: A Convict's Story. *Although he escaped the death penalty himself, Runyon was acutely aware of other, less fortunate prisoners on death row.*

Death Row looked ordinary enough. Composed of eight regular cells on the ground floor of cell house D, it was enclosed by wire screen that formed a four-foot-wide exercise corridor in front of the cells. We luckier ones strolled past the Row whenever our twice-weekly yard periods fell on stormy days, and even at close range it did not *look* extraordinary. But, at least to me, there was something intangible there, something not

Demonstrators protesting against capital punishment at the governor's mansion in 1962. (Courtesy, State Historical Society of Iowa, Des Moines)

to be seen with physical eyes. Most men apparently felt nothing unusual about the place, but while many of them loitered past, staring curiously at the five men waiting for the noose, I disliked even walking by.

. . . .

Time had about run out for four of the five. Two were no doubt counting the hours left to them. All routine efforts—a one-year delay after sentence was automatic—to save their lives with new trials and supreme-court reversals had failed. Only the Governor's clemency could prevent their taking that last walk, and that was unlikely. So, while the hours ran out, special death watch guards sat in the corridor outside the screened cage in eight-hour shifts, lest someone cheat the State by suicide.

. . . .

The knocked-down gallows was kept outside the walls, to be erected in the stockade by guards just before it had work to do. We couldn't see from the tailorshop, but on a quiet day we could hear the hammers erecting it. ...

Aside from innate hatred of capital punishment, we convicts had a legend—backed by many records—that a prisoner who helped install an electric chair or build a gas cage or erect a gallows stood a better-than-even chance of later dying on it. Even the guards, most of them, hated touching the gallows and dodged the erecting assignment when they could. Officials couldn't duck executions. The Deputy Warden and an assistant fastened the straps on arms and legs, put on the hood, and held the rope ... just so ... behind the victim's left ear. The sheriff from the convicting county would pull the lever that dropped the trap.

As the time edged close for a double execution I found the macabre business on my mind more and more. And then, the day before the two young men "went," I received a real shock.

The two condemned youngsters—Mercer was in his twenties; Wheaton had just celebrated his twenty-first birthday—were being taken through the crowded yard by a guard during the noon hour. I saw them coming toward me, laughing and talking to each other, taking time to wave or speak to someone or to answer a shouted greeting. I paid them no mind until they were about five feet away. Then there was shocked recognition, and I suddenly felt a little sick. If those kids had a care in this world it did not show

Officials at the Fort Madison penitentiary prepare an inmate for hanging. Capital punishment was abolished for the second time in Iowa in 1965. (Courtesy, State Historical Society of Iowa, Des Moines)

on their faces or in their voices, but I saw them as walking dead men. I knew that in about eighteen hours, just as the sun topped the Illinois hills across the river, they would be side by side, as they were now, swaying beneath the gallows before the eyes of a morbidly-curious crowd. They would wear hoods instead of smiles. Their non-waving arms would be stilled at their sides by heavy straps. ...

By standing on my bed I could just see the two youngsters, surrounded by guards, as they left the cell house. Then my eyes blinked under the glare of flash bulbs as photographers started their work. All told, the boys would walk perhaps five hundred yards before reaching the foot of the thirteen steps leading up to the gallows. They would stop at the Deputy's office to receive coffee and perhaps a sandwich, and to be dressed in their "going out" suits. Then they would start walking again. ...

There were a few scattered, angry yells in the cell house, and some talking from cell to cell, and then there was quiet once more as men drifted back into sleep or lay and thought their thoughts. Just as on a holiday, we were more than an hour late in going to work that morning. The whole nasty business was over with and everything was straightened up before we were allowed to leave our cells. We went to breakfast as usual, and I was the only man on my table who did not eat. With my mind filled with pictures of those two boys on the gallows, all I could force down was coffee. ...

Later, we heard that Wheaton was buried at his own request in the same cemetery that held Wild Bill Hickok and Calamity Jane, in South Dakota's Black Hills. An Iowa Quaker family, having failed to save Mercer's life, claimed his body and buried it in their private cemetery in their apple orchard. We cons thought very kindly indeed of that family.

Reprinted from *In For Life: A Convict's Story* by Tom Runyon, pp. 138-42, with the permission of W. W. Norton & Company, Inc. Copyright 1953 by Tom Runyon, renewed copyright 1981 by Thomas Runyon, Jr.

A number of amendments to Iowa's constitution were ratified during the 1960s, and some aroused fierce debate. A more than decade-long struggle to reapportion the General Assembly involved alike the federal and state courts, the legislature, and the voters. Constitutional amendments in 1968 established a 50-member Senate and 100-member House of Representatives and made apportionment plans subject to Supreme Court review, but not for several years was a satisfactory plan achieved consistent with the "one man-one vote" principle.

A constitutional amendment ratified by the voters in 1962 made a key change in Iowa's legal system. The amendment provided that district and Supreme Court judges henceforth would be nominated by judicial nominating commissions and appointed by the governor, subject to periodic retention votes. This change from the direct popular election of judges was a controversial departure from tradition, and it was hotly debated in the press as the vote on the proposed constitutional amendment drew near.

Judges Differ on Judicial Plan

Urges 'No' Vote

To the Editor:

Why give up a sound judicial system for one that could be arbitrary and destructive? Both proponents of and objectors to the proposed constitutional amendment fully agree that we have in Iowa a sound and effective judicial system under democratic government. It has stood unblemished for more than 100 years.

What will the proposed amendment do?

It will create 22 new commissions, at taxpayers' expense. ...

It will make it possible for four men to control the appointment of a supreme court judge; four men could control the appointment of district court judges in each of 21 judicial districts. Commissioners will be appointed one-half by the governor and one-half by members of the bar. We have too many bureaus and commissions now running our government—why not the people? ...

It will make it difficult to remove an incompetent or tyrannical judge. It will destroy the voter's present right to vote in a free and competitive election for judges. To vote for a judge "shall he be retained?" without opposition, is a denial of voter's right. ...

Mr. Voter, I warn you before you vote to examine carefully the subtle, misleading and high-sounding proposal which is being so widely disseminated by the State Bar Association. I urge you [t]o save your present God-given and constitutional right of selecting and voting for judges and preserving the present sound judicial system in Iowa. Vote "No."
Judge James P. Gaffney, Chairman,
Iowans to Preserve Constitution.
Marengo

Urge 'Yes' Vote
To the Editor:

We, the judges of the Eighteenth judicial district serving Linn, Jones and Cedar counties, want the citizens of these counties to know how we stand on the adoption of the judicial amendment .... We unqualifiedly endorse the plan and urge its adoption because:

1. We want the people of our counties to be able to vote for or against us on our own records and not because we may be affiliated with or endorsed by any political party. If the plan is adopted we will not be identified by a party label and each citizen will vote on the questions, "Shall Judge —— be retained in office?" We believe this assures each citizen an effective vote on our qualifications and not on our politics.

2. In the event of a judicial vacancy a non-partisan committee headed by a senior judge and composed of a given number of citizens chosen by the governor and an equal number selected by the lawyers of our district will consider the qualifications of those lawyers available for the position and recommend the two best qualified to the governor, who will then appoint one of the nominees to fill the vacancy. ...

3. Under the present system a vacancy is now filled by the governor. Since the governor is in politics, he is always under pressure to make appointments on political grounds or to serve political ends. ...

4. ... The changes urged are based on a 10-year study by the board of governors of the Iowa State Bar Association working with the District Court Judges Association. ...

We urge the voters of Linn, Jones and Cedar

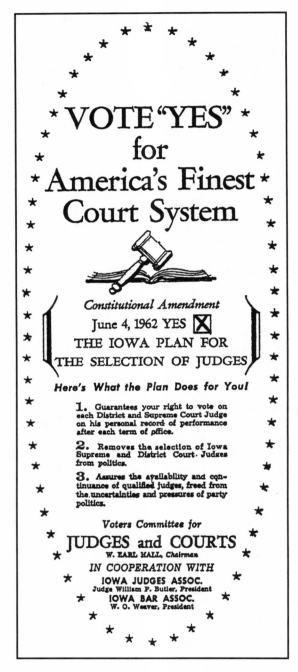

An advertisement in support of the constitutional amendment that changed the method of selecting Iowa judges. (*Boone News-Republican*, May 21, 1962)

counties to acquaint themselves with this proposal and vote "yes" on June 4.

Judge Charles Penningroth
Judge B. J. Maxwell
Judge Donald Barnes

Cedar Rapids Gazette, June 1, 1962.

*O*ne of the most enduring photographic im-
ages of the 1960s is the Des Moines Register *photo of Amish schoolchildren flee-
ing into the cornfields to avoid being transported
to a Hazleton public school. The episode was
part of a continuing state effort to enforce compulsory education laws against the Amish. In No-*

*vember 1962, several Amish men whose children
attended two private, one-room schools taught by
non-certified teachers were arrested and jailed
for refusing to comply with the state requirements.*

Independence, IA—Eight bearded Amish men
went to jail here Saturday afternoon rather than
pay fines for failure to send their children to
state-approved schools.

Justice of the Peace Joseph Koeppel gave each
man the alternative of paying a fine and costs totaling
$18.50.

When they refused, he sentenced each to serve
three days in the Buchanan County Jail.

. . . .

The hearing here resulted from a charge by J. J.
Jorgensen, county superintendent of schools, that the

Amish children flee into a cornfield near their rural school to avoid being taken to a
public school in Hazleton. (*Des Moines Register,* November 20, 1965)

Amish were sending 37 children to two private, one-room schools where they were being taught by teachers who are not certified by the state.

Iowa law requires that any pupil under 16, in public or private schools, be taught by a state-certified teacher.

. . . .

In his opening statement, County Attorney William O'Connell told the court that neither he nor Jorgensen wrote the law but that it was their duty to enforce it.

. . . .

Then O'Connell summed up the state's case:

"Our forefathers came to this country in order to be able to exercise a freedom of choice. But the Scriptures say render unto God that which is God's and render unto Caesar that which is Caesar's.["]

. . . .

Koeppel's decision drew no comment from the Amish. They strode one by one to the table where the justice was making out the court record.

He informed each one that the fine was $10, plus $4 court costs, plus $4.50 sheriff's cost—a total of $18.50.

Since each man already had posted a $25 bond, payment of the fine would have amounted simply to taking a refund of $6.50 from the bond.

. . . .

Twenty minutes later, the men followed a deputy sheriff to the third-floor jail, where four men were put in each of two cells.

Sheriff Emery A. Hart said the men will be released after the noon meal Tuesday. He said in his 18 years as sheriff and deputy he does not recall an Amish being in jail before.

_____

Excerpted from *Des Moines Register*, November 25, 1962 (Gene Raffensperger, reporter).

D ecision On Amish Schools Next Week
In a written statement of "articles of protest" submitted as evidence in Tuesday's district court hearing on a motion to close two of their schools, a group of area Amish parents claimed they have been "persecuted for our religious convictions."

. . . .

"We Amish have since the earliest days lived

peacefully and lawfully, tilling the soil under God's laws, only proclaiming God as our Lord and Educator and Guide ... ," the articles of protest opened.

"Now we are forced against our most intimate beliefs to submit our children to be instructed in a system of education which places values in ideas which violate our faith."

This conviction was also voiced on the witness stand by Menno Hershberger, who with Dan Borntreger, spokesman for the Amish at their trial last month, provided the defense in the hearing.

"We don't object to anyone else having all the education they want," said Mr. Hershberger. "Our children will be farmers or perhaps a few will be carpenters. We don't expect to get any high office of any kind, so we feel that an eighth grade education is all that is really necessary.["]

. . . .

On the witness stand Mr. Borntreger said high costs of bringing in certified teachers and the Amish belief that there has been "a decline in the morals of the Amish children taught by certified teachers" (in other area schools) led to the decision to retain [two non-certified teachers] in the two schools.

"We thought we were really in a land of freedom of religion," said Mr. Borntreger. "We believe in only going through the eighth grade. If someone else wants to go to high school, we don't interfere with them."

_____

The [*Independence*] *Bulletin-Journal*, December 14, 1962.

A fter years of controversy over the enforcement of compulsory school laws against the Amish, the Iowa legislature in 1967 enacted the so-called "Amish exception."

E XEMPTIONS FROM COMPULSORY EDUCATION.
Be It Enacted by the General Assembly of the State of Iowa:
Section 1. Chapter two hundred ninety-nine (299), Code 1966, is hereby amended by adding thereto the following new section.

"When members or representatives of a local congregation of a recognized church or religious denomination established for ten (10) years or more

Eight Amish men were jailed in November 1962 for violating Iowa's compulsory education law. Here some of the men are shown at the Buchanan County courthouse in Independence. (Photo by W. Ward, courtesy, *Cedar Rapids Gazette,* November 25, 1962)

within the state of Iowa prior to July 1, 1967, which professes principles or tenents that differ substantially from the objectives, goals, and philosophy of education embodied in standards set forth in section two hundred fifty-seven point twenty-five (257.25) of the Code, and rules adopted in implementation thereof, file with the state superintendent of public instruction proof of the existence of such conflicting tenents or principles, together with a list of the names, ages, and post office addresses of all persons of compulsory school age desiring to be exempted from the compulsory education law and the educational standards law, whose parents or guardians are members of the congregation or religious denomination, the state superintendent, subject to the approval of the state board of public instruction, may exempt the members of the congregation or religious denomination from compliance with any or all requirements

of the compulsory education law and the educational standards law for two (2) school years. When the exemption has once been granted, renewal of such exemptions for each succeeding school year may be conditioned by the state superintendent, with the approval of the board, upon proof of achievement in the basic skills of arithmetic, the communicative arts of reading, writing, grammar, and spelling, and an understanding of United States history, history of Iowa, and the principles of American government, by persons of compulsory school age exempted in the preceding year, which shall be determined on the basis of tests or other means of evaluation selected by the state superintendent with the approval of the board. …

Approved July 26, 1967.

Acts of the Sixty-Second General Assembly, 1967, ch. 248, § 1.

Perhaps no case originating in Iowa has achieved a more prominent place in American constitutional law than Tinker v. Des Moines Independent Community School District. *Born of the controversy over U.S. involvement in Vietnam, this case concerned the rights of high school students to protest an unpopular war through the wearing of a symbol—a black armband. More than just a legal proceeding, the* Tinker *case illustrated an intense political movement and the clash of values that divided a nation.*

Black Armbands, Free Speech, and School Discipline: The *Tinker* Case

IN DECEMBER 1965, MARY BETH TINKER, HER brother, John, and Chris Eckhardt defied the rules and wore black armbands to their schools in Des Moines. The purpose of the bands was to mourn the dead in Vietnam and to support a Christmas truce in that war-torn country. The episode led all the way to the U.S. Supreme Court and to a historic ruling on students' rights of free speech.

With casualties mounting in the Vietnam War, the Women's International League for Peace and the Students for a Democratic Society called nationally for the wearing of black armbands during a two-week period, beginning on Thursday, December 16. Fifteen-year-old Chris Eckhardt was then a student at Roosevelt High School in Des Moines. His mother, Margaret Eckhardt, was president of the Des Moines Chapter of the Women's International League for Peace. His father, William Eckhardt, was an assistant professor of psychology at the College of Osteopathic Medicine and Surgery in Des Moines. Chris and his mother had traveled to Washington, D.C., in November 1965 to a massive anti-war rally.

The story of the black armbands began with a meeting at the Eckhardt house in Des Moines on Saturday, December 11. Chris Eckhardt and the Tinkers did not attend, but two students from Chris's high school—Bruce Clark and Ross Peterson—were there. It was suggested at the meeting that black armbands be worn from December 16 until New Year's Day in support of a Christmas truce in Vietnam.

The following evening, Sunday, December 12, the "Liberal Religious Youth"—a Unitarian high school group—met at the Eckhardts' house. Chris Eckhardt, Bruce Clark, and Ross Peterson were all present at this meeting. The group decided to adopt and enlarge upon a statement that had been read in the First Unitarian Church that morning. Ross Peterson wrote up the statement as a draft editorial for publication:

WE MOURN
ATTENTION, STUDENTS!

Some students who are interested in expressing their grief over the deaths of soldiers and civilians in Vietnam will fast on Thursday, December 16th. They will also wear black armbands starting on that same day. The National Liberation Front (Vietcong) recently proposed a 12-hour truce on Christmas Eve. The United States has not yet replied to their offer. However, Senator Robert Kennedy has suggested that the truce be extended indefinitely pending negotiations. If the United States takes this action the armbands will be removed. If it does not, the bands will be worn throughout the holiday season .... [1]

Ross told his journalism teacher at Roosevelt High School that he wanted to publish the editorial in the school newspaper. As a result of his request, the proposed armband protest reached the ears of the school authorities. On Tuesday, December 14, Des Moines high school principals and the Director of Secondary Education met and decided that high school students would not be permitted to wear black armbands at school. The next morning, the *Des Moines Register* carried a report of the meeting under the heading, "D.M. Schools Ban Wearing of Viet Truce Armbands." The director was quoted as saying, "The schools are no place for demonstrations. ... We allow for free discussion of these things in classes."[2]

Mary Beth Tinker, then a thirteen-year-old student at Warren Harding Junior High School, read the director's statement in the newspaper. Mary Beth was the fourth of six children of the Reverend Leonard and Mary Jean Tinker. The Tinker parents had been activists in the civil rights movement, which apparently contributed to the Reverend Tinker leaving his position at Epworth Methodist Church in Des Moines. In 1964, he had become peace education coordinator for the American Friends Service Committee based in Des Moines. Mary Beth attended the Des Moines Valley Friends meeting and herself had taken part in civil rights and anti-Vietnam War demonstrations.

On the day Mary Beth read of the ban on black armbands, much of her mathematics class was taken up with discussion of student protests. During the discussion, the teacher said that he would send any student who demonstrated out of class. At this, Mary Beth asked if he considered wearing a black armband as a demonstration, and he said "yes."[3]

That evening, Bruce Clark and Ross Peterson talked to Mary Beth, her brother, John, and the Tinker parents about students' plans to wear black armbands. The next morning, Thursday, December 16, Mary Beth decided she would wear an armband that day. She cut off a strip of black ribbon and pinned it on her arm.

D. M. Schools Ban Wearing Of Viet Truce Armbands Wear Black Arm Bands, Two Students Sent Home BAN ON ARM BANDS UPHELD EXTEND BAN ON ARM BANDS

Des Moines newspaper headlines react to the unfolding drama following the banning of students' black armbands by school officials in December 1965.

At school, Mary Beth went through her first classes with virtually no comment. Then, in homemaking class, the teacher pointed to the armband and her fellow students noticed it. During lunch in the cafeteria, some boys teasingly made some "smart remarks."[4] In the afternoon came Mary Beth's mathematics class.

Wearing the black armband, Mary Beth sat in the rear of the room; her teacher stood nearby. When the bell rang, he laid a pass on Mary Beth's desk instructing her to go to the school office. She did so, and a few minutes later spoke to the vice-principal. He asked Mary Beth to give him the armband, and she said, "I suppose, if you want it,"[5] and handed it over.

Mary Beth then returned to her class, until the girl's advisor came to take her to the school office. The advisor was "real nice,"[6] explaining that she understood Mary Beth's point of view, but had to follow the rules. The advisor gave Mary Beth a suspension notice and sent her home.

On that same Thursday, Chris Eckhardt also wore a black armband at school. For some days he had been thinking about Ross Peterson's editorial, and he had made his decision the previous evening. On Thursday morning, "fearful and trembling,"[7] he set off for Roosevelt High School with a black armband on his sleeve.

When Chris arrived, instead of going to class, he went straight to the school office. There, the vice-principal asked him to remove his armband. Chris refused, and the vice-principal said he would have to suspend him. He telephoned Mrs. Eckhardt, who said that her son was acting out of conscience and had a constitutional right to wear the armband. After further unsuccessful attempts to persuade him to remove the band, Chris was suspended and sent home.

That evening, Bruce Clark and Ross Peterson joined twenty or more others—including fifteen-year-old John Tinker—in a meeting at the Tinkers' house. Bruce and Ross telephoned Ora Niffenegger, the president of the school board. They said that the students had been denied their constitutional right to wear armbands, and asked him to call an emergency meeting. Niffenegger said he wouldn't, but told them that the regular school board meeting would be held the following Tuesday.

John Tinker had not worn an armband that Thursday, because he had felt it would be open defiance of the principals' ruling. However, on the morning of Friday, December 17, when he read in the *Des Moines Register*, "Niffenegger said it wasn't important enough to require a special board meeting,"[8] his mind was made up. He left for North High School, where he put a black armband on the sleeve of his jacket.

In the locker room after gym, two or three students made unfriendly comments, but there were no threats of violence. John's friends warned him to take off the armband. Instead, he removed his jacket, put the band on the sleeve of his shirt, and went to lunch at the student center. There, a few boys made "smart remarks" and called him names like "Commie."[9] But when an older football player told the boys to leave him alone, they did so.

After lunch, John went to English class, where the teacher said: "They are waiting for you in the office."[10] John telephoned his father, telling him he expected to be sent home shortly. He went to the office of the principal, who said John must either remove the armband or be sent home. He added, "I don't suppose you will," and John said, "No."[11] Soon Reverend Tinker arrived and took his son home.

On the same day, Roosevelt High School suspended Bruce Clark and a girl named Christine Singer for wearing black armbands. A Lincoln High School student also wore a band, but removed it when requested to do so. Apparently the only other students in Des Moines who wore armbands were the two youngest Tinker children—Hope, aged eleven, and Paul, aged eight—but their school ignored them.

After the schools sent John Tinker and the others home on Friday, the Iowa Civil Liberties Union called on the school board to recognize "the students' right to freely express themselves."[12] The I.C.L.U. asked an assistant law professor at Drake University Law School, Craig Sawyer, to represent the students at the school board hearing.

The school board met on Tuesday, December 21. Two hundred people—many of them wearing black armbands—jammed the room. Mary Beth, her mother, and the Eckhardts were photographed wearing armbands. A *New York Times* correspondent joined a crowd of local press at the packed meeting.

For two hours the participants clashed on the question of student rights versus school discipline. Speaking on behalf of the Tinkers and the Eckhardts, Craig Sawyer demanded the immediate reinstatement of the suspended students, repeal of the ban on armbands, and a new policy permitting all means of peaceful expression. He termed the suspensions "an unconstitutional violation of free speech and free expression."[13]

Among others giving their views at the meeting, a World War II veteran spoke

Mary Beth Tinker and her mother listen to the Des Moines School Board debate about black armbands on December 21, 1965. (*Des Moines Register,* December 22, 1965)

of the need for discipline in schools, and the president-elect of the Roosevelt Student Council said that armbands were disruptive. An older man supported the ban, "to maintain law and order in the schools."[14] But most speakers from the floor—including Bruce Clark, Mrs. Tinker, and the father of Christine Singer (who had returned to school)—favored allowing armbands.

In response, the Des Moines school superintendent explained that the bands were forbidden, because "we thought it was a potentially disturbing element in our schools." Of the seven school board members, two spoke in favor of lifting the ban. One of them, a Methodist pastor, said: "Controversy is at the heart of education and the disturbance of set thinking is the catalyst." An attorney on the board called the matter "a clear issue of an individual's constitutional right of freedom of expression." But another board member, a children's doctor, spoke for the majority: "Schools should not and cannot be used for demonstrations [which] will be disruptive to some degree."[15] In the end, the board postponed taking a final decision, but voted four-to-three to continue temporarily the ban on armbands.

As people streamed out of the meeting room, members of the Students for a Democratic Society from Drake University and Iowa State University paraded in the street, carrying signs that read: "Why Conformist Education?" and "Freedom Begins at Home." Some of the arm-banded students and their supporters sang the civil rights anthem, "We Shall Overcome."

The following day—Wednesday, December 22—schools closed for the Christmas vacation. On December 23, the United States military command in Vietnam ordered a thirty-hour cease-fire. As soon as it ended, Mrs. Tinker told the press that the students would resume wearing black armbands until New Year's Eve to support Senator Robert Kennedy's proposal for an extended truce. On New Year's Eve, the school board met in secret session at the Hotel Savery. Their lawyer advised them that freedom of speech was not an absolute right, and that legally the board had authority to suspend the students. On New Year's day, Mrs. Eckhardt announced that some students would continue to wear armbands to mourn the dead in Vietnam, while others would do so "to mourn the death of freedom in the Des Moines public schools .... "[16]

When school resumed on Monday, January 3, 1966, Bruce Clark returned without an armband. But Mary Beth and John Tinker and Chris Eckhardt stayed away. That evening, the school board met in the Board of Education offices. Two hundred people again packed the meeting, and CBS television cameras filmed the event. After a repetition of the previous arguments, the board voted—this time by five-to-two—in favor of keeping the ban.

The lawyers for the Iowa Civil Liberties Union urged Mary Beth, John, and Chris to go back to school wearing black clothes, promising that the I.C.L.U. would shortly test the case in court. They assured them: "You have aroused the conscience of the nation as well as the conscience of the community."[17] The next day, dressed in black—but without armbands—the three students reluctantly returned to school.

The stage now moved to the federal courtroom. John and Mary Beth Tinker and Chris Eckhardt (represented by their fathers as "next friends") brought a lawsuit in the U.S. District Court for the Southern District of Iowa against the Des Moines Independent Community School District and other defendants. The students' complaint, filed by Des Moines attorney Dan Johnston, claimed they were deprived of their right to free speech under the U.S. Constitution. They sought an injunction against the enforcement of the armband regulation.

Following an evidentiary hearing, Chief Judge Stephenson on September 1, 1966, denied the students' request for relief and dismissed their complaint. The judge reasoned that although the wearing of an armband was a symbolic act that fell within the protection of the First Amendment's free speech clause, this constitutional guarantee was not absolute. The school district had a duty to maintain "a scholarly, disciplined atmosphere within the classroom."[18] If the defendants' acts were not unreasonable, the court would not interfere.

Judge Stephenson's opinion concluded: "While the armbands themselves may not be disruptive, the reactions and comments from other students as a result of the armbands would be likely to disturb the disciplined atmosphere required for any classroom. ... The school officials involved had a reasonable basis for adopting the armband regulation."[19]

The students appealed to the Eighth Circuit Court of Appeals. The case was heard before a regular panel of the court, then was re-argued and submitted to the court en banc. On November 3, 1967, the appellate court—dividing evenly four votes to four—affirmed without opinion the judgment of the court below.[20]

The students sought a review of this decision in the U.S. Supreme Court, and the Court agreed to hear the case. On February 24, 1969, the Court handed down its decision in the case of *Tinker v. Des Moines Independent Community School District.*[21] In an opinion written by Justice Fortas, the Court in a seven-to-two decision reversed the lower courts' dismissal of the case. In so doing, the Court set forth key principles governing school students' freedom of speech and expression.

The Court stated that the wearing of armbands "was closely akin to 'pure speech' which, we have repeatedly held, is entitled to comprehensive protection under the First Amendment."[22] These First Amendment rights were available to students and teachers alike. "It can hardly be argued that either students or teachers shed their constitutional rights to freedom of speech or expression at the schoolhouse gate."[23]

On the other hand, it was equally clear that school officials, consistent with constitutional safeguards, had authority to maintain discipline in the schools. "Our problem lies in the area where students in the exercise of First Amendment rights collide with the rules of the school authorities."[24]

The students' conduct in this case was not aggressive or disruptive, nor did it involve group demonstrations. Instead, "school officials banned and sought to punish [the students] for a silent, passive expression of opinion, unaccompanied by any disorder or disturbance .... There is here no evidence whatever of [the students'] interference, actual or nascent, with the schools' work or of collision with the rights of other students to be secure and to be left alone .... "[25]

The district court had deemed the school officials' action reasonable, because they had feared the armbands would create a disturbance. "But, in our system, undifferentiated fear or apprehension of disturbance is not enough to overcome the right to freedom of expression."[26] Where, as here, there was no showing that the conduct would "materially and substantially interfere with the requirements of appropriate discipline in the operation of the school,"[27] the prohibition could not be sustained.

The Court resoundingly affirmed the constitutional rights of students. "Students in school as well as out of school are 'persons' under our Constitution. They are possessed of fundamental rights which the State must respect .... In the absence of a specific showing of constitutionally valid reasons to regulate their speech, students are entitled to freedom of expression of their views."[28]

Justice Black wrote a long dissenting opinion. He warned that the Court's holding "ushers in what I deem to be an entirely new era in which the power to control pupils ... is in ultimate effect transferred to the Supreme Court."[29] In his view, the evidence showed that the armbands had caused comments and teasing, had disrupted Mary Beth's math class, and had distracted the students from their lessons. "[T]he armbands did exactly what the elected school officials and principals foresaw they would, that is, took the students' minds off their classwork and diverted them to thoughts about the highly emotional subject of the Vietnam war. [I]f the time has come when pupils of state-supported schools ... can defy and flout orders of school officials to keep their minds on their own school work, it is the beginning of a new revolutionary era of permissiveness in this country fostered by the judiciary."[30]

When the *Tinker* case was decided on February 24, 1969, the national press gave it extensive coverage. *Time Magazine* did an entire photo session of Mary Beth Tinker in her chemistry class at her new school in St. Louis. Photos of Mary Beth wearing a black armband appeared in *Time*, *Newsweek*, and the *New York Times*. The Tinker family itself celebrated the case with ice cream.

The *Harvard Law Review* summarized the importance of the case in American constitutional law: "*Tinker* was the first decision to establish that high school students have a positive, though limited, constitutional right to express themselves both on the campus and in the classroom."[31] *Tinker's* dictum that students do not "shed their constitutional rights ... at the schoolhouse gate" has been cited by the U.S. Supreme Court as recently as in a 1995 decision.[32]

Mary Beth Tinker grew up to become a nurse, and she looked back at the armband episode without regret. She said in an interview two decades later: "I work with a lot of paraplegics and quadriplegics, and some of them were injured in the Vietnam war. One guy I worked with today was amputated from the trunk down; his spine was shot up in the war. So I don't have any regrets about it all. I'm proud to have been part of anything that stopped the war."[33]

CHAPTER TEN

Toward the Sesquicentennial

1970–1996

"The work that we are about is neither women's work, nor men's work, but a solemn responsibility that we share equally ...."

— IOWA SUPREME COURT JUSTICE Linda K. Neuman

1970-1996

ETWEEN 1970 AND 1972, PRESIDENT
Nixon fulfilled his pledge to reduce United States troop numbers in Vietnam. However, the invasion of Cambodia by U.S. and South Vietnamese troops in April 1970 was met by intense and violent reaction in the United States. One protest demonstration on the campus of Kent State University ended with Ohio national guardsmen firing into the crowd, killing four students and wounding many others. Huge anti-war demonstrations ignited on other college campuses, resulting in the closing of a number of institutions.

Buoyed by the progress toward peace in Vietnam and his overtures toward China and the Soviet Union, President Nixon won decisive re-election in November 1972 against his Democratic opponent, Senator George McGovern. In January 1973, a peace agreement was signed in Paris by the United States and North Vietnam.

President Nixon's second term in office was dominated by the "Watergate" affair. A break-in at the Democratic National Committee offices in the Watergate complex in June 1972 by men associated with the Committee to Re-elect the President, and charges of an official "cover-up," led to Nixon's resignation from office in August 1974. He was succeeded by Vice-President Gerald Ford, who the previous year had been appointed to replace resigning Vice-President Spiro Agnew.

The year 1976 was celebrated as the bicentennial of the signing of the American Declaration of Independence. President Ford—whose popularity was hurt by his decision to pardon former President Nixon for any illegal acts committed while in office—lost the 1976 election to former Georgia Governor Jimmy Carter.

Although both of Iowa's U.S. Senate seats were held by Democrats in the post-Watergate era (including former Governor Harold Hughes for the period 1969-75, succeeding Republican Senator Bourke B. Hickenlooper), Republicans retained their traditional hold on most state offices. Republican Governor Robert Ray held office from 1969 to 1983, confronted in his last term by a state budget crisis, high unemployment, and a worsening farm crisis that followed upon the high inflation/high interest economy of the 1970s.

President Jimmy Carter's single term in office was marked alike by foreign policy triumph and disaster. In March 1979, Egyptian President Anwar Sadat and Israeli Prime Minister Menachem Begin signed a historic peace treaty in Washington, D.C. In October, the United States agreed to relinquish control over the Panama Canal Zone. In November, militant Iranians took over the American Embassy in Tehran, holding many Americans hostage. The hostage crisis weakened the Carter presidency, and Republican Ronald Reagan was elected President in the November 1980 election. The hostages were released on his inauguration day.

President Reagan—the fortieth American President—was wounded in an assassination attempt two months after taking office. In September 1981, Associate Justice Sandra Day O'Connor was sworn in as the first woman member of the U.S. Supreme Court. Five years later this historic legal event was mirrored in Iowa, with the appointment by Governor Terry Branstad of Linda K. Neuman as the first woman to sit on the Iowa Supreme Court.

The two terms of President Reagan witnessed dramatic economic and foreign affairs developments: major tax reform in 1981; a terrorist attack on U.S. Marine headquarters in Beirut, Lebanon; the invasion of Grenada in 1983; economic expansion; a severe farm debt crisis; and, in October 1987, a stock market crash. Vice-President George Bush was elected President in 1988. His single term in office saw the collapse of Communist regimes in eastern Europe, the tearing down of the Berlin Wall in November 1989, the Persian Gulf War against Iraq in early 1991, and the break-up of the former Soviet Union later that year.

In the 1992 presidential election, President Bush faced Democrat opponent Bill Clinton and independent candidate Ross Perot (who captured nearly twenty percent of the popular vote). Bill Clinton, Governor of Arkansas, was elected the forty-second President of the United States. He placed health care reform at the top of his domestic agenda, and named the First Lady, Hillary Rodham Clinton, as chair of a committee to develop a national health care policy.

America in the 1990s was still the greatest economic and military power, but it faced an uncertain future in a changing world, and its nearly 250 million citizens were confronted with serious domestic concerns about crime, health care, immigration, education, and the economy. Buoyed by electoral dissatisfaction, in 1994 the Republicans gained control of both houses of Congress from the Democrats.

Iowans and other midwesterners faced an additional challenge from nature when, in the summer of 1993, severe floods inundated towns and temporarily cut off Des Moines's water supply. With fewer than 2,800,000 residents, Iowa ranked only thirtieth in population among the fifty states, but its influence far outweighed its numbers as it drew near the 150th year of statehood in 1996. One of the dominant agricultural producers of the world, a leader in education and academic performance, with prosperous cities, high employment, clean air, natural beauty, and devotion to commerce and the arts, Iowa prepared to celebrate its Sesquicentennial.

A large group of anti-Vietnam War demonstrators outside the capitol building in Des Moines protest the visit of President Richard Nixon to the Iowa legislature in March 1971. (Courtesy, State Historical Society of Iowa, Des Moines)

Student protests of America's involvement in the Vietnam War were held on many Iowa college campuses, and were particularly intense at the University of Iowa. Following a demonstration in February 1971, a student was convicted of desecrating the American flag. The Iowa Supreme Court affirmed the conviction, holding that Iowa's flag desecration statute was constitutional as applied to the student's conduct. After the U.S. Supreme Court vacated this opinion, the Iowa Supreme Court was asked to reconsider its position. It responded with a resounding indictment of the student's flag-burning conduct.

We here accord further consideration to State v. Farrell ... pursuant to a directive issued August 6, 1974, by the Supreme Court of the United States (citations omitted).

More particularly, this court is called upon to now reevaluate its position in *Farrell, supra,* in light of Spence v. State of Washington, 418 U.S. 405 (1974).

... We again respectfully affirm [the defendant Farrell's conviction of flag descration].

State v. Farrell, *supra,* unquestionably involved the *mutilation by burning of a United States flag in a public place.* In other words, the offense occurred in an open courtyard of a dormitory in which an unknown number of university students occupied quarters facing upon the aforesaid incident-related area.

Conversely, *Spence, supra,* dealt with the *non-mutilative removable taping of a peace symbol on a flag then displayed on defendant's privately occupied premises.* ...

Significantly, defendant Farrell made no pretense of displaying our national emblem in a manner akin to that historically done to express a personal belief. Rather, she permanently and contumaciously, in a public place, destroyed our symbol of patriotism, of pride in the history of our country and of the service, sacrifice and valor of millions of Americans. ...

It is also to us evident a "*risk of breach of the peace*" attended Farrell's aforesaid flag desecration in a public place.

[T]his court is persuaded the State of Iowa does have a viable interest in the preservation of peace and order within this jurisdiction. Otherwise, the general public would have little or no assurance of orderly behavior on the part of others or of that tranquility which the people are entitled to enjoy. ...

A review of the record in *Farrell* ... reveals two individuals were seen leaving the main body of the instantly involved assemblage and that one of those departees pulled a dormitory fire alarm. There resultantly followed an immediate emergence of residents from the housing facility.

Upon the foregoing factual basis we are persuaded defendant Farrell's conduct created a *risk of* breach of the peace.

[A]s aforesaid, Patricia Farrell's incendiary flag mutilating conduct does not approach the degree of tranquility attendant upon that denoted in *Spence*.

On the contrary, Farrell manifested a total disregard for the flag as a symbol of patriotism, and by the same token espoused disunity. ...

[W]e are persuaded the State of Iowa has a substantial interest in preserving the flag of this Nation, and § 32.1, Code of Iowa, is to us sufficiently justified upon that basis. It furthers an important governmental interest unrelated to free expression and, as applied in the case now before us, any incidental restriction on First Amendment freedoms was no greater than essential to the furtherance of this State's interest in the protection of our national emblem.

State v. Farrell, 223 N.W.2d 270, 271-73 (Iowa 1974).

Almost as controversial as the war itself were the long hair styles adopted by many young men in the Vietnam era. Schools enacted dress and hair codes; some students responded by challenging the constitutionality of these rules in court. In one such case, an Iowa federal court struck down the school's hair rule as unconstitutional.

There is no question but that plaintiff's hair length violates that part of the school regulation requiring a male student's hair to be cut above the collar in back. ... The Court views the issue before it to be thus: Does the Adel Community School District's regulation requiring a male student's hair to be cut above his collar in the back violate that student's constitutionally protected rights?

... With very few exceptions, the courts recognize that a student's right to wear long hair is entitled to constitutional protection and the particular hair regulation is carefully scrutinized to ascertain whether a reasonable basis in fact exists for the rule. ...

[D]efendants' contention that a definite correlation exists between long hair and academic achievement is not only unsupported by any competent evidence but borders on the ridiculous. An argument that long hair produces absenteeism or a lower intelligence level is nothing short of ludicrous. ...

There is no evidence in this case that plaintiff's long hair was dirty or unsanitary and thus constituted a health problem. Certainly long hair and health are not synonymous per se.

In regard to distraction, there is very little evidence that classwork was disrupted to any significant extent. No students testified that long hair worn by other students would or did distract them in their school work. ...

[The] school board President ... testified that "rightly or wrongly", Adel residents draw associations between long hair and school riots, the "hippie class", and the "drug element" ....

There is no evidence that [plaintiff] has anything to do with drugs or riots. He has a right to be judged as an individual citizen, not for what others may have done. Community prejudices and stereotypes are not permissible criteria for classifying citizens under the Fourteenth Amendment.

. . . .

[I]t is common knowledge and evident to all concerned from the mass media as well as personal observation and contact that for whatever reason, men, young and old, in every profession and walk of life, have and are changing their personal appearance as it relates to hair growth and style in varying degrees. This individual right to govern one's appearance is constitutionally protected. In the final analysis, a student is entitled to the same protection unless good reasons can be shown for some restriction. ...

In conclusion, defendants have not demonstrated the reasonableness of the hair rule as it pertains to hair over the collar. The rule is thus unconstitutional and impermissible.

Turley v. Adel Community School District, 322 F. Supp. 402, 404-405, 407, 409-11 (S. D. Iowa 1971).

One of the more controversial decisions of the Iowa Supreme Court during the Vietnam era had nothing whatever to do with the war. The case of Katko v. Briney *concerned the right of the owner of a vacant farmhouse to protect its contents against intruders through the use of a shotgun trap. The plaintiff had broken into the boarded-up house, intending to steal antique bottles. He opened a bedroom door, which was rigged to trigger a shotgun blast, and his right leg was seriously wounded.*

After pleading guilty to a larceny charge, the plaintiff brought a civil action for damages. In the famous "Spring Gun Case," the Iowa Supreme Court affirmed the jury's verdict of $20,000 actual and $10,000 punitive damages in favor of the plaintiff. One justice filed a lengthy dissent, objecting in particular to the award of punitive damages.

I respectfully dissent ....

In the case at bar the plaintiff was guilty of serious criminal conduct, which event gave rise to his claim against defendants. Even so, he may be eligible for an award of compensatory damages which so far as the law is concerned redresses him and places him in the position he was prior to sustaining the injury. The windfall he would receive in the form of punitive damages is bothersome ....

When such a windfall comes to a criminal as a result of his indulgence in serious criminal conduct, the result is intolerable and indeed shocks the conscience. If we find the law upholds such a result, the criminal would be permitted by operation of law to profit from his own crime.

Furthermore, if our civil courts are to sustain such a result, it would in principle interfere with the purposes and policies of the criminal law. ...

We cannot in good conscience ignore the conduct of the plaintiff. He does not come into court with clean hands, and attempts to make a claim to punitive damages in part on his own criminal conduct. In such circumstances, to enrich him would be unjust, and compensatory damages in such a case itself would be a sufficient deterrent to the defendant or others who might intend to set such a device.

The criminal law can take whatever action is appropriate in such cases, but the civil law should not compound the breach of proper social conduct by rewarding the plaintiff for his crime. I conclude one engaged in a criminal activity is an unworthy object of largesse bestowed by punitive damages and hold the law does not support such a claim to enrichment in this case.

Katko v. Briney, 183 N.W.2d 657, 662, 672 (Iowa 1971) (Larson, J., dissenting).

*I*n the post-Vietnam War era, the issue of abortion came to the forefront of public debate. After the 1973 U.S. Supreme Court decision in the case of Roe v. Wade, *the Iowa criminal statute prohibiting abortions except to save the mother's life was challenged in federal court. The court declared that the Iowa statute was unconstitutional, and the legislature later amended the statute to conform to the guidelines of* Roe.

Abortion foes gather in the state capitol rotunda on the fifth anniversary of the U.S. Supreme Court's decision in *Roe v. Wade.* (*Des Moines Register,* January 23, 1978)

This action comes before this Court upon a Complaint challenging the Iowa abortion law, which Complaint appears to be based upon the recent United States Supreme Court decisions in Roe v. Wade, 410 U.S. 113 (1973) and Doe v. Bolton, 410 U.S. 179 (1973) ....

Jane Doe instituted this action on her own behalf and others similarly situated, alleging her own pregnancy, and her attempt to procure a legal, medically safe abortion within the State of Iowa. She alleges that she has been advised by attending physicians that absent a clear statement as to the viability of Iowa's abortion law in reference to the above cited cases and holdings, that such physicians could not perform such an operation upon them without fear of prosecution by the defendants ....

Chapter 701.1 of the Code of Iowa, 1973 provides:

"Administration of drugs—use of instruments. If any person, with intent to produce the miscarriage of any woman, willfully administer to her any drug or substance whatever, or, with such intent, use any instrument or other means whatever, unless such miscarriage shall be necessary to save her life, he shall be imprisoned in the penitentiary for a term not exceeding five years, and be fined in a sum not exceeding one thousand dollars."

. . . .

Roe v. Wade sets out how a state may restrict the performance of an abortion:

"1. A state criminal abortion statute of the current Texas type, that excepts from criminality only a *life saving* procedure on behalf of the mother, without regard to pregnancy state and without recognition of the other interests involved, is violative of the Due Process Clause of the Fourteenth Amendment.

(a) For the stage prior to approximately the end of the first trimester, the abortion decision and its effectuation must be left to the medical judgment of the pregnant woman's attending physician.

(b) For the stage subsequent to approximately the end of the first trimester, the State, in promoting its interest in the health of the mother, may, if it chooses, regulate the abortion procedure in ways that are reasonably related to maternal health.

(c) For the stage subsequent to viability the State, in promoting its interest in the potentiality of human life, may, if it chooses, regulate, and even proscribe, abortion except where it is necessary, in appropriate medical judgment, for the preservation of the life or health of the mother. ..."

The Iowa statute on its face is identical in substance to the Texas statute struck down by the United States Supreme Court and it would appear that this Court is compelled to reach the same conclusion, that Chapter 701 of the Iowa Code, 1973 is unconstitutional and as a unit must fall.

... The statute makes no distinction between abortions performed early in pregnancy and those performed later, and it limits to a single reason, "saving" the mother's life, the legal justification for the procedure. The statute, therefore, cannot survive the constitutional attack made upon it here.

Doe v. Turner, 361 F. Supp. 1288, 1289-92 (S. D. Iowa), *appeal denied*, 488 F.2d 1134 (8th Cir. 1973).

In 1977, the case of an Iowan convicted of the abduction and murder of a ten-year-old girl in Des Moines received national attention when the United States Supreme Court overturned his conviction, holding that evidence obtained in violation of his constitutional rights had wrongly been admitted at trial.

Arrested in Davenport, the defendant, Robert Anthony Williams, was being transported to Des Moines when police officers persuaded him to show them where the little girl's body was, urging that she was entitled to a "Christian burial." The U.S. Supreme Court affirmed the issuance of a writ of habeas corpus, finding that Williams had been deprived of his right to assistance of counsel under the Sixth Amendment. (The defendant later would be re-tried and again convicted; the U.S. Supreme Court in Nix v. Williams, *467 U.S. 431 (1984) upheld the conviction.) The case of the "Christian burial speech" remains a key decision in U.S. constitutional and criminal law.*

On the afternoon of December 24, 1968, a 10-year-old girl named Pamela Powers went with her family to the YMCA in Des Moines, Iowa, to watch a wrestling tournament in which her brother was participating. When she failed to return from a trip to the washroom, a search for her began. The search was unsuccessful.

Robert Williams, who had recently escaped from a mental hospital, was a resident of the YMCA. ...

On the morning of December 26, a Des Moines lawyer named Henry McKnight went to the Des Moines police station and informed the officers present that he had just received a long-distance call from Williams, and that he had advised Williams to turn himself in to the Davenport police. ...

In the meantime Williams was arraigned before a judge in Davenport on the outstanding arrest warrant. ... Before leaving the courtroom, Williams conferred with a lawyer named Kelly, who advised him not to make any statements until consulting with McKnight back in Des Moines.
. . . .

The two detectives, with Williams in their charge, then set out on the 160-mile drive [to Des Moines]. ... Detective Leaming knew that Williams was a former mental patient, and knew also that he was deeply religious.

The detective and his prisoner soon embarked on a wide-ranging conversation covering a variety of topics, including the subject of religion. Then, not long after leaving Davenport and reaching the interstate highway, Detective Leaming delivered what has been referred to in the briefs and oral arguments as the "Christian burial speech." Addressing Williams as "Reverend," the detective said:

"I want to give you something to think about while we're traveling down the road. ... Number one, I want you to observe the weather conditions, it's raining, it's sleeting, it's freezing, driving is very treacherous, visibility is poor, it's going to be dark early this evening. They are predicting several inches of snow for tonight, and I feel that you yourself are the only person that knows where this little girl's body is, that you yourself have only been there once, and if you get a snow on top of it you yourself may be unable to find it. And, since we will be going right past the area on the way into Des Moines, I feel that we could stop and locate the body, that the parents of this little girl should be entitled to a Christian burial for the little girl who was snatched away from them on Christmas [E]ve and murdered. ... "

... The car continued towards Des Moines, and as it approached Mitchellville, Williams said that he would show the officers where the body was. He then directed the police to the body of Pamela Powers.
. . . .

[I]t is clear that the judgment before us must ... be affirmed upon the ground that Williams was deprived of ... the right to the assistance of counsel.
. . . .

There can be no doubt in the present case that judicial proceedings had been initiated against Williams before the start of the automobile ride from Davenport to Des Moines. ...

There can be no serious doubt, either, that Detective Leaming deliberately and designedly set out to elicit information from Williams just as surely as—and perhaps more effectively than—if he had formally interrogated him. Detective Leaming was fully aware before departing for Des Moines that Williams was being represented in Davenport by Kelly and in Des Moines by McKnight. Yet he purposely sought during Williams' isolation from his lawyers to obtain as much incriminating information as possible. ...

[S]o clear a violation of the Sixth and Fourteenth Amendments as here occurred cannot be condoned. The pressures on state executive and judicial officers charged with the administration of the criminal law are great, especially when the crime is murder and the victim a small child. But it is precisely the predictability of those pressures that makes imperative a resolute loyalty to the guarantees that the Constitution extends to us all.

Brewer v. Williams, 430 U.S. 387, 390-93, 397-99, 406 (1977).

A significant change in Iowa's court system occurred in 1976, when the legislature established the Iowa Court of Appeals. This intermediate appellate court—consisting initially of five judges (increased to six in 1983)—was deemed necessary due to the heavy caseload faced by the Iowa Supreme Court.

In 1978, Janet Johnson, a professor at Drake University Law School, was appointed an associate judge of the Iowa Court of Appeals, thus becoming the first woman to be appointed to an appellate court in Iowa. Another important first was the appointment in 1986 of Scott County district judge Linda K. Neuman as the first woman to serve on the Iowa Supreme Court. (She would be joined on the Court in 1993 by a second woman appointee, attorney Marsha Ternus of Des Moines.) The historic significance of Justice Neuman's appointment was reported by the Iowa press.

Linda Kinney Neuman was sworn in Thursday as the first woman on Iowa's Supreme Court, and the historical significance did not go unnoticed.

"We have turned another—and a landmark—page in the history of the court," said Chief Justice W. W. Reynoldson during a 45-minute ceremony inside the high court's packed 100-year-old courtroom in the Capitol.

"Today we are making history," said Gov. Terry Branstad, who appointed Neuman and administered the oath.

Smiling broadly and wearing the robe she wore as Scott County District Court judge, the state's newest justice made her way to the handcarved bench, pulled out one of the heavy upholstered chairs and sat down with the robed court.

"I accept this grave new responsibility with a reverence and respect for those who have gone before me," said Neuman, the 98th justice appointed to the court.

Neuman added a second—and possibly a third—historical footnote: At 38, she's the youngest to join the court, and at 5 feet tall, she may be the shortest. Before the ceremony, court aides adjusted her chair to make certain she would not appear "small" among the justices.

The Iowa Supreme Court in 1995. *Back row (left to right):* James H. Andreasen, Linda K. Neuman, Bruce M. Snell, Jr., and Marsha K Ternus. *Front row (left to right):* James H. Carter, David Harris, Chief Justice Arthur A. McGiverin, Jerry L. Larson, and Louis A. Lavorato. (Courtesy, Iowa Supreme Court)

. . . .

Reynoldson told the courtroom, "Ordinarily this room is filled with the thrust and parry of legal warriors, and that special and unforgettable mix of anxiety, tensions and sweaty palms." But, he added, "today is one of those rare and memorable occasions when the courtroom shines with happiness and good will."

. . . .

A short time later, in a scene repeated through the decades, the spouse of the newest justice—this time a husband—placed the judicial robe on the new member. Neuman then went to an empty chair at the far end of the bench traditionally left open for the junior justice.

"The work that we are about is neither women's work, nor men's work, but a solemn responsibility that we share equally, male and female, black and white, young and old, to uphold the dignity and freedom of every person and to preserve and strengthen the democratic society which we have inherited," Neuman said.

She thanked family members and others who have supported her and said it "has given me the confidence to seek the joy and duty of life."

Quoting Oliver Wendell Holmes, who served as a U.S. Supreme Court justice for 30 years beginning in 1902, Neuman said, "To use one's talents to the fullest—the only question as to whether one's life is worth living is whether you've had enough of it."

Excerpted from *Des Moines Register*, August 15, 1986 (Frank Santiago, reporter).

The age of technology and mass communication brought new challenges to the legal profession. A hotly debated (and litigated) issue was the extent to which attorneys should be allowed to advertise in the media, particularly on television. Iowa's ethical rules concerning lawyer advertising—which bar a visual display other than print on television—generally were regarded as among the most restrictive in the nation.

In the case of Committee on Professional Ethics v. Humphrey, the ethics committee of the Iowa State Bar Association sought to enjoin a lawyer from using dramatic advertisements on television. The Iowa Supreme Court rejected the lawyer's challenge to the constitutionality of the advertising restrictions. After the U.S. Supreme Court remanded the case for further consideration, the Iowa Supreme Court in 1985 ratified its prior order restraining the advertisement. The Chief Justice, in a special concurring opinion, gave a passionate defense of Iowa's more restrictive rule.

I join the majority opinion, and write further only to express my deep philosophical concern for the future of state courts if [a recent U.S. Supreme Court] holding is to be extended to the uncontrollable and inevitable machinations of television advertising, absent the safeguards provided by our rules challenged here.

Surely no one will dispute there is a compelling state interest that state courts be, *and should be perceived to be,* forums in which controversies will be seriously and dispassionately resolved, and justice administered, in a structured, disciplined, and dignified environment. ...

Solemn forums for the litigation of cases whose lawyer-officers resemble carnival barkers at the doors scarcely can avoid being viewed as carnivals, or at least, places where justice is bought and sold as in any marketplace. Judicial systems are not equipped, nor do they have the time, to police Madison Avenue.

. . . .

Iowa long has been in the forefront with protective measures for persons involved in its legal processes, all with the support of its organized, vol-untary bar association. The Iowa Supreme Court was the second in the nation to mandate continuing legal education for lawyers and judges. It was the first in the United States to mandate compulsory audits of lawyer trust accounts. This step was ancillary to court rules which created a client security fund, now totaling over $1,400,000, to reimburse embezzled clients. As of July 1, 1985, through supreme court order, Iowa became one of a handful of states mandating that interest on lawyer trust accounts be combined through a commission and used primarily to provide legal services to the poor in civil cases. ...

The effectiveness of state courts, which have only moral suasion and public respect for the ultimate vindication of their judicial power, is enhanced by the perception that courts are served by a cadre of professional court officers. These professionals in turn should be perceived in the light described by Justice Frankfurter:

> From a profession charged with such responsibilities there must be exacted those qualities of truth-speaking, of a high sense of honor, of granite discretion, of the strictest observance of fiduciary responsibility, that have, throughout the centuries, been compendiously described as "moral character."

... The television advertising exposed in the record before us hardly projects the above-described qualities. ... Our rules are designed to permit television advertising while avoiding the excesses and dangers otherwise so inherent and accepted in that media. These rules reasonably protect defendants' first amendment rights. At the same time, they protect the integrity of Iowa's courts in "the primary governmental function of administering justice."

Committee on Professional Ethics and Conduct of the Iowa State Bar Association v. Humphrey, 377 N.W.2d 643, 647-48, 650-52 (Iowa 1985) (Reynoldson, C. J., specially concurring).

[*Above*] The University of Iowa College of Law, Iowa City, dedicated in 1986. (Courtesy, University of Iowa College of Law) [*Right*] The Dwight D. Opperman Hall and Law Library, Drake University Law School, Des Moines, dedicated in 1993. (Courtesy, Drake University Law School)

An issue equally controversial as that of attorney advertising was the question of allowing cameras in Iowa courtrooms. Following a two-year experiment begun in January 1980, the judicial rules allowing expanded media coverage were made permanent.

In a 1992 appeal to the Iowa Supreme Court, the defendant—convicted of first-degree murder—argued that the placement of microphones at the counsel table violated his constitutional rights. While finding that the microphones had not prejudiced the defendant's rights, the Court expressed deep concern over the delicate balance between a free press and a fair trial.

The final assignment of error is that the placement of media microphones at the counsel table violated Douglas's due process rights and his right to effective assistance of counsel. ...

We have granted expanded media coverage by our rules. Broadcasting, televising, recording, and photographing are permitted in the courtroom during sessions of the court under certain conditions. ...

Douglas's trial counsel ... vehemently objected to the presence of live microphones at the counsel table. ...

Defense counsel noted that the microphones were equipped with cut-off switches but complained that it placed an unfair burden on counsel to perform trial duties and to have to remember to operate microphones simultaneously. ... A response was given by media personnel that confidential discussions between counsel and the defendant detected by the microphones would not be publicized. ...

After the second day of trial, defense counsel ... heard a television news broadcast .... On the screen she observed the image of herself conferring with co-counsel. She believed she heard co-counsel['s] voice during the broadcast. Knowing that co-counsel had not participated in the questioning that day, she concluded that a confidential communication had been broadcast.

... Although clearly a nuisance, the microphone's presence do[es] not appear in this case to have prevented or even impeded Douglas's counsel in the presentation of his defense. Not a single instance is cited where the defendant's claims or evidentiary proof were adversely affected from this cause. ...

Nevertheless, we view with alarm the disdainful attitude displayed by the media in this case. The impression given is that once expanded media coverage was granted, media conduct was above reproach and beyond review. Despite assurances of responsibility, the media representative's promise to not broadcast confidential communications was apparently violated. ...

It is clear that the presence of live microphones at the counsel table creates a real potential for prejudicing a defendant's constitutional rights. Further complicating this issue is the fact that proving a negative, i.e., that counsel was prevented from adequately representing the defendant, is difficult. ...

Viewed in retrospect, the trial court would have been well advised in denying the media's request for the type of live microphones at the counsel table used in this case.

Our rules allowing expanded media coverage have been drafted to give the public increased access to judicial proceedings. This access is, nevertheless, subject to the duty and authority of the presiding judge to control the conduct of proceedings, to prevent distractions, and to ensure the fair administration of justice. [We] encourage trial judges to assiduously exercise their authority over the judicial proceedings in order to assure a fair trial to the parties.

State v. Douglas, 485 N.W.2d 619, 623-26 (Iowa 1992).

In the 1980s and 1990s, the courts often were confronted with issues involving religion and the schools. The offering of prayers during public school graduation ceremonies provoked numerous lawsuits, as both proponents and opponents of prayer claimed constitutional protection for their positions. One such lawsuit was filed in an Iowa federal court by a parent and a graduating student, who claimed that graduation prayers violated the First Amendment prohibition against the "establishment of religion."

This is a civil rights action under 42 U.S.C. § 1983, challenging the constitutionality of including an invocation and benediction at high school graduation ceremonies conducted by the defendant. Plaintiffs seek a declaratory judgment that including an invocation and benediction at the ceremonies violates the Establishment Clause of the First Amendment to the United States Constitution, which applies to the states through the Fourteenth Amendment, and they seek preliminary and permanent injunctive relief. ...

For at least the past twenty years, and probably for much longer, the defendant's graduation ceremonies ... have been opened with an invocation prayer by a Christian minister and closed by a Christian minister's benediction. ...

In 1984 the Iowa Civil Liberties Union wrote to the defendant's board about the invocation and benediction at commencement exercises, and on March 5, 1985 the Iowa Civil Liberties Union demanded that defendant abandon that practice. Defendant rejected the demand.

Attendance at the graduation ceremony is and always has been voluntary. Attendance by a graduating senior is not required to receive a diploma.

. . . .

The First Amendment to the Constitution of the United States provides, *inter alia:* "Congress shall make no law respecting an establishment of religion, or prohibiting the free exercise thereof." ...

[T]he invocation and benediction portions of defendant's commencement exercises serve a Christian religious purpose, not a secular purpose. This finding and conclusion is supported not only by the great weight of the evidence in this case, but by the undeniable truth that prayer is inherently religious. ...

Defendant suggests that if this court grants plaintiffs injunctive relief, the rights of others to freely exercise their religion will be infringed. That is not so. The First Amendment right of the people to the free exercise of religion does not give them a right to have government provide them public prayer at government functions and ceremonies, even if the majority would like it. ...

It may well be that the majority of graduating seniors and the majority of the population in the defendant school district would like to have an invocation and benediction as part of the commencement exercises. However, the enforcement of constitutional rights is not subject to the pleasure of the majority. It would be the antithesis of the concept of constitutional law to apply the protection of the Constitution, which is the fundamental law of our land, in any given situation only if the majority at the relevant time and place approved. ...

It is the declaratory judgment of the court that the defendant's inclusion of a religious invocation and a religious benediction as part of its graduating ceremonies violates the Establishment Clause of the First Amendment of the United States Constitution.

Graham v. Central Community School District of Decatur County, 608 F. Supp. 531, 532, 534-35, 537 (S. D. Iowa 1985).

The compulsory education law that was the center of conflict between state officials and the Amish in the 1960s became the focus for challenge by other, predominately fundamentalist, religious groups in the 1980s. In a 1985 case, a Baptist pastor and members of his church argued that the "Amish exception" should apply to exempt their parochial school from the state's compulsory attendance law. The Iowa Supreme Court rejected this contention, distinguishing the plaintiffs' educational needs from those of the Amish.

Plaintiffs are the pastor and certain members of a fundamentalist Baptist church in Charles City. The controversy arose following their organization of a parochial school. ...

When it was set up in the fall of 1980 the school was not incorporated separately from the church. The curriculum chosen, the Accelerated Christian Education Program, has not as yet been challenged as inadequate by any state authorities. At the bottom of this litigation is the fact that plaintiffs are unwilling to submit to any state inquiry on the matter. In their view, the educational content and process of their school, because it is so central to their religion, is not properly subject to state oversight. ...

In view of the historical background for section 299.24 (the plaintiffs themselves call it the "Amish exception") we do not think the legislature intended the exemption to be available to any and all church groups who seek to provide for a religiously oriented education. ...

To obtain an exemption under section 299.24, plaintiffs had to prove their church "professes principles or tenets that differ substantially from the objectives, goals, and philosophy of education embodied in standards set forth in section 257.25, and rules adopted in implementation thereof .... "

We conclude ... that the plaintiffs have not established any substantial dissimilarity between their educational goals and those specified for public schools, certainly none which sets them apart from all the many other parochial schools in the state. ...

... Sincerity of belief is the only factor wholly common to both the Amish and these plaintiffs. The beliefs of the plaintiffs are greatly less interwoven with their daily mode of life. The Amish culture is greatly more isolated from mainstream American life. Plaintiffs' children, for all the distinctive religious convictions they will be given, will live, compete for jobs, work, and move about in a diverse and complex society. Their educational needs are plainly not as circumscribed as those of Amish children. Neither does exposure to the more general American culture pose such an immediate threat to plaintiffs' mode of living as is the case with the Amish.

Whatever they may feel about their children's religious needs, the plaintiffs have not established that their children's educational needs are significantly different from those of other children. The superintendent's determination not to grant plaintiffs an Amish exception did not infringe upon their religious rights under the first amendment.

Johnson v. Charles City Community Schools Board of Education, 368 N.W.2d 74, 75-76, 82-84 (Iowa 1985).

Some parents whose children remained in the public schools became active in challenging the content of the school curriculum and textbooks. These battles often were fought during elections of school board officials and at school board meetings. In one such case in 1983, parents objected to a school film as being contrary to their religious beliefs about creation.

The primary focus of testimony, evidence and argument at the [District Board of Directors] hearing centered around the film entitled, "Apemen of Africa." The film is not owned by the District, but is loaned to District staff members for classroom use by Area Education Agency 11. The film itself is relatively short and portrays various anthropological discoveries which tend to substantiate the theory of evolution of man from lower forms of life. ...

The film was presented by the teacher to students in a fourth grade social studies class as a demonstration of methods used by social scientists in making discoveries by digging up and analyzing evidence of the past. ... The film is not a requirement in all fourth grade social studies classrooms, but was utilized by teachers on an individual basis.

The record is not totally clear as to the teacher's actions or remarks to the students regarding the issue of evolution theory presented in "Apemen of Africa." It is obvious, however, that the teacher was somewhat sensitive to the issue of potential conflict with students' personally held beliefs because she warned the students before showing the film that it presented one theory about the way man came into being. She emphasized that other theories do exist.

. . . .

The term "creationism" and the phrase "creation science" generally refer to a body of theory and evidence which allegedly substantiates the Biblical version of the creation of the earth and all living things in six days. An important part of this view is that a world-wide flood occurred as a result of the sinful nature of man.

. . . .

The primary focus of the First Amendment provisions regarding the establishment and free exercise of religion is to make governmental bodies, such as public schools, neutral toward religion. ...

This neutrality is breached when state government attempts to force public schools to teach creationism along side the theory of evolution. ... The courts have consistently rejected arguments that the theory of evolution is a religion and should not be taught in the public schools and that creation science meets the essential characteristics of being a true scientific theory which should be taught along side the theory of evolution. ... The Iowa Attorney General's office has stated in an official opinion that teaching the creationist theory in science class in a public school would violate the First Amendment prohibition against the establishment of religion. Fleming to Anderson, No. 82-10-1, October 1, 1982.

While the First Amendment prohibits the District from teaching creation science on the same basis as the scientific theory of evolution as the [parents] have requested, so does practicality prevent the teaching of alternate theories of how things came to be. There are certainly more theories of how the world, man and living things came into being than just those involved in evolution and creationism. To require the public schools to teach all such theories is totally unrealistic.

. . . .

In conclusion, we find that the [parents'] request with regard to the removal of evolution from the curriculum or the teaching of alternate theories should not and cannot be granted.

Burgett v. Des Moines Independent Community School District, 3 D.P.I. App. Dec. 196, 205-06, 208-10 (Iowa State Board of Public Instruction 1983).

Perhaps no case originating in Iowa has aroused more national interest and controversy than the custody battle over "Baby Jessica." During a two-and-one-half-year period, courts in Iowa and Michigan considered whether the child should remain with the DeBoers, her would-be adoptive parents in Michigan, or be returned to her natural parents in Iowa. While a nation watched, transfixed, the case finally ended in August 1993 with the DeBoers bidding an emotional farewell to the child.

The decisive ruling in the case—ultimately followed by the Michigan Supreme Court—was the 1992 Iowa Supreme Court decision holding that the adoption proceedings were fatally flawed because the natural father's parental rights had not been terminated.

This case is, we observe thankfully, an unusual one. It involves the future of a baby girl, B.G.C., who was born on February 8, 1991. Her mother, Cara, who was not married, decided to give up the baby for adoption and signed a release of parental rights. ... She named "Scott" as the father of the baby, and Scott also signed a release of parental rights. Later, both Cara and Scott signed waivers of notice of the termination hearing. After the hearing, the court ordered the termination of the parental rights of both Cara and Scott. Custody of the child was given to the potential adoptive parents, R.D. and J.D.

Cara moved to set aside the termination, asserting that her release was defective for several reasons. She also asserted, for the first time, that the real father was "Daniel," not Scott. ...

In the meantime, the adoption case proceeded.

The district court found that Daniel was in fact the real father, that he had not released his parental rights, and that he had not abandoned the baby. The court denied the adoption and ordered the baby to be surrendered to Daniel. ... The baby has remained in the custody of R.D. and J.D. virtually from the time of her birth.

. . . .

As tempting as it is to resolve this highly emotional issue with one's heart, we do not have the unbridled discretion of a Solomon. Ours is a system of law, and adoptions are solely creatures of statute. As the district court noted, without established procedures to guide courts in such matters, they would "be engaged in uncontrolled social engineering." This is not permitted under our law; "[c]ourts are not free to take children from parents simply by deciding another home offers more advantages." [citation omitted] We point out that this case does not invalidate an adoption decree. Adoption of the baby was denied by the district court because the father's rights were not terminated.

. . . .

The argument that the best interests of the baby are best served by allowing her to stay with R.D. and J.D. is a very alluring argument. ...

[A]s the district court found, R.D. and J.D. "have provided exemplary care for the child [and] view themselves as the parents of this child in every respect."

What R.D. and J.D. ask us to do, however, is to bypass the termination requirements of chapter 600A and order the granting of the adoption without establishment of any of the grounds for termination specified in section 600A.8 because it would be in the baby's best interest.

. . . .

We empathize with the district court, which observed that:

> The court had an opportunity to observe [R.D. and J.D.] at the time of hearing and the court is under no illusion that this tragic case is other than an unbelievably traumatic event. ... While cognizant of the heartache which this decision will ultimately cause, this court is presented with no other option than that dictated by the law in this state. Purely equitable principles cannot be substituted for well-established principles of law.

The parental rights of this father may not be dismissed without compliance with our termination statute, and the court correctly ordered that the petition for adoption be dismissed.

In the Interest of B.G.C., A Child, 496 N.W.2d 239, 240-41, 245-46 (Iowa 1992).

Proponents of an Equal Rights Amendment to the Iowa constitution, which would have added to Article I, §1 the sentence— "Neither the State nor any of its political subdivisions shall, on the basis of gender, deny or restrict the equality of rights under the law"—were disappointed when the amendment failed to win voter approval in 1980 and again in 1992. Numerous other constitutional amendments were ratified, including those that increased the governor's term to four years (1972), permitted county home rule (1978), provided for joint election of the governor and lieutenant governor (1988), and repealed the disqualification from public office of citizens who had engaged in a duel (1992).

Despite the defeat of the Equal Rights Amendment, the Iowa legislature passed a number of laws removing gender inequality in the Iowa Code, including "An Act Relating to Statutory Provisions Affecting the Legal Treatment of Male and Female Persons" (1974), and "An Act Requiring the Code Editor to Amend Certain Words in the Code ... to Reflect Both Genders" (1982). This trend worked in favor of men as well as women, as shown by some additions made to the "Mother's Day" statute in 1985.

GENDER AND MARITAL STATUS DISCRIMINATION.
Be It Enacted by the General Assembly of the State of Iowa:
Section 31.4, Code 1985, is amended to read as follows [additions are emphasized ...]:
    31.4 MOTHER'S DAY—*FATHER'S DAY*
The governor of this state is authorized and requested to issue annually a proclamation calling upon

Don't Let Them Take Away Your Rights! VOTE YES ON ①

A majority of Iowans support equal rights for men and women. The Iowa Legislature passed Amendment ① by overwhelming margins and placed it before the voters for approval November 3.

WHY DO THE RADICAL FEMINISTS *REALLY* WANT THE E.R.A. IN IOWA?

Iowa voters soundly defeated the Equal Rights Amendment (E.R.A.) in November, 1980. Now the same radical feminist groups such as the National Organization for Women (N.O.W.) are forcing us to vote again on E.R.A. this Tuesday, November 3.

Pro- and anti-ERA (Equal Rights Amendment) advertisements compete for attention in the 1992 referendum. The proposal to add an equal rights amendment to Iowa's constitution was defeated by voters in 1992, as it had been in 1980. (*Des Moines Register,* November 1, 1992)

our state officials to display the American flag on all state and school buildings, and the people of the state to display the flag at their homes, lodges, churches, and places of business, on the second Sunday in May, known as Mother's Day, *and on the third Sunday in June, known as Father's Day,* as a public expression of reverence for the homes of our state, and to urge the celebration of Mother's Day *and Father's Day* in *the* proclamation in such a way as will deepen home ties, and inspire better homes and closer union between the commonwealth, its homes, and their children.

   . . . .
Approved May 9, 1985.

Acts of the Seventy-First General Assembly, 1985, ch. 99, § 1.

In the 1980s, Iowans suffered from the worst farm debt crisis since the Great Depression. Dramatically falling land prices between 1981 and 1985 threatened to precipitate a round of farm mortgage foreclosures unlike any seen in fifty years. Iowa, like many other states, took steps to ease the crisis, including the passage in 1985 of amendments to Iowa's depression-era moratorium law, and the establishment of a mandatory farm debt mediation program in 1986. In October 1985, Governor Terry Branstad activated the provisions of the foreclosure moratorium law as to farm real estate loans by issuing a "declaration of a state of economic emergency."

EXECUTIVE ORDER #20
        WHEREAS, high interest rates, embargoes, an overvalued dollar and declining farm receipts have created an economic crisis in agriculture; and

WHEREAS, farm asset value[s] have dropped by over 50% since 1981, draining over $35 billion in wealth from Iowa; and

WHEREAS, this level of asset liquidation is three to four times the amount that can be handled by the market; and

WHEREAS, farmers, through no fault of their own, are having loans called because the value of their collateral is declining below the amount required to secure outstanding loans; and prices received at liquidation sales are so low as to further reduce the value of collateral securing outstanding farm loans; and

WHEREAS, agriculture affects 65% of all jobs in the State of Iowa and Iowans in small towns to large cities are threatened by the farm crisis.

NOW, THEREFORE, I, Terry E. Branstad, Governor of the State of Iowa, on this 1st day of October, 1985, by virtue of the authority granted to me by the Constitution of the State of Iowa, and in light of the current condition of the economy of the State of Iowa, … hereby declare that a state of economic emergency now exists.

The purpose behind this declaration is to stabilize the economy of this state, by permitting the implementation of the Moratorium Continuance provision in Chapter 654.15 of the Code of Iowa. The continuance should give mortgagors additional time to stabilize their indebtedness.

This declaration of a state of economic emergency is limited to farm real estate loans. The state of economic emergency will formally exist upon the signing of this statement.

IN TESTIMONY WHEREOF, I have hereunto subscribed my name and caused the Great Seal of Iowa to be affixed. Done at Des Moines this 1st day of October in the year of our Lord one-thousand nine hundred and eight-five.
Terry E. Branstad
Governor

Executive Department, State of Iowa, Executive Order #20, October 1, 1985.

In the quarter century preceding Iowa's Sesquicentennial, the General Assembly passed many acts of key importance to the state, including divorce law reform, consumer credit legislation, the adoption of an Iowa Administrative Code, domestic abuse laws, anti-smoking regulations, and home schooling legislation. Consistent with the growing national interest in issues of "death and dying," the legislature also enacted a law to give Iowans more control over the prolongation of their lives by medical technological means—the so-called "Living Will" Act.

LIFE-SUSTAINING PROCEDURES ACT.
        Be It Enacted by the General Assembly of the State of Iowa:
        Section 1. The legislature finds that all adults have the fundamental right to control the decisions relating to their own medical care, including the decision to have medical or surgical means or procedures calculated to prolong their lives provided, withheld or withdrawn. This right is subject to certain interests of society, such as the protection of human life and the preservation of ethical standards in the medical profession. The legislature further finds that the artificial prolongation of life for persons with a terminal condition may secure only a precarious and burdensome existence, while providing nothing med-

ically necessary or beneficial to the patient. In order that the rights and intentions of persons with such conditions may be respected even after they are no longer able to participate actively in decisions concerning themselves, and to encourage communications between these patients, their families, and their physicians, the legislature declares that the laws of Iowa shall recognize the right of an adult to make a written declaration instructing the adult's physician to provide, withhold, or withdraw life-sustaining procedures or to designate another to make treatment decisions, in the event the person is diagnosed as suffering from a terminal condition.

. . . .

Sec. 4. Any competent adult may execute a declaration at any time directing that life-sustaining procedures be withheld or withdrawn. The declaration may be given operative effect only if the declarant's condition is determined to be terminal and the de-

clarant is not able to make treatment decisions. The declaration must be signed by the declarant or another at the declarant's direction in the presence of two persons who shall sign the declaration as witnesses. ...

Sec. 12. Death resulting from the withholding or withdrawal of life-sustaining procedures pursuant to a declaration and in accordance with this chapter does not, for any purpose, constitute a suicide or homicide.

. . . .

This chapter shall not be construed to condone, authorize or approve mercy killing or euthanasia, or to permit any affirmative or deliberate act or omission to end life other than to permit the natural process of dying.

Approved March 4, 1985.

Acts of the Seventy-First General Assembly, 1985, ch. 3, §§ 1, 4, 12.

Of all the changes made by the Iowa legislature during the period 1970 to 1995, none was more dramatic than the change in laws governing gambling. From its earliest territorial days, Iowa's laws were strongly anti-gambling. A prohibition against lotteries was even included in the Constitutions of 1846 and 1857, which stood for well over a century. However, as Iowa neared the 1996 Sesquicentennial, the state had set its face in a direction diametrically opposed to that of its founders. The reason for this great change began with many Iowans' wish to legalize the simple game of bingo.

Opening the Door:
The Repeal of the Constitutional
Ban on Lotteries

AN IOWAN WHO FELL ASLEEP AT THE beginning of the 1970s would be amazed to awaken as the state's Sesquicentennial approached and find the great range of legal gambling taking place in Iowa. Prior to 1973, strict laws had long forbidden even the simplest gambling. In that year, the Iowa General Assembly legalized bingo for qualified organizations and the games of skill and chance played at fairs.[1]

Thereafter, the legislature passed a plethora of acts: in 1983, to authorize pari-mutuel betting on horse and dog races and to provide for a state racing commission; in 1985, to create a state lottery; in 1989, to allow limited-stakes gambling games—including slot machines and roulette—on riverboats; in the same year, to permit the introduction at Iowa's racetracks of simultaneous telecasts and pari-mutuel betting on horse and dog racing from other states.[2]

Then, in 1991-1992, the state of Iowa entered into compacts with Indian tribes to enable them to open casinos on their lands, as allowed under a 1988 federal law. In 1994, the legislature (subject to local approval) made riverboat gambling stakes unlimited and permitted slot machines and certain other gambling games at horse and dog racing tracks.[3] The 1970 Iowan would be astonished at the proliferation of floating casinos, racing tracks, state lotteries, and casinos on Indian lands.

A seemingly innocuous vote in 1972 was the key that opened the door to this host of gambling measures. That year, Iowans wanted to enable the General Assembly to pass a law permitting bingo. Accordingly, they paved the way for such legislation by voting in a referendum to adopt the so-called "bingo amendment," which removed the long-standing prohibition on lotteries from Iowa's constitution. This was the first step favorable to any form of gambling since the beginning of territorial Iowa.

At the founding of the Territory of Iowa in 1838, a strong movement against lotteries had grown up in many states. Lotteries had been used since colonial times to finance public projects. However, fraud in private lotteries and compulsive gambling, coupled with the financial ruin they gave rise to, led in 1833 to the abolition of lotteries in Pennsylvania, New York, and Massachusetts. By 1840, twelve states had abolished lotteries. (At the time of the Civil War, only Delaware, Kentucky, and Missouri still had lotteries, and in 1894, the last legal lottery was abolished.)

Against this background, Iowa's first territorial governor, Robert Lucas, gave his first annual message to the legislature on November 12, 1838. He emphasized his abhorrence of all gambling: "[W]e frequently see the most disastrous consequences proceed from practices, that in some places are considered as only fashionable vices—namely: *gambling and intemperance*. These two vices may be considered the fountains from which almost every other crime proceeds …. Could you in your wisdom devise ways and means to check the progress of gambling and intemperance in this Territory, you will perform an act that will immortalize your names and entitle you to the gratitude of posterity."[4]

The Territorial Assembly of 1838 promptly passed Iowa's first anti-gambling statute. Then, in 1843, the Assembly added to the territorial laws a ban on lotteries and the sale of lottery tickets. Iowa's first state constitution in 1846 provided that "[n]o lottery shall be authorized by this state; nor shall the sale of lottery tickets be allowed," and the new state's criminal code included separate sections with strict prohibitions on "gaming and betting" and "lotteries." The constitutional ban on lotteries continued unamended in the Iowa Constitution of 1857.[5]

In the 1860 decision of *P. & C. Guenther v. Dewein*, the Iowa Supreme Court explained the policy behind the constitutional and statutory prohibition of lotteries: "The reason and policy of this constitutional provision and this statute … is found in the preamble to New York Act upon the same subject … 'Whereas experience has proved that private lotteries occasion idleness and dissipation, and have been productive of frauds and impositions.' "[6]

Eighty years later, the Iowa Supreme Court's attitude toward lotteries had not changed. In the 1940 decision of *St. Peter v. Pioneer Theater Corporation*, the Court reaffirmed that "the source of the evil which attends a lottery is that it arouses the gambling spirit and leads people to hazard their substance on a mere chance."[7]

But if the Iowa Supreme Court retained the traditional hostility toward lotteries, more and more Americans during the 1940s and 1950s came to accept at least one form of lottery. Although bingo had widely been held by the courts to be an illegal lottery, efforts in some states during the 1940s and 1950s to legalize the game primarily for charitable purposes were successful. After a referendum in 1957 to allow charitable bingo, New York became the ninth state to permit the game. At the end of the decade, an estimated twenty million Americans regularly played bingo in church or professional groups, while forty million others played it occasionally. As one writer put it in 1957: "The word bingo has … become as much a part of the American idiom as strike-out or home run."[8]

Bingo came before the Iowa Supreme Court in February 1953 in the case of *State v. Mabrey*.[9] The appeal was from a decision of the Council Bluffs municipal court acquitting the defendant for keeping a gambling house. The defendant operated a recreational club where bingo was played.

The gambling provision under which the defendant was charged did not list "bingo" among the prohibited games. The trial judge, in acquitting the defendant, maintained the legislature had a duty to be specific: "If 'Bingo' is to be illegal in Iowa, it is not a difficult matter to include it specifically in [the statute]. The game has become of age and worthy of christening and either specifically prohibited or openly tolerated .... " The lack of specific prohibition in the statute forced the court "to apply its personal opinion as to whether bingo as played in the present case was gambling."[10]

The Iowa Supreme Court, reversing on a point of law, held that this ruling ignored the words of general prohibition in the statute: "to play ... other game for money .... " Accordingly, "we hold the game of bingo would receive no immunity merely because it was not specifically named."[11]

The Court further considered whether the defendant's bingo game also constituted a lottery. The defendant conceded prizes were given and the recipients were determined by chance. But he urged that this was not a lottery, because the participants had paid only for dinner, and the bingo was "free." The Court rejected this interpretation: "It is enough that whoever purchased a dinner ticket, purchased a chance for the prize. The three elements of lottery were present: the payment of consideration for a chance to win a prize."[12]

The following month, in March 1953, a committee of the Iowa House of Representatives introduced a joint resolution to amend the constitutional prohibition on lotteries. The amendment would have permitted the legislature to authorize bingo "even though a consideration is paid by participants in such a game."[13] The joint resolution only received a first reading, but the opening salvo in a long war had been fired.

In both 1961 and 1963, joint resolutions were introduced in the Senate to amend the lottery provision and permit bingo conducted by charitable, religious, or veterans organizations. These joint resolutions got no further than being read a first and second time. However, another attempt begun in 1965 came far nearer to success.

In that year, the Senate and the House both considered a joint resolution for a charitable bingo amendment. Senator Eugene M. Hill (D-Newton), in opposition, quoted from Meredith Wilson's *The Music Man*: legalized bingo "spells TROUBLE for Iowa,"[14] because pari-mutuel betting on horse and dog races would follow. Senator Peter Hansen (D-Manning), sponsor of the resolution, replied that not even commercial bingo—let alone other forms of gambling—would be permitted under his amendment. Other senators urged that bingo was not really gambling, and that it provided people with great fun. The Senate approved the resolution by forty-four votes to fourteen.

In the House, supporters of the measure urged: "[L]et the middle-aged women of Iowa enjoy themselves." Despite the counterargument that to allow bingo "would be opening the gate to all forms of gambling,"[15] the House by seventy-seven to forty-two voted in favor of the resolution. The charitable bingo amendment had now passed both houses of the Sixty-First General Assembly. To become part of the Iowa constitution, the proposed amendment also would have to be approved by the next succeeding legislature and then be ratified by the electorate in a referendum.

During the summer of 1965, a police raid on a bingo club in Davenport caused a stir throughout the state. One hundred and forty-four bingo players—139 of them women—were loaded into relays of squad cars and patrol wagons and taken to police headquarters for booking. One woman was eighty-seven years old, and four others were over eighty. Some were amused, but others cried as they climbed into

The arrest of nearly 150 bingo players in Davenport in June 1965 caused some Iowans to re-think the state's policy on banning the game. In this photograph, police squad cars line up outside the Capitol Club in Davenport to transport the offenders to police headquarters. (*Davenport Times-Democrat,* June 4, 1965)

the patrol wagon. To the fury of many of the women, they were initially charged as "inmates of a disorderly house." The charge was later changed to "gaming and betting."[16]

In the courtroom, awaiting trial, a woman in a flowered hat said: "At least I got my name in the paper before my death notice." Another woman commented: "I'm glad I won before they made the raid."[17] Two others were livid that when booked they had had to give their age and weight. Each bingo player received a suspended sentence of $5.

In March 1967, the charitable bingo amendment came back before the Senate. One senator said: "The issue is legalized gambling in Iowa."[18] Another argued: "[S]ome old ladies will take their whole week's paycheck to a bingo game."[19] The Senate passed the resolution by forty-four votes to fifteen.

However, the House Committee on Constitutional Amendments, without discussion, voted thirteen to four indefinitely to postpone the bingo amendment. The chairman afterwards explained that he had received a large anti-bingo mail. Not one of the 124 representatives protested the committee's recommendation within three legislative days, as required under the rules. "And so," said the *Cedar Rapids Gazette,* "bingo died, quietly and without friends."[20]

But reports of bingo's death were premature. During the first session of the Sixty-Third General Assembly (which met annually from 1969 onward), Representative Theodore Ellsworth (R-Dubuque) introduced a resolution to permit a charitable bingo amendment. In February 1970, during the second session of the Sixty-Third General Assembly, the amendment came before the House. At the urging of Representative Elizabeth Shaw (R-Davenport), who objected to putting the word "bingo" in the constitution, and others, the House debated a substitute amendment proposed by the Committee on Constitutional Amendments. This amendment would totally repeal the constitutional prohibition on lotteries, thereby allowing the legislature to legalize bingo—and indeed, any other type of lottery. Both sides agreed that bingo was played right across the state. Representative Ellsworth said: "The only lobby I've been subjected to on this resolution is the little old ladies and a lot of them." He went on: "They have come to me literally with tears in their eyes, and all they want to do is play this innocent game." Representative Shaw, recalling that more than a hundred "little old ladies" had been arrested in Davenport for playing bingo, said: "An unenforceable law always promotes disrespect for the law."

Members on the other side argued that the "little old ladies" would spend too much of their pension money on bingo, and that illegal forms of gambling would thrive under cover of legalized bingo. Representative Charles Grassley (R-New Hartford) declared: "[L]egalized gambling fosters and promotes illegal gambling. … Gambling feeds on the boredom and loneliness of those who are socially maladjusted and the poor. … " Another representative said: "Gambling is like garlic—there is no such thing as a little."[21]

The House voted by seventy-three to forty-three to repeal the constitutional ban on lotteries. The Senate followed suit by thirty-six votes to twenty-two.

The next succeeding General Assembly, the Sixty-Fourth, met for its first session in 1971. In February, the lottery amendment again came before the House. During a five-minute debate, Representative Ellsworth said: "It is silly of us not to let the senior citizens play this innocent game." Against him, Representative Richard Radl (D-Lisbon) argued: "This is but the opening step to legalize bingo, and that is but the opening step to pari-mutuel betting. Make no mistake about it you are opening the door to legalized gambling in Iowa."[22] The amendment passed by fifty-nine votes to twenty-five.

The Senate did not consider bingo again that year—but bingo was in the news nonetheless. On the afternoon of Sunday, September 5, 1971, a *Des Moines Register* reporter telephoned Attorney General Richard Turner. The reporter told him that illegal gambling was taking place at the annual Catholic church picnic in the tiny town of North Buena Vista (population 118), twenty-five miles north of Dubuque. As the attorney general noted shortly afterwards: "The D M Register reported the matter to me & asked what I was going to do about it."[23] So he sent two agents of the Iowa Bureau of Criminal Investigation to raid the church premises. At 9:30 that evening, the agents found 1,500 people on the grounds of the Church of the Immaculate Conception. They saw roulette, poker, and dice being played. The second story of the parish hall was being used as a bingo parlor.

The agents seized the roulette wheels, dice, decks of cards, and bingo machine. As there were so many bingo cards, they just took seven to represent them. They also took $595.95 from the various gambling locations. The following day, the

THIS MAY BE THE MOST EXCITING EVENT OF THE 1972 IOWA STATE FAIR

[*Left*]Attorney General Richard Turner's crackdown on bingo and gambling games at church picnics and fairs led to calls for reform of the state's gambling laws. (Courtesy, *Des Moines Register*) [*Right*] A Frank Miller editorial cartoon summarizes many Iowans' views about the Attorney General's crackdown on carnival games at the 1972 Iowa State Fair. (*Des Moines Register,* August 8, 1972)

parish priest, Father Carl Ruhland, was charged with operating and keeping a place resorted to for the purpose of gambling.

The raid received great publicity. The North Buena Vista parishioners were furious—half their church's income came from the annual picnic, which had raised $11,000 the previous year. A member of the parish complained after the arrest that the state gambling law should be changed "to use a little common sense."[24] One irate woman from Grinnell wrote to Turner: "Really, Mr. Atty. Gen. there must be bigger 'crooks' than bingo players running around!"[25]

Governor Robert Ray backed Turner's decision to uphold the law. However, he urged the Senate to pass the lottery repeal amendment, thus paving the way for the legislature to pass a bill legalizing bingo. "The public demand is there," he said. "Bingo isn't something that involves crime. This is something that people like to do."[26]

On September 18, Father Ruhland had a court appearance at the Clayton County courthouse in Elkader. A cavalcade of thirty cars brought 150 supporters from North Buena Vista and the surrounding area. Father Ruhland pleaded guilty.

His attorney said of the crowd in the packed courthouse: "These people don't feel they were doing anything wrong .... They felt the laws are antiquated and should be changed to allow this type of activity." The judge said that those dissatisfied with the laws should work to change them; he fined Father Ruhland $100. The priest, smiling, raised his fingers in a "V" sign and said: "Everybody up to Angie's [an Elkader cafe] for drinks [and] coffee."[27]

The following day, the attorney general told the *Des Moines Tribune* that many North Buena Vista residents had complained to him that similar games were played every year at the Iowa State Fair in Des Moines. "I think these people have a very good point," he said. "In light of this incident I'll probably have occasion to meet with [the State Fair secretary]. Certainly we can't be allowing violations of the law by the state."[28]

In March 1972, during the second session of the Sixty-Fourth General Assembly, the lottery amendment—after long being held up in committee—was again debated in the Senate. It ran into stern opposition. Senator Marvin Smith (R-Paulina) complained that the resolution had become known as the "bingo bill" because its main supporters said they wanted the lottery clause repealed to permit legal bingo. "If you call this a bingo bill you've got rocks in your head. How are you going to legalize little gambling and not big gambling?" Senator Eugene Hill (D-Newton) agreed. "I tell you, friends, this bingo game soon gets out of hand .... Other forms of gambling will run rampant in this state if we take this prohibition out of the Constitution."[29] But the Senate, on March 22, voted to pass the resolution by the slim majority of twenty-six to twenty-three.

Both houses in two successive General Assemblies had thus approved a resolution to repeal the lottery prohibition in Iowa's constitution. The final constitutional requirement was ratification by popular referendum, which was to take place on November 7, 1972.

The summer of 1972 saw gambling constantly in the headlines. In May, Attorney General Turner announced a planned crackdown on gambling at the State Fair in August. Anybody caught gambling would be arrested, and gambling devices would be seized. In addition to bingo, roulette, and slot machines, people would be arrested for playing games in which marbles were rolled into holes, claws were lowered into candy and toys, pennies were pitched to win teddy bears, and balls were thrown at bottles.

On June 12, Turner ordered a raid on a church picnic at St. Patrick's Catholic parish at Epworth, not far from Dubuque, and a large quantity of bingo and roulette equipment was seized. Local officials shut down or forbade small gambling games or bingo at carnivals and similar events in Story City, Davenport, Spirit Lake, and Burlington.

At the end of June, the Association of Iowa Fairs and other fair groups sought a permanent injunction in the Polk County district court to prevent the Attorney General from closing down carnival games played at Iowa fairs. Initially, Judge A.B. Crouch granted a temporary injunction for twenty days, ordering the Attorney General not to interfere with such carnival games as hoop-la, balloon dart, bear pitch, basketball shoot, six cat game, fishpond, and tic-tac-toe. The judge reasoned that it would be inequitable to jeopardize the county fairs without a hearing.[30]

The hearing on the permanent injunction was set for July 5, 1972. In his ruling on July 17, Judge Crouch considered the language of section 726.3 of the Iowa Code, which, except for the penalty, had remained unchanged since the Code of 1851: "If any person play at any game for any sum of money or other property of any value or make any bet or wager for money or other property of value, he shall be guilty .... "[31] The judge ruled that the term "any game" in this provision applied to the enumerated carnival games. "[N]o decisions in this state clearly decide the meaning of 'any game.' But there is language in several cases that indicates whether the game involves skill is not material to the question."[32] The attorney general's enforcement efforts therefore could continue.

The fair associations immediately appealed this ruling to the Iowa Supreme Court, asking for a stay until the Court gave its decision (which was not expected for several months). On July 25, the Court denied the request for a stay without giving reasons.[33] But Chief Justice C. Edwin Moore told the Associated Press: "The court hesitates to prevent enforcement of a state statute."[34]

With the Iowa Supreme Court appeal not likely to be heard until winter, the fair associations turned to the federal courts, claiming in a lawsuit filed in the United States District Court for the Southern District of Iowa that the 121-year-old Iowa gambling law was impermissably vague, contrary to the Fourteenth Amendment of the U.S. Constitution. The federal court on August 12 handed down its decision. By a two-to-one majority, the court abstained from granting relief prior to the final disposition of the Iowa Supreme Court.[35]

The fair associations went back to the Polk County district court and again asked for a temporary injunction to bar Turner from interfering with fair games. This time, the fair associations raised an argument similar to that in federal court— that the Iowa anti-gambling law was "so vague, overbroad, indefinite, and without any ascertainable standards or guidelines to determine what games or activities are covered" as to be unconstitutional.

Judge Leo Oxberger granted the temporary injunction for the period of the State Fair and set a hearing for August 28 to consider the constitutional issue. His ruling stated: "The plaintiffs have a due process right to operate their fairs and game concessions ... free from interference by the law enforcement officials unless they are violating a constitutional statute that actually encompasses the activity in which they are engaged."[36] He added in an interview: "It hasn't been such a threat to society that we needed to impose this restriction for the last 100 years. It seems to me it could wait until [the Iowa Supreme Court's decision in] wintertime."[37]

Charging that Judge Oxberger committed a "gross use of discretion,"[38] a furious attorney general promptly appealed the judge's ruling to the Iowa Supreme Court. On August 18, the day before the Iowa State Fair was to open, the Court set aside the temporary injunction and stayed Oxberger's August 28 hearing. The Court, citing the strong presumption in favor of the constitutionality of statutes, noted that courts are reluctant "to interfere by injunction with law enforcement officials in enforcing criminal laws."[39]

In a final effort to halt Turner's crackdown, the fair associations sought an injunction from the United States Supreme Court, which was denied on September 5.[40] As Governor Ray later put it: "I think it is a safe bet to state that our gambling laws made news in 1972."[41]

The attorney general's reaction to the Iowa Supreme Court's decision was that if the injunction had not been stayed, there would have been "discrimination against the Immaculate Conception Church at North Buena Vista and other fairs and carnivals that have complied with the law."[42]

Judge Crouch, in the first Polk County court hearing, had applied Iowa's *gambling* laws to carnival games, but had noted that the laws dealing with *lotteries* did not apply to the case.[43] Turner had agreed with this distinction, observing that the gambling statutes could be modified, regardless of whether the constitutional ban on lotteries was repealed. "Lots of games while gambling are not lotteries." He added: "Maybe this will all result in some amendments to our [gambling] law."[44]

Despite Turner's emphasis on changing the gambling law, many Iowans believed that his crackdown on bingo (which *was* a lottery) and carnival games was actually prompted by a desire to get support for the constitutional lottery amendment in November. In an interview in June, Turner denied that he had ordered the crackdown to affect the referendum, but he added that his campaign would make the voters "better informed."[45]

An article that appeared during the State Fair reported that Attorney General Turner had garnered fewer votes than any other unopposed Republican candidate for a major state office in the August 1 primary election. Realizing his showing was because of the crackdown, Turner responded that he hoped Iowans would "vote for [the lottery amendment] but not against me."[46]

Republican Governor Robert Ray had already voiced his support for the amendment in June, viewing it as a necessary step before legalizing bingo and carnival games. Later that month, a former Democratic leader of the state Senate, Andrew Frommelt, announced the formation of a group based in Dubuque called Citizens for Legal Bingo, with an array of former politicians on its board. In July, both Democratic candidates for governor announced themselves in favor of the lottery amendment, as did Turner's Democratic opponent for attorney general.

During a government symposium at Drake University later in July, the legislative chair of the League of Women Voters of Iowa backed repeal of the lottery prohibition as being inappropriate in the constitution, although the League took no position on changes in Iowa's gambling law. At the same meeting, Representative Theodore Ellsworth, who had steered the amendment through the House of Representatives, said Iowa would not become "a little or a big Las Vegas" if the amendment passed. He stressed that the lottery amendment "was explained and sold to the Legislature as the 'bingo amendment' .... "[47]

During the State Fair, Governor Ray predicted that the amendment would pass in November. A straw poll taken among fair goers showed 624 in favor of the lottery amendment and 251 against. An Iowa opinion poll published on August 28 showed sixty-three percent in favor of the amendment and twenty-seven percent against.

The following week, at the invitation of Father Ruhland, the attorney general attended the annual Catholic church picnic at North Buena Vista. This time no gambling took place, but Father Ruhland urged the crowd to vote for the lottery amendment in November. Turner said he was sorry for what had happened the previous year. "I can't, however, apologize for enforcing the law. If we don't like those laws, and believe, as I do, that they are antiquated and need to be revised, then we should get them changed."[48]

One year after the famous raid at the North Buena Vista Immaculate Conception Church picnic, the flyer advertising the 1972 picnic spoofed the prior year's problems. Pictured in the fake currency: Father Ruhland, the arrested priest, and Attorney General Richard Turner. (Courtesy, State Historical Society of Iowa, Des Moines, Richard Turner Papers)

In mid-September, groups opposed to the lottery amendment announced their plans. The Iowa Council of Churches, the state's largest organization of Protestant churches, said that it had sent a letter to pastors of its 2,500 member churches asking them to preach sermons on the lottery amendment. The letter gave both sides of the issue, but stressed as a reason for opposition that the legislature would then be free to vote for new types of gambling whenever it wanted. The Council planned a second letter to remind pastors of its strong stand against gambling.

A group called the Citizens Committee Against Legalized Gambling announced a fall campaign to defeat the lottery amendment. Its president, Harry Beardsley of West Des Moines, a former state representative, said repeal "would really be a blank check for the legislature to approve any type of gambling that anyone chose to present."[49]

In late October, leaders from four major Protestant denominations—United Methodists, Presbyterians, Lutherans, and Baptists—urged Iowans to vote against the lottery amendment. Dr. Robert Finch of the United Presbyterian Church said: "Under the guise of allowing a few little old ladies to have some fun at the bingo tables, an effort is being made to take away all restraints on gambling." Likewise, Bishop James Thomas of the Iowa Area United Methodist Church said that repealing the ban on lotteries "even if it were only to legalize bingo would open the door to organized gambling in Iowa."[50]

However, the opposition efforts failed to catch fire. Two days before the referendum, the *Davenport Times-Democrat* reported: "In the last couple of weeks a few sparsely attended meetings have been held by anti-gambling forces throughout the state. But organized resistance has failed to materialize."[51] On November 7, 1972, Iowans cast 585,966 (67.13 percent) votes in favor of the lottery amendment, and 286,959 (32.87 percent) against. Of Iowa's ninety-nine counties, only Osceola and Sioux counties opposed the amendment. The following year, the General Assembly passed the act legalizing bingo and fair games.

And two decades after the referendum on the lottery amendment, the prophecies of its opponents were fulfilled. By the 1990s, Iowa was deluged by laws permitting various forms of gambling. When, in 1972, Iowans removed the lottery prohibition from their constitution, the floodgates indeed were opened.

EPILOGUE

The Mound Builders

"You will plant corn where my dead sleep ...."

— Chief Poweshiek

The Mound Builders

WHEN CHIEF POWESHIEK LEARNED
that the cause for celebration of his white neighbors on July 4, 1838, was the creation of the new
Territory of Iowa, he well knew what this meant for the land and for his Meskwaki people. "Soon
I will go to a new home," he said. "You will plant corn where my dead sleep, our towns, the paths
we have made, the flowers we have loved will soon be yours."[1]

The Meskwaki did leave, and the Sauk, the Winnebago, the Potawatomi, the Ioway, and the
Sioux—pushed beyond the boundaries of the Territory (and then the state) of Iowa by a series of
treaties. Some Meskwaki eventually did return and, with the aid of an Iowa statute in 1856, purchased back a tiny part of the land they had inhabited before the displacement.

But others, still, had never left. Buried beneath the rich black earth of Iowa were the remains
of Indian ancestors, some as old as thousands of years. Their presence and their importance
weren't appreciated or perhaps even known by those settlers who rushed onto the Iowa lands after the Black Hawk Purchase in 1832. The riches beneath the soil were less important than the soil
itself. If the mounds were noticed, and were in the way of the plough, they were destroyed. The
artifacts and bones beneath were, at best, curiosities; at worst, obstacles to progress. "You will
plant corn where my dead sleep .... "

But decade gave way to decade and, as Iowans moved toward the Sesquicentennial of statehood, the state's archeological heritage loomed larger in importance. Now laws were enacted and
enforced to protect the historical riches buried deep within the earth.

In 1976, the Iowa legislature passed a law that gave the state archaeologist responsibility for
"investigating, preserving and reinterring discoveries of ancient human remains," defined as remains over 150 years old. Two years later, another law gave the state archaeologist authority "to
deny permission to disinter human remains that the state archaeologist determines have state and
national significance .... " Anyone who intentionally disinterred such remains without the permission of the state archaeologist was deemed guilty of a criminal offense. [2]

In 1994, the case of *Hunziker v. State of Iowa* came before the Iowa Supreme Court. The plaintiffs had purchased land in 1988 for development. In 1991, it was discovered that one of the lots contained a burial mound made between 1,000 and 2,500 years ago by Native Americans of the Woodland Period. The state archaeologist prohibited disinternment of the burial mound and its surroundings. The developers brought a lawsuit to compel the state formally to condemn the property, claiming that the state's action was an unconstitutional "taking" of property without just compensation.

The Iowa Supreme Court disagreed. The statutes restricting the plaintiffs' use "were in existence and therefore part of Iowa's property law" well before the plaintiffs had purchased the land. So, the Court reasoned, "the 'bundle of rights' the plaintiffs acquired by their fee simple title did not include the right to use the land contrary to the provisions [of the ancient human remains statutes]."[3]

Chief Poweshiek is gone, and his people, and the settlers who streamed over the Mississippi River after 1832 to occupy the newly opened Iowa lands. But there remain—protected by law—the substance and spirit of those who found this land first, and who left their mounds as permanent reminders that the earth can be occupied, but never really owned.

Iowa law now protects ancient Indian mounds, such as those pictured here near McGregor, Iowa. (Courtesy, State Historical Society of Iowa, Iowa City)

NOTES

ABBREVIATIONS

AI—Annals of Iowa
IJH—Iowa Journal of History
IJHP—Iowa Journal of History and Politics
IHR—Iowa Historical Record
ILR—Iowa Law Review
ISU—Iowa State University
PAL—The Palimpsest
SHSI—State Historical Society of Iowa

QUOTATIONS IN CHAPTER HEADINGS

Prologue: Chief Poweshiek, "Poweshiek's Oration," Memoirs of M. Etta Cartwright Coxe, SHSI, Manuscript Division, Iowa City.

Chapter One: Territorial Governor Robert Lucas, "Reminiscence," Memoirs of M. Etta Cartwright Coxe, SHSI, Manuscript Division, Iowa City.

Chapter Two: Amelia Bloomer, "Editorial Correspondence," *The Lily*, June 15, 1855, p. 93.

Chapter Three: Inscription on the Iowa stone, 110' level, Washington Monument, Washington, D.C.

Chapter Four: Coger v. The North West. Union Packet Co., 37 Iowa 145, 158 (1873).

Chapter Five: Governor William Larrabee, First Inaugural Address, Jan. 14, 1886, reprinted in Benjamin F. Shambaugh (ed.), *The Messages and Proclamations of the Governors of Iowa* (Iowa City, 1904), vol. VI, p. 29.

Chapter Six: Governor Albert Baird Cummins, Second Inaugural Address, Jan. 14, 1904, reprinted in *Iowa Documents* (Des Moines, 1904), vol. 1, p. 6.

Chapter Seven: Governor William L. Harding, Address to the Iowa State Bar Association, *Proceedings of the Twenty-Fourth Annual Session of the Iowa State Bar Association* (Iowa City, 1918), Session of June 28, 1918, p. 171.

Chapter Eight: Milo Reno, "Is the New Deal a Square Deal?," Radio Broadcast, May 13, 1934, reprinted in Roland A. White, *Milo Reno: Farmers Union Pioneer* (New York, 1975), p. 186.

Chapter Nine: Paul Engle, "For the Iowa Dead," reprinted in *Out Of This World: Poems From the Hawkeye State* (Ames, 1975), p. 55.

Chapter Ten: Hon. Linda K. Neuman, Swearing-in speech, Iowa Supreme Court, Aug. 14, 1986, reprinted in *Des Moines Register*, Aug. 15, 1994, pp. 1, 8A.

Epilogue: Chief Poweshiek, "Poweshiek's Oration," Memoirs of M. Etta Cartwright Coxe, SHSI, Manuscript Division, Iowa City.

ESSAYS: ENDNOTES AND SOURCES

Chapter One: "'To Go Free': The Case of Ralph, a Former Slave" [This essay was first published as Richard Acton, "To Go Free," *Pal* 70 (1989):51]

(1) Bill of Sale, William Montgomery to J.J. Montgomery, certified by Lincoln County, Kentucky Clerk, Nov. 5, 1830; filed Marion County, Missouri Circuit Clerk, Deed Record "B", pp. 151-152, May 21, 1832.

(2) "Address of Judge T.S. Wilson at the Opening of the Supreme Court-room," *IHR* III (1887):457, 460.

(3) Lucius H. Langworthy, "Dubuque: its history, mines, Indian legends, etc." Lecture, Dubuque Literary and Scientific Society, Feb. 26, 1855, reprinted in *IJHP* 8 (1910):366, 417.

(4) Address of Judge T.S. Wilson, *op. cit.*, p. 461.

(5) 1 Bradford 3 (Iowa 1839). The case also appears at 1 Morris 1 (Iowa 1839).

(6) An Ordinance for the Government of the Territory of the United States, Northwest of the River Ohio (1787), art. 6, reprinted in Benjamin F. Shambaugh, *Documentary Material Relating To The History of Iowa* (Iowa City, 1897), vol. I, p. 55.

(7) An Act to Authorize the People of the Missouri Territory to Form a Constitution and State Government, and for the Admission of Such State into the Union on an Equal Footing with the Original States, and to Prohibit Slavery in Certain Territories [hereafter the "Missouri Compromise"] (1820), *U.S. Statutes at Large*, vol. 3, p. 548.

(8) 1 Morris 1, 3 (Iowa 1839).

(9) *Statute Laws of the Territory of Iowa 1838-39* (Dubuque, 1839), p. 69.

(10) Missouri Compromise, proviso to sec. 8.

(11) Supreme Court Order Book, vol. A (1838-53), p. 6 (SHSI, Manuscript Division, Des Moines).

(12) Quotations from the Court's opinion are from 1 Morris at 4-7.

(13) [*Burlington*] *Iowa Patriot*, July 18, 1839.

(14) Address of Judge T.S. Wilson, *op. cit.*, p. 461.

(15) Diary of Richard Bonson, entries of Aug. 16, 1841, Aug. 4, 1842, Oct. 5, 1844, May 8, 1845, July 14, 1845 (typed manuscript, Dubuque County Historical Society, Dubuque).

(16) *Dubuque Daily Times*, July 24, 1870.

(17) *Proceedings of the Grand Lodge of the State of Missouri, Oct. 30, 1845* (St. Louis, 1845), pp. 13-14 (copy located at Masonic Library, Cedar Rapids, Iowa).

(18) For the case of Rachel Bundy *see* William Salter, *Iowa: The First Free State in the Louisiana Purchase* (Chicago, 1905), p. 244. For the case of Jim White *see* J.P. Walton, "Unwritten History of Bloomington (Now Muscatine) in Early Days," *AI* 2d Series, vol. 1 (1882-84):44, 47-49; D.C. Cloud, "A Fugitive Slave Case," (typed manuscript, SHSI, Manuscript Division, Des Moines, CL 6245 Cloud D.C.).

(19) 60 U.S. (19 Howard) 393 (1856).

(20) Quoted in Don E. Fehrenbacher, *The Dred Scott Case: Its Significance in American Law and Politics* (New York, 1978), p. vii.

(21) Hon. John F. Dillon, "Early Iowa Lawyers and Judges," *The American Lawyer* 14 (1906):250, 251.

(22) An Act to Divide the Territory of Wisconsin and to Establish the Territorial Government of Iowa (1838), § 5, reprinted in Benjamin F. Shambaugh, *Documentary Material Relating to the History of Iowa* (Iowa City, 1897), vol I, pp 105-06; An Act to Regulate Blacks and Mulattoes (1839), § 1; An Act Providing for the Establishment of Common Schools (1839), § 1; An Act to Organize, Discipline and Govern the Militia of This Territory (1839), sec. 6; An Act Regulating Practice in the District Courts of the Territory of Iowa (1839), § 38, reprinted in *The Statute Laws of the Territory of Iowa, 1838-39, op. cit.*, pp. 69, 191, 352, 404; An Act Regulating Marriages (1840), § 13, reprinted in *Laws of the Territory of Iowa 1840* (Burlington, 1840), p. 33; An Act for the Relief of the Poor (1842), § 2, reprinted in *Revised Statutes of the Territory of Iowa* (Iowa City, 1843), p. 491.

(23) An Act to Incorporate the City of Du Buque (1840), § 1, reprinted in *Laws of the Territory of Iowa 1840* (Burlington, 1840), p. 124.

(24) Address of Judge T.S. Wilson, *op. cit.*, p. 461.

ADDITIONAL SOURCES: Contemporary Dubuque and Burlington newspaper accounts; Marion County, Missouri Circuit and County Court records; federal censuses; Hon. John F. Dillon, "Early Iowa Lawyers and Judges," *The American Lawyer* 14 (1906):250; Robert R. Dykstra, "Dr. Emerson's Sam: Black Iowans Before the Civil War," *Pal* 63 (1982):66; Robert R. Dykstra, "White Men, Black Laws: Territorial Iowans and Civil Rights, 1838-1843," *AI* 46 (1982):403; Lucius H. Langworthy, "Dubuque: its history, mines, Indian legends, etc." *IJHP* 8 (1910):366; *The History of Dubuque County Iowa* (Chicago, 1880); R.I. Holcombe, *History of Marion County Missouri 1884* (Hannibal, reprint 1979); Frank T. Oldt (ed.), *History of Dubuque County Iowa* (Chicago, 1911); Harrison Anthony Trexler, *Slavery in Missouri, 1804-1865* (Baltimore 1914).

Chapter Two: "A Lawyers' Convention: The Making of the Iowa Constitution of 1857"

(1) William Salter, *The Life of James W. Grimes* (New York, 1876), p. 95.

(2) Benjamin F. Shambaugh (ed.), *Fragments of the Debates of the Iowa Constitutional Conventions of 1844 and 1846* (Iowa City, 1900), p. 349.

(3) Benjamin F. Shambaugh (ed.), *The Messages and Proclamations of the Governors of Iowa* (Iowa City, 1903), vol.I, p. 446.

(4) *Ibid.*, p. 477.

(5) Salter, *op. cit.*, p. 34.

(6) Salter, *op. cit.*, p. 35.

(7) W. Blair Lord (ed.), *The Debates of the Constitutional Convention of the State of Iowa, Assembled at Iowa City, Monday, January 19, 1857*, (Davenport, 1857), vol. II, p. 1031.

(8) *Ibid.*, vol. I, p. 8.

(9) *Ibid.*

(10) *Ibid.*, vol. I, p. 12.

(11) *Ibid.*, vol. I, p. 13.

(12) *Ibid.*, vol. I, p. 115.

(13) *Ibid.*, vol. II, p. 648.

(14) *Ibid.*, vol. I, p. 350.

(15) *Ibid.*, vol. I, p. 349.

(16) *Ibid.*, vol. I, p. 390.

(17) *Ibid.*, vol. I, p. 346.

(18) *Ibid.*, vol. I, p. 355.

(19) Benjamin F. Shambaugh, *The Constitutions of Iowa* (Iowa City, 1934), pp. 235-36.

(20) Lord, *Debates, op. cit.*, vol. I, p. 173.

(21) *Ibid.*, vol. II, p. 651.

(22) *Ibid.*, vol. I, p. 172.

(23) *Ibid.*, vol. II, p. 825.

(24) *Ibid.*, vol. I, p. 641.

(25) Salter, *op. cit.*, p. 34.

(26) Lord, *Debates, op. cit.*, vol. I, pp. 450, 454.

(27) *Ibid.*, vol. I, p. 452.

(28) *Ibid.*

(29) Shambaugh, *Messages, op. cit.*, vol. II, pp. 37-38.

(30) Lord, *Debates, op. cit.*, vol. I, p. 267.

(31) *Ibid.*, vol. II, p. 805.

(32) *Ibid.*

(33) *Ibid.*, vol. II, pp. 923, 926.

(34) *Ibid.*, vol. II, p. 931.

(35) *Ibid.*, vol. II, p. 925.

(36) Shambaugh, *Fragments, op. cit.* p. 358.

(37) Lord, *Debates, op. cit.*, vol. II, p. 1052.

(38) "Letters of James W. Grimes," *AI* 3rd Series, vol. XXII (1940-41):469, 477.

(39) Letter from John Edwards to William Penn Clark, May 17-18, 1857, reprinted in Robert R. Dykstra, *Bright Radical Star: Black Freedom and White Supremacy on the Hawkeye Frontier* (Cambridge, London, 1993), p. 172.

(40) [*McGregor*] *North Iowa Times*, July 24, 1857, quoted in Mildred Throne (ed.), "Contemporary Editorial Opinion of the 1857 Constitution," *IJH* 45 (1957):115, 119.

(41) [*Davenport*] *Daily Iowa State Democrat*, Aug. 31, 1857, reprinted in Erling A. Erickson, *Banking In Frontier Iowa 1836-1865* (Ames, 1971), p. 90.

(42) [*Davenport*] *Daily Gazette*, July 22, 1857.

(43) Salter, *op. cit.*, p. 95.

ADDITIONAL SOURCES: [*Burlington*] *Daily State Gazette*, June 10, 11, 17, 1857; "The Constitutional Convention of 1857," *IHR* XII (1896):481; John E. Briggs, "A History of the Constitution of Iowa," *Iowa Code Annotated* (St. Paul, 1949), vol. 1, p. 1; Erik McKinley Eriksson, "The Framers of the Constitution of 1857," *IJHP* 22 (1924):52; Emlin McClain, "The Constitutional Convention and the Issues Before It," reprinted in Benjamin F. Shambaugh (ed.), *Proceedings of the Fiftieth Anniversary of the Constitutions of Iowa* (Iowa City, 1907), p. 155; Russell M. Ross, "The Development of the Iowa Constitution of 1857," *IJH* 55 (1957):97; Mildred Throne (ed.), "Contemporary Editorial Opinion of the 1857 Constitution," *IJH* 55 (1957):115; Eli C. Christoferson, *The Life of James W. Grimes*, (Univ. of Iowa Doctoral Thesis, 1924, SHSI, Iowa City); Robert R. Dykstra, *Bright Radical Star: Black Freedom and White Supremacy on the Hawkeye Frontier* (Cambridge, London, 1993); Erling A. Erickson, *Banking in Frontier Iowa 1836-1865* (Ames, 1971); Herbert S. Fairall, *The Iowa City Republican Manual of Iowa Politics 1881* (Iowa City, 1881); Morton M. Rosenberg, *Iowa On the Eve of the Civil War: A Decade of Frontier Politics* (Norman, 1972); Edward H. Stiles, *Recollections and Sketches of Notable Lawyers and Public Men of Early Iowa* (Des Moines, 1916).

Chapter Three: "Iowa and Southern Secession: The Story of Barclay Coppoc" [This essay was adapted in part from Richard Acton, "The Story of Ann Raley: Mother of the Coppoc Boys," *Pal* 72 (1991):20]

(1) Declaration of Causes Which Induced the Secession of South Carolina, reprinted in Frank Moore (ed.) *The Rebellion Record* (New York: 186?), vol. I, p. 4 (emphasis added).

(2) *William Wade Hinshaw Index to (Iowa) Quaker Meeting Records*, Springdale Monthly Meeting, p. 33 (Microfilm, SHSI, Iowa City).

(3) Ralph Keeler, "Owen Brown's Escape From Harper's Ferry," *Atlantic Monthly* 33 (1874):342, 345.

(4) *Ibid.*, p. 357.

(5) *Ibid.*, p. 362.

(6) Letter from William McCormick of Muscatine, Iowa to Governor Wise of Virginia, Dec. 23, 1859, quoted in C.B. Galbreath, "Barclay Coppoc," *Ohio Archaeological and Historical Quarterly* 30 (1921):459, 469.

(7) Letter from Ann L. Raley to James Whinnery, Jan. 22, 1860, quoted in *ibid.*, p. 469.

(8) *Hinshaw Index, op. cit.*, p. 33.

(9) First Inaugural Message, Jan. 11, 1860, reprinted in Benjamin F. Shambaugh (ed.), *The Messages and Proclamations of the Governors of Iowa* (Iowa City, 1903), vol. II, p. 241.

(10) Message to the House of Representatives, March 3, 1860, reprinted in *ibid.*, p. 383.

(11) Benjamin F. Gue, "John Brown and His Iowa Friends," *Midland Monthly* 7 (1897):274.

(12) *Muscatine Daily Journal*, Feb. 20, 1860; *Chicago Press and Tribune*, Feb. 17, 1860.

(13) "Governor John Letcher's Communication Relative to the Refusal of the Governor of Iowa to Surrender a Fugitive From Justice," Feb. 13, 1860, reprinted in Shambaugh, *Messages, op. cit.*, vol. II, pp. 397, 400, 401 (emphasis added).

(14) L.R. Witherell, "'Old John Brown': Incidents, Sketches and Relics of Freedom's Hero and His Martyr Band," ch. XIX, "Barclay Coppoc," *serialized in Davenport Gazette*, Feb. 2, 1878.

(15) *Muscatine Daily Journal*, March 23, 1860.

(16) *Ibid.*, April 6, 1860.

(17) Richard J. Hinton, *John Brown and His Men With Some Account of the Roads They Traveled to Reach Harper's Ferry* (New York, rev. ed. 1894), p. 555.

(18) Quoted in Edward Stone, *Incident At Harper's Ferry* (Englewood Cliffs, 1956), p. 164 (emphasis added).

(19) Declaration of Causes, *op. cit.*

ADDITIONAL SOURCES: Contemporary Davenport, Des Moines, Iowa City, Muscatine, Tipton, Chicago, New York, and Richmond, Virginia newspaper accounts; Undated affidavit of Jont Maxson, E.R. Harlan Correspondence, Accessions File 36A Portraits Part 2 1909, SHSI, Des Moines; Undated letter of the Deputy Clerk, Court of Common Pleas, Columbiana County, Ohio, Probate Division, to the author; *U.S. Senate Committee Reports*, 36th Cong, 1st Sess., Rep. Com. No. 278 (1859-60), sec. II; Richard Acton, "An Iowan's Death at Harpers Ferry," *Pal* 70 (1989):186; C.B. Galbreath, "Edwin Coppoc," 30 *Ohio Archaeological and Historical Quarterly* (1921):397; Ransom L. Harris, "John Brown and His Followers in Iowa," *Midland Monthly* 2 (1894):267; Frederick Lloyd, "John Brown Among the Pedee Quakers," *AI* 1st ser., vol. 4 (1866):665; Thomas Teakle, "The Rendition of Barclay Coppoc," *IJHP* 10 (1912):503; L.R. Witherell, "'Old John Brown' etc.," ch. XVIII, "Edwin Coppoc," serialized in *Davenport Gazette*, Jan. 26, 1878, *William Wade Hinshaw Index to (Iowa) Quaker Meeting Records*, Salem (Iowa) Monthly Meeting, pp. 36, 147 (Microfilm, SHSI, Iowa City); *Ibid.*, Upper Springfield Monthly Meeting, pp. 977, 943; *The Life, Trial and Execution of Captain John Brown* (New York: 1859); C. Ray Aurner (ed.), *A Topical History of Cedar County* (Chicago, 1910) vol. 1; Louis Thomas Jones, *The Quakers of Iowa* (Iowa City, 1914); Stephen B. Oates, *To Purge This Land With Blood* (New York, 1970); Irving B. Richman, *John Brown Among the Quakers, and Other Sketches* (Des Moines, 1894); Oswald Garrison Villard, *John Brown, 1800-1859: A Biography Fifty Years After* (New York, reissue 1943).

Chapter Four: "The Death Penalty in Early Iowa: Abolition and Restoration, 1872-1878" [This essay is a shortened version of Richard Acton, "The Magic of Undiscouraged Effort: The Death Penalty in Early Iowa, 1838-1878," *AI* 50 (1991):721]

(1) An Act Defining Crimes and Punishments, §§ 1, 2, 101, reprinted in *The Statute Laws of the Territory of Iowa, 1838-39*, pp. 150, 151, 180.

(2) *Code of 1851*, §§ 2565, 2569-70.

(3) *Daily Iowa State Register*, April 3, 1872.

(4) *Ibid*. The Iowa press apparently forgot about the 1865 execution of Benjamin McComb at Ottumwa.

(5) *Daily Iowa State Register*, March 19, 1872.

(6) *Ibid.*, March 29, 1872.

(7) Cyrus Clay Carpenter diary (entry of April 4, 1872), Carpenter papers, SHSI, Manuscript Division, Iowa City.

(8) *Daily State Leader*, April 5, 1872.

(9) *Daily Iowa State Register*, April 5, 1872.

(10) *[Iowa City] Press*, April 8, 1872.

(11) *Daily State Leader*, April 5, 1872.

(12) *Dubuque Herald*, April 10, 1872.

(13) *Dubuque Times*, April 13, 1872.

(14) *Muscatine Journal*, April 11, 1872.

(15) *Dubuque Times*, April 16, 1872.

(16) *Muscatine Journal*, April 11, 1872.

(17) *Ibid*.

(18) *Ibid*.

(19) *Keokuk Constitution*, April 23, 1872.

(20) *Iowa Daily State Register*, Dec. 15, 1874.

(21) *Keokuk Constitution*, quoted in *Iowa Daily State Register*, Dec. 17, 1874.

(22) *Warren County Record*, Dec. 24, 1874.

(23) *Report of the First Annual Meeting of the Iowa State Bar Association* (Davenport, 1895), Session of June 27, 1895, p. 59 (Statement by Iowa Supreme Court Judge Josiah Given).

(24) *Ottumwa Daily Courier*, June 30, 1875; *Ottumwa Democrat*, June 30, 1875.

(25) *Iowa Daily State Register*, Jan. 29, 1876.

(26) *Dubuque Times*, Jan. 21, 1876.

(27) *Davenport Gazette*, Jan. 24, 1876.

(28) *Iowa State Register*, Feb. 27, 1876.

(29) *Dubuque Times*, Feb. 26, 1876; *Iowa State Register*, Feb. 26, 1876.

(30) *Muscatine Journal*, Feb. 28, 1876.

(31) *Webster County Gazette*, Nov. 30, 1877.

(32) *Iowa State Register*, Nov. 20, 1877.

(33) *Iowa State Leader*, Feb. 28, 1878.

(34) *Ibid.*, Feb. 27, 1878.

(35) *Ibid*.

(36) *Iowa State Register*, March 2, 1878.

(37) *Ibid.*, Feb. 28, 1878.

(38) *Ibid.*, March 9, 1878.

(39) *Iowa State Leader*, March 9, 1878.

(40) *Daily Iowa State Register*, April 21, 1872.

(41) *Iowa State Register*, March 27, 1878.

(42) John Irish, quoted in *[Iowa City] Press*, April 8, 1872.

ADDITIONAL SOURCES: *State v. Stanley*, 32 Iowa 532 (1871); An Act in Relation to Capital Punishment, and Regulating Pardons, ch. 242, *Laws of Iowa 1872*, p. 139; An Act to Restore Capital Punishment, ch. 165, *Laws of Iowa 1878*, pp. 150-51; contemporary reports from approximately fifty newspapers from all parts of the state; Elwood R. McIntyre, "A Farmer Halts the Hangman: The Story of Marvin Bovee," *Wisconsin Magazine of History* 42 (1958-59):3; Leland L. Sage, "The Clarksons of Indiana and Iowa," *Indiana Magazine of History* 50 (1954):429; *Des Moines Bulletin Legislative Supplement* No. 49 (Des Moines, 1870), March 11, 1870, House; *ibid*. No. 43, March 28, 1870, Senate; *Iowa House Journal 1850-51*; *ibid., 1870, 1872, 1873, 1874, 1876, 1878*; *Iowa Senate Journal 1850-51; ibid., 1870, 1872, 1873, 1874, 1876, 1878*; *History of Polk County, Iowa* (Des Moines, 1880); Eric F. Goldman, *Rendezvous With Destiny: A History of Modern American Reform* (New York, 1953); Philip English Mackey, *Voices Against Death: American Opposition to Capital Punishment 1787-1975* (New York, 1976); W.O. Payne, *The History of Story County, Iowa* (Chicago, 1911), vol. 1.

Chapter Four: "Judge Wright's Vision: The Founding of Iowa's First Law School" [This essay was first published as Richard, Lord Acton, "Justice Wright's Law School," *The Iowan* vol. 40, no. 2 (1991):8]

(1) George G. Wright, "Judge Wright and His Contemporaries," *Sixtieth Anniversary Celebration of the College of Law 1865-1925, Bulletin of the State University of Iowa* No. 372 (Oct. 9, 1926):40.

(2) "George Grover Wright," *IHR* XII (1896):433, 443.

(3) Millard Winchester Hansen, "The Early History of the College of Law, State University of Iowa 1865-1884," *ILR* 30 (1944-45):31, 38.

(4) *Daily State Register*, Dec. 6, 1866.

(5) *[Iowa City] State Democratic Press*, Sept. 30, 1868.

(6) "William G. Hammond," *IHR* X (1894):97, 105.

(7) W.W. Baldwin, "The Beginnings of the Iowa Law School," *Sixtieth Anniversary Celebration, op. cit.*, p. 23.

(8) "The Law Department of the Iowa State University," *The Western Jurist* 2 (Dec. 1868):325, 334.

(9) *The University Reporter*, June 1869, p. 36.

(10) *Ibid.*, Nov. 15, 1875, p. 22.

(11) *Ibid.*, Dec. 15, 1875, p. 33.

(12) *William G. Hammond's Records Iowa Law School*, p. 203, Univ. of Iowa Law Library, Manuscript Division, Iowa City.

(13) *Muscatine Weekly Journal*, June 27, 1884.

(14) *The Vidette-Reporter*, Oct. 20, 1883, p. 5.

ADDITIONAL SOURCES: Contemporary Iowa City, Des

Moines, Anamosa, Muscatine and University newspaper accounts; "The Origin of the Law College of the State University of Iowa—Two Communications From John P. Irish," *IJHP* 8 (1910):553; "Dicta From the Dean—Iowa Law School 125 Years Young," *Iowa Advocate* (Fall-Winter 1989-90):3; Marilyn Jackson, "Alexander Clark: A Rediscovered Black Leader," *The Iowan,* vol. 23, no. 3 (1975):43; Emlin McClain, "Law Department of the State University of Iowa," *The Green Bag* I (1889):374; Helen S. Moylan, "A Manuscript Record of the Early Days of the Iowa Law School," *ILR* 22 (1936-37):108; Teresa Opheim, "Portias of the Prairie: Early Women Graduates of the University Law Department," *Pal* 67 (1986):28; Rollin M. Perkins, "The Story of the Iowa Law School," *ILR* XV (1929-30):257; *History of the Law Department," Year Book of the Law Department of Iowa State University for 1877-8* (Iowa City, 1878); *Catalogue of the Iowa State University at Iowa City for 1868-9* (Des Moines, 1869); *Pioneer Law-Makers Association of Iowa: Reunions of 1886 and 1890* (Des Moines, 1890); *Proceedings of the Iowa State Bar Association Held at Des Moines, Iowa 1874-1881* (Iowa State Bar Assoc., 1912); Edward H. Stiles, *Recollections and Sketches of Notable Lawyers and Public Men of Early Iowa* (Des Moines, 1916).

Chapter Five: "Hans Reimer Claussen: The Story of an Immigrant Lawyer" [A version of this essay was first published as Richard, Lord Acton, "A Remarkable Immigrant: The Story of Hans Reimer Claussen," *Pal* 75 (1994):87]

(1) Charles August Ficke, *Memories of Fourscore Years* (Davenport, 1930), pp. 189-90.

(2) Letter from Wilhelm Fisher, quoted in *ibid.*, pp. 6-7.

(3) Hildegard Binder Johnson, "German Forty-Eighters in Davenport," *IJHP* 44 (1946):3, 17.

(4) Thomas P. Christensen, "A German Forty-Eighter in Iowa," *AI* 3rd Series, vol. 26 (1945):245, 252.

(5) Edward H. Stiles, *Recollections and Sketches of Notable Lawyers and Public Men of Early Iowa* (Des Moines, 1916), p. 753.

(6) Letter of Claussen to Sen. James Harlan, March 31, 1860, quoted in F.I. Herriott, "The Conference of German-Republicans In The Deutsches Haus, Chicago May 14-15, 1860," *Transactions of the Illinois State Historical Society* 35 (1928):101, 143.

(7) *Davenport Gazette*, Feb. 3, 1872.

(8) *Revision of 1860*, §§ 4392-93.

(9) *Iowa Senate Journal 1870*, pp. 343-45.

(10) Geebrick v. State of Iowa, 5 Clarke 491 (Iowa 1858).

(11) State v. Weir, 33 Iowa 134 (1871).

(12) *Des Moines Bulletin Legislative Supplement* No. 45 (Des Moines, 1870), Friday April 1, 1870, Senate.

(13) *Davenport Gazette*, May 2, 1871; *Davenport Democrat*, May 2, 1871.

(14) *Davenport Gazette*, Jan. 30, 1872.

(15) *Daily Iowa State Register*, March 30, 1872.

(16) Ficke, *op. cit.*, pp. 168-69.

(17) *Davenport Gazette*, Feb. 2, 1873.

(18) *Ibid.*, Jan. 29, 1879.

(19) *Ibid.*, May 11, 1882.

(20) *Davenport Democrat*, Aug. 1, 1882.

(21) "Hon. Hans R. Claussen," *Biographical History and Portrait Gallery of Scott County, Iowa* (Chicago & New York, 1895), pp. 230, 237. The Iowa Supreme Court decision holding that the prohibition amendment was not constitutionally enacted was Koehler & Lange v. Hill, 60 Iowa 543 (1883).

(22) *Davenport Democrat*, March 15, 1894.

(23) *Ibid.*

ADDITIONAL SOURCES: Contemporary Davenport, Des Moines, Dubuque and Schleswig-Holstein newspaper accounts; "Hans Reimer Claussen," *The Western Life-Boat* 1 (1873):56; Dan Elbert Clark, "History of Liquor Legislation in Iowa 1861-1878," *IJHP* 6 (1908):339; F.I. Herriott, "Iowa and the First Nomination of Abraham Lincoln," *AI* 3rd Series, vol. VIII (1907-08):186; F.I. Herriott, "A Forceful Influence," in Harry E. Downer, *Davenport and Scott County, Iowa* (Chicago, 1910), vol. 1, p. 839; Hildegard Binder Johnson, "Hans Reimer Claussen," *The American-German Review,* vol. X, no. 5 (1944):30; Hildegard Binder Johnson, "List of Lectures and Debates Given Before the Davenport Turngemeinde," *IJHP* 44 (1946):54; Joachim Reppmann, "The Concept of Liberty and Idea of Democracy of the Schleswig-Holstein 'Forty Eighters' in the U.S.A." (unpublished essay); Augustus P. Richter, "A True History of Scott County," serialized in *Davenport Democrat and Leader* (Sundays, 1920-22); Theodore Schreiber, "Early German Pioneers of Scott County, Iowa," *American-German Review*, vol. VIII, no. 2 (1941):20; *Iowa Senate Journal 1870; ibid., 1872, 1873; Code of Iowa 1873; The United States Biographical Dictionary, Iowa Volume* (Chicago, 1878); *The History of the First National Bank in the United States* (Chicago, 1913); *History of Scott County, Iowa* (Chicago, 1882); W. Carr, *Schleswig-Holstein 1815-1848* (Manchester, 1963); Carl N. Degler, *At Odds: Women and Family in America From the Revolution to the Present* (New York, 1989); Joseph Eiboeck, *Die Deutschen von Iowa und deren Errungenschaften* (Des Moines, 1900); Frank Eyck, *The Frankfurt Parliament 1848-49* (New York, 1968); Louise R. Noun, *Strong-Minded Women: The Emergence of the Woman-Suffrage Movement in Iowa* (Ames, 1969); Carl Wittke, *Refugees of Revolution: The German Forty-Eighters in America* (Philadelphia, 1952).

Chapter Five: "The Legendary Jones County Calf Case"

(1) Charles E. Wheeler, "The Jones County Calf Case," *in Proceedings of the Twenty-Sixth Annual Session of the Iowa State Bar Association* (Iowa City, 1920), Session of June 24, 1920, pp. 141, 142.

(2) Johnson v. Miller, 63 Iowa 529, 531 (1884).

(3) Wheeler, *op. cit.*, p. 150.

(4) *Ibid.*, p. 153.

(5) Johnson v. Miller, 63 Iowa 529, 533 (1884)

(6) Johnson v. Miller, 63 Iowa 529 (1884).

(7) Johnson v. Miller, 69 Iowa 562, 574 (1886).

(8) Johnson v. Miller, 69 Iowa 562 (1886).

(9) Johnson v. Miller, 82 Iowa 693 (1891).

(10) Johnson v. Miller, 93 Iowa 165 (1894).

(11) *History of Jones County, Iowa Past and Present* (Chicago, 1910), vol. I, p. 218.

(12) Wheeler, *op. cit.*, p. 152.

ADDITIONAL SOURCES: Contemporary newspaper reports in the *Anamosa Eureka, Iowa State Register*, and *Des Moines Register & Leader*; Records of the Clerk, Jones County District Court, Appearance Docket District Court B., pp. 265, 281, District Court Record F., p. 521, District Court Record G., p. 226, Judgment Index C.C., index pp. "F" (Foreman), "J" (Johnson); Jasper H. Ramsey, "Jones County Calf Case," *Pal* XXXIII (1952):369; J.A. Swisher, "The Jones County Calf Case," *Pal* VII (1926):197; Bertha Finn, "The Jones County Calf Case: Forward," *Anamosa 1838-1988 ... A Reminiscence* (Monticello, 1988), pp. 151-52; Mary Shanney, "A Man's Character Restored," *ibid.*, pp. 152-54.

Chapter Six: "The Cherry Sisters: A Case of Libel"

(1) Effie Cherry, unpublished memoirs, final version, p. 7, Rennie Collection, MS 178, box #3, folder #3, SHSI, Manuscript Division, Iowa City (hereafter "Rennie Collection").

(2) Winnifred Van Etten, "The Queens of Corn," unpublished biography, p. 47, Rennie Collection, box #4, folder #1.

(3) *Cedar Rapids Gazette*, Feb. 22, 1893.

(4) *Ibid.*, March 15, 1893.

(5) *Dubuque Herald*, May 18, 1893, quoted in Van Etten, *op. cit.*, pp. 5-6.

(6) *Center Point Tribune* and *Marion Sentinel* (undated), quoted in Van Etten, *op. cit.*, p. 80.

(7) Unnamed newspaper, quoted in Van Etten, *op. cit.*, p. 81.

(8) Van Etten, *op. cit.*, p. 95.

(9) *New York Times*, Nov. 17, 1896.

(10) Van Etten, *op. cit.*, chap. vii, p. 11.

(11) *Odebolt Chronicle*, Feb. 17, 1898 (reprinted in *Des Moines Leader*, Feb. 23, 1898).

(12) Addie Cherry v. Des Moines Leader et al., Petition, *Abstracts and Arguments*, Supreme Court of Iowa, Jan. Term 1901, Des Moines, p. 288 (hereafter "*Abstracts and Arguments*").

(13) *Ibid.*, p. 290.

(14) *Des Moines Daily News*, April 20, 1899.

(15) *Abstracts and Arguments*, Plaintiff's Evidence, pp. 290-96; Effie Cherry, p. 296; Jessie Cherry, pp. 296-97; Defendant's Evidence, William E. Hamilton, pp. 297-99.

(16) *Des Moines Leader*, April 21, 1899.

(17) Cherry v. Des Moines Leader, 114 Iowa 298, 300-01 (1901).

(18) *Ibid.*, p. 304.

(19) *Ibid.*, p. 305.

(20) Robert H. Phelps & E. Douglas Hamilton, *Libel: Rights, Risks, Responsibilities* (New York, 1978), p. 213.

(21) *New York Times*, Aug. 7, 1944.

ADDITIONAL SOURCES: Orville and Jane Rennie Collection: Personal papers of the Cherry sisters with material related to their lives and careers, SHSI, Manuscript Division, Iowa City [Boxes ##1-5 containing correspondence, diaries, flyers, press clippings, Effie Cherry unpublished memoirs, and miscellaneous papers]; contemporary newspaper reports in the *Odebolt Chronicle, Des Moines Daily News, Des Moines Leader, Des Moines Weekly Leader*; Winnifred Van Etten, "The Queens of Corn," unpublished biography of the Cherry sisters, Rennie Collection, box #4, folders ##1-2; Addie Cherry v. Des Moines Leader et al., *Abstracts and Arguments*, Supreme Court of Iowa, Jan. Term 1901, Des Moines, pp. 287-329 (district court record).

Chapter Seven: "Governor Harding's Proclamation and the School Language Law, 1918-1923"

(1) *Des Moines Capital*, June 20, 1917.

(2) *Ibid.*, Aug. 9, 1917.

(3) *Ibid.*, Sept. 10, 1917.

(4) *Ibid.*, Nov. 24, 1917.

(5) *Ibid.*, Dec. 24, 1917.

(6) *Ibid.*, Jan. 14, 1918.

(7) *Washington Post*, April 4, 1918; *New York Times*, April 4, 1918; *Des Moines Register*, April 4, 1918.

(8) *Washington Post*, April 5, 1918; *Des Moines Register*, April 5, 1918.

(9) *Des Moines Capital*, April 25, 1918.

(10) Nancy Ruth Derr, *Iowans During World War I: A Study of Change Under Stress* (Ph.D. Dissertation, May 1979, SHSI, Iowa City), vol. 2, p. 396.

(11) "Language Proclamation," Benjamin F. Shambaugh (ed.), *Iowa and War: War Proclamations By Governor Harding* (Iowa City, July 1918), no. 13, pp. 43-46.

(12) Letter of Jos Mekota to Governor Harding, May 27, 1918, File #136, Council of Defense Gov. W.L. Harding Administration, County Organization Linn, Foreign Language Proclamation (SHSI, Des Moines).

(13) *Cedar Rapids Gazette*, May 30, 1918.

(14) *Council Bluffs Nonpareil*, May 31, 1918.

(15) *Des Moines Register*, May 31, 1918.

(16) *Des Moines Capital*, May 31, 1918.

(17) *Waterloo Times Tribune*, June 23, 1918.

(18) *Ibid.*

(19) State Council of National Defense Circular Letter, June 13, 1918, File #370, Council of Defense Gov. W.L. Harding Administration, Other States, Foreign Language Misc. 4-15-18 to 6-27-18 (SHSI, Des Moines).

(20) *Davenport Democrat and Leader*, June 14, 1918.

(21) *Marshalltown Times-Republican*, July 5, 1918.

(22) File #109, Council of Defense Gov. W.L. Harding Administration, County Organization Dickinson, Foreign Language Proclamation (SHSI, Des Moines).

(23) *Waverly Independent Republican*, June 21, 1918.

(24) Letter of Rev. P. Blaufuss to Governor Harding, July 15, 1918, File #88, Council of Defense Gov. W.L. Harding Administration, County Organization Bremer, Foreign Language Proclamation (SHSI, Des Moines).

(25) Letter of Rev. P. Blaufuss to Gov. Harding, Aug. 3, 1918, in *ibid.*

(26) Letter of Rev. P. Blaufuss to Gov. Harding, Aug. 15, 1918, in *ibid.*

(27) Copy letter of Gov. Harding to Rev. P. Blaufuss, Aug. 20, 1918, in *ibid.*

(28) Letter of Rev. P. Blaufuss to Gov. Harding, Sept. 24, 1918, in *ibid.*

(29) State Council of Defense Circular Letter, Aug. 2, 1918, File #39, Council of Defense Gov. W.L. Harding Administration, Bulletins, State Gov. & Metcalf H.J. (SHSI, Des Moines).

(30) *Sac Sun*, July 11, 1918.

(31) *Des Moines Tribune,* Nov. 11, 1918, quoted in John E. Visser, *William Lloyd Harding and the Republican Party in Iowa, 1906-1920* (Ph.D. Dissertation, Feb. 1957, Univ. of Iowa Library), vol. 1, p. 245.

(32) *Iowa Senate Journal 1919*, pp. 87-88.

(33) *Des Moines Register*, Jan. 17, 1919.

(34) *The Lutheran Witness*, March 18, 1919, vol. XXXVIII, p. 88; *Des Moines Capital*, March 12, 1919.

(35) *Ibid. See* Acts 38th G.A., 1919, ch. 198.

(36) *Proceedings Iowa District Missouri Lutheran Synod*, No. 25-34 (1915-1930), vol. III, p. 287 (District Archives, Iowa East District, Cedar Rapids).

(37) Letter of Rev. August Bartels to John Kimberly, June 3, 1918, File #88, Council of Defense Gov. W.L. Harding Administration, County Organization Bremer, Foreign Language Proclamation (SHSI, Des Moines).

(38) State of Iowa v. Bartels, 191 Iowa 1060, 1072 (1919).

(39) Meyer v. Nebraska, 262 U.S. 390 (1923).

(40) *Ibid.*, p. 400-01.

(41) Bartels v. Iowa, 262 U.S. 404 (1923).

(42) *Ibid.*, p. 412 (Holmes, J., dissenting).

(43) *Lutheran Herald*, June 23, 1923.

(44) Letter of Rev. August Bartels to John Kimberly, *op. cit.*

ADDITIONAL SOURCES: Contemporary reports in Cedar Rapids, Charles City, Council Bluffs, Decorah, Des Moines, Fort Dodge, Iowa City, Ottumwa, Sac City, Sioux City, Story City, Waterloo, Waverly, and Webster City newspapers, and in the *Chicago Tribune, Des Moines Capital, Lutheran Herald, Lutheran Witness,* and *New York Times*; Czech letters and telegrams in File #136, Council of Defense Gov. W.L. Harding Administration, County Organization Linn, Foreign Language Proclamation (SHSI, Des Moines); State Council of National Defense Circular Letter, June 13, 1918, File #370, *ibid.*, Other States; Letter from Pres. of Norwegian Lutheran Church of Am. to Gov. Harding, Aug. 24, 1918, *ibid.*, Other States; Letter from "An American Patriot" of Williamsburg to Gov. Harding, July 11, 1918, File #127, *ibid.*, County Organization Iowa; Letter of J.P. Conner to Gov. Harding, June 19, 1918, File #103, *ibid.*, County Organization Crawford; Letter from Earl R. Ferguson to Gov. Harding, Aug. 7, 1918, File #152, *ibid.*, County Organization Page; Report of H.V. Yackey to Gov. Harding, Aug. 19, 1918, File #139, *ibid.*, County Organization Lyon; Blaufuss-Harding Correspondence, June 4, 1918 to Sept. 24, 1918, File #88, *ibid.*, County Organization Bremer; "Notable Deaths", *AI* 3rd Series, vol. 15 (1925-1927):631; "Emil Henry Rausch," *AI* 3rd Series, vol. 21 (1937-39):560; "The Transition from German to English in the Missouri Synod from 1910 to 1947," *Concordia Historical Institute Quarterly*, XXII, No. 3 (1949):97; *Proceedings of the Twenty-Fourth Annual Session of the Iowa State Bar Association* (Iowa City, 1918); *Iowa House Journal 1919*; *Iowa Senate Journal 1919*; *Proceedings Iowa District Missouri Lutheran Synod* (1915-1930), vol. III (located at District Archives, Iowa East District, Cedar Rapids); Charles August Ficke, *Memories of Fourscore Years* (Davenport, 1930); Frederick C. Luebke, *Bonds of Loyalty: German-Americans and World War I* (De Kalb, 1974); Nathaniel R. Whitney, *The Sale of War Bonds in Iowa* (Iowa City, 1923).

Chapter Eight: "Judge Bradley Upholds His Oath of Office"

(1) *Des Moines Register*, Jan. 5, 1933.

(2) George Mills, "Comment," *AI* 3d Series, vol. 47 (1983):128, 130.

(3) Acts of the Forty-Fifth General Assembly, 1933, chs. 179, 182.

(4) Curtis Harnack, *We Have All Gone Away* (New York, 1973), p. 133.

(5) John L. Shover, *Cornbelt Rebellion: The Farmers' Holiday Association* (Urbana, 1965), p. 116.

(6) *Des Moines Register*, June 6, 1933.

(7) *Sioux City Tribune*, April 28, 1933.

(8) *Des Moines Register*, April 28, 1933.

(9) *Ibid.,* April 29, 1933.

(10) *Le Mars Sentinel*, May 2, 1933.

(11) *Des Moines Register*, April 28, 1933.

(12) George Mills, *op. cit.*, p. 131.

(13) *Sioux City Tribune*, April 28, 1933. Accounts of the incident differ in some of the details. The account given here represents the most consistent order of events gleaned from several contemporary newspaper reports and Judge Bradley's own statement given during the trial of A.A. Mitchell, reported in the *Le Mars Globe-Post*, July 20, 1933 and the *Le Mars Sentinel*, July 21, 1933.

(14) *Sioux City Journal*, April 29, 1933.

(15) *Des Moines Register*, April 29, 1933.

(16) *Le Mars Globe-Post*, July 20, 1933; *Le Mars Sentinel*, July 21, 1933.

(17) *Le Mars Globe-Post*, July 20, 1933.

(18) *Des Moines Register*, April 29, 1933.

ADDITIONAL SOURCES: Contemporary reports in the *Le Mars Sentinel, Le Mars Globe-Post, Sioux City Tribune, Sioux City Journal, Council Bluffs Nonpareil, Des Moines Register, Des Moines Tribune, Chicago Tribune, New York Times*; Patrick B. Bauer, "Farm Mortgagor Relief Legislation in Iowa During the Great Depression," *AI* 3d Series, vol. 50 (1989):23; Frank D. DiLeva, "Attempt To Hang An Iowa Judge," *AI* 3d Series, vol. 32 (1954):337; Rodney D. Karr, "Farmer Rebels In Plymouth County, Iowa, 1932-1933," *AI* 3d Series, vol. 47 (1985):637; Joseph F. Wall, "The Iowa Farmer in Crisis 1920-1936," *AI* 3d Series, vol. 47 (1983):116; Milton S. Eisenhower (ed.), *United States Department of Agriculture Yearbook of Agriculture 1935* (Washington, 1935); John L. Shover, *Cornbelt Rebellion: The Farmers' Association* (Urbana, 1965).

Chapter Eight: "'Enough Blood and Hell': Bonnie and Clyde in Iowa" [This essay was first published as Richard, Lord Acton, "'Hell' in Dexfield Park," *The Iowan*, vol. 42, no.3 (1994):14]

(1) Bonnie Parker, "The Story of Bonnie and Clyde," reprinted in John Treherne, *The Strange History of Bonnie and Clyde* (New York, 1985), pp. 192, 194.

(2) W.D. Jones, "Riding With Bonnie and Clyde," *Playboy* (Nov. 1968):151, 165.

(3) Jan I. Fortune (ed.), *The True Story of Bonnie and Clyde As Told by Bonnie's Mother and Clyde's Sister* (New York, 1968), p. 78.

(4) W.D. Jones, *op. cit.*, p. 165.

(5) *Stuart Herald*, July 28, 1933.

(6) *Des Moines Register*, July 25, 1933.

(7) *Ibid.*

(8) *Dexter Sentinel*, July 28, 1933, reprinted in *Dexfield Review Sentinel*, Oct. 5, 1967.

(9) *Des Moines Register*, July 25, 1933.

(10) *Perry Daily Chief*, July 25, 1933.

(11) W.D. Jones, *op. cit.*, p. 165.

ADDITIONAL SOURCES: W.D. Jones Statement, Police Report, Dallas, Texas, Nov. 18, 1933; contemporary reports in the *Dallas County News, Des Moines Register, Des Moines Tribune; Dexter Sentinel, Dexfield Review Sentinel, Earlham Echo, Fort Dodge Messenger & Chronicle, Perry Daily Chief, Redfield Review, Spencer News-Herald,* and *Stuart Herald*; Donald E. Fish, "A Stakeout For Bonnie and Clyde," *Pal* 72 (1991):104; Debra Sanborn, "The Barrows Gang's Visit to Dexter," May 14, 1976 (privately published, available at Weesner Pharmacy, Dexter); Miriam Allen De Ford, *The Real Bonnie and Clyde* (New York, 1968); H.G. Frost & J.H. Jenkins, *I'm Frank Hammer: The Life of a Texas Police Officer* (Austin & New York, 1968); Jay Robert Nash, *Bloodletters and Badmen* (New York, 1973); John Toland, *The Dillinger Days* (New York, 1963); John Treherne, *The Strange History of Bonnie and Clyde* (New York, 1985).

Chapter Nine: "Black Armbands, Free Speech, and School Discipline: The *Tinker* Case"

(1) Reprinted in William Eckhardt, "The Black Arm Band Story: A Community Case Study of Conflicting Ideologies and Values," *Journal of Human Relations* 17 (1969):495.

(2) *Des Moines Register*, Dec. 15, 1965.

(3) Tinker v. Des Moines Independent Community School District (Civil No. 7-1810-C-1, U.S. District Court, Southern District of Iowa), Transcript of Non-Jury Trial, July 25, 1966, pp. 55, 65 (hereafter "Transcript").

(4) *Ibid.*, p. 52.

(5) *Ibid.*, p. 120.

(6) Peter H. Irons, *The Courage of Their Convictions* (New York & London, 1988), p. 247.

(7) Eckhardt, *op. cit.*, p. 496.

(8) *Des Moines Register*, Dec. 17, 1965.

(9) Transcript, *op. cit.*, p. 16, 34.

(10) *Ibid.*, p. 17.

(11) *Ibid.*, p. 19.

(12) *Des Moines Register*, Dec. 18, 1965.

(13) *New York Times*, Dec. 22, 1965.

(14) *Des Moines Register*, Dec. 22, 1965.

(15) *Ibid.*

(16) *Des Moines Register*, Jan. 2, 1966.

(17) Eckhardt, *op. cit.*, p. 507.

(18) Tinker v. Des Moines Independent Community School District, 258 F. Supp 971, 972 (S.D. Iowa 1966).

(19) *Ibid.*, p. 973.

(20) Tinker v. Des Moines Independent Community School District, 383 F.2d 988 (8th Cir. 1967).

(21) 393 U.S. 503 (1969).

(22) *Ibid.*, p. 505-06.

(23) *Ibid.*, p. 506.

(24) *Ibid.*, p. 507.

(25) *Ibid.*, p. 508.

(26) *Ibid.*

(27) *Ibid.*, p. 509 (quoting Burnside v. Byars, 363 F.2d 744, 749 (5th Cir. 1966)).

(28) 393 U.S. at 511.

(29) *Ibid.*, p. 515 (Black, J., dissenting).

(30) *Ibid.*, p. 518.

(31) "The Supreme Court, 1968 Term," 83 *Harvard L. Rev.* 7, 157 (1969).

(32) Vernonia School District 47J v. Acton, 1995 WL 373274, *6 (U.S. June 26, 1995).

(33) Irons, *op. cit.*, p. 252.

ADDITIONAL SOURCES: Court Records, Court Papers and Transcript of Non Jury Trial, Tinker v. Des Moines Community School District (Civil No. 7-1810-C-1, U.S. Dist. Ct, Southern Dist. of Iowa, Complaint filed March 14, 1966); Contemporary reports in the *Des Moines Register, Des Moines Tribune*, and *New York Times*; "The Supreme Court, 1968 Term," 83 *Harvard L. Rev.* 7, 154 (1969); "How to Deal With Student Dissent," *Newsweek*, March 10, 1969, p. 66; "The Supreme Court," *Time*, March 7, 1969, p. 47; William Eckhardt, "The Black Arm Band Story: A Community Case Study of Conflicting Ideologies and Values," *Journal of Human Relations* 17 (1969):495; Thomas J. Flygare, "Schools & the Law—John Tinker Still an Idealist," *Phi Delta Kappan* (Nov.1979):210; Peter H. Irons, *The Courage of Their Convictions* (New York & London, 1988).

Chapter Ten: "Opening the Door: The Repeal of the Constitutional Ban on Lotteries"

(1) *Laws of the Sixty-Fifth General Assembly*, 1973, ch. 153.

(2) *Laws of the Seventieth General Assembly*, 1983, ch. 187; *Laws of the Seventy-First General Assembly*, 1985, ch. 33; *Laws of the Seventy-Third General Assembly*, 1989, ch. 67; *Laws of the Seventy-Third General Assembly*, 1989, ch. 216.

(3) Indian Gaming Regulatory Act, 25 U.S.C. §§ 2701-21; 18 U.S.C. §§ 1166-68 (1988); *See* Note, "State Authority to Regulate Gaming Within Indian Lands: The Effect of the Indian Gaming Regulatory Act," 41 Drake L. Rev. (1992):317; *Acts of the Seventy-Fifth General Assembly*, 1994, ch. 1021.

(4) Benjamin F. Shambaugh (ed.), *The Messages and Proclamations of the Governors of Iowa* (Iowa City, 1903), vol. I, pp. 83-84.

(5) *The Statute Laws of the Territory of Iowa, 1838-1839* (Du Buque, 1839), pp. 234-38; *Revised Statutes of the Territory of Iowa, 1842-43* (Iowa City, 1843), p. 191; Constitution of 1846, art. 4, § 29; *Code of 1851*, ch. 145, §§ 2723, 2730; Constitution of 1857, art. 3, § 28.

(6) 11 Iowa 133, 134 (1860).

(7) 227 Iowa 1391, 1401-02 (1940).

(8) Robert Daley, "Bingo Binge is Big Business," *New York Times Magazine*, Dec. 8, 1957, pp. 61, 67.

(9) 244 Iowa 415 (1953), *rehearing denied*, 245 Iowa 428 (1954).

(10) 244 Iowa at 419.

(11) *Ibid.*

(12) *Ibid.*, p. 421.

(13) *Iowa House Journal 1953*, p. 905.

(14) *Cedar Rapids Gazette*, Jan. 27, 1965.

(15) *Ibid.*, Feb. 24, 1965.

(16) *Des Moines Register*, June 6, 1965.

(17) *Ibid.*

(18) *[Davenport] Times-Democrat*, March 7, 1967.

(19) *Cedar Rapids Gazette*, March 6, 1967.

(20) *Ibid.*, March 30, 1967.

(21) *[Davenport] Times-Democrat*, Feb. 10, 1970.

(22) *Ibid.*, Feb. 9, 1971.

(23) Attorney General Richard Turner's annotation on Letter of Ann Trebon, Grinnell, Iowa, Sept. 6, 1971, File "Gambling-Buena Vista Father Ruhland," Richard Turner Papers, SHSI, Des Moines.

(24) *Des Moines Register*, Sept. 7, 1971.

(25) Letter of Ann Trebon, *op. cit.*

(26) *Des Moines Register*, Sept. 9, 1971.

(27) *[Dubuque] Telegraph-Herald*, Sept. 19, 1971.

(28) *Des Moines Tribune*, Sept. 18, 1971.

(29) *Ibid.*, March 22, 1972.

(30) *Des Moines Register*, June 29, 1972.

(31) Iowa Code § 726.3 (1971).

(32) *Des Moines Tribune*, July 17, 1972.

(33) *Ibid.*, July 25, 1972.

(34) *[Davenport] Times-Democrat*, July 26, 1972.

(35) Century 21 Shows, Inc. v. State of Iowa, 346 F. Supp. 1050 (S.D. Iowa 1972).

(36) *Des Moines Register*, Aug. 16, 1972.

(37) *Ibid.*

(38) *Des Moines Tribune*, Aug. 17, 1972.

(39) *Des Moines Register*, Aug. 18, Aug. 19, 1972.

(40) *Thirty-Ninth Biennial Report of the Attorney General for the Biennial Period Ending December 31, 1972* (Des Moines, 1972).

(41) *Iowa House Journal 1973*, p. 47.

(42) *[Davenport] Times-Democrat*, Aug. 18, 1972.

(43) *Des Moines Tribune*, July 17, 1972.

(44) *[Burlington] Hawk-Eye*, July 18, 1972.

(45) *Des Moines Register*, June 21, 1972.

(46) *Ibid.*, Aug. 22, 1972.

(47) *Ibid.*, July 19, 1972.

(48) *[Dubuque] Telegraph-Herald*, Sept. 3, 1972.

(49) *Des Moines Tribune*, Sept. 14, 1972.

(50) *Des Moines Register*, Oct. 28, 1972.

(51) *[Davenport] Times-Democrat*, Nov. 5, 1972.

ADDITIONAL SOURCES: Correspondence on North Buena Vista Raid, File "Gambling-Buena Vista Father Ruhland," Richard Turner Papers, SHSI, Des Moines; contemporary Burlington, Cedar Rapids, Council Bluffs, Davenport, Des Moines, and Dubuque newspaper accounts; *New York Times*; "Legalized Gambling is Still Immoral," *The Christian Century* 74 (Nov. 20, 1957):1373; *Iowa Senate Journals*, 1961-1972; *Iowa House Journals*, 1965-1971; *Thirty-Sixth Biennial Report of the Attorney General for the Biennial Period Ending December 31, 1966* (Des Moines, 1966); *Thirty-Ninth Biennial Report 1972, op. cit.*; *Iowa Official Register*, 1973-74; John Ezell, *Fortune's Merry Wheel: The Lottery in America* (Cambridge, 1960); Lee Ann Osbun & Steffen W. Schmidt (eds.), *Issues in Iowa Politics* (Ames, 1990).

Epilogue: The Mound Builders

(1) "Poweshiek's Oration," Memoirs of M. Etta Cartwright Coxe, SHSI, Manuscript Division, Iowa City.

(2) 1976 Iowa Acts ch. 1158, §7, Iowa Code § 263B.7 (1993); 1978 Iowa Acts ch. 1029, §26, Iowa Code §263B.9 (1993); 1978 Iowa Acts ch. 1029, § 50, Iowa Code §716.5(2) (1993).

(3) Hunziker v. State of Iowa, 519 N.W. 2d 367, 371 (Iowa 1994), *cert. denied,* 115 S. Ct. 1313 (1995).

INDEX

Cases

A

Amos v. Prom, Inc., 117 F. Supp 615 (N.D. Iowa 1954), 277n

Anderson v. Tyler, 223 Iowa 1033 (1937), 265n

B

Bartels v. Iowa, 262 U.S. 404 (1923), 232, 335n

Bell v. Wheeler, 15 illus.

Bremmer v. Journal-Tribune Publishing Co., 247 Iowa 817 (1956), 277-78, 278n

Brewer v. Williams, 430 U.S. 387 (1977), 301-2, 302n

Brown v. The J.H. Bell Company, 146 Iowa 89 (1910), 201n

Burgett v. Des Moines Independent Community School District, 3 D.P.I. App. Dec. 196 (Iowa State Board of Public Instruction 1983), 308-9, 309n

Burnside v. Byars, 363 F.2d 744 (5th Cir. 1967), 291, 336n

C

Century 21 Shows, Inc. v. State of Iowa, 346 F. Supp. 1050 (S.D. Iowa 1972), 320, 337n

Cherry v. Des Moines Leader, 114 Iowa 298 (1901), 208, 334n

Chicago, Burlington & Quincy Railroad Co. v. Attorney General, 5 F. Cas. 594 (Cir. Ct. D. Iowa 1875), aff'd, 94 U.S. 155 (1876), 160n

Chouteau v. Molony, 57 U.S. (16 Howard) 203 (1853), 8n, 65-66

Clark v. The Board of Directors, 24 Iowa 266 (1868), 130-31, 131n

Coger v. The North West Union Packet Co., 37 Iowa 145 (1873), 125, 131-32, 132n, 329n

Cole v. Cole, 23 Iowa 433 (1867), 133n

Committee on Professional Ethics and Conduct of the Iowa State Bar Association v. Humphrey, 377 N.W.2d 643 (Iowa 1985), 304n

D

Daggs v. Frazier (D. Iowa, Southern Div., 1850), 64-65, 65n

Dickson v. Yates, 194 Iowa 910 (1922), 222n

Doe v. Turner, 361 F. Supp. 1288 (S.D. Iowa), appeal denied, 488 F.2d 1134 (8th Cir. 1973), 300-301, 301n

Dred Scott v. Sandford, 60 U.S. (19 Howard) 393 (1856), 48, 95, 330n

Dunham v. State of Iowa, 6 Clarke 245 (Iowa 1858), 94-95, 95n

E

Emmet County, Iowa v. Dally, 216 Iowa 166 (1933), 255-56, 256n

Ex Parte Anderson, 16 Withrow 595 (Iowa 1864), 122-23, 123n

F

First Trust Joint Stock Land Bank v. Arp, 225 Iowa 1331 (1939), 256-57, 257n

Frink & Co. v. Coe, 4 Greene 555 (Iowa 1854), 94n

G

Geebrick v. State of Iowa, 5 Clarke 491 (Iowa 1858), 72n, 173, 333n

Graham v. Central Community School District of Decatur County, 608 F. Supp. 531 (S.D. Iowa 1985), 306-7, 307n

H

Heller v. Town of Portsmouth, 196 Iowa 104 (1923), 234-35, 235n

Hill v. Smith, 1 Morris 70 (Iowa 1840), 35n

Hunt v. Hunt, 4 Greene 216 (Iowa 1854), 74n

Hunziker v. State of Iowa, 519 N.W.2d 367 (Iowa 1994) cert. denied, 115 S. Ct. 1313 (1995), 326, 337n

I

In re Lelah-Puc-Ka-Chee, 98 F. 429 (N.D. Iowa 1899), 178-79, 179n

In the Interest of B.G.C., A Child, 496 N.W.2d 239 (Iowa 1992), 309-10, 310n

In the matter of Ralph (a colored man) on Habeas Corpus. See Jordan J. Montgomery v. Ralph, a man of color

J

Johnson v. Charles City Community Schools Board of Education, 368 N.W.2d 74 (Iowa 1985), 307-8, 308n

Johnson v. Miller, 63 Iowa 529 (1884), 187-88, 189, 333n, 334n

Constitutions and Statutes

General Entries